Treasures

Treasures

of

THE NEW YORK PUBLIC LIBRARY

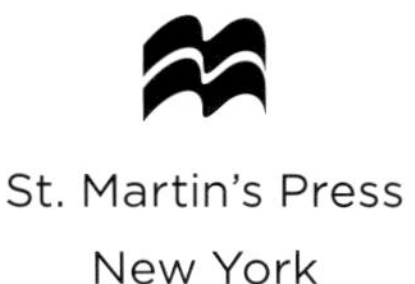

St. Martin's Press
New York

First published in the United States by St. Martin's Press, an imprint of St. Martin's Publishing Group

www.stmartins.com

The Library of Congress Cataloging-in-Publication Data is available upon request.

ISBN 978-1-250-62377-5 (hardcover)
ISBN 978-1-250-62378-2 (ebook)

Our books may be purchased in bulk for promotional, educational, or business use. Please contact your local bookseller or the Macmillan Corporate and Premium Sales Department at 1-800-221-7945, extension 5442, or by email at MacmillanSpecialMarkets@macmillan.com.

First Edition: 2021

10 9 8 7 6 5 4 3 2

This book was created with a generous gift from Dr. Georgette Bennett in honor of her husband, Dr. Leonard Polonsky, CBE, and the Polonsky Exhibition of the Treasures of The New York Public Library.

THE NEW YORK PUBLIC LIBRARY

TREASURES

THE POLONSKY EXHIBITION

Curiosity Required

by Anthony W. Marx, President and Chief Executive Officer

Public libraries are at the foundation of our democracy of informed citizens, making information, fact, knowledge, and opportunity available to all. The New York Public Library is one of the oldest and largest public library systems in the country, and at its heart are its extraordinary and diverse collections.

For over a century, The New York Public Library has collected, preserved, and made accessible the world's history, documenting our collective experience via manuscripts, rare books, photography, maps, audio and moving images, ephemera, unusual objects, and more.

These collections are more than the documenting, musings, writings, and thoughts of universally accepted great writers and historic leaders, but often the work of "everyday" people, chronicling day-to-day life in New York City, the United States, and beyond.

The Library has always taken seriously its role to preserve history from varying perspectives and to make that knowledge and education accessible to all. The only requirement for accessing our research collections is curiosity. Any individual can view, study, learn from, and be inspired by these collections, as have countless scholars and researchers of all ages and backgrounds.

An immeasurable number of works of fiction and nonfiction, art, performance, scholarship, and more were inspired and informed by the collections preserved by The New York Public Library. In the broadest sense, the Library has shaped our cultural and educational landscape. In a personal sense, the Library sparks excitement through these collections every day. There is nothing like the wonder of serendipitous discovery, of learning something new from our past, of uncovering a gem that can help us better navigate today's waters.

That noble mission of our research libraries is arguably more important than ever, as truth and fact continue to be blurred, and too often we are forgetting the vital lessons of our past. But those lessons are still here, captured through the vast array of material that has withstood time.

This is why it is so important to the Library—and to me personally—that we keep on permanent display a rotating collection of some of our most profound, rich, inspiring research collection items in the *Polonsky Exhibition of The New York Public Library's Treasures*. The exhibition's first iteration ranges from the seemingly mundane to the monumental, and provides unique perspectives and glimpses into the places, events, and lives of people over history.

Visitors will be transported thousands of years into the past to the day-to-day lives of now-ancient civilizations while viewing cuneiform tablets, one of the earliest examples of the written word. They will get a sense of how Thomas Jefferson felt during that hot summer in Philadelphia writing the Declaration of Independence, and actually see that this venerable document was, in fact, debated until the last moment. They will peek into the minds of Malcolm X, Virginia Woolf, Charles Dickens, Phillis Wheatley, and so many other luminaries, leaders, and writers through their notes, drafts, manuscripts, typescripts, photographs, and letters. They will see and hopefully better understand what it was like to be an African American traveling in the Jim Crow South by viewing our *Green Books*, and discover early documentation of the fight for LGBTQ rights. And that's just a small sample.

In this exhibition, one will get direct access to figures from history. Information, fact, and knowledge from the primary sources. The first drafts of history. The history you may not learn in school. It's here.

It has been my personal goal since I joined the Library to ensure that every visitor to its iconic 42nd Street library experiences these treasures and is motivated to learn more about our past, our heroes, our mistakes, and our world. We can't build on the foundation created by those who came before us without understanding that foundation. These items—and over 46 million others in our research collections—have always been and will always be accessible to anyone who wants to learn from them. This book documenting some of the exhibition is a first step toward that end, providing all readers and visitors with the small taste they need to provoke questions, inspire curiosity, and drive future visits to dig deeper into our collections.

I hope everyone enjoys and appreciates the Polonsky Exhibition and this gorgeous memento of its highlights, and I hope many will be inspired to visit or return to our research libraries to learn more.

Treasures of The New York Public Library

by William P. Kelly, Andrew W. Mellon Director of the Research Libraries, and Declan Kiely, Director, Special Collections and Exhibitions

What constitutes a treasure? How is it defined? The word *treasure* has been around for centuries. Its origin lies in the Greek word *θησανρός* (*thēsauros*), meaning "treasure, treasury, storehouse or collection." The word was Latinized as *thēsaurus,* a term that Peter Mark Roget adopted in 1852 to describe his treasure trove of synonyms. It thence evolved from Anglo-French into Middle English as *tresor.* In the popular imagination, the word *treasure* conjures up images of chests overflowing with precious metals, jewels, or money. We may think of the quest for Captain Flint's buried treasure in Robert Louis Stevenson's *Treasure Island*, or the dragon Smaug curled atop his golden hoard in *The Hobbit*.

We can go as far back as Chaucer's *Canterbury Tales* to find the term used in just this way, as in "The Pardoner's Tale": "This tresor hath Fortune unto us yiven / In myrthe and joliftee oure lyf to lyven" ("This treasure has Fortune unto us given / In mirth and jollity our life to live.") In Chaucer's moral exemplum on the dangers of cupidity, this interpretation of the meaning of "tresor" proves to be a fatal misunderstanding. The word functions as a similarly loaded term in "The Merchant's Tale," in which Chaucer tells us that "a wyf is the fruyt of his tresor" ("a wife is the best part of his treasure").

"Treasuring Up"

Treasure, then, is a word often associated with opportunity, risk, danger, avarice, or mere contented acquisitiveness. But what does it mean in the context of The New York Public Library, and the permanent, rotating exhibition of the Library's treasures that the Polonsky Foundation has underwritten? If the Library were to assemble and display a group of items based purely on their appraised value, it would be a gratuitous exercise lacking coherence. It is better to think of the Library's treasures in the word's verbal sense: "to hold as precious, to collect and store up something of value for future use." This is the meaning that one encounters (courtesy of Milton) at the threshold of the Rose Main Reading Room on the Library's third floor: "A good Booke is the pretious life-blood of a master spirit, imbalm'd and treasur'd up on purpose to a life beyond life."

We who serve at the Library are not so much concerned with determining what constitutes a treasure per se; rather, we are actively engaged in collecting, preserving, and making accessible the widest possible range of research materials, art, and artifacts. Our purpose is to "treasure up" those materials for present and future generations of researchers and visitors.

Rising to Truth

Abbot Suger, the 12th-century superior of the Basilica of Saint-Denis—the burial place of French monarchs—was responsible for recording and describing the treasures of the cathedral. In the course of his work, Abbot Suger wrote in *De Administratione* (*Of Administration*, ca. 1144–1148) that "the dull mind rises to truth through that which is material." As Kenneth Clark noted in *Civilisation*, his landmark television documentary series, Suger's observation "was really a revolutionary concept in the Middle Ages. It was the intellectual background of all the sublime works of art of the next century and in fact has remained the basis of our belief in the value of art . . ."

The New York Public Library is, in every sense, a republic of books. But we preserve so much more than books. We operate in the world of materiality, in all the fullness that the word suggests—illuminated manuscripts, painted miniatures, prints, photographs, sculpture, audio and moving images, and, in recent times, a vast amount of born-digital materials. Most often, these artifacts have to do with language—the written transmission of knowledge and information. Sometimes we value these materials for their beauty or rarity, rather than their contents or meaning. At other times, meaning is everything: How did these words change history, lead to actions, inspire beliefs? How did this choreographer advance the possibilities of modern dance? How did this painting, or map, or photograph change people's perceptions of the world around them?

Research is never complete—it is always about finding missing pieces, pursuing avenues of inquiry that appear opaque at the start of the process, and then making hitherto unseen connections. The essence of research is exploring winding paths in order to make unexpected discoveries. It is in the nature of the Library to value and encourage the open-ended research of these winding paths. To that end, we acquire widely and deeply, following our governing principles of access and utility. We collect in the belief that all knowledge is worth preserving, because what we know today and discover tomorrow are fundamentally rooted in the preservation of the material documenting our shared human experience.

Access to a Shared Heritage

The permanent exhibition in Gottesman Hall of the Library's treasures provides us with an opportunity to showcase this vast range, and to elucidate for our visitors—whether they are first-time tourists or researchers who have spent decades engaged in scholarly study—the crucial role the Library plays in collecting, preserving, and providing access to our shared cultural heritage.

While all items in our vast collections have value, this exhibition is meant to highlight some of our more than 46 million objects that stand out as especially rare, significant, beautiful, or unusual—our treasures. We invite our visitors to ask such questions as: What is it that makes a particular object special? Is it its age, or its rarity? Its uniqueness or beauty? Is it of great scholarly importance? Does it provoke strong emotions? Is it a curiosity? Has it made a significant impact as an art or literary form? Does it demonstrate the potential to enhance the lives of future generations? Is there an extraordinary story it tells about the workings of science or the culture in which we live?

The exhibition and this book provide a unique opportunity for visitors to view treasures that have heretofore largely been hidden. The Library is, indeed, a treasure house of sorts, a museum of acquisitions. But, more compelling than that, it is a living library and not a reliquary. Our treasures are both objects to be viewed, admired, and appreciated, and also scholarly resources that are available to researchers in our reading rooms. They help to demonstrate the Library's mission to inspire lifelong learning, advance knowledge, and strengthen our communities.

The archives of the museum of the Palais de Chaillot in Paris are inscribed with these lines by the poet Paul Valéry:

It depends on those who pass
Whether I am tomb or treasure;
Whether I speak or am silent.
The choice is yours alone.
Friend, do not enter without
desire.

We invite all our visitors and readers to view the Library's treasures in the same spirit—as a portal to further inquiry and discovery, some of which may, in turn, become tomorrow's treasure.

Treasures

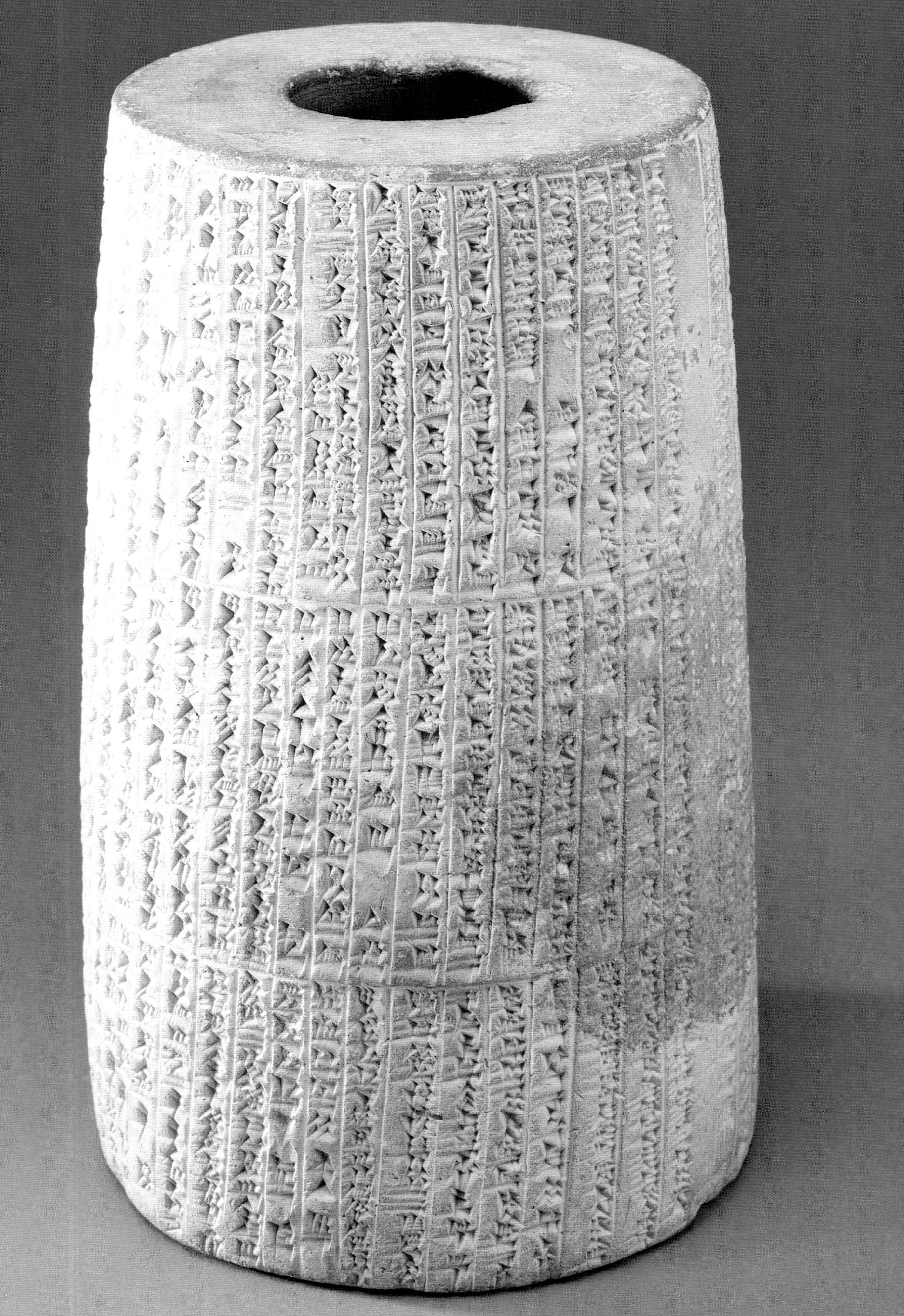

Cuneiform tablets

Clay, Iraq, 3rd–2nd millennia BCE
Wilberforce Eames Babylonian collection,
Manuscripts and Archives Division

The Manuscripts and Archives Division of the New York Public Library holds approximately 700 artifacts inscribed in an ancient writing system known as cuneiform (Latin *cuneus*, "wedge"). The script was invented in the mid-fourth millennium BCE in the region known as Mesopotamia, the "Land between the Rivers," in what is now Iraq. These artifacts were bequeathed by the Library's chief bibliographer, Wilberforce Eames. Today, we are able to re-engage with the societies of ancient Mesopotamia—their beliefs, art, literature, scientific accomplishments, and much more—thanks to the pioneering work of 19th-century scholars to decipher cuneiform.

Mesopotamian cuneiform was mainly used during the 3rd–1st millennia BCE to write texts in the Sumerian and Akkadian languages, but was adapted to other languages such as Elamite or Hittite. Students of cuneiform learned up to 1,000 different characters impressed by styli made of reed or bone into damp clay.

Royal inscriptions were deposited in the foundations of official architecture, where they could be rediscovered during later renovations. This large clay barrel cylinder from the reign of Nebuchadnezzar II (r. 605–562 BCE) mentions his restoration of a temple in Marad (modern Tell Wannat as-Sadun in southern Iraq). According to this inscription, he looked for the original ground plan of the temple and found an inscription of a previous ruler, King Naram-Sin, who reigned some 1,600 years earlier:

> *As for Lugal-Marada, my lord, whose temple in Marad and whose ancient foundation platform no former king had seen since the days of old, at that time I looked for and found its ancient foundation platform, and upon the platform of King Naram-Sin, my ancient ancestor, I fixed its (new) foundations. I created an inscription written in my name and put it therein.*

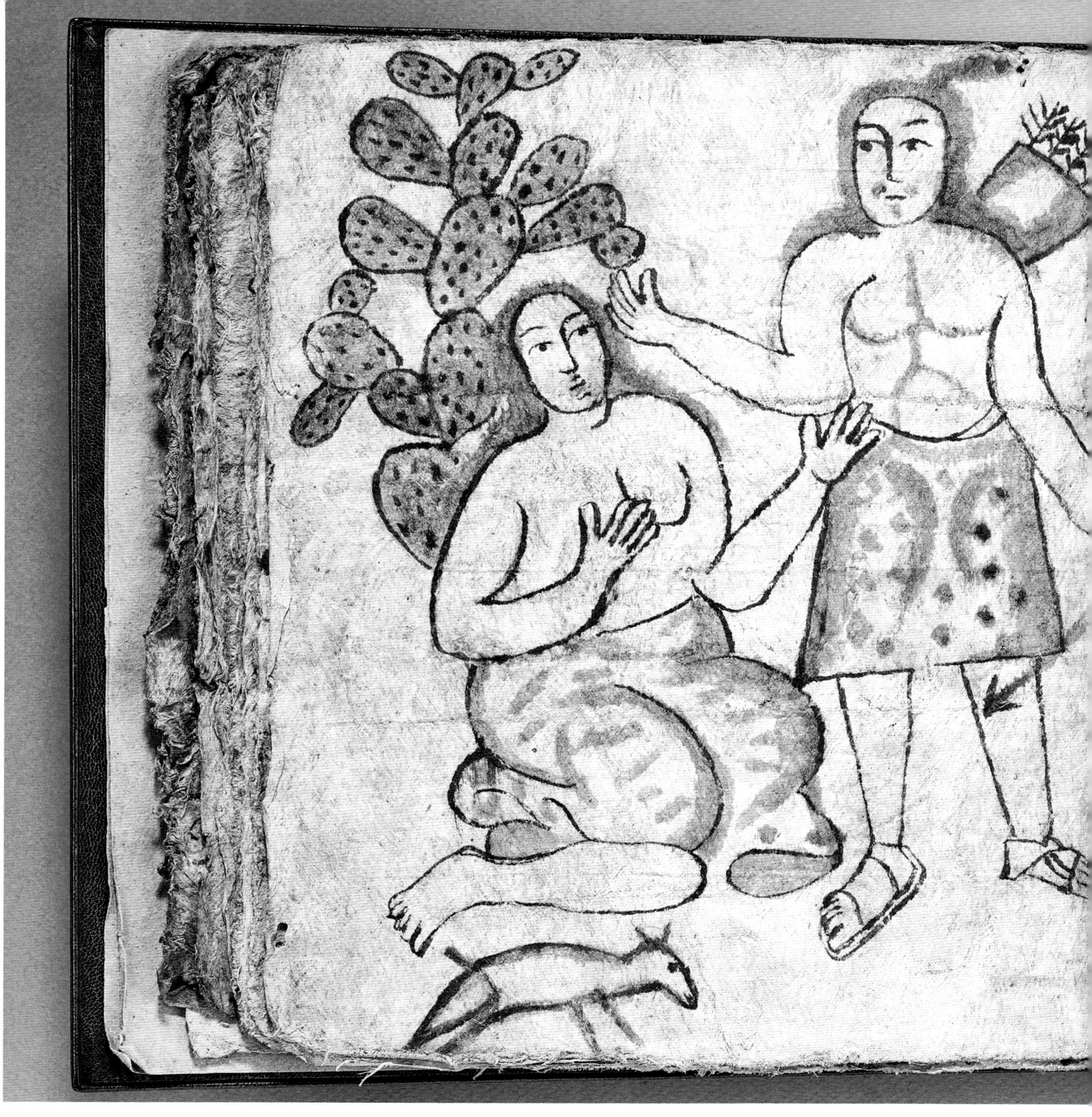

Anonymous (Mexican (Toluca))
Council House of Santa Maria Toluca
Ink and pigments on amatl paper, early 18th century
The Miriam and Ira D. Wallach Division of Art, Prints and Photographs, Spencer Collection

In pictures and words, this manuscript records the history and defines the boundaries and landholding titles of a village in the Valley of Mexico. Although its text contains the date 1535, which may reiterate earlier claims, scholars have convincingly assigned

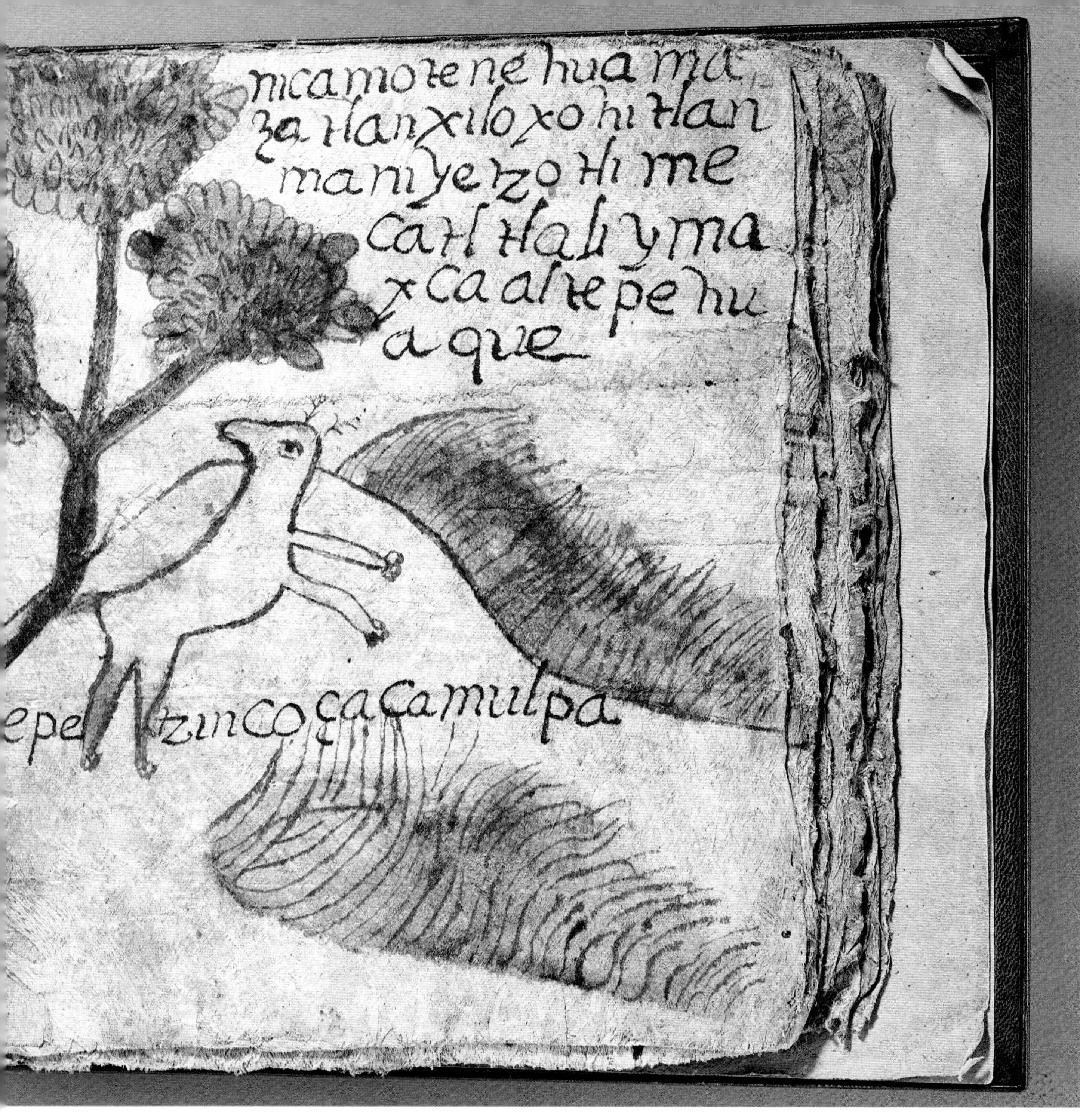

the manuscript to the early 18th century—a time of frequent challenges to village land titles that were thus reissued by leaders of pueblo council houses. It is an important example of a Colonial Mexican codex, written in the Central American Indian language Nahuatl and illustrated in a manner that reflects its maker's contact with examples of European art. The work is executed on indigenous, coarse-grained, unsized, cloth-like *amatl* paper, manufactured from tree bark fiber. Its views offer powerful evidence for what the Aztecs thought about the European conquest of their lands and an important counterpoint to the Library's significant holdings of works relating to the discovery of the New World.

ne quando dicat inimi cus meus p̄ ua lui ad

uersus e um. CO Oportet te fili gaudere

quia frater tuus mortuus fuerat et reuixit. perierat et

cy hi mei Dominica .III. Inuent̄ ē.

semper ad dominum quia ipse euellet de la

queo pedes me os respi ce in me et misere

re me quoniam uni cus et pau per sum ego.

Ad te dn̄e leuaui animam meā deus meus in te confido n̄e

GR Exurge domine non preua leat ho

mo iudice tur gentes in

conspec tu tu o y In

conuertendo inimicum meum retror sum

infirmabuntur et perient a facie

TRA Ad te le uaui oculos me os qui habitas

in ce lis y Ecce si cut o culi ser

uorum in manibus domino rum suorum

y Et sicut oculi ancille in manibus do mine sue

y I ta oculi nos tri ad dominum deum nos

trum donec misereatur nostri y Miserere

no bis do mine mi se rere nobis

OF Iusticie domi ni rec te leti ficantes cor da et

dulcio ra super mel et fa uum nam et ser

et de pre can tem

minor glo ri

le ecce nunc di

R. Peccaui do mi

me Quid fa ciam

quia ma gna et

Quoniam ini

um coram me est

de mus in me lu

pre occupatis di e

inuenire non p

quia pecca uimi

stris iniuste egi

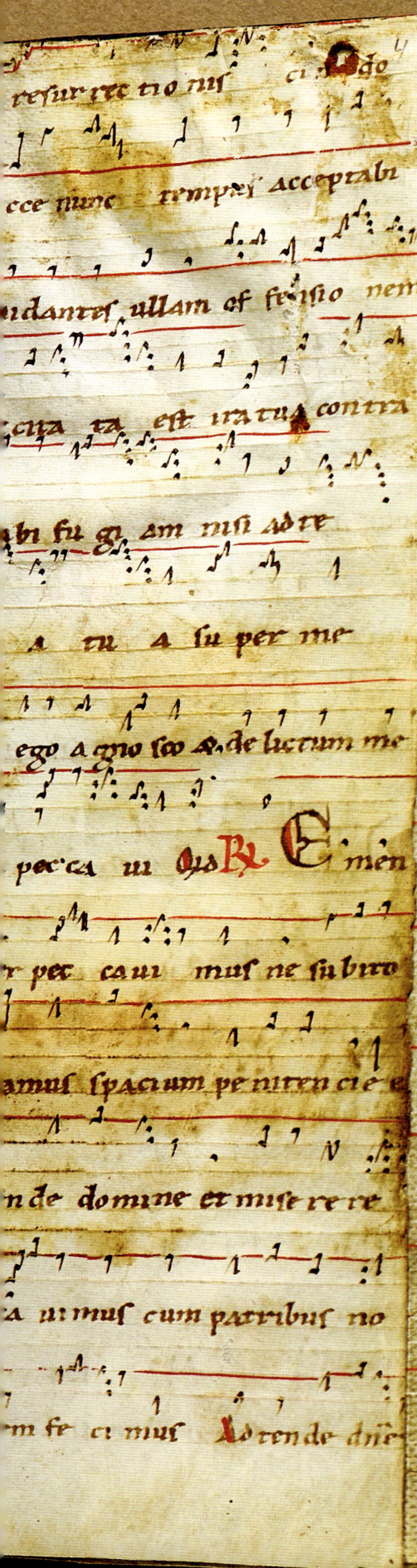

Book of chant fragments
11th–12th centuries
Music Division, The New York Public Library for the Performing Arts, Dorothy and Lewis B. Cullman Center

This volume consists of fragments from three separate sources sewn together in a 19th-century binding, and is the oldest known item held at the Library for the Performing Arts. The first two sources likely originated in Swiss or German regions, while the third probably derives from northern Italy or southern France. The left-hand page displayed here comes from the second of the three sources in the volume and dates from approximately 1050. Though likely created soon after Guido of Arezzo's invention of musical staff notation, this page is notated without staves. The source comes from a book containing chants from the Proper of the Mass, with words and music that would have been specific to certain days of the year. The "Oculi mei" chant shown here is from an Introit, sung during the second and third weeks of Lent. The pictured page features marginalia that outline melodic filigree—ornamental notes that emphasize the primary pitch—to be sung on certain syllables, and a drawing of a man's face in the "O" of "Oculi mei." The right-hand page comes from the third of the three sources and dates from the 12th century; its later date is indicated by the use of staves. This source contains chants intended for the first and second Sundays of Lent and the Sunday before Ash Wednesday.

Biblia Latina

Mainz: Johannes Gutenberg, 1455

Rare Book Division

Johannes Gutenberg, a goldsmith from the city of Mainz in what is now Germany, undertook the development of a new method of printing in the late 1430s that would revolutionize the production of books and other materials. His combined innovations—conceiving the use and manufacture of movable metal type, formulating oil-based printing ink, and employing a mechanical printing press—enabled the mass production of identical texts, facilitating the spread of knowledge and literacy.

As the cornerstone of printing in the West, the Gutenberg Bible embodies its creator's achievements. Collector and Library founder James Lenox acquired the Library's copy, the first one brought to the Americas, in 1847. Its arrival in New York City occasioned not only great excitement but also a romantic legend: that Lenox's agent instructed the Custom House workers to remove their hats upon seeing it—a fitting tribute, given the book's historical importance.

Liber generationis ihesu xpi
filij david: filij abraham.
Abraham genuit ysaac:
ysaac autē genuit iacob.
Iacob aūt genuit iudā et fratres eiꝰ:
iudas aūt genuit phares et zara de
thamar. Phares aūt genuit esrom:
esrom aūt genuit aram. Aram aūt
genuit aminadab: aminadab aūt genuit naasō. Naason aūt genuit salomon: salomō aūt genuit booz de raab.
Booz aūt genuit obeth ex ruth: obeth
aūt genuit iesse. Iesse autē genuit da-
uid regē: david autē rex genuit salo-
monē ex ea q̄ fuit urie. Salomō aūt
genuit roboam: roboam aūt genuit
abyam. Abyas aūt genuit asa: asa
aūt genuit iosaphat. Iosaphat aūt
genuit ioram: ioram aūt genuit ozi-
am. Ozias autē genuit ioathan: ioathan aūt genuit achaz. Achaz autē
genuit ezechiam: ezechias aūt genuit
manassen: manasses aūt genuit ammon. Ammon aūt genuit iosyam:
iosias aūt genuit iechoniā et fres eiꝰ
ī trāsmigratione babilonis. Et post
transmigrationē babilonis iechonias
genuit salathiel: salathiel aūt genuit
zorobabel. Zorobabel aūt genuit abiud: abiud autem genuit eliachim. Eliachim aūt genuit azor: azor aūt genuit sadoch. Sadoch autem genuit a-
chim: achim aūt genuit eliud. Eliud
aūt genuit eleazar: eleazar aūt genuit
mathan. Mathan aūt genuit iacob:
iacob aūt genuit ioseph virū marie:
de qua natꝰ est ihesus: qui vocatur
xpc. Omnes itaq; generationes ab a-
braham usq; ad david generationes
q̄tuordecim: et a david usq; ad transmigrationē babilonis generationes
q̄tuordecī: et a trāsmigratione babilonis
usq; ad xpm generationes quatuor-
decim. Xpi autem generatio sic erat.
Cum esset desponsata mater ihesu maria ioseph: antequā convenirent inventa ē
ī utero habēs de spiritu sancto. Ioseph
autem vir eiꝰ cū esset iustus et nollet
eam traducere: voluit occulte dimitte-
re eam. Hec aūt eo cogitante: ecce āgelus dn̄i apparuit ī somnis ioseph di-
cens. Ioseph fili david: noli timere ac-
cipere mariā coniugem tuā. Qd̄ eni in
ea natū est: de spiritu sancto est. Pariet aūt filiū: et vocabis nomē eius ihesum. Ipse eni salvū faciet pplm suum
a peccatis eorū. Hoc autem totū factū
est: ut adimpleretur qd̄ dictū esset a domino p prophetā dicentem. Ecce vir-
go in utero habebit et pariet filiū: et vo-
cabit nomē eius emanuel: qd̄ est in-
terpretatū nobiscum deus. Exurgens
aūt ioseph a somno fecit sicut precepit
ei āgelus dn̄i: et accepit coniugem suā.
Et non cognoscebat eam donec pepe-
rit filium suum primogenitum: et
vocavit nomen eius ihesum. II
Cum natus esset ihesus in bethleem iude ī diebꝰ herodis regis: ecce magi ab oriente venerūt ierosoli-
mam dicentes. Ubi est qui natus est
rex iudeorū? Vidimus eni stellā eius
in oriente: et venimꝰ adorare eū. Au-
diens autem herodes rex turbatus ē:
et omnis ierosolima cū illo. Et cōgre-
gans omnes principes sacerdotū et
scribas ppli: sciscitabat ab eis ubi xpus
nasceretur. At illi dixerūt ei. In bethleem
iude. Sic eni scriptū est p prophetam.
Et tu bethleem terra iuda: nequaq̄ mi-
nima es ī principibꝰ iuda. Ex te eni exi-
et dux qui regat pplm meum israhel.
Tūc herodes clam vocatis magis dili-
genter didicit ab eis tempus stelle q̄

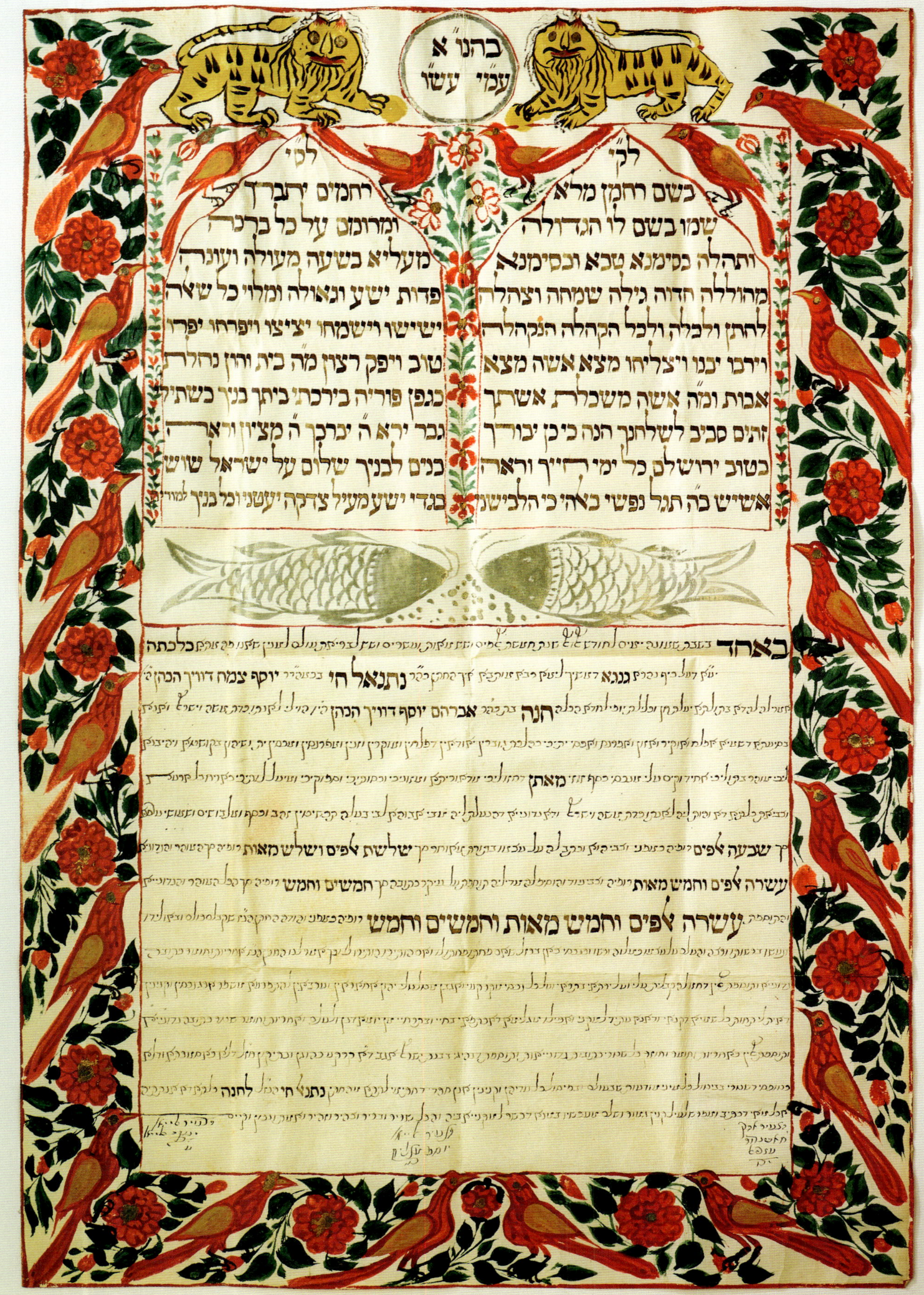

ברהנ״א
עמ״י עש״ו

לק״י
בשם רחמן מרא
שמו בשם לו הגדולה
ותהלה בסימנא טבא ובסימנא
מהוללה חדוה גילה שמחה וצהלה
לחתן ולכלה ולכל הקהלה הנקהלה
וירבו יבנו ויצליחו מצא אשה מצא
אבות ומ״ה אשה משכלת אשתך
זתים סביב לשלחנך הנה כי כן יבורך
כטוב ירושלם כל ימי חייך וראה
אשיש בה׳ תגל נפשי באהי כי הלבישני

לס״י
רחמים יתברך
ומרומם על כל ברכה
מעליא כשעה מעולה ועונה
פדות ישע וגאולה ומלוי כל שאלה
ישישו וישמחו יציצו ויפרחו יפרו
טוב ויפק רצון מה׳ בית והון נחלת
כגפן פוריה בירכתי ביתך בניך כשתילי
גבר ירא ה׳ יברכך ה׳ מציון וראה
בנים לבניך שלום על ישראל שוש
בגדי ישע מעיל צדקה יעטני וכל בניך למודי

Ketubbah
1866
Dorot Jewish Division

The bond of matrimony marks a new beginning. The *ketubbah*, the Jewish wedding contract, outlines the legal and financial responsibilities of a husband to his wife. Signed by witnesses, the document is typically hung prominently in a couple's home, since Jewish law forbids a couple from cohabitating if their *ketubbah* is lost or destroyed. This particular contract, between a bride named Hanah bat Avraham Yosef Dvek ha-Kohen [Hanna Dwek] and a groom, Netanel Hai ben Yosef Tsemah Dvek ha-Kohen [Netanel Hai Dwek], was signed on 8 Elul, 5626 [August 19, 1866], in Calcutta, India. The pair of fish symbolizes fertility, and the tigers, strength.

Antiphoner
Illuminated manuscript, late 15th century
Music Division, The New York Public Library for the Performing Arts, Dorothy and Lewis B. Cullman Center

This single sheet of chant contains a series of antiphons—melodies intended to be performed in a call-and-response between sections of a choir. These particular antiphons would have been sung in the Catholic service on Christmas, the Feast of St. Stephen, the Sunday after Christmas, and the Epiphany.

The extraordinary gold leaf decoration of the "M" (that begins the word "Magi") helps to approximate the date for this fragment. The illuminator depicted one of the three kings with dark skin, an illustrative practice that became common across Europe during the 16th century. The coat of arms along the bottom of the fragment may provide a clue to its location of origin: the scholar Anne Levitsky suggests that it may link the fragment to the Benedictine abbey of St. Aegidius in Braunschweig, Germany. One of several illuminated manuscripts held by the Library's Music Division, this fragment is of special importance because of the extent and variety of its visual symbolism.

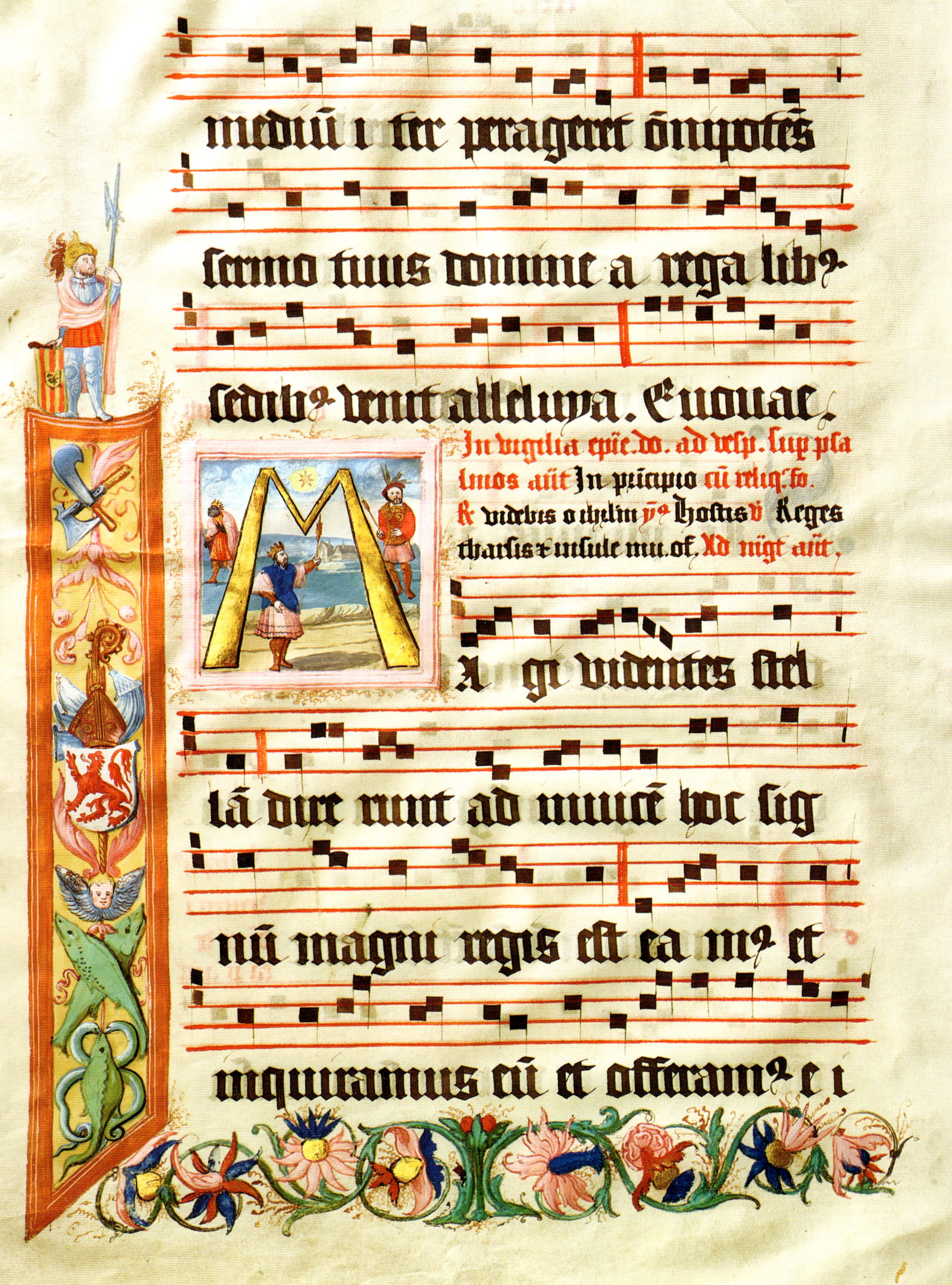
mediū i ter peragerēt ōnipotēs
sermo tuus domine a rega lib⁹
sedib⁹ venit alleluya. Euouae.
agi videntes stel
lā dixe runt ad invicē hoc sig
nū magni regis est ea m⁹ et
inquiramus eū et offeram⁹ e i

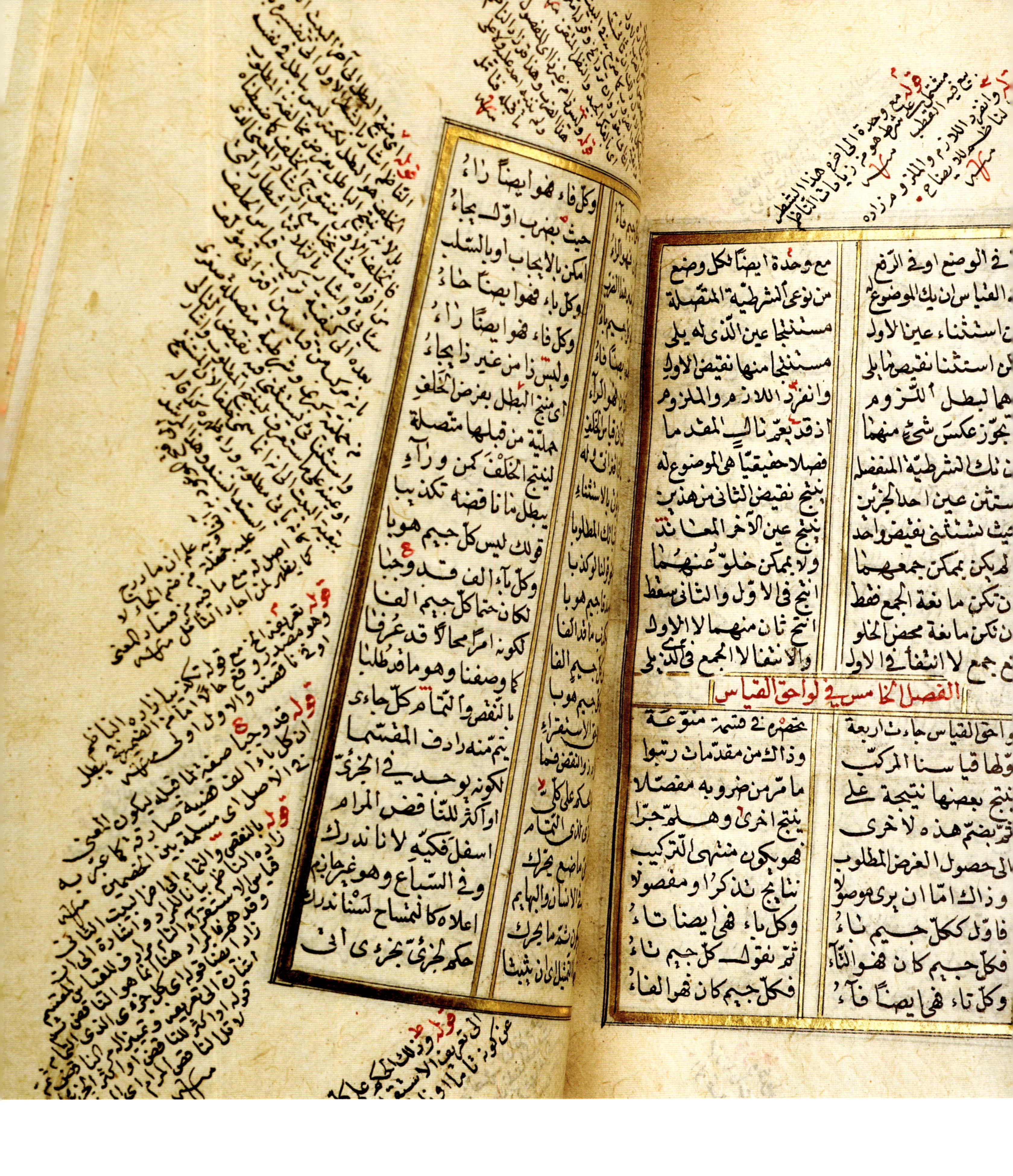

في الوضع او في الرفع
القياس ان ذلك الموضوع له
ان استثناء عين الاول
ان استثنا نقيض ما يلي
هما لبطل اللزوم
يجوز عكس شيء منهما
ان تلك الشرطية المنفصلة
ستثنى عين احد الجزئين
حيث تستثنى نقيض واحد
لم يكن يمكن جمعهما
ن تكن مانعة الجمع فقط
ن تكن مانعة محض الخلو
ع جمع لا انتفا في الاول

مع وحدة ايضا لكل وضع
من نوعي الشرطية المتصلة
مستنتجا عين الذي له يلي
مستنتجا منها نقيض الاول
وانفرد اللازم والملزوم
اذ قد يعم تالي المقدما
فصلا حقيقيا هي الموضوع له
ينتج نقيض الثاني من هذين
ينتج عين الآخر المعاند
ولا يمكن خلو عنهما
انتج في الاول والثاني سقط
انتج ثان منهما لا الاول
والانتفا لا الجمع في الذي يلي

الفصل الخامس في لواحق القياس

لواحق القياس جاءت اربعة
اولها قياسنا المركب
ينتج بعضها نتيجة على
ترتيب بضم هذه لاخرى
الى حصول الغرض المطلوب
وذاك اما ان يرى موصولا
فاول ككل جيم تاء
فكل جيم كان هو التاء
وكل تاء هي ايضا فاء

مختصر في قسمة متنوعة
وذاك من مقدمات رتبوا
ما مر من ضروبه مفصلا
ينتج اخرى وهلم جرا
هو يكون منتهى التركيب
نتائج تذكرا ومفصولا
وكل باء هي ايضا تاء
ثم نقول كل جيم تاء
فكل جيم كان هو الفاء

وكل فاء فهو ايضا راء
حيث يضرب اول بجاء
امكن بالايجاب او بالسلب
وكل باء فهو ايضا حاء
وكل فاء فهو ايضا راء
وليس ذا من غير ذا بجاء
اي ينتج البطل بفرض الخلف
حملية من قبلها متصلة
لينتج الخلف كمن وراء
يبطل ما ناقضه تكذيبا
قولك ليس كل جيم هو با
وكل باء الف قد وجبا
لكان حتما كل جيم الفا
لكونه امرا محالا قد عرفا
كما وصفنا وهو ما قد طلبا
بالنقص والتمام كل جاءي
يتم منه رادف المقسما
لكونه بوحده في الجزئي
او اكثر للناقص المرام
اسفل فكيه لانا ندرك
وفي السباع وهو غير جازم
اعلاه كالتمساح لسنا ندرك
حكم لجزئي بجزئي اي

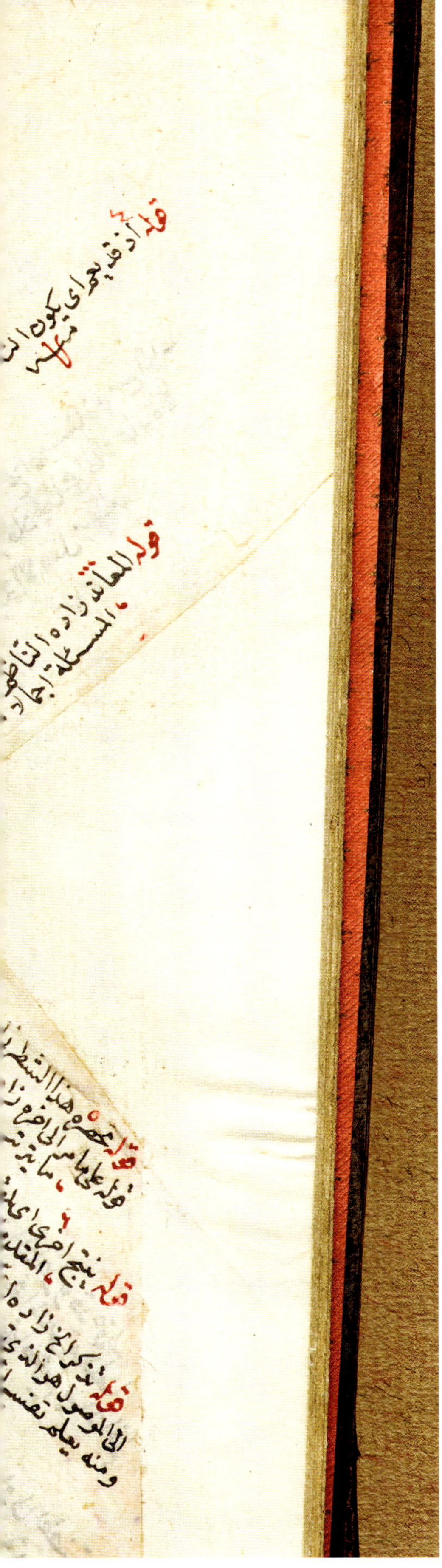

Yūsuf ibn Muhammad al-Qudāmī al-Shāmī (d. after 1675)
al-Bāriqah al-qudsīyah nāzimat la'āli al-shamsīyah
(A commentary on 'Ali ibn 'Umar al-Kātibī al-Qazwīnī's *a-Risālah al-shamsīyah fī al-qawā'id al-mantiqīyah*)
Illuminated manuscript, copied 1090/1679
Manuscripts and Archives Division

The Library's collection of Islamic manuscripts—written in Arabic, Persian, and Ottoman Turkish, on vellum and on paper—span more than a millennium. The earliest texts in the collection were written in the 7th century and the most recent in the late 19th century. Bound in more than 200 volumes, this collection of manuscripts includes copies of the Qur'an and the Bible, as well as religious commentaries and treatises, prayers, and prayer books. Among Arabic literary writings are poems, proverbs, biographical accounts, and jurisprudence. Other learned works concern astronomy, astrology, magic, science, philosophy, logic, and metaphysics. This Ottoman manuscript, which a scribe copied in 1679, is Yūsuf ibn Muhammad al-Qudāmī's commentary on 'Ali ibn 'Umar al-Kātibī al-Qazwīnī's (d. 1276/77) work on logic, titled *al-shamsīyah*. The *mise-en-page*, two columns flanked by commentary written diagonally, is more commonly seen in texts of poetry.

Flavius Josephus
(ca. 37/38–100 CE)
De bello Judaico
Paris: Antoine Vérard, 1492
Rare Book Division

Written by Flavius Josephus at the conclusion of the First Jewish-Roman War (66–73 CE), *De bello Judaico* offers a firsthand account of the Jewish revolt against the Roman occupation of Judea. Josephus, a soldier and historian, divided the work into seven sections, opening with a summary of Jewish history and concluding with a detailed recounting of the rebellion itself.

De bello Judaico first appeared in print in 1470 and was published in at least a dozen editions across Europe in the 15th century. This 1492 edition from the press of Antoine Vérard is printed on vellum, or calfskin, and contains particularly beautiful rubricated (hand-colored) initials and miniatures. A treasure in its own right, it highlights not only the Library's splendid holdings of incunabula, or 15th-century printing, but also its Judaica collections, which are known internationally for their depth and breadth.

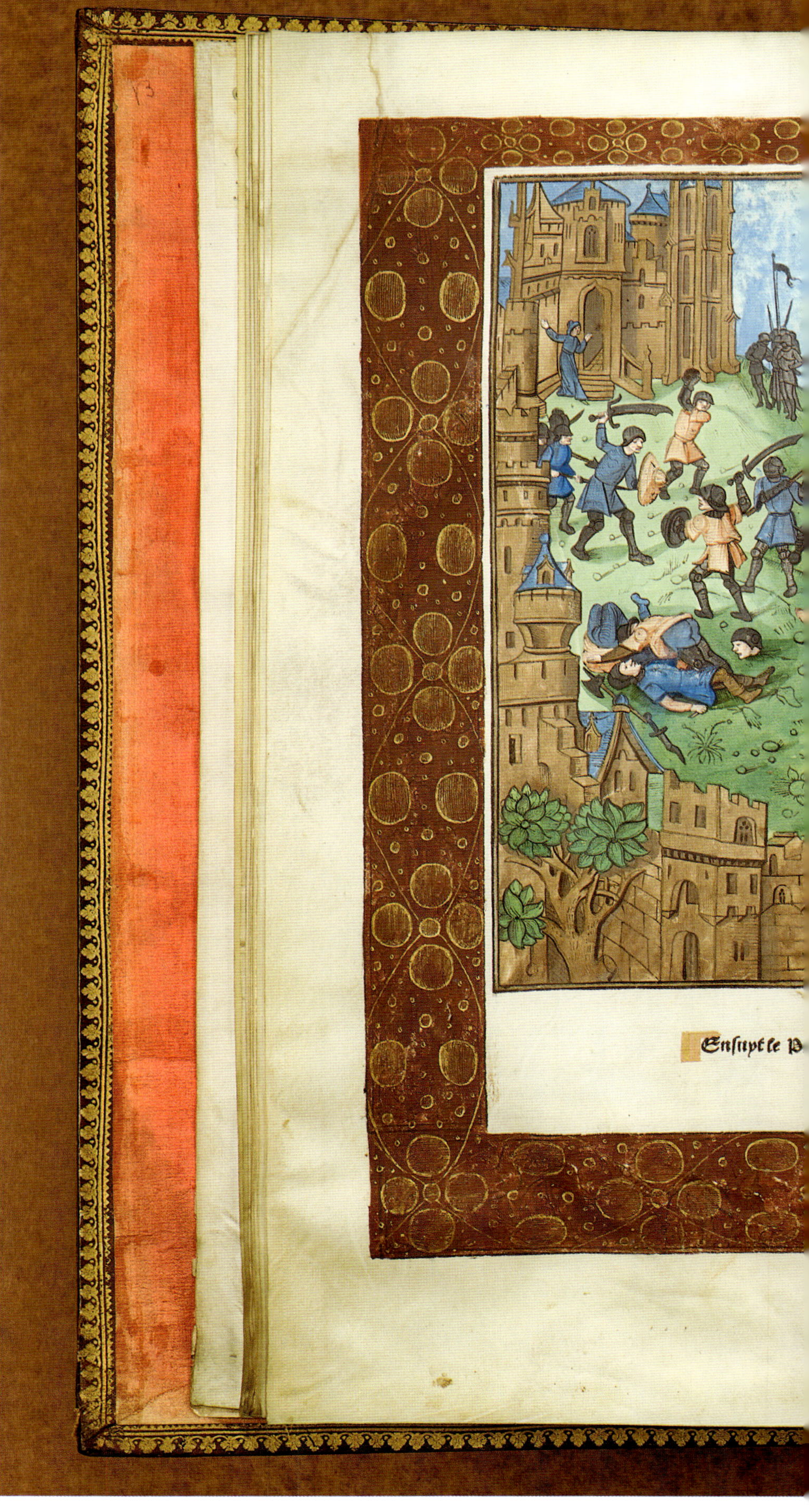

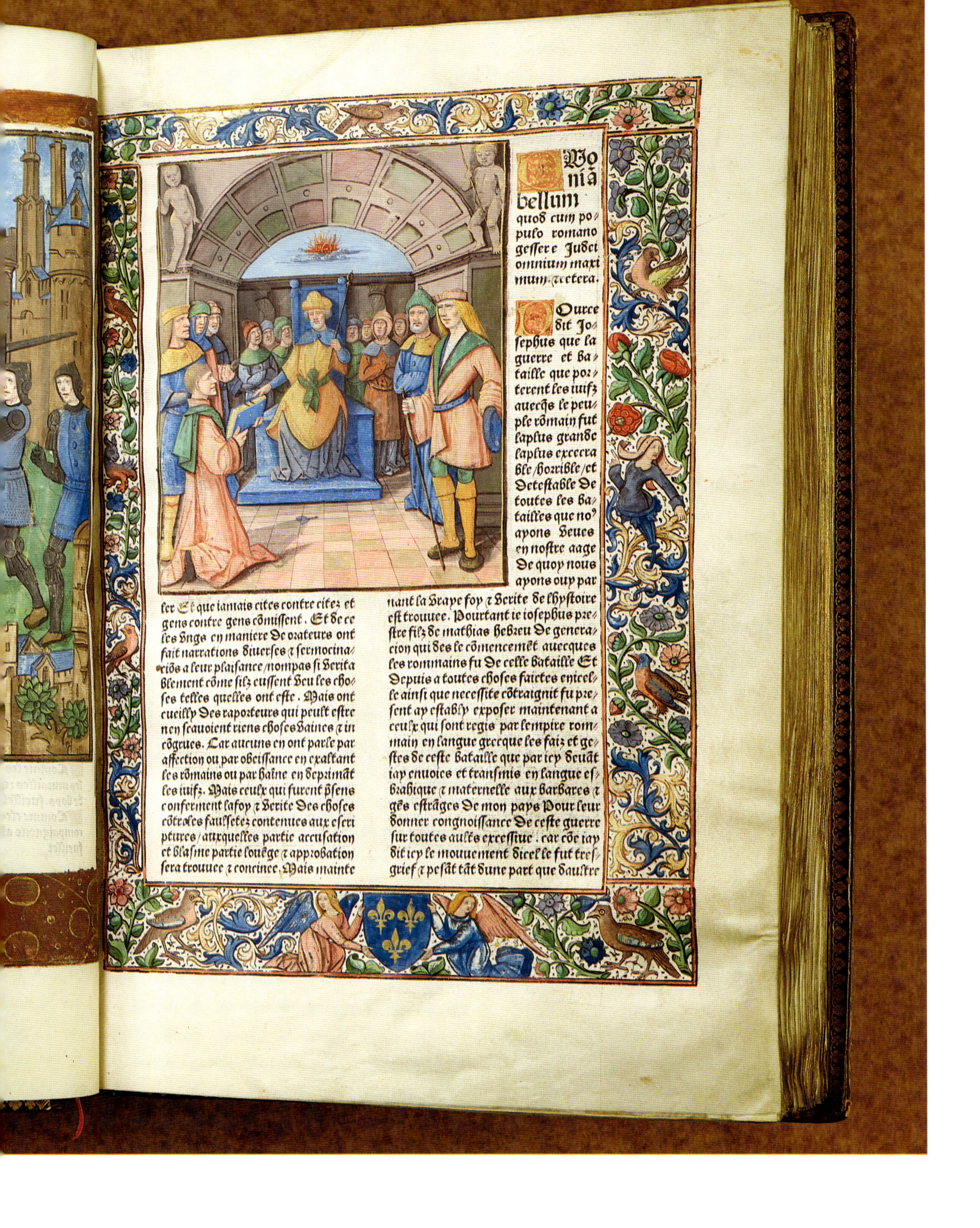

[B]ohiā
bellum
quos cum po-
pulo romano
gessere Judei
omnium maxi
mum. ⁊cetera.

[P]ource
dit Jo-
sephus que la
guerre et ba-
taille que por-
terent les iuifz
avecqs le peu-
ple rõmain fut
laplus grande
laplus execra
ble/horrible/et
detestable de
toutes les ba-
tailles que no⁹
avons veues
en nostre aage
de quoy nous
avons ouy par-
ler. Et que iamais cites contre citez et
gens contre gens cõmissent. Et de ce-
les vngs en maniere de orateurs ont
fait narrations diverses ⁊ sermocina-
ciõs a leur plaisance/nompas si verita
blement cõme silz eussent veu les choses telles quelles ont este. Mais ont
cueilly des raporteurs qui peult estre
nen scavoient riens choses vaines ⁊ in
cõgrues. Car aucuns en ont parle par
affection ou par obeissance en exaltant
les rõmains ou par haine en deprimãt
les iuifz. Mais ceulx qui furent p̃sens
conferment lafoy ⁊ verite des choses
cõtraires faulsetez contenues aux escri
ptures/auxquelles partie accusation
et blasme partie louẽge ⁊ approbation
sera trouvee ⁊ contenue. Mais maintenant la vraye foy ⁊ verite de lhystoire
est trouvee. Pourtant ie iosephus pre-
stre filz de mathias hebreu de genera-
cion qui des le cõmencemẽt avecques
les rommains fu de celle bataille Et
depuis a toutes choses faictes en icel-
le ainsi que necessite cõtraignit fu present ay estably exposer maintenant a
ceulx qui sont regis par lempire rom-
main en langue grecque les faiz et ge-
stes de ceste bataille que par icy devãt
iay envoies et transmis en langue e-
brahique ⁊ maternelle aux barbares ⁊
gẽs estrãges de mon pays Pour leur
donner congnoissance de ceste guerre
sur toutes aultres excessive. car cõe iay
dit icy le mouvement dicelle fut tres-
grief ⁊ pesãt tãt dune part que daultre

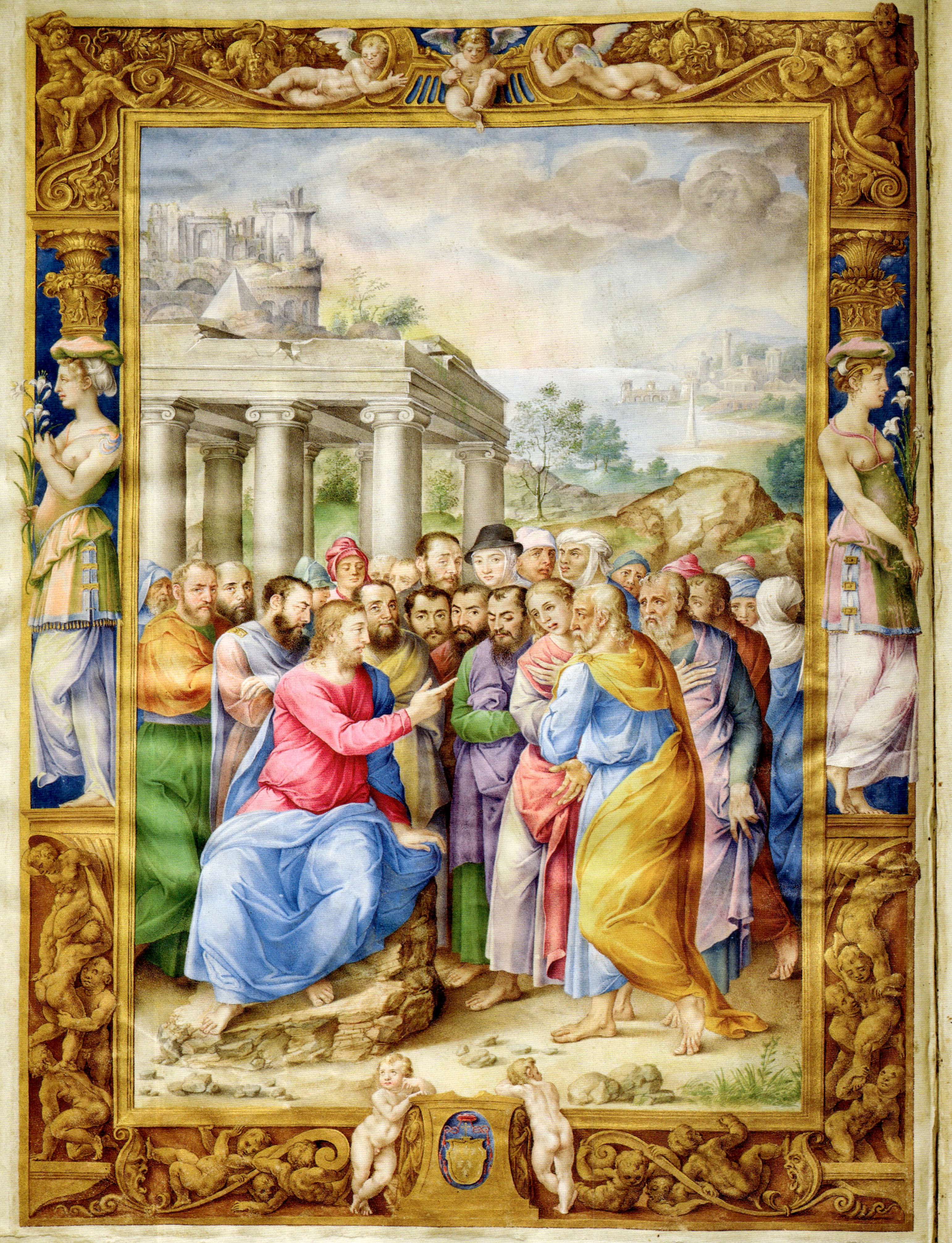

Giulio Clovio (ca. 1498–1578), illustrator

Lectionarium Evangeliorum

Illuminated manuscript, ca. 1540

Manuscripts and Archives Division

Giulio Clovio, a native of present-day Croatia and resident artist in the Farnese Palace in Rome, created this illuminated work for Cardinal Alessandro Farnese (1520–1589), who later bequeathed it to the College of Cardinals for use in the Sistine Chapel. Clovio's prodigious talent had drawn him to Italy, where Michelangelo befriended him. Clovio's use of color in his miniatures would eventually prompt the contemporaneous art scholar Giorgio Vasari to call him "a Michelangelo in little." Although books made the transmission of knowledge cheaper and more efficient than manuscripts, wealthy collectors like Cardinal Farnese continued to commission deluxe handwritten texts from artists they patronized; the practice would continue for a century after the print revolution. The prayer book is composed of lections, or scriptural readings, for each of the feast days of the Catholic Church's calendar. After Napoleon's victories in Italy, the book was stored in Spain, where the Englishman John Towneley purchased it at the turn of the 19th century.

Joseph ben Kalonymus ha-Nakden, of Xanten (d. after 1294), calligrapher and illuminator

Xanten Bible

Manuscript on vellum, 1294

The Miriam and Ira D. Wallach Division of Art, Prints and Photographs, Spencer Collection

The colophon of this very early two-volume manuscript of the Hebrew Bible states: "I, Joseph of Xanten, son of Kalonymus from Neuss have written and illustrated these twenty-four books for my friend Moses, Son of Jacob." The text is arranged in three columns to the page, with scattered historiated initials and charming pen-and-ink miniatures of flora and fauna. The minuscule writing that appears around the main text forms the Masorah ("Tradition")—notes for the reader intended to ensure the accurate transmission of the text, its grammar, and pronunciation. The first Hebrew manuscript to enter the Library's Spencer Collection, the Xanten Bible is an important addition to the Library's rich collections of Judaica and complements the broad range of Christian devotional literature that the collection also holds.

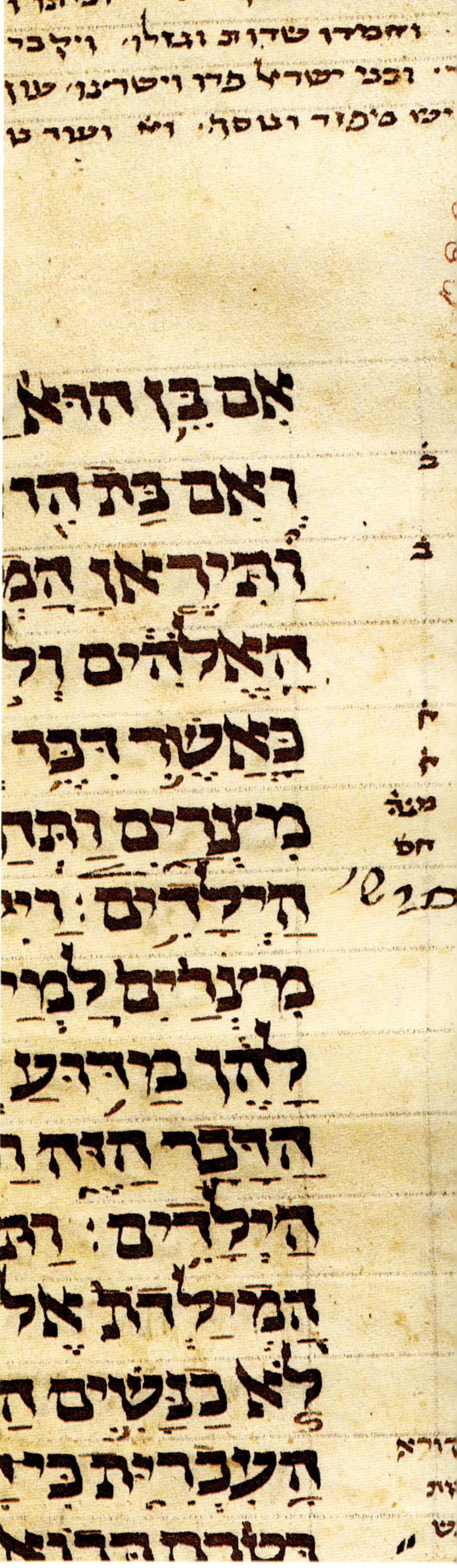

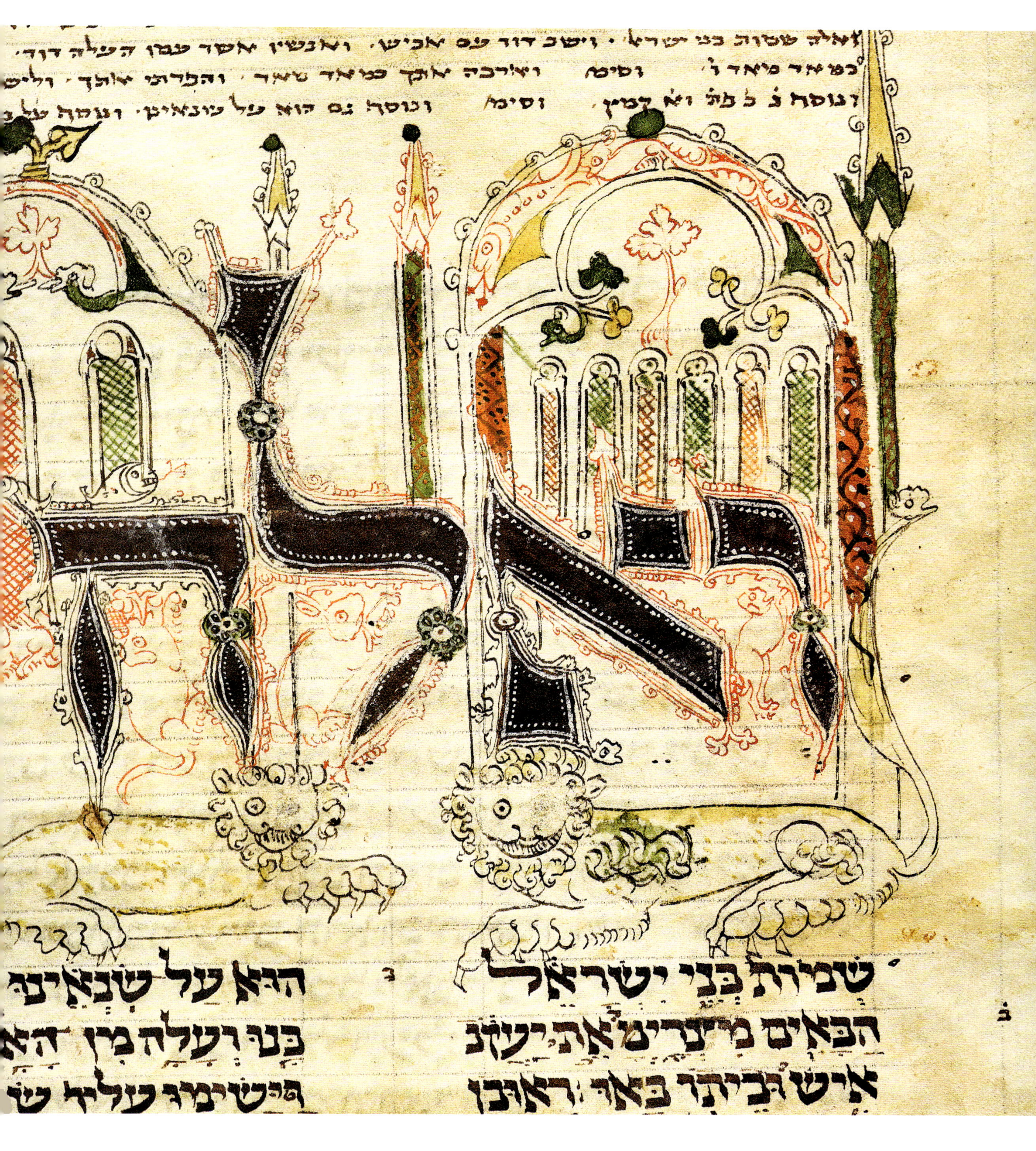

AD LECTOREM PIUM

CATHOLICI

ATQVE INVICTISSIMI

Philippi stemmata.

Omnib⁹ grata.

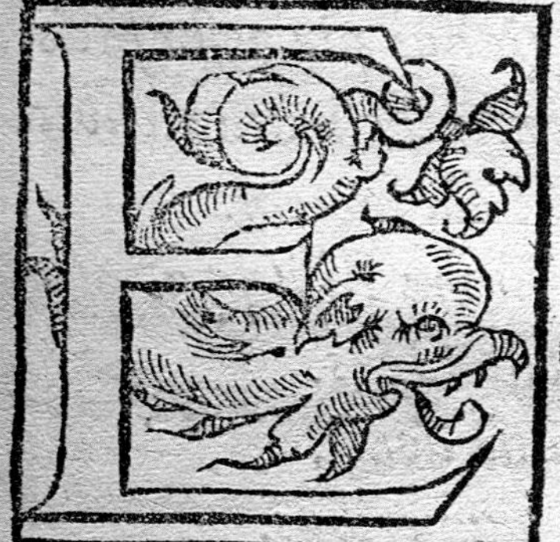

Cce tibi occurrunt, lector p[ia]

da Philippi

Regis terrarum stem[mata]

in orbe timor.

Vtpote Catholica.

Quæ sola Ecclesiæ vener[ata]

numine patrem,

Sanctam tutantur p[er]

Victricia semper.

iura Fidem.

Hæreticos, Mauros, Turcas, victosq; Tyrannos

Sub iuga nunc mittunt, paret vbiq; mare.

Fernandus victurus Deo.

Fernandum Christus, sceptrum, nomenq; Philipp[o]

Seruat, quò victor seruiat ille Deo.

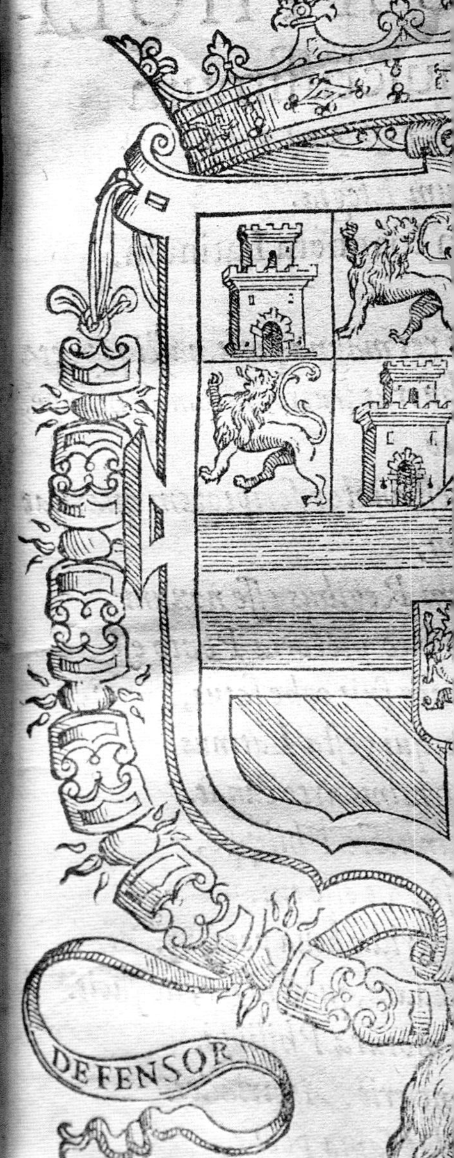

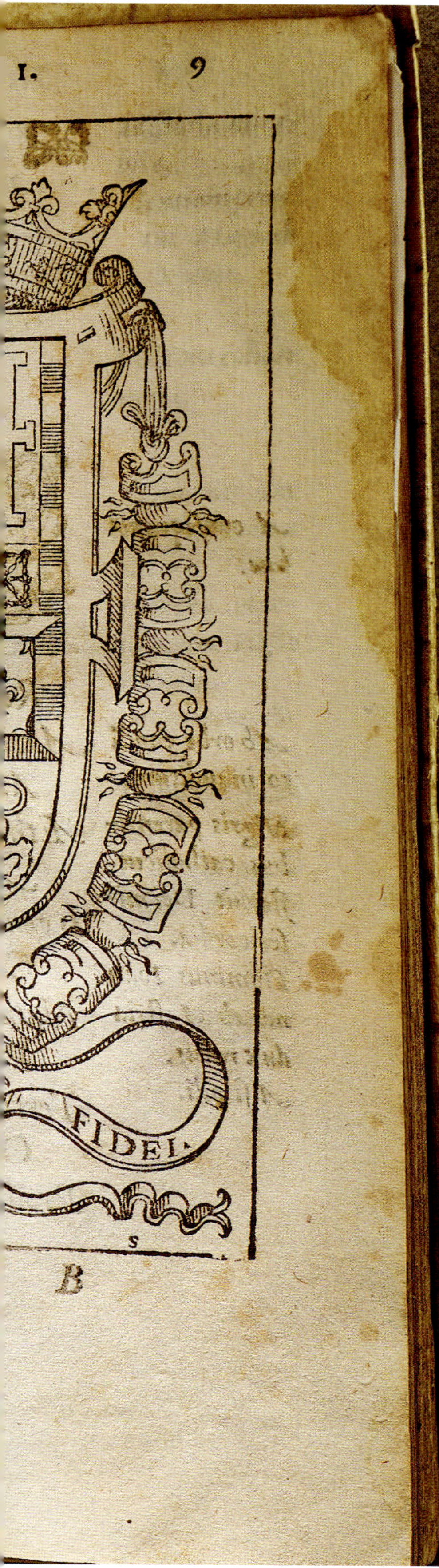

Juan Latino (ca. 1518–1596)

Ad Catholicum

1573

Manuscripts, Archives and Rare Books Division, Schomburg Center for Research in Black Culture

Panegyric verses—or poems of praise—like this one were common from the 15th to 18th centuries, when writers, painters, and musicians had to seek aristocratic patrons to underwrite their artistic endeavors. *Ad Catholicum*'s appeal to King Philip II of Spain is unique because its author, the humanist scholar Juan Latino, was the son of enslaved African parents. Latino's master, a Spanish count, educated him along with the count's own son, the Duke of Sessa. In 1546, the University of Granada in Spain awarded Latino a baccalaureate, and he later married a noblewoman. Latino's complete mastery of Latin is evident in the epigrams published in *Ad Catholicum*, of which only one other copy is known to have survived. Considered one of the rarest books in the world, *Ad Catholicum* is the earliest imprint by a black author in the Library's collection.

David Bar Pesah, scribe and decorator

Mahzor

Illuminated manuscript, 14th century

Dorot Jewish Division

The *mahzor* is a prayer book that Jews use on the High Holy Days of Rosh ha-Shanah and Yom Kippur, and on the three pilgrimage festivals of Sukkot, Passover, and Shavuot. This superb vellum *mahzor* in two volumes appears to be an example of the large-format, illuminated *mahzorim* created in Ashkenaz (Germany and Central Europe) in the mid-13th to mid-14th centuries. The only explicit information that has survived is the name of the scribe: a pair of illuminated letters incorporate the signature, "I, David Bar Pesah the scribe."

This panel illuminates the word *kol*—the initial word of the Kol Nidre declaration annulling the vows between penitent and God for the coming year. It is chanted three times at the beginning of the Yom Kippur evening service. With its hunting scene and grotesque images of diverse creatures, the volume's illustrations exhibit graphic elements common to much medieval book design. Bezalel Narkiss (author of *Hebrew Illuminated Manuscripts*) notes that "animal headed figures became one of the main Jewish motifs in South-German Hebrew illumination of the 13th and 14th centuries." It is possible that the hunting scene represents the persecution of the Jews. The New York manufacturer and bibliophile Louis Rabinowitz (1887–1957) purchased this treasure from the Jewish community of Padua, Italy, and donated it to the Library.

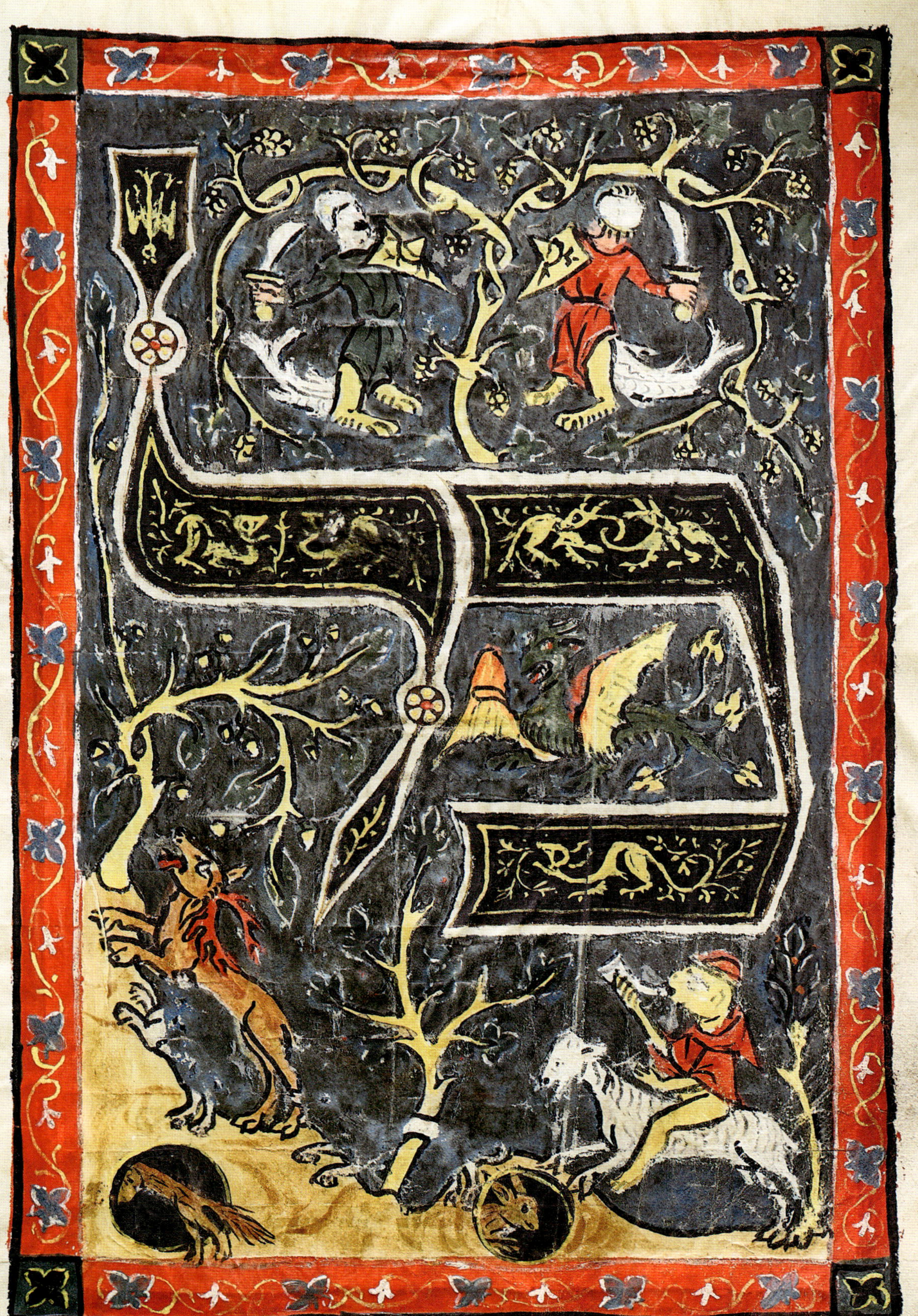
בישיבה של
מעלה׳ בישיב׳
של מטה׳ על
דעת המקום׳
ועל דעת הקהל
אנו מתירין ל
להתפלל עם
עברינים

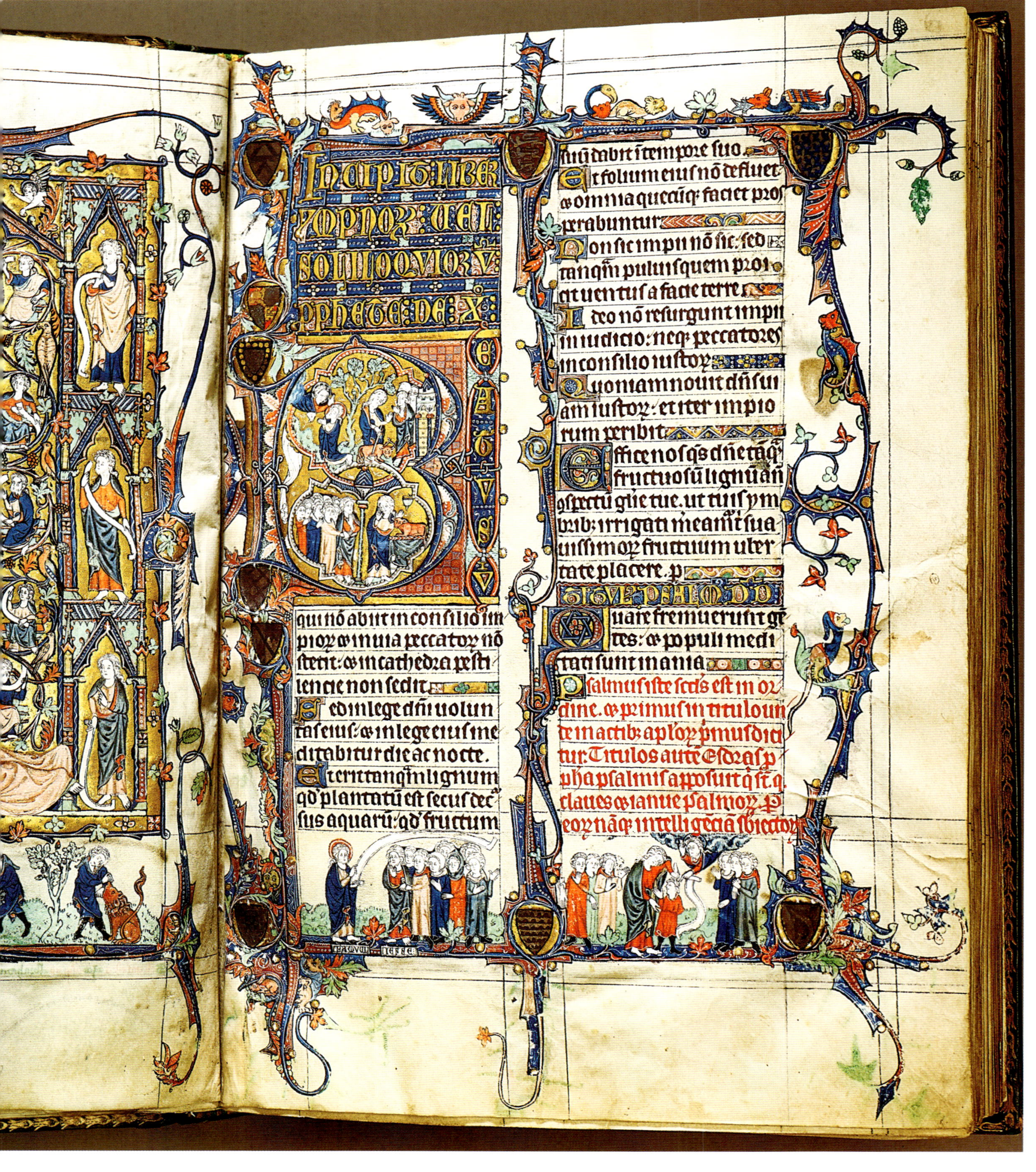

John de Tickhill (fl. early 14th century)
Tickhill Psalter
Illuminated manuscript, ca. 1310
The Miriam and Ira D. Wallach Division of Art, Prints and Photographs, Spencer Collection

Named after John de Tickhill, the prior of the Augustinian Canon Priory of Worksop in Nottinghamshire, the *Tickhill Psalter* is among the most lavishly illuminated of all 14th-century English manuscripts. Tickhill was elected prior in 1303 but discharged from his position in 1314 as a result of fiscal misconduct, a wrongdoing to which the steep costs of the manuscript likely contributed. A work of gargantuan ambition, the manuscript features pictorial and textual decorations that include large historiated initials and *bas-de-page* scenes forming a continuous narrative, commencing with the Old Testament. This astonishingly opulent, full-page opening illustration of the Tree of Jesse notwithstanding, the Psalter has numerous unfinished sheets that offer an unrivaled opportunity to study the genesis of the medieval illuminated manuscript. Acquired by the Library in the early 1930s, the work is among the Spencer Collection's most valuable holdings.

Pāli, Buddhist prayer boards
18th century
Manuscripts and Archives Division

Buddhist scriptures, or sutras, have been recorded on palm leaves and bamboo slivers for more than 2,000 years. The Pāli Canon is the standard collection of scriptures in the Theravada Buddhist tradition, preserved in the Pāli language. The lacquered palm leaves with large script inscribed in tamarind-seed ink were often used in the ordination of Buddhist monks. These texts detail principles that monks in Burma (now Myanmar) were required to follow, as well as sutras from the Buddha for use in instruction and meditation. The text itself is read horizontally from left to right.

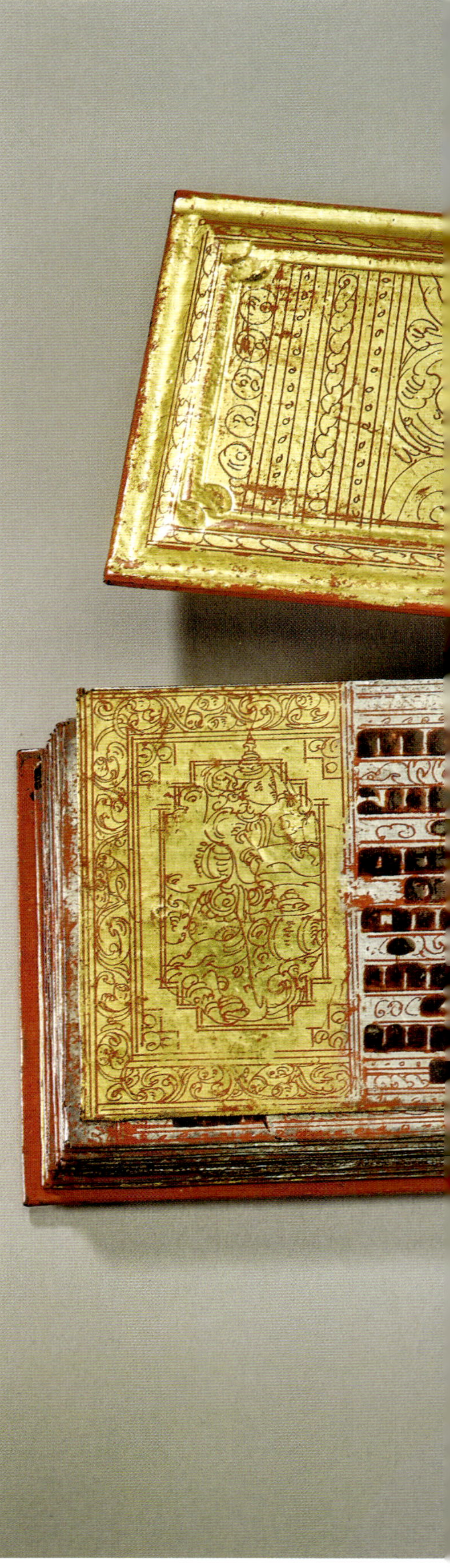

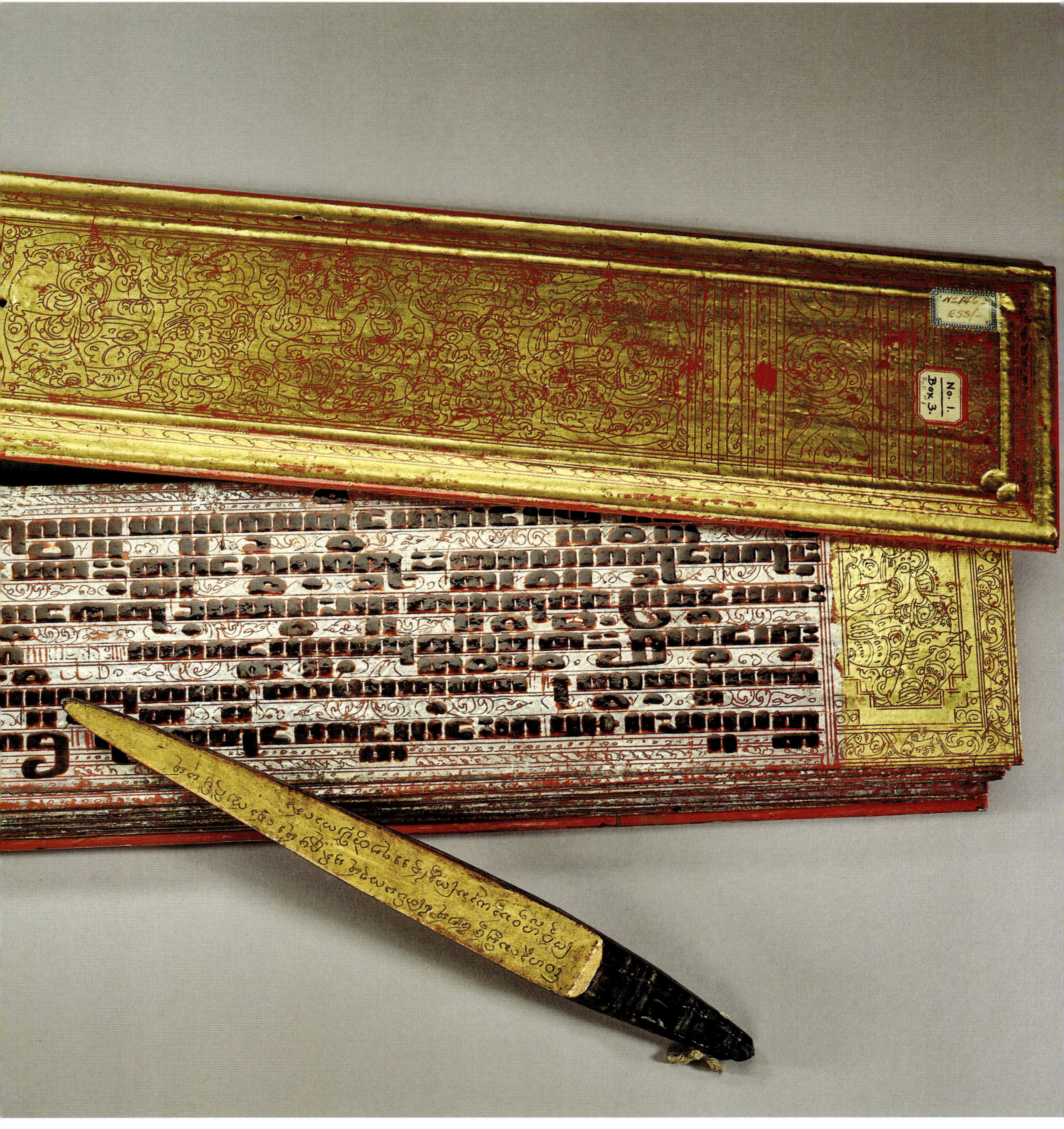
No. 1.
Box 3.

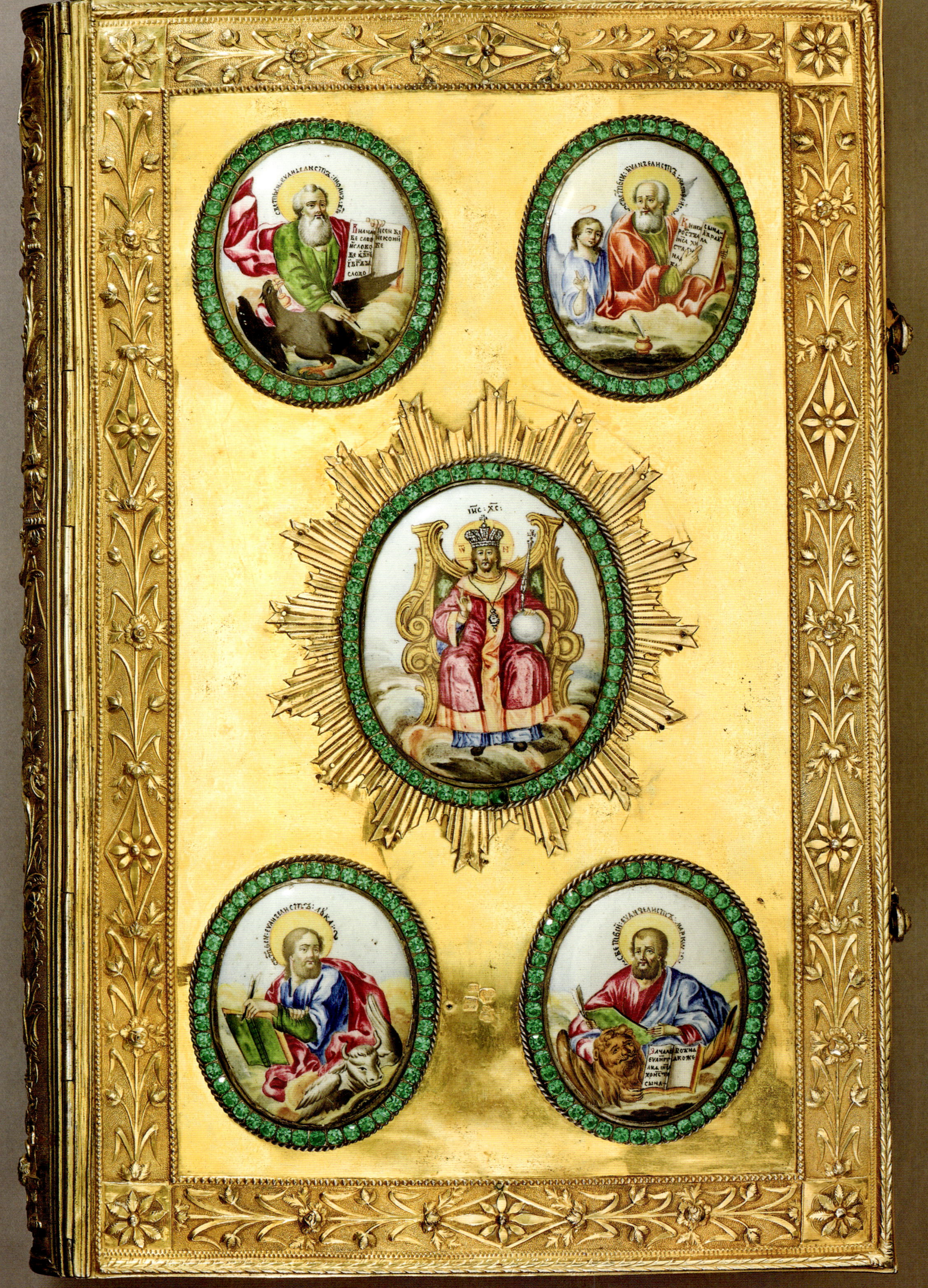

Evangelie naprestol'noe
Moscow, 1791
Rare Book Division

This sumptuous binding, the work of French-influenced Muscovite craftsmen, intentionally draws attention to the Word of God and signals the importance of the Gospels. Displayed prominently on the altar during the Divine Liturgy, it would have been raised and held aloft just prior to that day's gospel reading, to be seen by the entire congregation—hence its alternate name, the Elevation Gospels.

The binding of heavily gilded silver incorporates five enameled miniatures in surrounds of green semiprecious stones. The central medallion depicts Christ in Majesty—on a throne as a ruler—in the vestments of a Russian bishop. The four corner medallions encircle the four Evangelists (Matthew, Mark, Luke, and John), each with his respective symbols, or attributes. The clasps represent Saints Peter and Paul.

Mustafâ Darîr (fl. 14th century), translator and elaborator
Abū al-Ḥasan al-Bakrī al-Baṣrī (fl. 6th/13th century), author
Siyer-i Nebī (Life of the Prophet)
Illuminated manuscript, 13th century, copied 1594–1595
The Miriam and Ira D. Wallach Division of Art, Prints and Photographs, Spencer Collection

This manuscript of the *Life of the Prophet* is a masterpiece of classical Ottoman illumination. The Spencer Collection's volume is the only example of the surviving five volumes to retain its original, decorated black morocco binding. This volume is the third out of six; the first two are in the Topkapı Library in Istanbul and the remaining three are now lost. The New York Public Library's volume was copied and illustrated for Sultan Murād III (r. 1574–1595), who was an avid bibliophile and patron of numerous works, at the imperial court scriptorium in Istanbul in 1594–1595. Several of its 128 full-page miniature paintings have been identified as the work of the master known as Hasan, and together they comprise the earliest illustrated version of the text, which begins with the story of the Prophet's night journey. Escorted by winged angels, Prophet Muḥammad can be seen mounted on his mare Burāq. His face has, according to tradition, been whitened out in this elaboration of a 9th-century account of the life of Muḥ ammad.

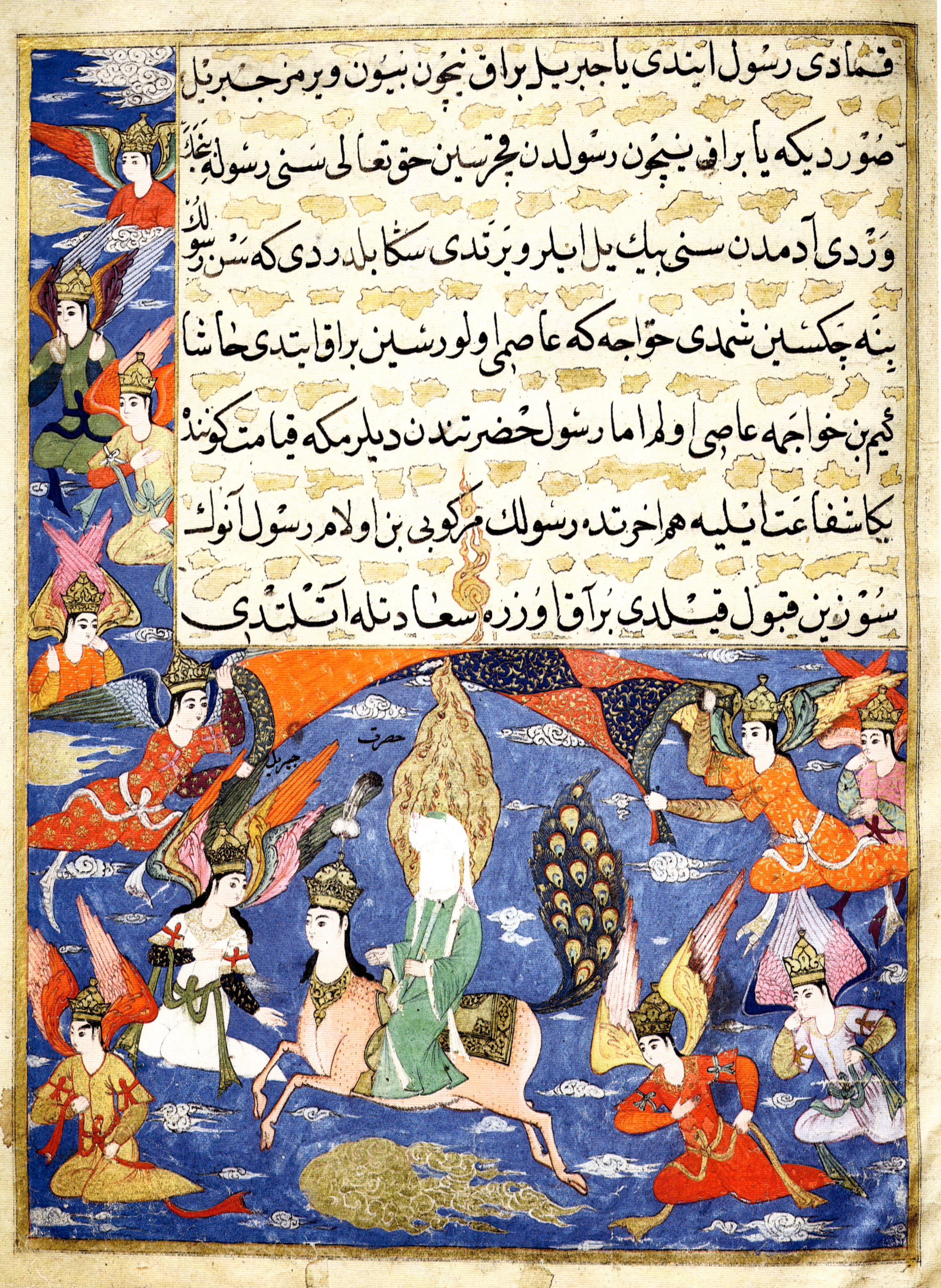

قمادی رسول ایندی یا جبریل براق نیچون بیون ویرمز جبریل
صوردیکه یا براق نیچون رسولدن فخر سین حق تعالی سنی رسولة بغش
وردی آدمدن سنی بنك یل ایلرو برتدی سڭا بلدردی که سن رسولك
بنه چکسین شمدی خواجه که عاصی اولورسین براق ایتدی حاشا
کیم بن خواجمه عاصی اولم اما رسول حضرتندن دیلرمکه قیامت کوننده
بکا شفاعت ایلیه هم احرتده رسولك مرکوبی بن اولام رسول آنوك
سوزین قبول قیلدی براق اوزره سعادتله آتلندی
حضرت
جبریل

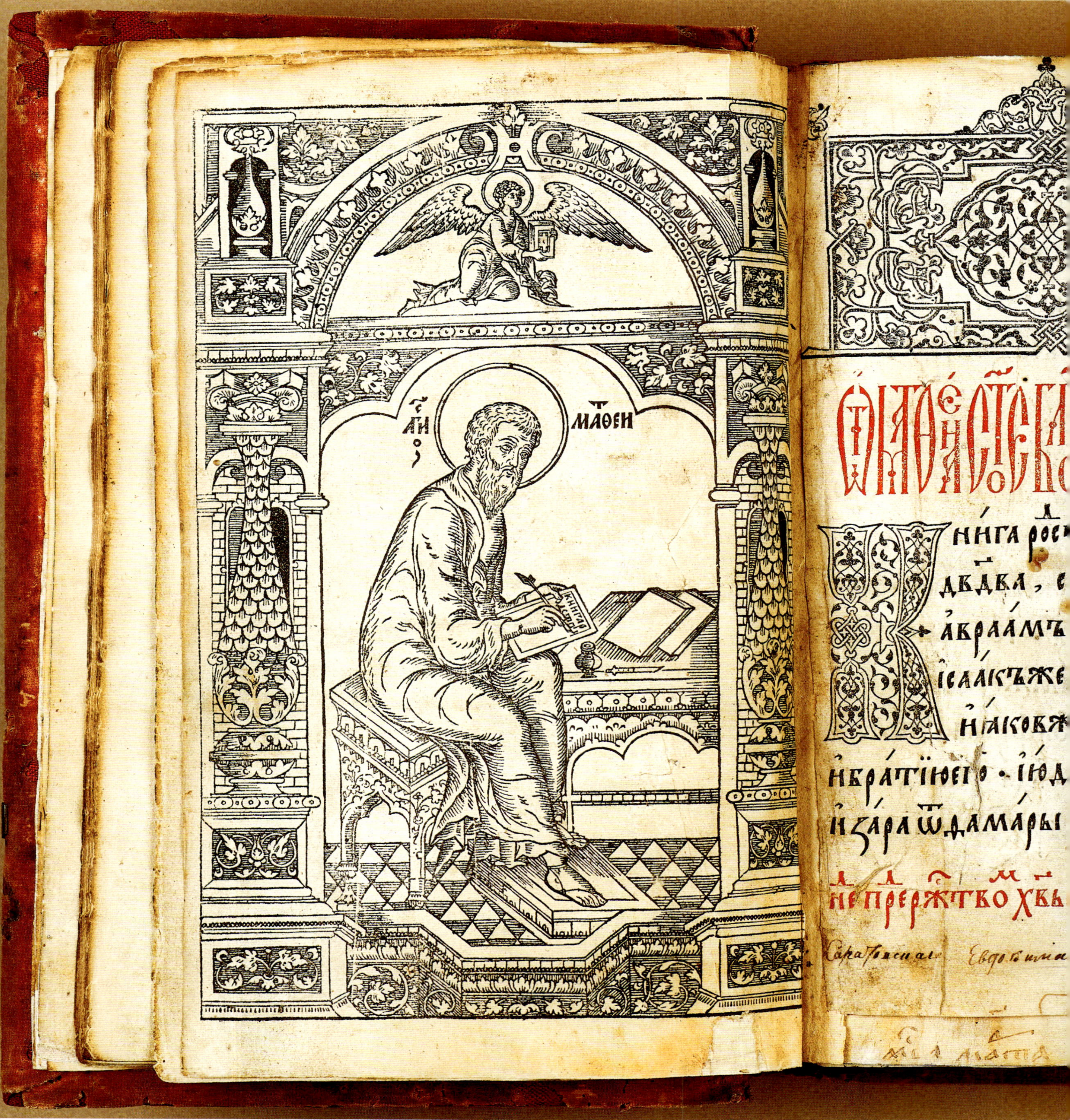

нига роси
двдва, с
авраамъ
исаакъже
иакова
ибратїю его. иуд
изара ѿ дамары

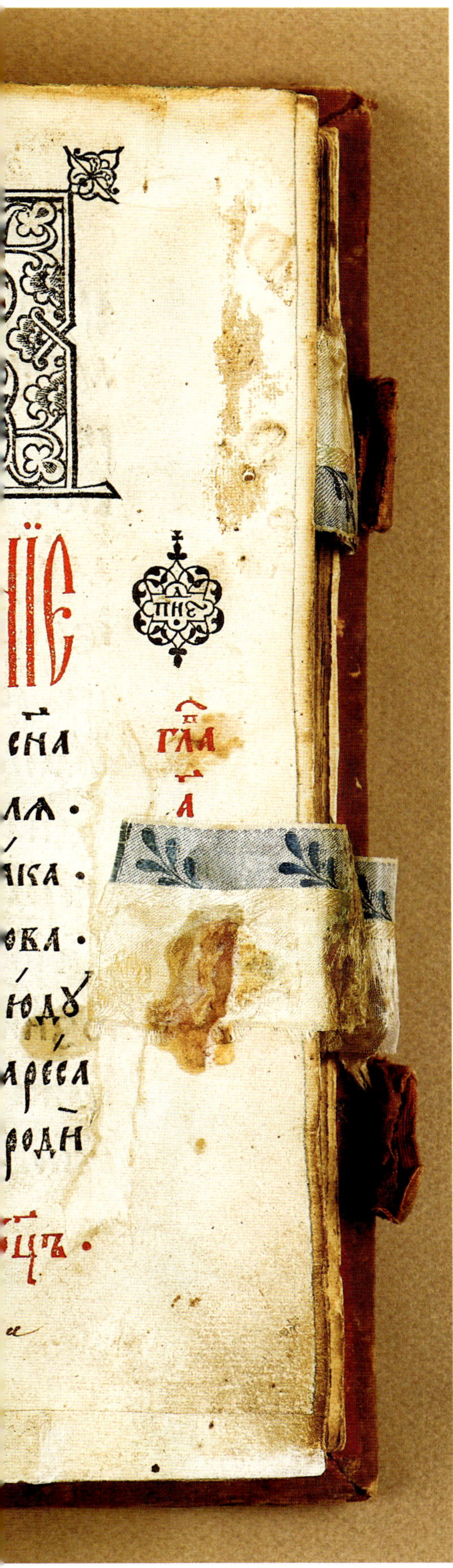

Vĕdomo būdi ʹi͡ako cheryre sut′ Evangeli͡e

Moscow: Ivan Fedorov, ca. 1564

Rare Book Division

The New York Public Library is fortunate to hold both the first dated book printed in Russia—*The Acts and Epistles of the Apostles*, issued in 1564 by Ivan Fedorov during the reign of Ivan the Terrible—and the present work, its undated predecessor, also published by Fedorov. Because it bears no imprint date or attribution, this latter volume is often referred to as the "Anonymous" Gospels. Both works stand as cornerstones of the Library's rich collections of Slavic-language holdings that document the history and culture of Imperial Russia.

A curious hieroglyphick Bible; or, Select passages in the Old and New Testaments, represented with emblematical figures, for the amusement of youth. . . .
Worcester, Massachusetts: Isaiah Thomas, 1788
Rare Book Division

A Curious Hieroglyphick Bible was published in 1788 by Isaiah Thomas, one of the premier printers in North America during the late colonial era and early years of the United States. The volume was intended to help juvenile readers learn both their ABCs and Scripture, and it functioned in part like a rebus—a puzzle in which words are represented by playful combinations of pictures and individual letters. It is notable, as well, for being the most heavily illustrated American book of its time, featuring nearly 500 woodcut illustrations.

While hieroglyphic Bibles were popular during the 18th century, with many thousands of copies printed in the Americas and England, only four examples of the present edition are known, making it one of the great rarities in all of children's literature.

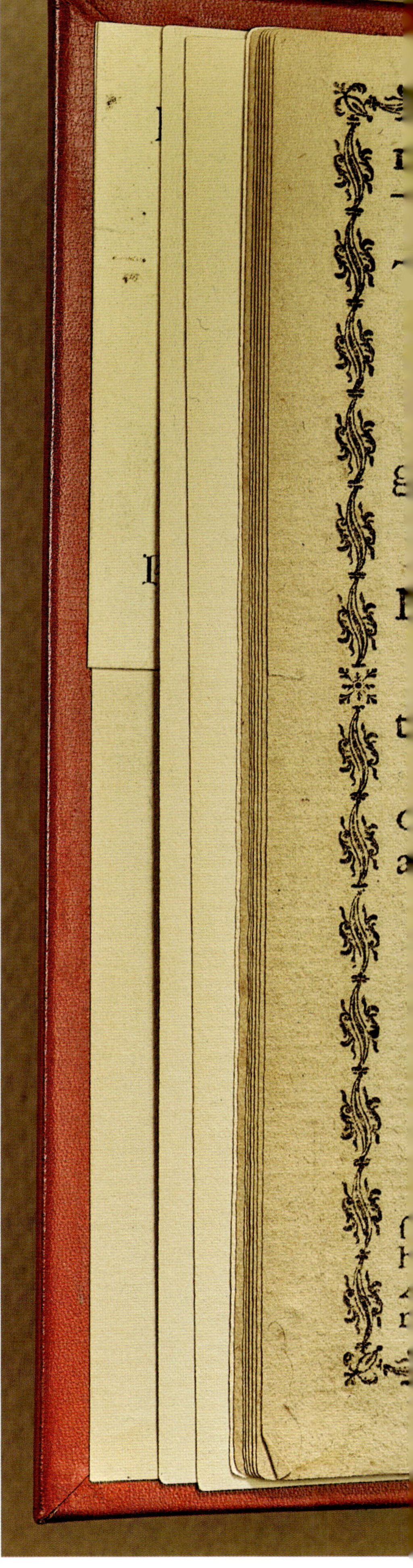

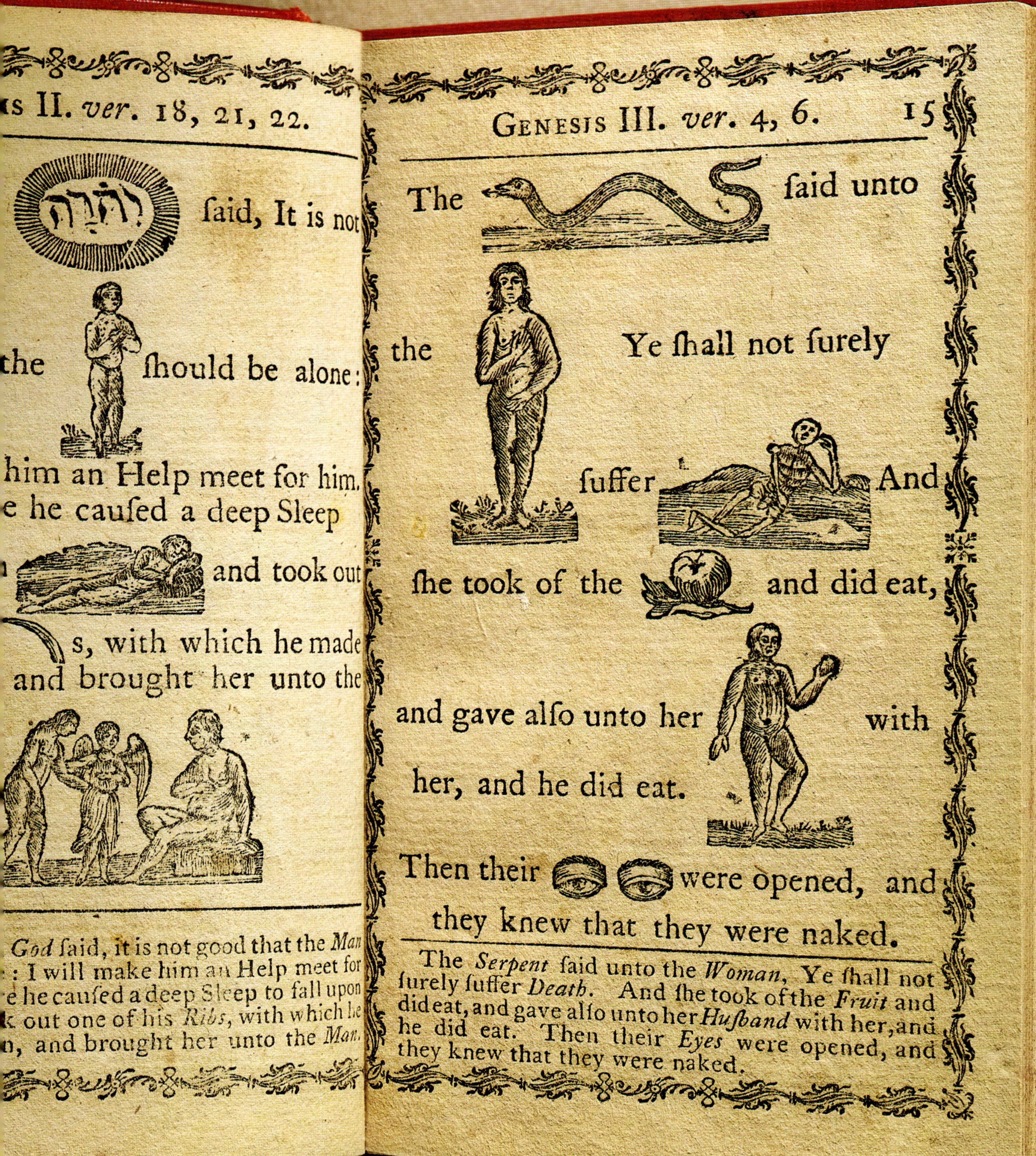

s II. *ver.* 18, 21, 22.

said, It is not

the should be alone:

him an Help meet for him.
e he caused a deep Sleep

and took out

s, with which he made
and brought her unto the

God said, it is not good that the *Man*
: I will make him an Help meet for
e he caused a deep Sleep to fall upon
k out one of his *Ribs*, with which he
n, and brought her unto the *Man*.

GENESIS III. *ver.* 4, 6. 15

The said unto

the Ye shall not surely

suffer And

she took of the and did eat,

and gave also unto her with

her, and he did eat.

Then their were opened, and
they knew that they were naked.

The *Serpent* said unto the *Woman*, Ye shall not
surely suffer *Death*. And she took of the *Fruit* and
did eat, and gave also unto her *Husband* with her, and
he did eat. Then their *Eyes* were opened, and
they knew that they were naked.

more full and emphaticall ſignification then any one engliſh word can or doth ſomtime expreſſe, hence wee have done that ſomtime which faithfull tranſlators may doe, *viz.* not only to tranſlate the word but the emphaſis of it; as אל *mighty God*, for God. ברך *humbly bleſſe* for *bleſſe*; *riſe to ſtand*, pſalm 1. for *ſtand truth and faithfullnes* for *truth*. Howbeit, for the verſe ſake wee doe not alway thus, yet wee render the word truly though not fully; as when wee ſomtime ſay *reioyce* for *ſhout for ioye*.

As for all other changes of numbers, tenſes, and characters of ſpeech, they are ſuch as either the hebrew will unforcedly beare, or our engliſh forceably calls for, or they no way change the ſence; and ſuch are printed uſually in an other character.

If therefore the verſes are not alwayes ſo ſmooth and elegant as ſome may deſire or expect; let them conſider that Gods Altar needs not our polliſhings: Ex. 20. for wee have reſpected rather a plaine tranſlation, then to ſmooth our verſes with the ſweetnes of any paraphraſe, and ſoe have attended Conſcience rather then Elegance, fidelity rather then poetry, in tranſlating the hebrew words into engliſh language, and Davids poetry into engliſh meetre;

that

that ſoe wee may ſing
ſongs of prayſe accor
will; untill hee take
and wipe away all c
bid us enter into
ioye to ſing
Halleluia

The Whole Booke of Psalmes Faithfully Translated into English Metre

Cambridge, Massachusetts Bay Colony: Stephen Day, 1640

Rare Book Division

The 1640 edition of *The Whole Booke of Psalmes Faithfully Translated into English Metre*—better known as the Bay Psalm Book—has the distinction of being the first book printed in British North America. Published in an edition of perhaps as many as 1,700 copies, only eleven are now known to survive, and only five of those are complete.

While the Bay Psalm Book is full of typographical errors and is far from being an aesthetically pleasing production, its importance cannot be overstated. The book symbolizes the early introduction of printing into the English colonies, which in turn reflects the importance that the Puritans placed on reading and education—and, somewhat later, on the concepts of freely available information, freedom of expression, and freedom of the press. All of these principles fed into the revolutionary impulse that gave rise 136 years later to the United States of America.

John Eliot (1604–1690), translator

Mamusse Wunneetupanatamwe Up-Biblum God Naneeswe Nukkone Testament Kah Wonk Wusku Testament. . . .

Cambridge, Massachusetts Bay Colony: Samuel Green and Marmaduke Johnson, 1663

Rare Book Division

The first Bible printed in the Americas, as well as the first Bible translated into a Native American language, resulted from the ecclesiastical efforts of John Eliot, one of the earliest Puritan proselytizers for Christianity in the English colonies.

Soon after his arrival in Boston in 1631, Eliot became convinced of the need for a translation of the Bible into the local Algonquin language. Eliot began his project in 1649 and proceeded to work diligently for the next ten years, not only learning the indigenous language, but also inventing a new orthography with which to write it. He completed the New Testament in 1661, followed by the Old Testament two years later. Although the dialect that he translated is now extinct, Eliot's Bible stands as a remarkable scholastic achievement.

MAMUSSE

WUNNEETUPANATAMWE

UP-BIBLUM GOD

NANEESWE

NUKKONE TESTAMENT

KAH WONK

WUSKU TESTAMENT.

Ne quoſhkinnumuk naſhpe Wuttinneumoh CHRIST
noh aſoowesit

JOHN ELIOT.

CAMBRIDGE:

Printeuoop naſhpe *Samuel Green* kah *Marmaduke Johnſon*.

1663.

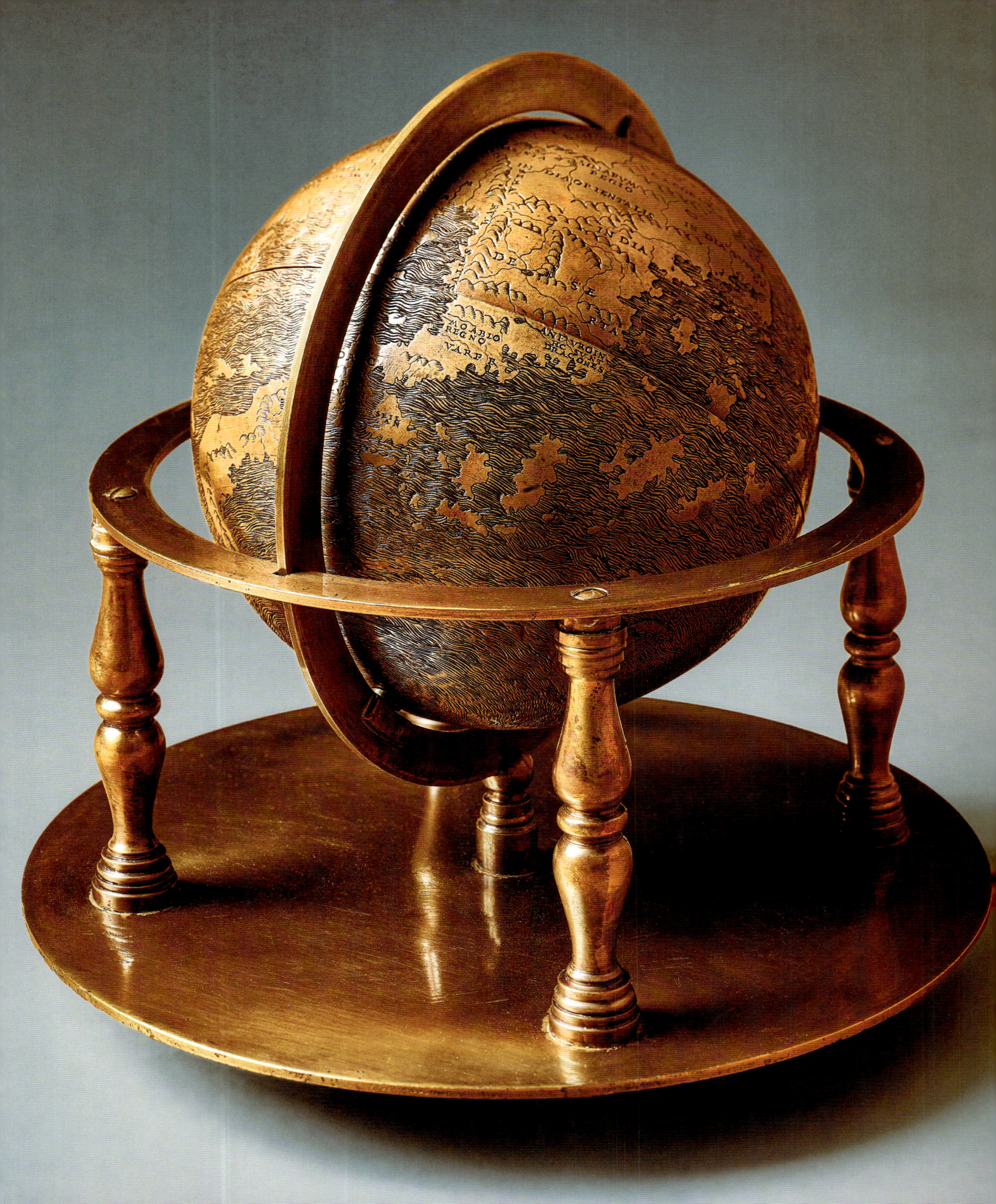

DIA ORIENTALIS
INDIA
MOABIO
REGNO
HC SVNT
DRACONES

Hunt-Lenox Globe
Copper, ca. 1508
Rare Book Division

The Hunt-Lenox Globe is recognized not only as one of the earliest surviving terrestrial globes, but also as one of the oldest known cartographic depictions of the Americas—specifically, the islands of Cuba and Hispaniola, along with the South American continent, which is assigned various regional names such as "Mundus Novus" and "Terra Brazil."

The Globe is also one of only two medieval or Renaissance-era maps or globes known to bear the famous motto *Hic Sunt Dracones*, or "Here be dragons." While today this phrase connotes images of the unknown, it may have originally referenced the Komodo dragons that inhabit portions of the Indonesian archipelago. Originally purchased in France during the 1850s by the noted American architect Richard Morris Hunt, the globe was subsequently gifted to the Library's progenitor James Lenox.

Letter from Christopher Columbus (1451–1506) to Luis de Santángel (d. 1498)
February 15, 1493
Rare Book Division

Christopher Columbus detailed his initial voyage to the Americas in the form of several long letters, including this one to Luis de Santángel, Treasurer of Aragon, who funded much of the voyage. Here, Columbus provides a brief account of the lands and peoples that he encountered, while also enjoining the Spanish court to fund a subsequent return expedition.

On receiving the letter in Barcelona in late March 1493, Santángel arranged to have it printed not only as a public announcement of Columbus's achievement, but also as a propaganda piece to further publicize and strengthen Spanish territorial claims. Though at least several hundred copies of the letter were issued, only the present example is known to survive, making it the rarest example of printed Americana in existence.

SEÑOR por que se que aureis plazer dela grand vitoria que nuestro señor me
ha dado en mi viaie vos escrivo esta por la ql sabreys como en .xxxiii. dias pase A
las indias cõ la armada q̃ los illustrissimos Rey e Reyna ñros señores me dieron
dõde yo falle muy muchas Islas pobladas cõ gente sin numero : y dellas todas
he tomado posesion por sus altezas con pregon y vãdera rreal estendida y non mefu
e cõtradicho Ala primera q̃ yo falle puse nonbre sant saluador a comemoracion desu alta mages
tat el qual marauillosamente todo esto andado los idios la llaman guanahani Ala segũda
puse nonbre la isla de santa maria deconcepcion ala tercera ferrandina ala quarta la isla bella
ala quita la Isla Juana e asi a cada vna nonbre nuevo Quando yo llegue ala Juana seg
ui io la costa della al poniente y la falle tan grande q̃ pense que seria tierra firme la prouicia de
catayo y como no falle asi villas y luguares enla costa dela mar saluo pequeñas poblaciones
con la gente delas q̃les nopodia hauer fabla por que luego fuyan todos: andaua yo a de
lante por el dicho camino pẽsado deuo errar grãdes Ciudades o villas y al cabo de muchas
leguas visto q̃ no hauia inouació i que la costa me leuaua alsetẽtrion de adõde mi voluntad
era cõtraria porq̃ el yuierno era ya ẽcarnado yo tenia proposito de hazer del al austro y tan biẽ
el viẽto medio adelãte determine deno aguardar otro tiẽpo y bolui atras fasta vn señalado puer
to de adõde ẽbie dos hõbres por la tierra para saber si hauia Rey o grãdes Ciudades ãdoui
erõ tres iornadas y hallarõ ĩfinitas poblaciões pequeñas i gẽte si nu mero mas no cosa de reg
imẽto por lo qual se boluierõ yo entẽdia harto de otros idios q̃ ia tenia tomados como conti
nuamẽte esta tierra era Isla e asi segui la costa della al oriẽte ciento i siete leguas fasta dõde fa
zia fin: del qual cabo vi otra Isla al oriẽte distĩcta de esta diez o ocho leguas ala qual luego
pu se nombre la spañola y fui alli y segui la parte del setentrion asi como dela iuana al oriente.
clxxviii grãdes leguas por linia recta del oriẽte asi como dela iuana la qual y todas las otras
sõ fortissimas en demasiado grado y esta enestremo en ella ay muchos puertos enla costa dela
mar si cõparació de otros q̃ yo sepa en cristianos y fartos rrios y buenos y grandes q̃ es mara
villa las tierras della sõ altas y ẽ ella muy muchas sierras y mõtañas altissimas si cõparació
de la isla de cẽtre fre todas fermosissimas de mil fechuras y todas ãdabiles y llenas de arbols
de mil maneras i altas i parecen q̃ llegã al cielo i tẽgo por dicho q̃ iamas pierdẽ la foia segun lo
puede cõprhẽder q̃ los vi tã verdes i tã hermosos como sõ por mayo en spaña i dellos stauã flor
ridos dellos cõ fruto i dellos enotro termino segũ es su calidad i cãtaua el rui señor i otros pa
xaricos demil maneras en el mes de nouiẽbre por alli dõde io ãdaua ay palmas de seis o de
ocho maneras q̃ es admiracion verlas por la diformidad fermosa dellas mas asi como los o
otros arboles y frutos e iervas en ella ay pinares amarauilla e ay canpiñas grãdissimas e ay mi
el i de muchas maneras de aues y frutas muy diuersas enlas tierras ay muchas minas deme
tales e ay gẽte istimabile numero La spañola es marauilla la sierras y las mõtañas y las uegas
i las campiñas y las tierras tan fermosas y gruesas para plantar y sẽbrar pa criar ganados de to
das suertes para hedificios de villas e lugares los puertos dela mar aqui no hauria crehencia sin
vista y delos rios muchos y grandes y buenas aguas los mas delos quales traẽ oro ẽ los arbo
les y frutos e yeruas ay grandes differencias de aquel las dela iuana en esta ay muchas specie
rias y grandes minas de oro y de otros metales. La gente desta ysla y de todas las otras q̃ he
fallado y hauido: ni aya hauido noticia andan todos desnudos hõbres y mugeres asi como
sus madres los parẽ haun que algunas mugeres se cobiian vn solo lugar cõ vna foia de yerr
ua: o vna cosa dealgodõ que pa ello fazen ellos no tienen fierro ni azero ni armas ni son para
ello no por que no sea gente bien dispuesta y de fermosa estatura saluo que sõ muy te merosos
a marauilla no tienẽ otras armas saluo las [illegible]as delas cañas quando estan cõ la simiente
qual ponen al cabo vn pa lillo agudo eno osan vsar de aq̃llas que m[illegible] veces [illegible]
cido embiar atierra dos otres hombres [illegible] alguna villa pa hauer fabl[illegible] y salir[illegible]

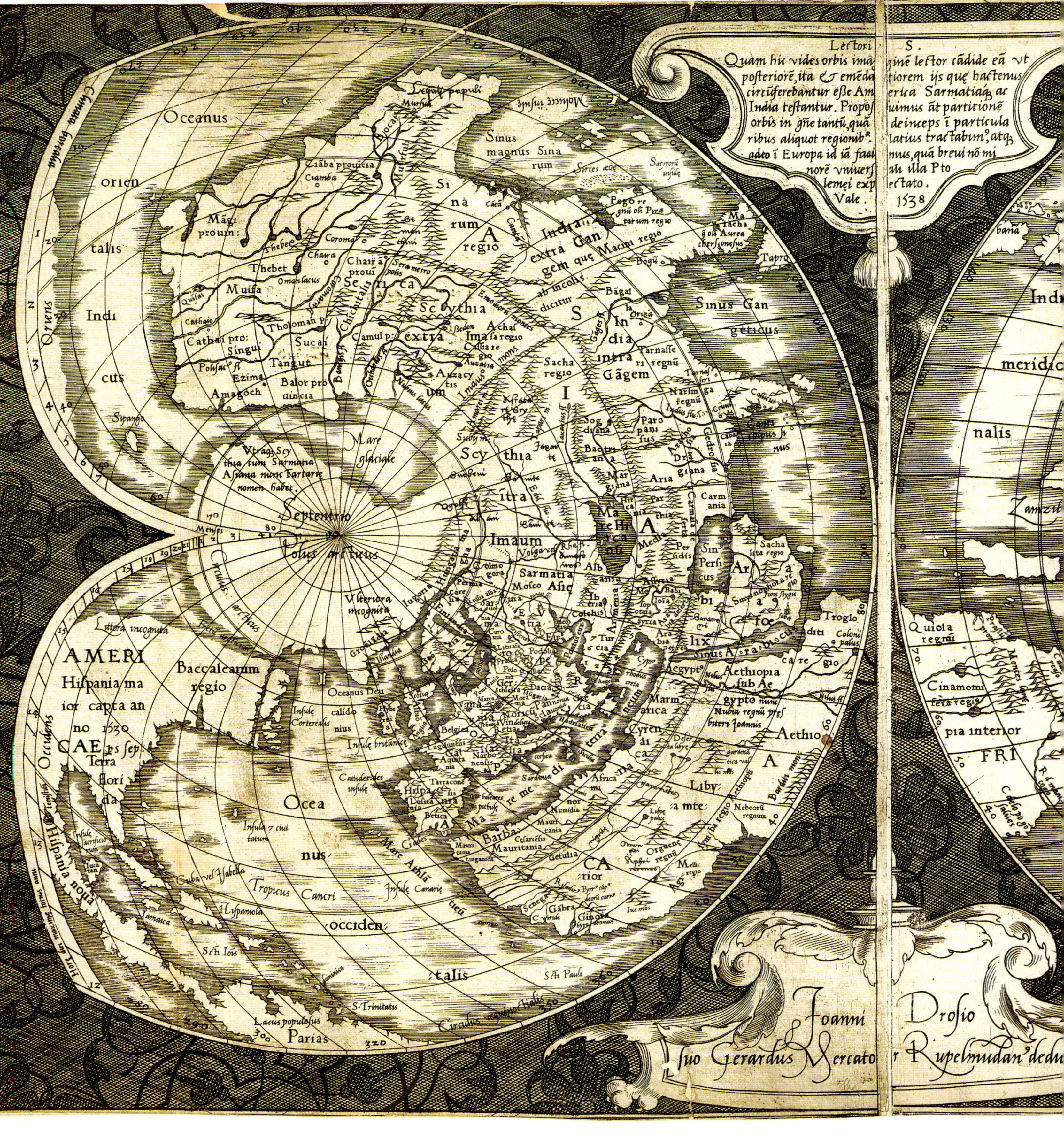

Lectori S.
Quam hic vides orbis ima gine lector cādide eā ut
posteriorē, ita & emēda tiorem ijs quę hactenus
circūferebantur esse Am erica Sarmatia ac
India testantur. Propo suimus āt partitionē
orbis in gñe tantū, quā deinceps ī particula
ribus aliquot regionib. latius tractabim. atq3
adeo ī Europa id iā faci mus, quā breui nō mi
norē vniuers ali illa Pto
lemei expe ctato.
Vale. 1538
Joanni Drosio
suo Gerardus Mercato r Rupelmudan' dedi
Oceanus
orien
talis
Indi
cus
Oriens
Septentrio
Polus arcticus
Mare glaciale
Scythia
Sarmatia Asię
India extra Gangem
India intra Gāgem
Sinus Gangeticus
AMERI
Hispania ma
ior capta an
no 1530
Terra flori da
Baccalearum regio
Occidens
Hispania noua
Ocea
nus
occiden
talis
Tropicus Cancri
Hispaniola
Parias
Aethiopia sub Aegypto
Libya
AFRICA
Indi
meridic
nalis

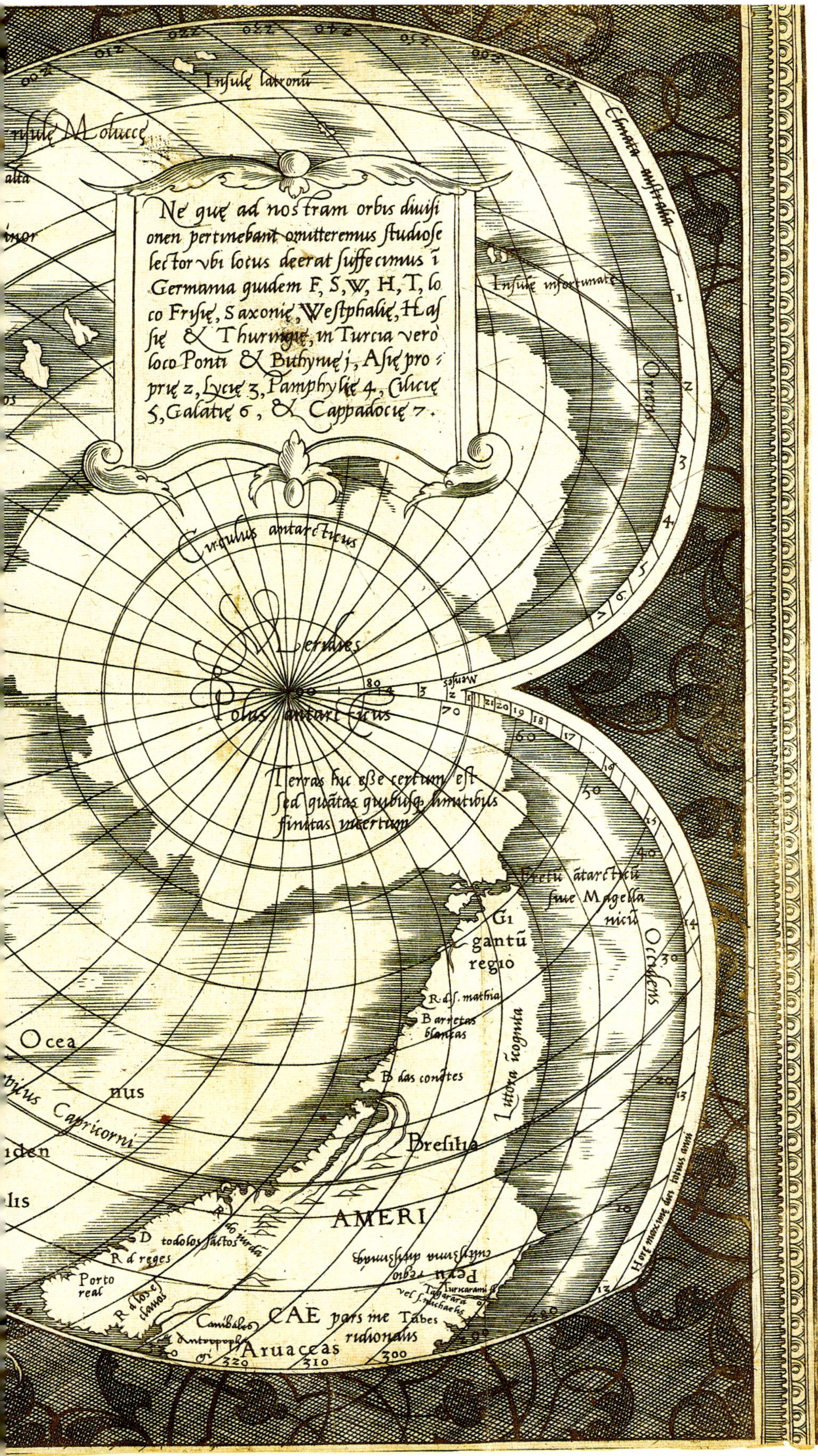

Gerardus Mercator (1512–1594)
Orbis Imago
Louvain, 1538
Rare Book Division

The *Orbis Imago* is the earliest dated map to apply the name "America" to both continents of the Western Hemisphere. Gerardus Mercator drew the map when he was only twenty-six years old, and it represents the Flemish cartographer's first published world map. The Library is honored to hold one of only two known copies of this cartographic milestone.

Today, Mercator is best known for the projection that bears his name, a representation that solved the problem of depicting the spherically shaped world on a flat surface. For this earlier map, however, Mercator used a double-cordiform (heart-shaped) projection, which breaks the world sphere into halves, with the equator as the common base, thus allowing for the illustration of both polar regions.

François Marie Arouet Voltaire (1694–1778)
Initial printing of *Candide, ou, L'optimisme / traduit de l'allemand de Mr. le docteur Ralph*
Geneva, 1759
Rare Book Division

Voltaire's satirical novel, first published anonymously, stands as one of the great literary achievements of the 18th century. The innocent hero's misadventures reveal human cruelty and greed, and he concludes that contentment comes only from tending one's own garden.

An instant success despite much controversy over its political and religious views, *Candide* appeared in seventeen editions within a year of its first publication. Voltaire, one of the great minds of the Enlightenment, promoted religious tolerance and legal equality at a time when church and king were powerful and corrupt. Late in life, he was responsible for freeing 12,000 serfs near his Swiss estate.

The New York Public Library is one of only two institutions in the world that hold all of these first-year printings. (The other is the Bodleian Library of Oxford University.) The volumes are held as part of the Rare Book Division's Martin J. Gross Collection, which contains the finest collection of contemporary editions of Voltaire's works to be found in any American institution.

CANDIDE,

OU

L'OPTIMISME,

TRADUIT DE L'ALLEMAND

DE

MR. LE DOCTEUR RALPH.

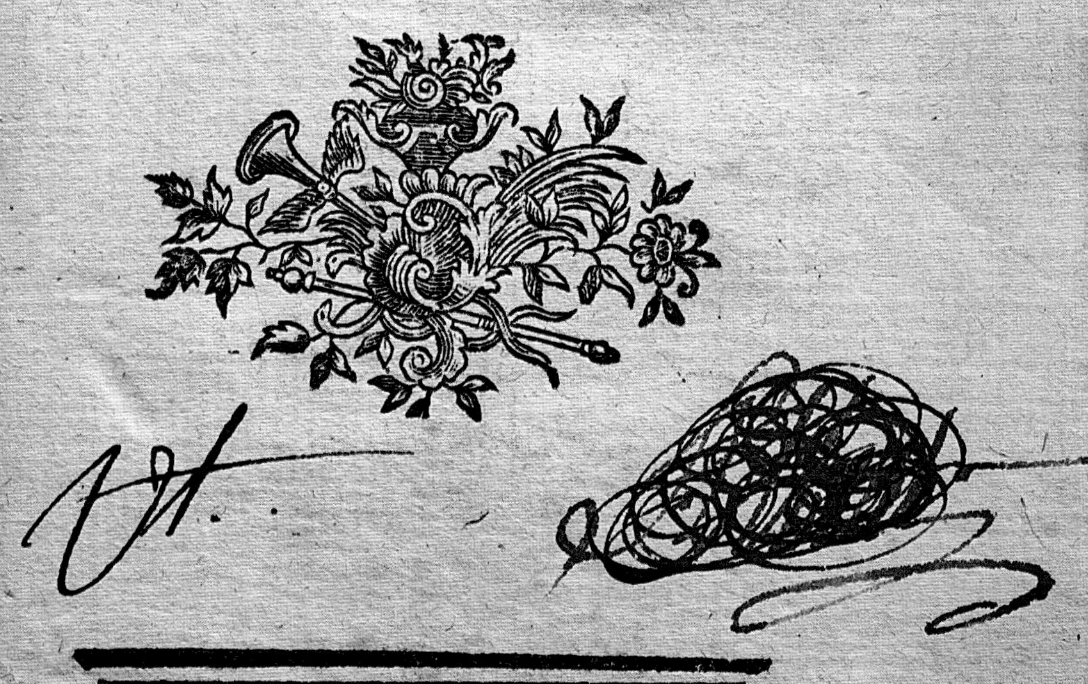

MDCCLIX.

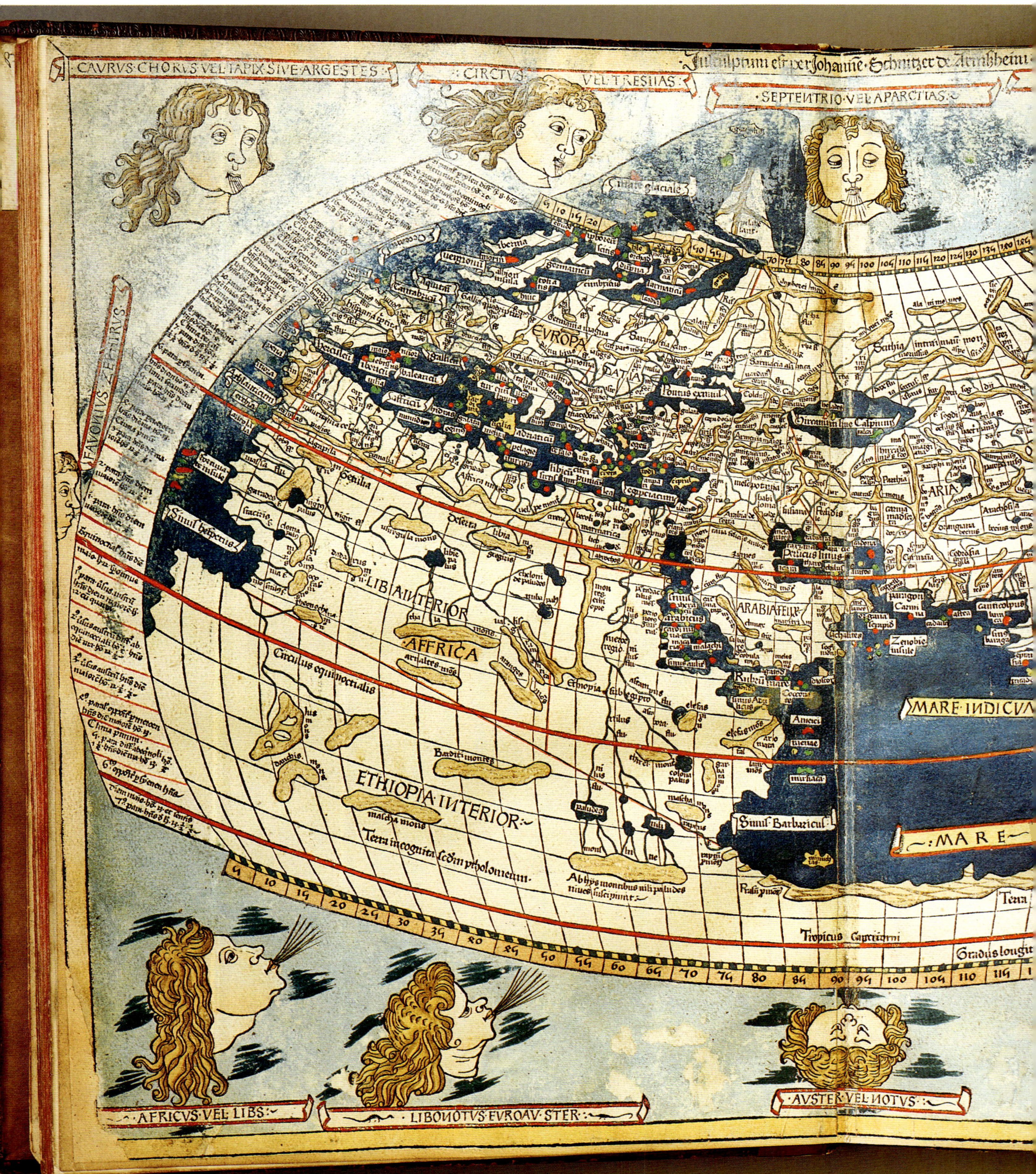
CAVRVS·CHORVS·VEL·IAPIX·SIVE·ARGESTES
CIRCIVS VEL·TRESIAS
SEPTENTRIO·VEL·APARCTIAS
FAVONIVS·ZEPHIRVS
EVROPA
LIBIA INTERIOR
AFFRICA
Circulus equinoctialis
ETHIOPIA·INTERIOR
Terra incognita secundum pholomeum
ARABIA FELIX
MARE·INDICVM
Sinus Barbaricus
MARE
Tropicus Capricorni
Gradus longit
AFRICVS·VEL·LIBS
LIBONOTVS·EVROAVSTER
AVSTER·VEL·NOTVS

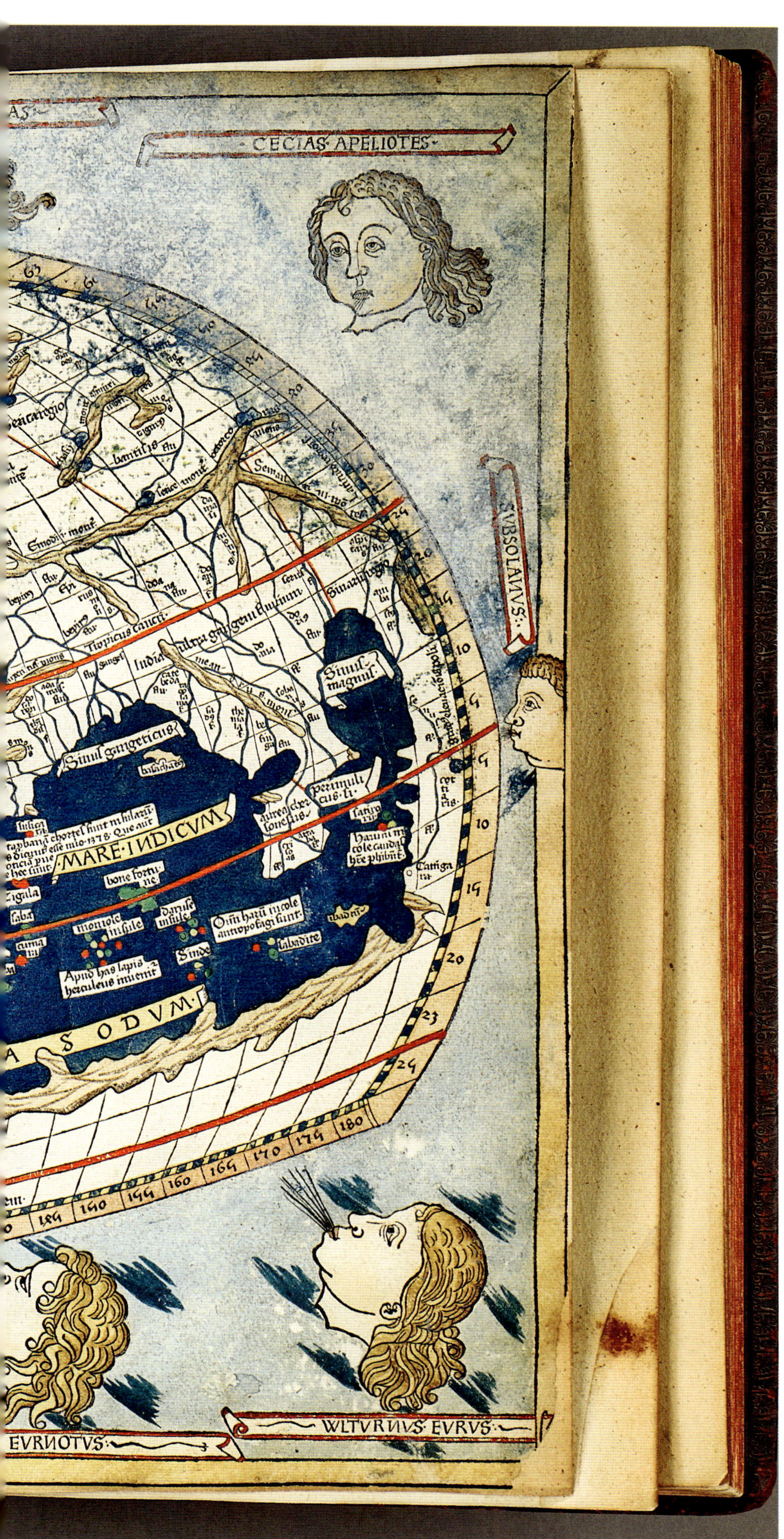

Ptolemy (ca. 100–ca. 170)
Cosmographia
Ulm: Lienhart Holle, 1482
Rare Book Division

Compiled during the 2nd century CE by astronomer and geographer Claudius Ptolemy, *Cosmographia* gained popularity during the Renaissance following its translation into Latin from Greek and Arabic sources. Indeed, the volume—which comprises an atlas, gazetteer, and scholarly treatise—proved highly influential, promoting mathematics as the basis for accurate mapmaking as well as increasing Europeans' overall geographic understanding.

The present edition of *Cosmographia*, issued in 1482 by Lienhart Holle of Ulm, a city in what is now Germany, is notable not only for its place in printing history—it was the first cartographic work to be published north of the Alps—but also for its beauty and sumptuousness: the intense blue coloration adorning many of the book's full-page maps derives from the use of ultramarine pigment, made from expensive lapis lazuli stone.

Miguel de Cervantes (1547–1616)

First edition of *El ingenioso hidalgo Don Quixote de la Mancha*

Madrid: Por Iuan de la Cuesta, vendese en casa de Francisco de Robles, librero del Rey nr̃o señor, 1605

Henry W. and Albert A. Berg Collection of English and American Literature

Don Quixote, the first part of which was published in 1605, is often called the first modern novel. Some say it is the finest ever written, and it is certainly the most influential work of literature in the Spanish language. Before 1605, Cervantes published a few poems and a pastoral novel (*La Galatea*, 1585), and saw some of his plays produced in Madrid, but much of his life leading up to the publication of *Don Quixote* was precarious. He spent time in the military, was enslaved for five years in Algiers, worked as a tax collector in Andalusia, and was interned in a Spanish prison. Little is known about his personal life, including when he had time to write his masterpiece.

EL INGENIOSO HIDALGO DON QVIXOTE DE LA MANCHA,

Compuesto por Miguel de Ceruantes Saauedra.

DIRIGIDO AL DVQVE DE BEIAR, Marques de Gibraleon, Conde de Benalcaçar, y Bañares, Vizconde de la Puebla de Alcozer, Señor de las villas de Capilla, Curiel, y Burguillos.

M. j. chavignac —

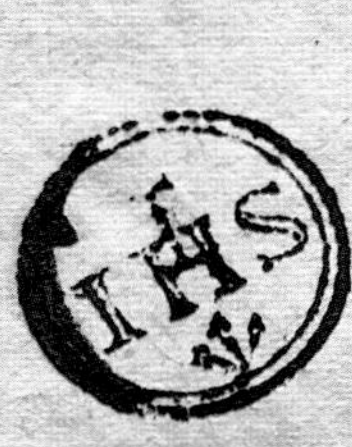

Año, 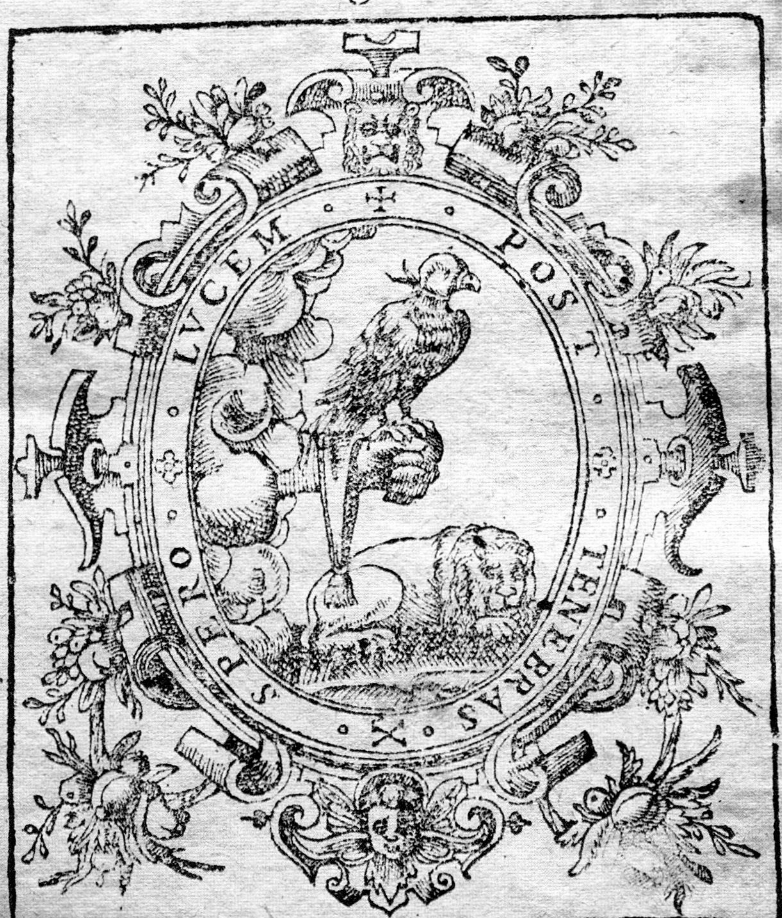

1605.

CON PRIVILEGIO,

EN MADRID, Por Iuan de la Cuesta.

Vendese en casa de Francisco de Robles, librero del Rey nro señor.

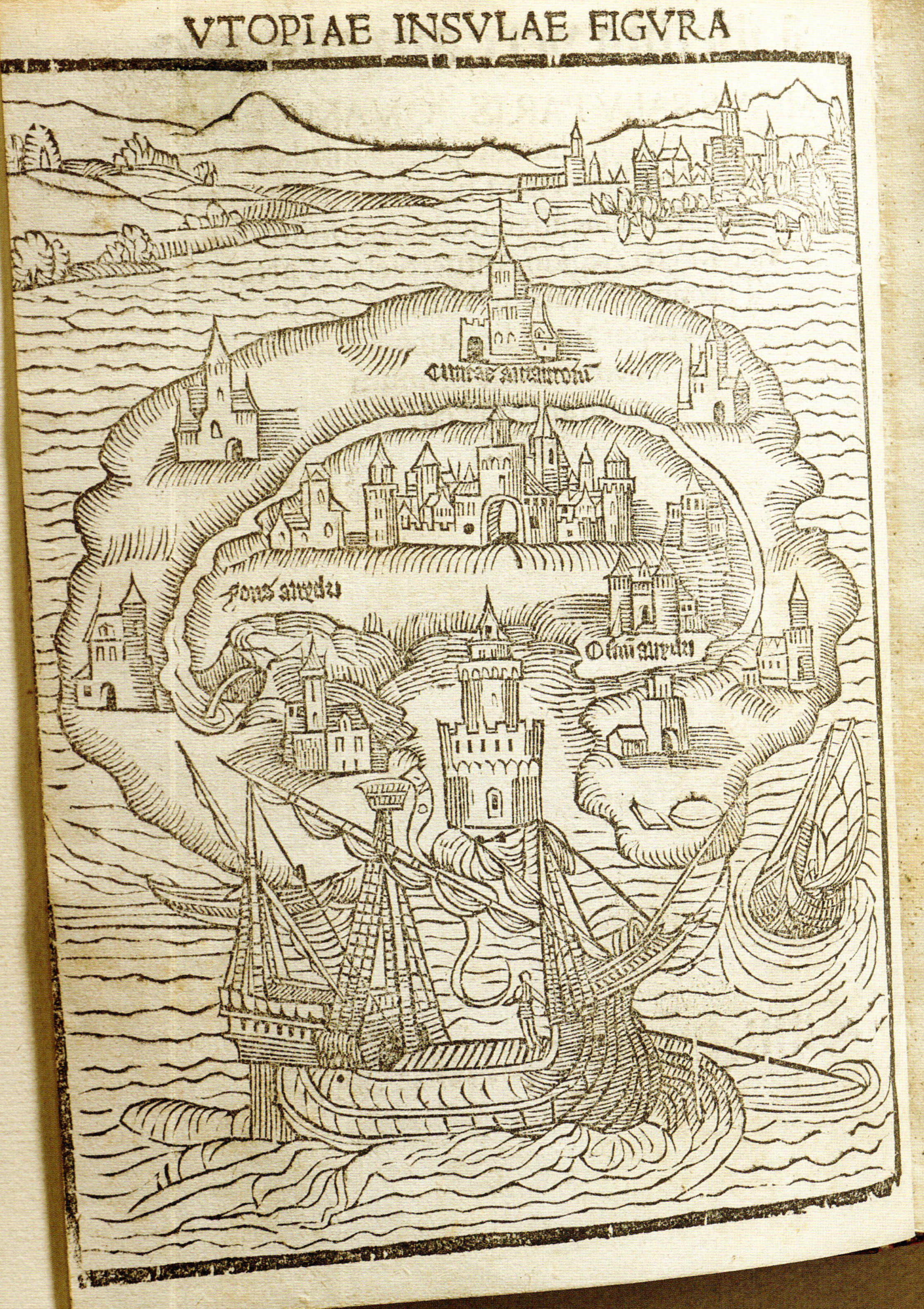
VTOPIAE INSVLAE FIGVRA

VTOPIENSIV
a b c d e f g h i
Tetrastichon ver
Vtopos ha
chama
Bargol he
ſoma gymn
Agrama gymnoſo
bodamilomi
Voluala barc
lauoluola
Horum verſuu
Vtopus me dux ex non
Vna ego terrarum om
Ciuitatem philoſophic
Libéter impartio mea.

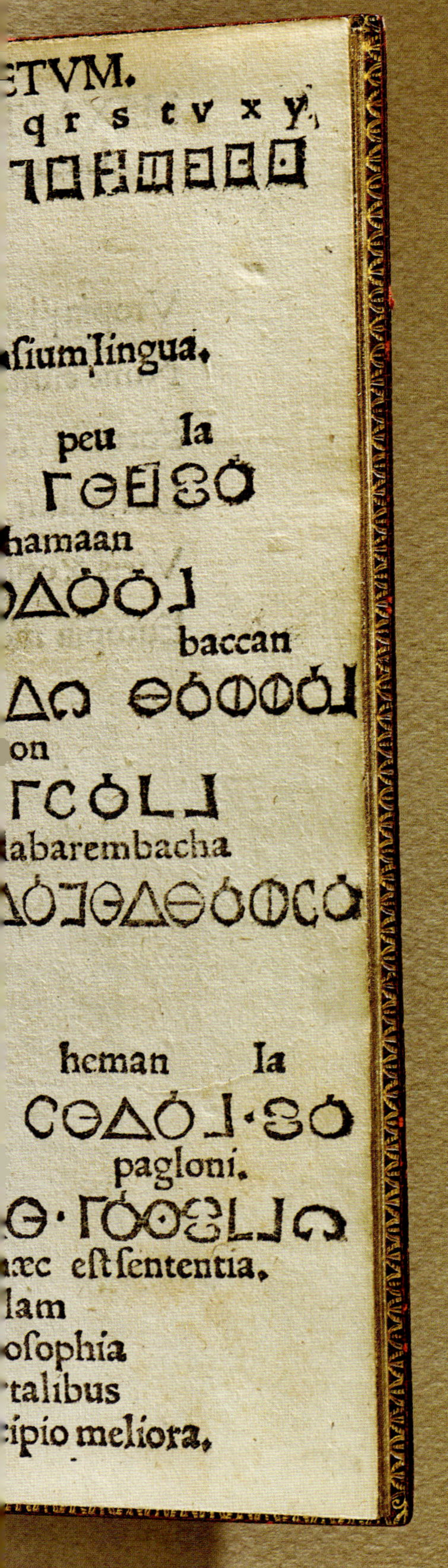

Thomas More (1478–1535)

First edition of *Libellus vere aureus nec minus salutaris quam festivus de optimo reip. statu, deq; nova insula Utopia*

Louvain: Arte Theodorici Martini, 1516

Henry W. and Albert A. Berg Collection of English and American Literature

Dreams of a just and peaceful community date to antiquity, but the most celebrated vision of a perfect community—a utopia—was imagined by Sir Thomas More during the Renaissance. Without private property, Utopians work no more than six hours a day—though their economy is possible only through the enslavement of criminals, foreigners, and adulterers. Hans Holbein the Younger's brother, Ambrosius, designed the woodcut map on the verso of the title page seen here, which faces a table of the twenty-two-letter Utopian alphabet. Scholars remain divided about whether More intended to praise or satirize the socialist society he invented, as the name "utopia" derives from two identically pronounced Greek words: *eu-topos* (meaning "good place") and *ou-topos* (meaning "no place" or "nowhere").

Jacques Le Moyne de Morgues (ca. 1533–ca. 1588)
Laudonnierus et rex athore ante columnam a praefecto prima navigatione locatam quamque venerantur floridenses
Gouache and metallic pigments on vellum with traces of black chalk outlines, 1564–1565
The Miriam and Ira D. Wallach Division of Art, Prints and Photographs, Print Collection

This rare gouache on vellum drawing is attributed to the esteemed botanical artist Jacques Le Moyne. He was appointed by King Charles IX of France to accompany the second French expedition of Jean Ribault and René de Laudonnière to northern Florida in 1564–1565 in order to establish a Huguenot colony. Le Moyne's task was to document the local population and exotic habitation. Here, Le Moyne depicts Athore, the son of the Timucuan king Saturiwa, showing Laudonnière the monument Ribault had erected after the first French expedition to Florida two years earlier. A veritable cornucopia of foods placed before the column suggests the origin of the tragic French misconception that the Timucua grew enough supplies to enable the French to survive on trade alone, rather than needing to plant their own crops.

This rare work may be the only surviving drawing Le Moyne produced while accompanying Laudonnière's voyage. Le Moyne later redrew from memory the majority of his impressions from Florida. After his death, they were published in Theodor de Bry's 1591 publication *Brevis narratio eorum quae in Florida Americai provincia Gallis acciderunt*, which became the most widely read and influential history of the region and depiction of its native peoples.

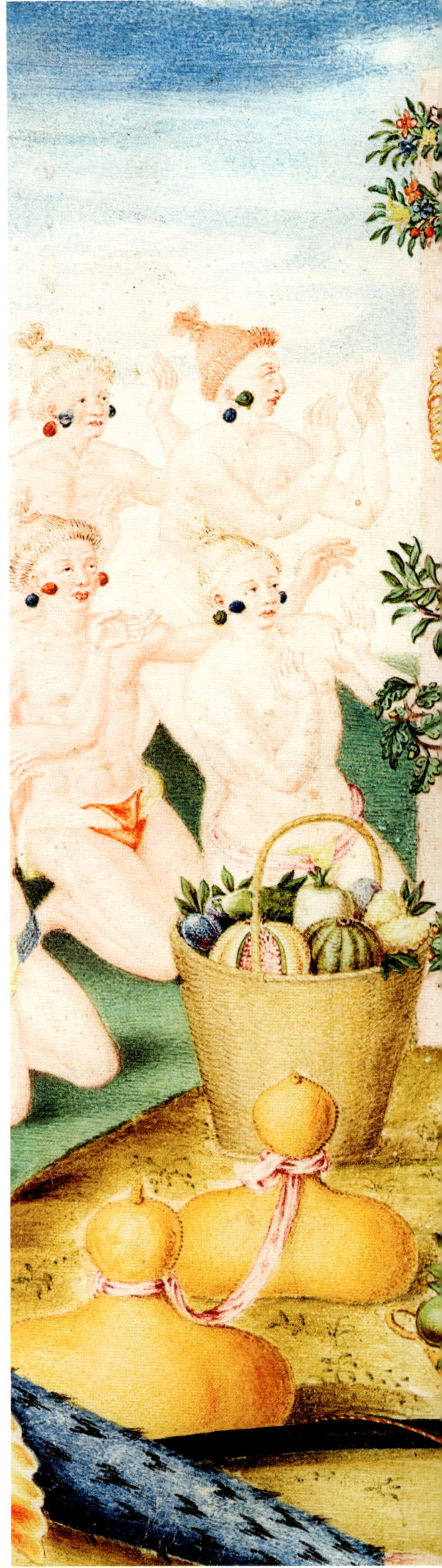

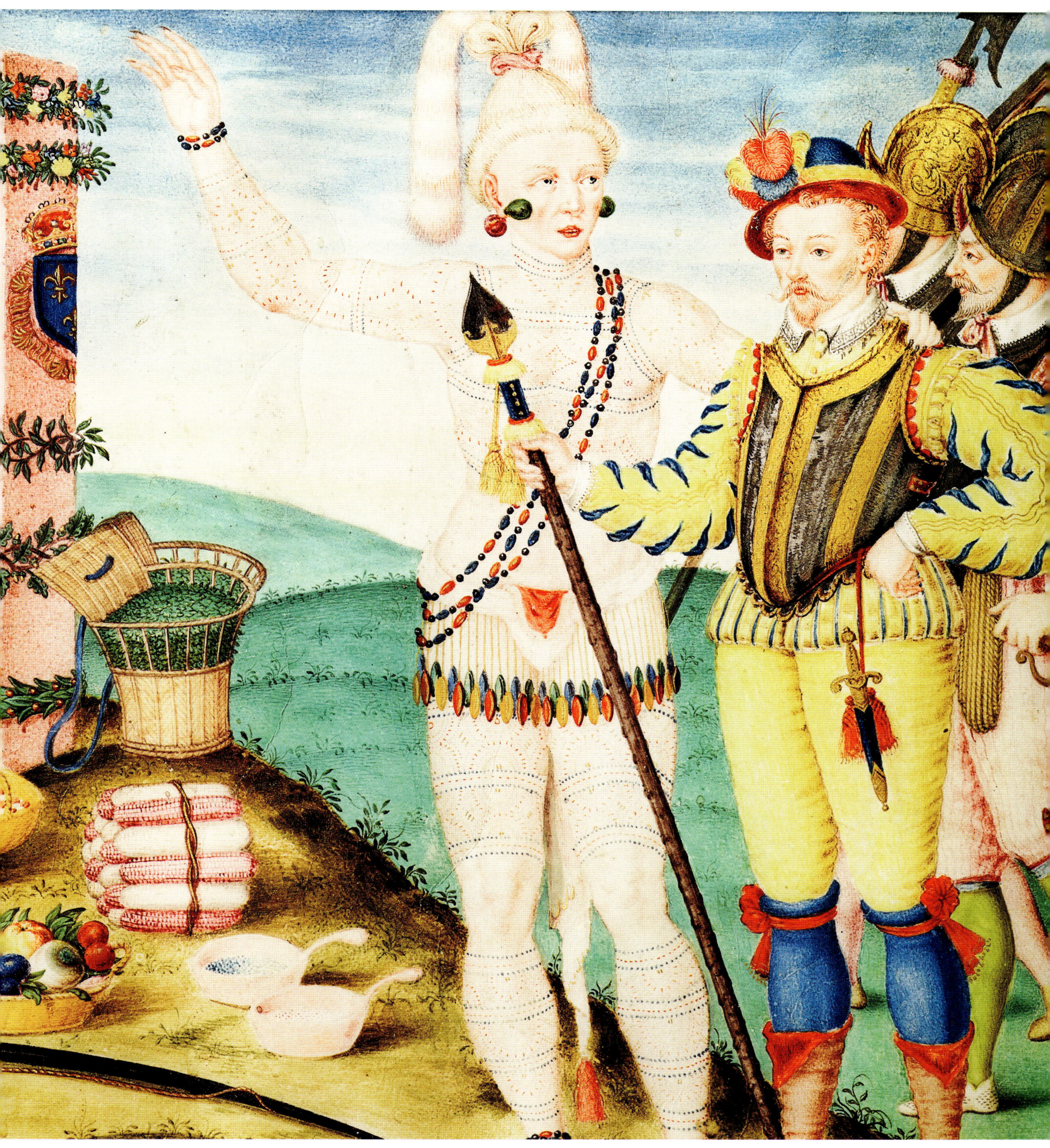

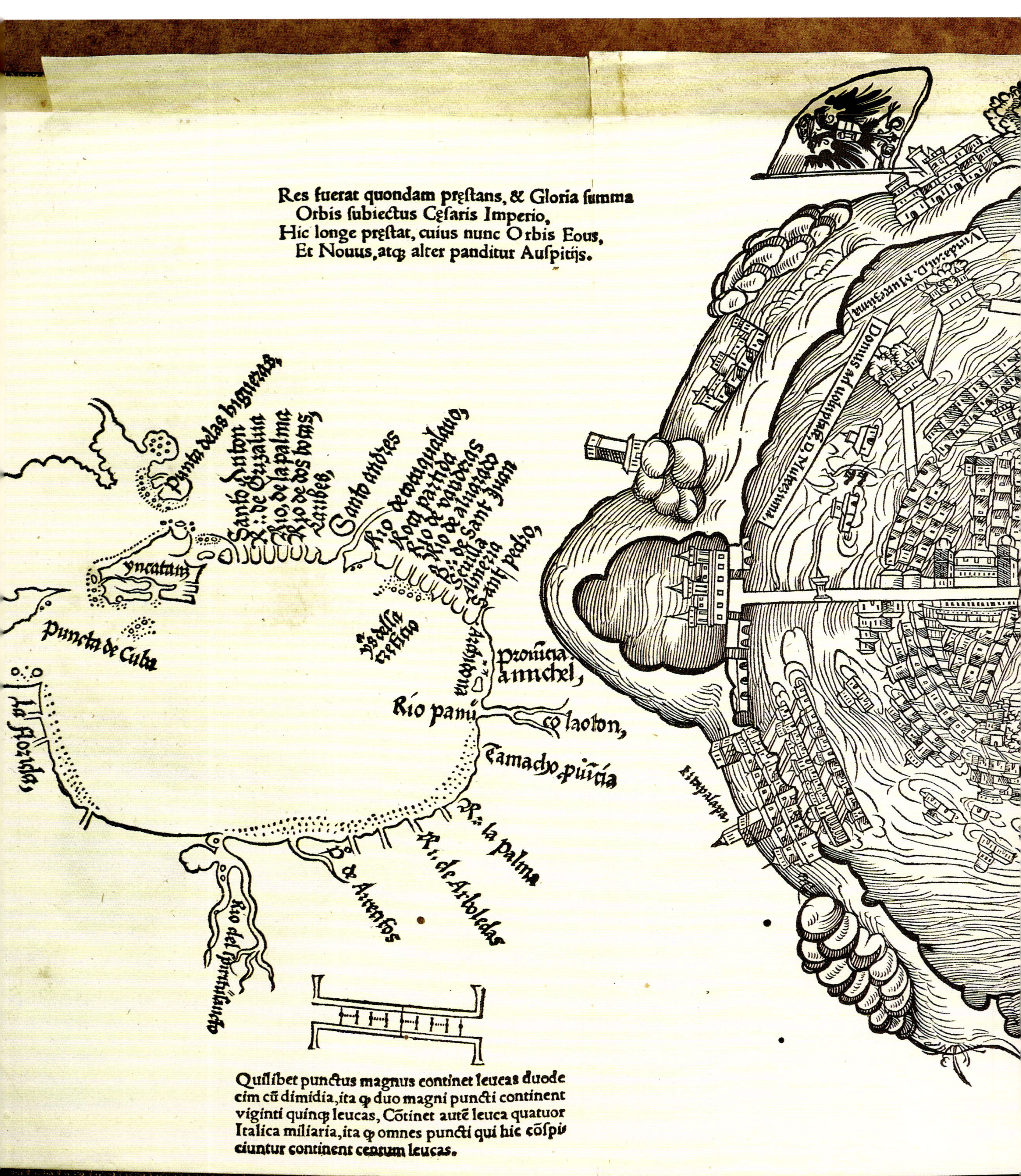
Res fuerat quondam pręstans, & Gloria summa
Orbis subiectus Cęsaris Imperio,
Hic longe pręstat, cuius nunc Orbis Eous,
Et Nouus, atq; alter panditur Auspitijs.
yucatan
Puncta de Cuba
La florida
Santo Anton
Rio de la palma
Rio de dos bocas
Santo andres
Almeria
Sant pedro
prouĩcia
amichel
Rio pani
co laoton
Tamacho puĩcia
R. la palma
R. de Arboledas
Quilibet punctus magnus continet leucas duodecim cũ dimidia, ita ꝙ duo magni puncti continent viginti quinq; leucas, Cõtinet autẽ leuca quatuor Italica miliaria, ita ꝙ omnes puncti qui hic cõspiciuntur continent centum leucas.

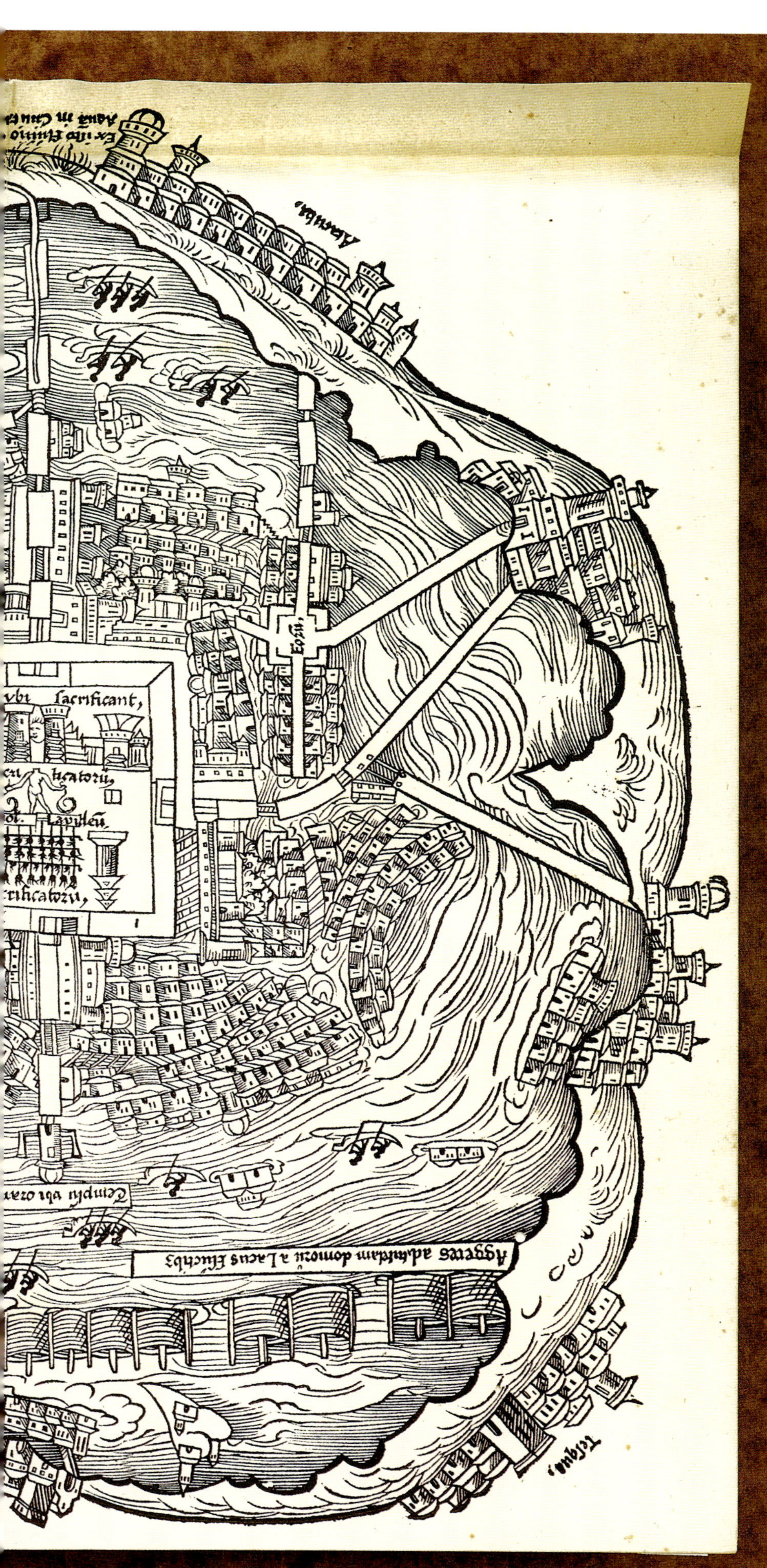

Hernán Cortés (1485–1547)
Praeclara Ferdinadi Cortesii de Nova Maris Oceani Hyspania Narratio
Nuremberg: Fredericum Peypus Arthemesimus, 1524
Rare Book Division

Hernán Cortés, a Spanish military officer, led an expedition to conquer and colonize the territories now known as Mexico. Ruthlessly ambitious, he ultimately forced the Aztec emperor Montezuma to acknowledge himself and his subjects as the vassals of Emperor Charles V of Spain. This elaborate woodcut of Tenochtitlán—present-day Mexico City—that appeared with the Latin printing of Cortés's second letter to Charles V is the first European depiction of a city in the Americas.

Cortés was awed by the architectural beauty of what he called "this noble city of Temixtitan." In his letter, he perhaps unexpectedly describes the indigenous peoples' conduct as "marked by as great an attention to the proprieties of life as in Spain." Founded two centuries before Cortés's arrival and boasting intricate urban planning, Tenochtitlán was successfully defended by the Aztecs on the Spaniards' first attempt to take the city.

Juan de Zumárraga (1468–1548)

Doctrina breve muy provechosa de las cosas que pertenecen a la fe Católica y a nuestra Cristiandad en estilo llano para común inteligencia (Short Compendium of Catholic Doctrine in both Nahuatl and Spanish)

Mexico City: Juan Pablos, 1543

Rare Book Division

Juan de Zumárraga, the first bishop of New Spain, established a printing press in Mexico City for the purpose of propagating Christianity. The *Doctrina breve*—a work outlining the essential tenets of the Catholic faith—was printed at Zumárraga's behest and expense by Juan Pablos, the viceroyalty's initial printer.

Pablos traveled from Spain to Mexico at the bishop's insistence in order to set up a branch office of the famous printing house of Juan Cromberger, arriving in the autumn of 1539. Soon afterward, his press issued a work entitled *Breve y mas compendiosa doctrina Christiana en lengua Mexicana y Castellana*, of which no copy has been located. Several other works followed, none of which survives in more than fragmentary copies. Published in 1543, the *Doctrina breve*, of which nine copies are recorded, is the earliest extant complete book printed in the Americas.

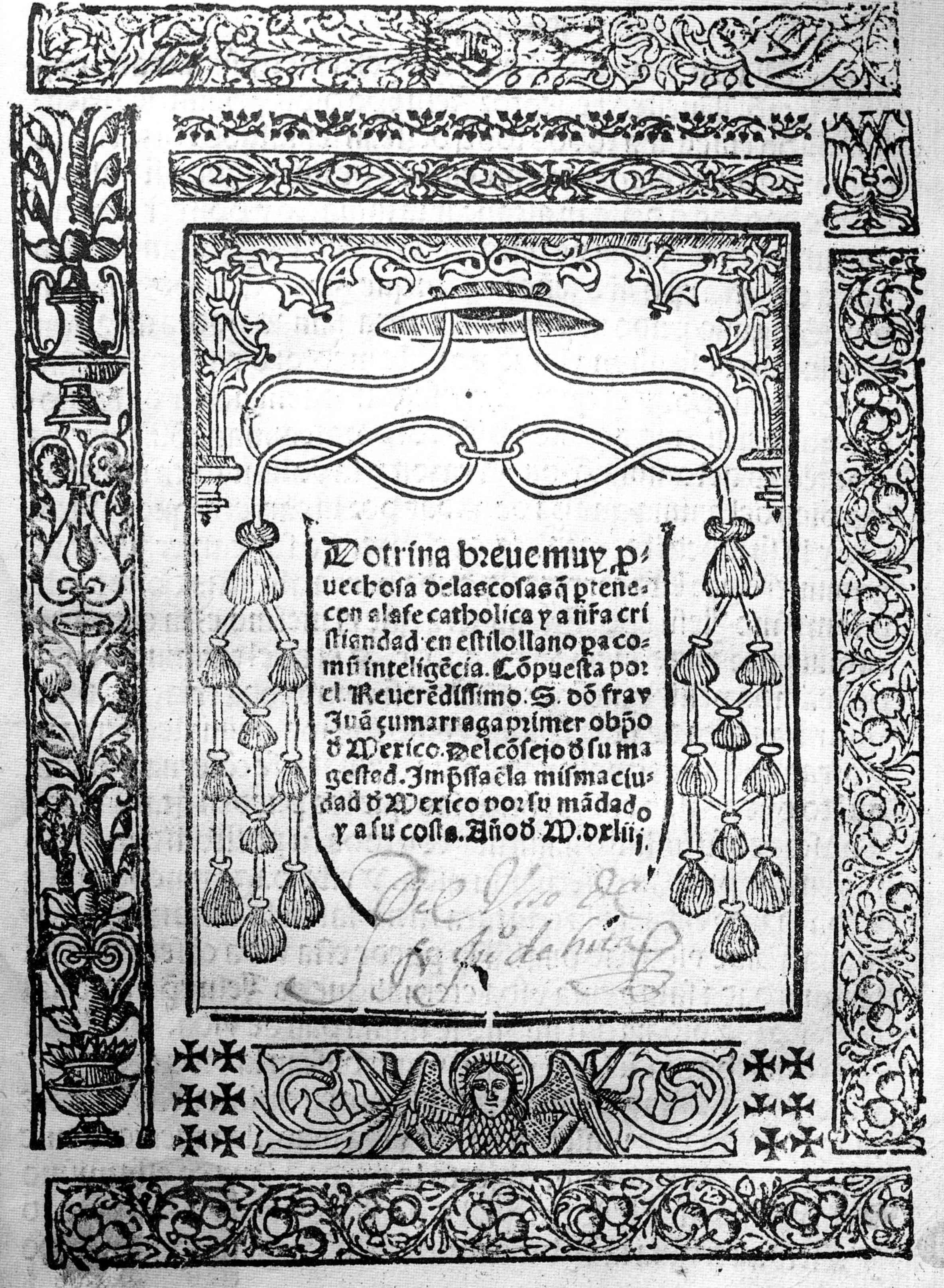

Dotrina breue muy p̄-
uechosa delas cosas q̄ ptene-
cen ala fe catholica y a nr̄a cri
stiandad en estilo llano pa co-
mū inteligēcia. Cōpuesta por
el Reuerēdissimo. S. dō fray
Juā çumarraga primer obpo
d Mexico. Del cōsejo d su ma
gestad. Impssa ēla misma ciu-
dad d Mexico por su mādado
y a su costa. Año d M.dxliij.

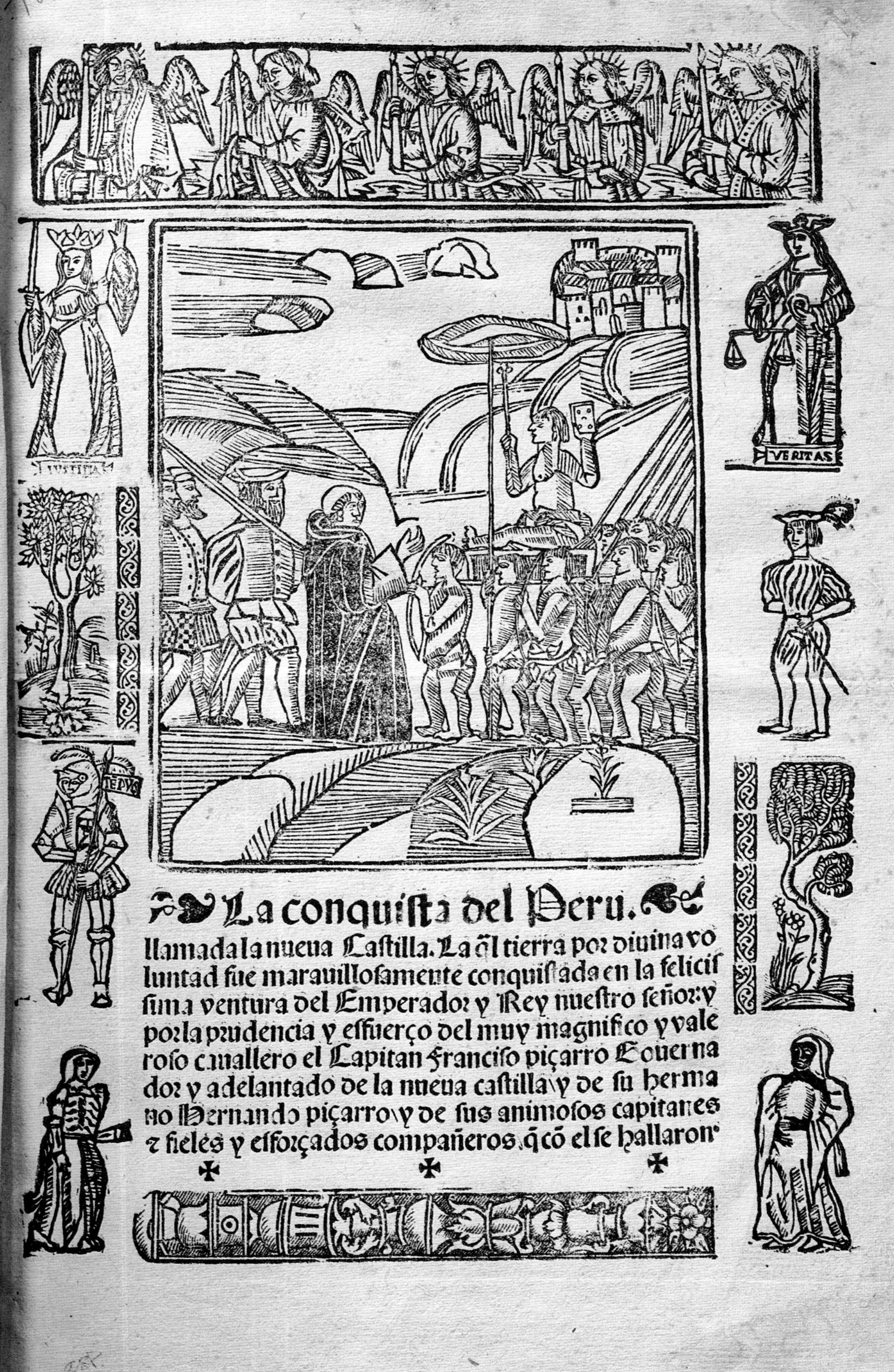

La conquista del Peru.

llamada la nueua Castilla. La q̃l tierra por diuina voluntad fue marauillosamente conquistada en la felicissima ventura del Emperador y Rey nuestro señor: y por la prudencia y esfuerço del muy magnifico y valeroso cauallero el Capitan Francisco piçarro Gouernador y adelantado de la nueua castilla y de su hermano Hernando piçarro y de sus animosos capitanes e fieles y esforçados compañeros q̃ cō el se hallaron.

✠ ✠ ✠

***La conquista del Perú* (*The Conquest of Peru*)**

Seville: Bartolome Perez, 1534

Rare Book Division

La conquista del Perú, printed in Spain in 1534, provides the earliest published account of European contact with, and subjugation of, the Inca Empire. The work was most likely written by Cristóbal de Mena, who was a captain in the fleet of the conquistador Francisco Pizarro.

In his brief narrative, the author recounts the capture and eventual execution of Atahualpa, the last ruler of the Incan Empire, whose fateful encounter with Pizarro's forces took place on November 16, 1532. The title page's woodcut illustration vividly depicts this pivotal event. An attending friar has offered a Catholic breviary to Atahualpa, who hurls the religious book to the ground in either confusion or defiance.

Mexican Declaration of Independence: ***La Regencia Del Imperio Se Ha Servido Dirigirme El Decreto Que Sigue . . . Acta De Independencia Del Imperio***
October 10, 1821
Rare Book Division

The Mexican Declaration of Independence was drafted and signed on September 28, 1821, formally ending 300 years of Spanish colonial rule. This printing, undertaken less than two weeks after its signing, marks the first official public appearance of the document. The Mexican Declaration of Independence often mirrors its American counterpart in themes and language, citing "unalienable" rights that are to be restored to the nation's citizens.

The present copy of the initial publication, dated October 10, 1821, is signed by José Manuel de Herrera, Secretary of Relations, or Foreign Minister, of the newly instituted government. One of only a handful of known surviving copies, it was added to the Rare Book Division in 2011, augmenting the Library's already rich holdings of Latin American imprints—one of the largest collections of its kind in any American institution.

Número 86 10.

La Regencia del Imperio se ha servido dirigirme el decreto que sigue:

La Regencia del Imperio Gobernadora interina por falta de Emperador, á todos los que las presentes vieren y entendieren, SABED: Que la Soberana Junta provisional gubernativa ha declarado lo siguiente:

„La Soberana Junta provisional gubernativa del Imperio Mexicano congregada en la Capital de él en 28 de septiembre inmediato anterior pronunció la siguiente

ACTA DE INDEPENDENCIA DEL IMPERIO.

La Nacion Mexicana que por trescientos años ni ha tenido voluntad propia, ni libre el uso de la voz, sale hoy de la opresion en que ha vivido.

Los heroicos esfuerzos de sus hijos han sido coronados, y está consumada la empresa eternamente memorable, que un genio superior á toda admiracion y elogio, amor y gloria de su pátria, principió en Iguala, prosiguió y llevó al cabo arrollando obstáculos casi insuperables.

Restituida pues esta parte del Septentrion al ejercicio de cuantos derechos le concedió el Autor de la Naturaleza, y reconocen por inenagenables y

Cancion a N.ra Señora de Guadalupe en Verso Mex.no
del M.ro Joseph Perez de la fuente año de 1717

19

Zuapilhueyhuacatzintle:
to quallituilizzyo yzeltzin,
Ca otonhualmonextitzino
Iuhqui theoyeyo tlanextli.
Ypan ynin teue-huacantli,
Ca zenca zentonalleti,
Ypampa mo zehuallotzin
Ca oconmochalchiuh mazehui.
Campa zenmahuizolloni
yn tonalli mo tlaquentzin
tontemotilitzinohua
yn metztli mo xopepechtzi
Yhuan yca mo qualyotzin
zenyamatzhca tzopelqui
Inmo tepalchuilitoc
huel Iuhqui yn tetechmone
tlacnellilcamatiliuhtim
Yolloceyotl zenca yhectli
tinitzon tomaquiliat
Manel tatlacnopillequil.
Yhuan yn to yollilhuatlo
yca mochi yn tlein to hueli
Mocxitlantzinco theoyoqui
Contlalia yn to tlaellehuil.

Moreno F.

Nican Mopohua

ca. 1550–1600

Manuscripts and Archives Division

The *Nican Mopohua* ("Here It Is Told") relates the earliest-recorded apparition in the Americas of the Virgin Mary. In this manuscript account, the Virgin appeared in December 1531 to Juan Diego, a Native American man, asking that he build a shrine in her honor on Tepeyac, a hill located on the outskirts of present-day Mexico City. The incident is recorded in Nahuatl, the imperial language of the Mexicas (later called Aztecs), with iron gall ink on European paper with other materials used in sacred rites. The document thus incorporated Aztec tradition into Catholic ritual, and it became an effective instrument for converting indigenous populations.

The document's authorship continues to inspire debate—it is widely, though not definitively, credited to the Colonial Mexican scholar Antonio Valeriano (1521–1605)—but the *Nican Mopohua*'s cultural and theological significance is without question. The work is considered a masterpiece of Nahuatl literature of the Spanish Colonial period, and the shrine first built in the 16th century, today much enlarged and known as the Basilica of Our Lady of Guadalupe, remains a cherished symbol of Mexico.

James Latimer Allen (1907–1977)
***Brown Madonna* (Madonna and Child)**
Gelatin silver print, 1930s
Photographs and Prints Division, Schomburg Center for Research in Black Culture

One of the three major photographers associated with the Harlem Renaissance (James Van Der Zee and Carl Van Vechten were the other two), James L. Allen captured many of the literary and artistic luminaries of the movement and conveyed the New Negro philosophy through his subjects and photographic techniques. *Brown Madonna*, reproduced on the cover of the December 1941 issue of *Opportunity* magazine, is far more than a religious image used to commemorate the Advent season. Allen pays homage to the black woman, defying the stereotype of the mammy so prevalent in Western iconography and elevating her image. Moreover, this depiction of the nurturing maternal figure harks back centuries to African art. Allen is one of the earliest African-American photographers to frame his work in the context of classical art, and his photographs housed in the Schomburg Center were among the first photographic acquisitions of the then-fledgling collection.

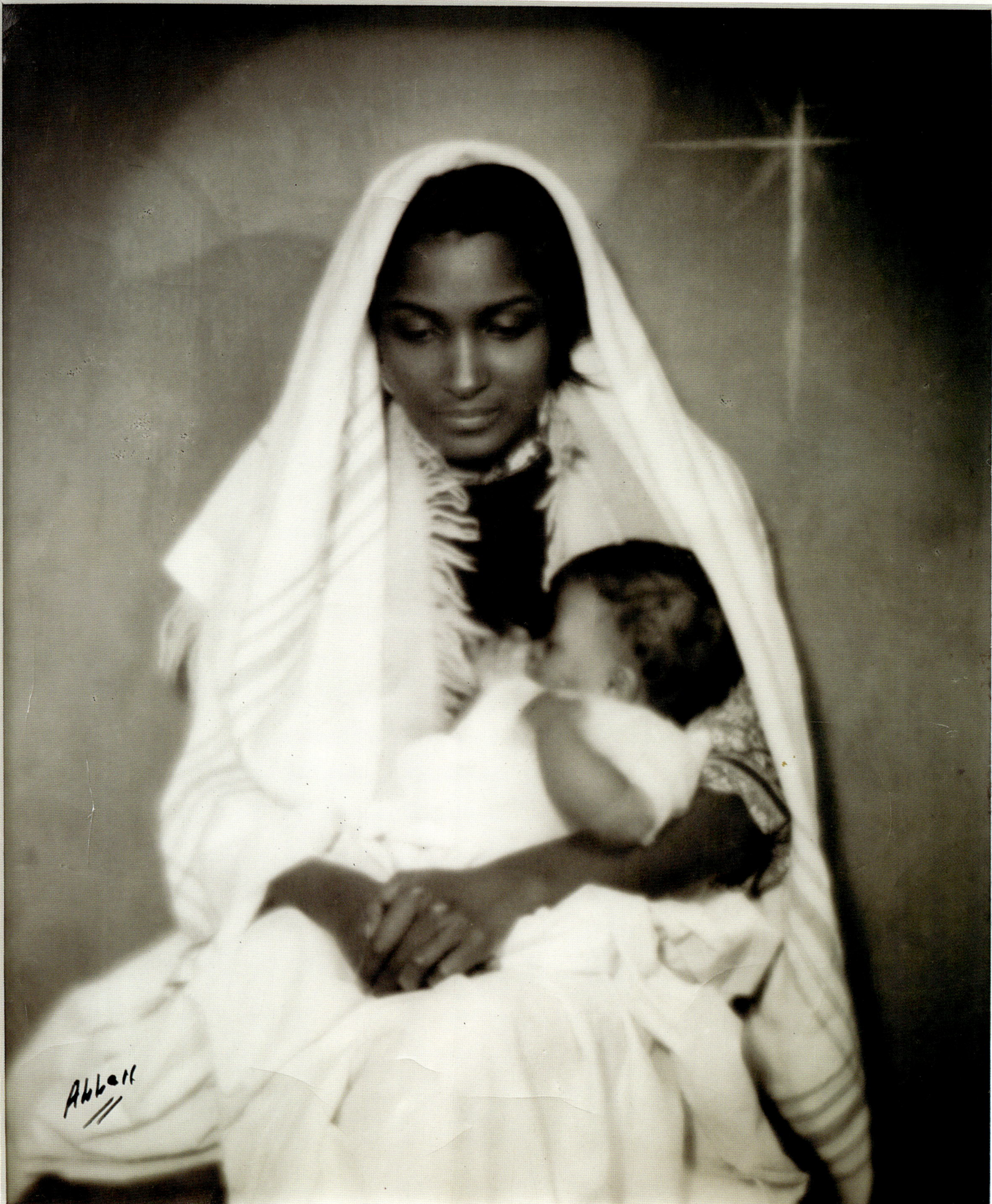

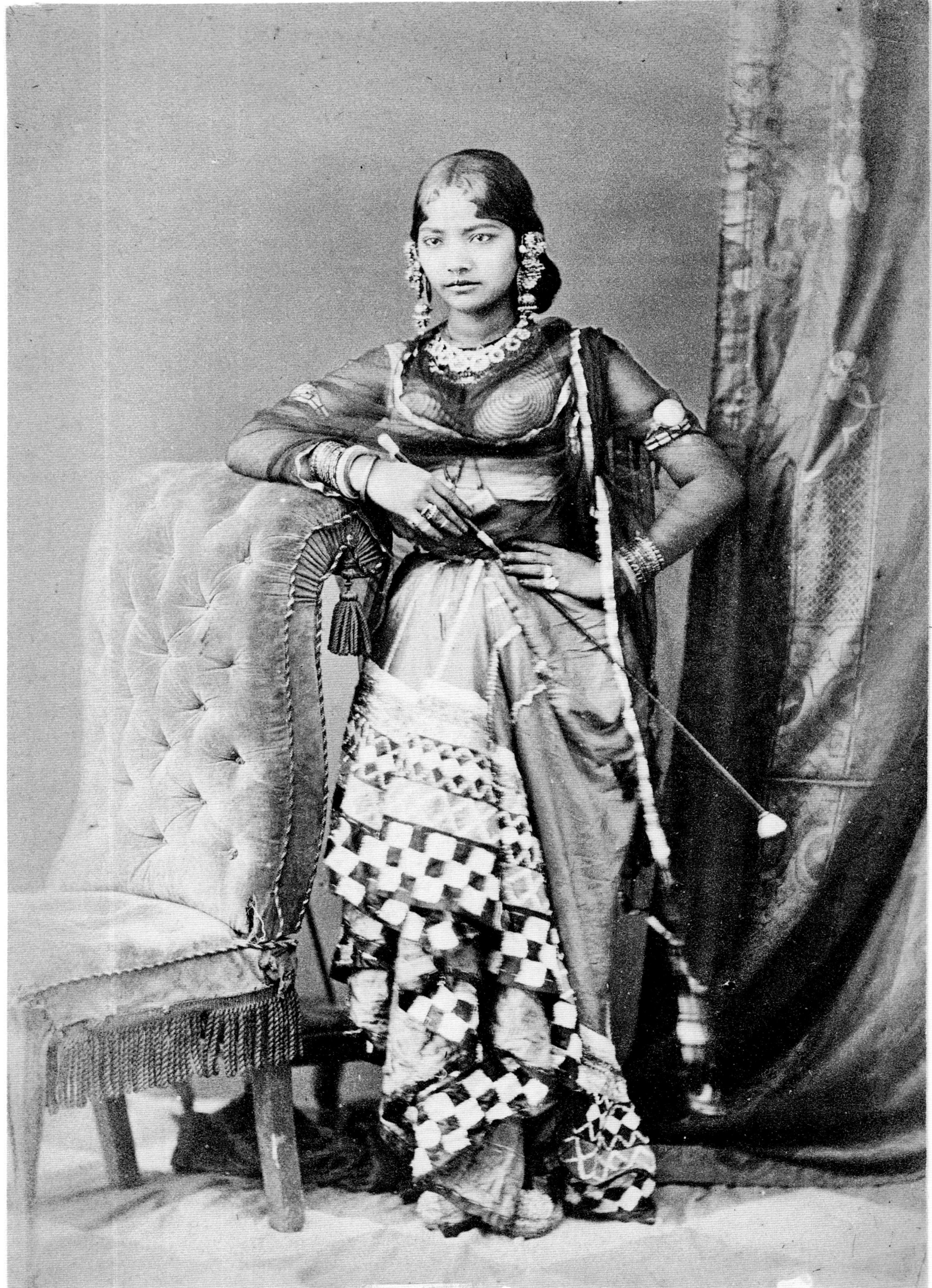

Juddan Dancing Girl*, from *Beauties of Lucknow, Calcutta

1874

Jerome Robbins Dance Division, The New York Public Library for the Performing Arts, Dorothy and Lewis B. Cullman Center

This photograph belongs to a series of twenty-one images of dancers taken at the Oudh Court of Lucknow. These, in turn, are part of a larger collection of twenty-four images that also includes portraits of actresses and musicians. The British annexation of Oudh in 1856 and the subsequent rebellion completely transformed the life of patronage that artists had typically enjoyed under the Mughal Empire (1526–1857). The region of Lucknow is steeped in rich dance history, particularly the evolution of the Indian classical dance style of *kathak*. One of the three *gharanas,* or forms, of *kathak* is named for Lucknow and is renowned for its expressiveness of the face and graceful mudras (the detailed hand movements that are the forte of Indian dancers). Lucknow was also a fertile site for the evolution of music that accompanied dance. A unique tabla (drum) technique developed in the early 19th century has become inextricably linked with *kathak* performance.

Anonymous artist of the Pahari school

Bhagavata Purana (Krishnagita)

18th century

The Miriam and Ira D. Wallach Division of Art, Prints and Photographs, Spencer Collection

This is a detail of one of twenty-two miniature paintings of scenes from the life of Lord Krishna (*Krishnagita*), one of the most popular and widely revered Indian divinities. These miniatures were created in the 1700s by an anonymous artist of the Pahari (or Rajput) school, a style of painting that developed and flourished in India's Punjab Hill states between the late 17th and 19th centuries. (*Pahari* means "mountain" in Hindi.)

Just as European Renaissance masters turned to the Bible for inspiration, so Indian painters found inspiration in their Sanskrit epics. Pahari miniaturists produced some of the finest images of legendary or religious narratives, and their delicate and lyrical compositions represent an accurate record of the social and cultural life of their time. The *Bhagavata Purana* was the first sacred Hindu text to be translated into a European language; a French translation by Maridas Poullé, an interpreter who worked for the French East India Company in Pondicherry, was the first to introduce many Europeans to Hinduism and 18th-century Hindu culture during Europe's colonial era.

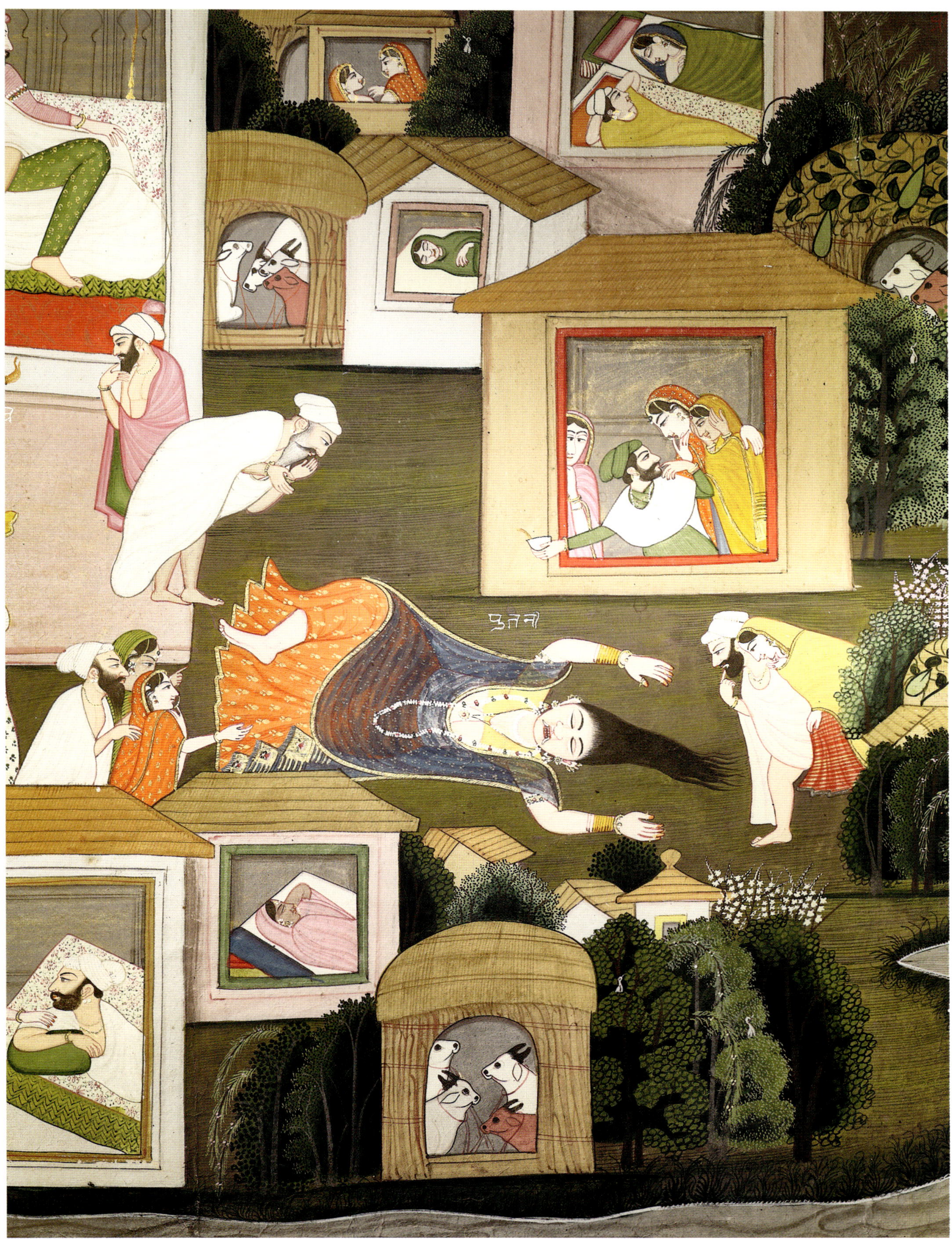

CANTO PRIMO DELLA PRIMA CANTICA O VE[...] COMEDIA DEL DIVINO POETA FIORENTINO DANTHE ALEGHIERI : CAPITOLO PRIMO :

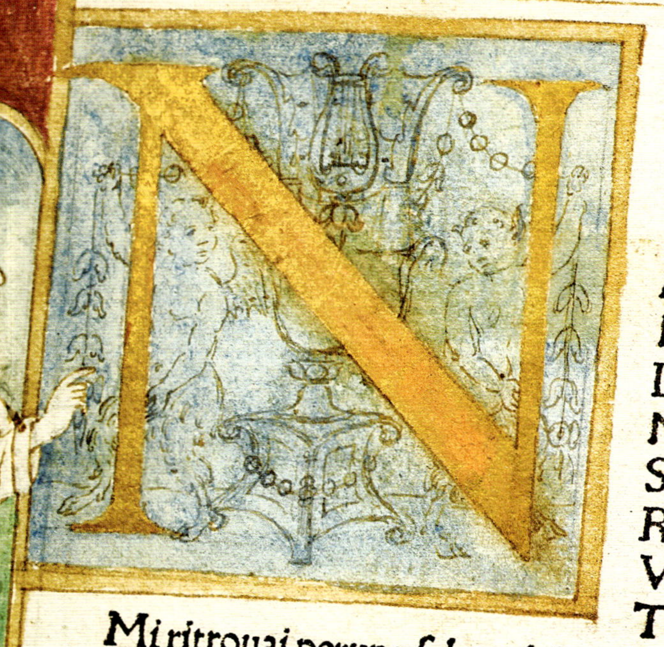

EL MEZO DEL CAMINO DI NOSTRA VITA

Mi ritrouai peruna selua obscura
che la diricta uia era smarrita
Et quanto adire quale era e/ cosa dura
esta selua seluaggia et aspra et forte
che nel pensier rinuoua lapaura
Tanto era amara che pocho e piu morte
ma per tractar del ben chio ui trouai
diro dellaltre cose chio uho scorte
I non so ben ridire chomio uentrai
tantera pien disonno insu quel puncto
che lauerace uia abbandonai
Ma poi chio fui appie dun colle giunto
la oue terminaua quella ualle
che mhauea dipaur el cor compuncto
Guardai inalto et uidi lesue spalle
coperte gia deraggi delpianeta
che mena dricto altrui per ogni calle
Allhor fu lapaura un pocho queta
che nellago del chuor mera durata
lanocte chio passai con tanta pieta

Habbiamo narrato non solament[e] poeta et eltitolo dellibro et che [...] eta Ma etiam quāto sia uetusta et ant[...] nobile et uaria quanto utile et iocon[...] trina. Quanto sia efficace a muouere [...] mēti; et quāto dilecti ogni liberale īge[...] giudicammo da tacere quanto in sī du[...] plina sia stata la excellentia dello inge[...] nostro poeta. Inche sisono stato piu br[...] forse non si conuerebbe; consideri chi le[...] lanumerosa et quasi infinita copia delle[...] le quali e necessario tractare misforza n[...] do chel uolume cresca sopra modo: a in[...] et inuilluppare piutosto che explicare: [...] dere moltecose et maxime quelle lequali [...] ben tacessi non pero ne restera obscura l[...] sitione del testo. Verremo adunque aq[...] Ma perche stimo non esser lectore alcuno [...] si basso ingegno: ne di si pocho giudicio: [...] uendo inteso; quanto sia et laprofondita [...] rieta della doctrina: et la excellentia et diu[...] dello ingegno delnostro toscano: et fioren[...] poeta: non si persuada che questo princ[...] delprimo canto debba per sublimita et gra[...] za esser pari alla stupenda doctrina dellech[...] che seguitano; pero con ogni industria in u[...] gheremo che allegoricho senso arechi seco [...] sto mezo delcamino: et che cosa sia selua Di[...] ueggio non piccola differentia essere stata [...] glinterpreti et expositori diquesta cantica. I[...] pero che alchuni dicono: che il mezo della ui[...] humana e el sonno mossi: credo dalla sentent[...] daristotele dicendo lui nellethica nessuna dif[...] rentia essere tra felici; et miseri nella meta del[...] uita per che lenocti che sono lameta del temp[...] cinducono sonno: et daquello nasce che ne ben[...] nemale sentir possiamo. Ilperche uogliono qu[...] sti: che el poeta pongha el mezo della uita per la [...] nocte: et lanocte pelsonno: ad notare che questo [...] poema non sia altro che una uisione che gliap[...] parue dormēdo per laquale hebbe cognitōe del[...] le cose dallui descripte ī queste tre comedie. Di[...] cono adūque che lui imita Ioanni euangelista el [...] quale dormēdo sopra elpecto di christo redemptore hebbe uisione delle chose celeste [...] ponghi lanocte dimostrando lui hauere cominciato e suo poema [...] lanimo insemedesimo et absoluendos[...] sententia [...]

Dante Alighieri (ca. 1265–1321)

First illustrated edition of *La Divina Commedia*

Florence: Niccolò di Lorenzo, 1481

The Miriam and Ira D. Wallach Division of Art, Prints and Photographs, Spencer Collection

The first illustrated edition of Dante's *Divine Comedy* was not a resounding success. Using engravings rather than woodcuts, Nicolaus Lorenz, a German printer from Breslau, had planned to illustrate all one hundred of Dante's cantos. He managed only nineteen. Successful with printing the first two, he then pasted in the remaining seventeen; printing them onto the volume's sheets in the spaces the compositor provided had proved overwhelming. Attributed to the Florentine engraver Baccio Baldini after drawings by Botticelli, the illustrations were designed to offer a figural commentary of each of the cantos in the poem. Only a very few copies, this being one, include all nineteen engravings. One of the last early modern attempts in Italy to use copper engravings as illustrations, it belongs to a trove of incunabula (books printed before ca. 1500) in the Library's Spencer Collection that offers rich avenues for research on the history of the book.

“Fujitsubo receives Prince Genji,” from *Genji monogatari: Sakaki no maki* (back cover)
17th century
The Miriam and Ira D. Wallach Division of Art, Prints and Photographs, Spencer Collection

Completed around 1019 by Murasaki Shikibu, a lady of the Imperial Court, *Genji Monogatari*, or *The Tale of Genji*, follows the life of Prince Genji, the son of an ancient Japanese emperor known to readers as Emperor Kiritsubo. A classic in its time and beyond, the work is sometimes described as the world’s first novel. This early 17th-century example demonstrates the sustained demand for deluxe manuscript editions of the work at a time when cheaper volumes executed with movable type and woodcut illustrations were just beginning to enter the market. The Library’s Spencer and Print Collections have a large and broad range of examples of *The Tale of Genji*, spanning from as early as the mid-16th century to the early 20th century, reflecting the enduring power of the story.

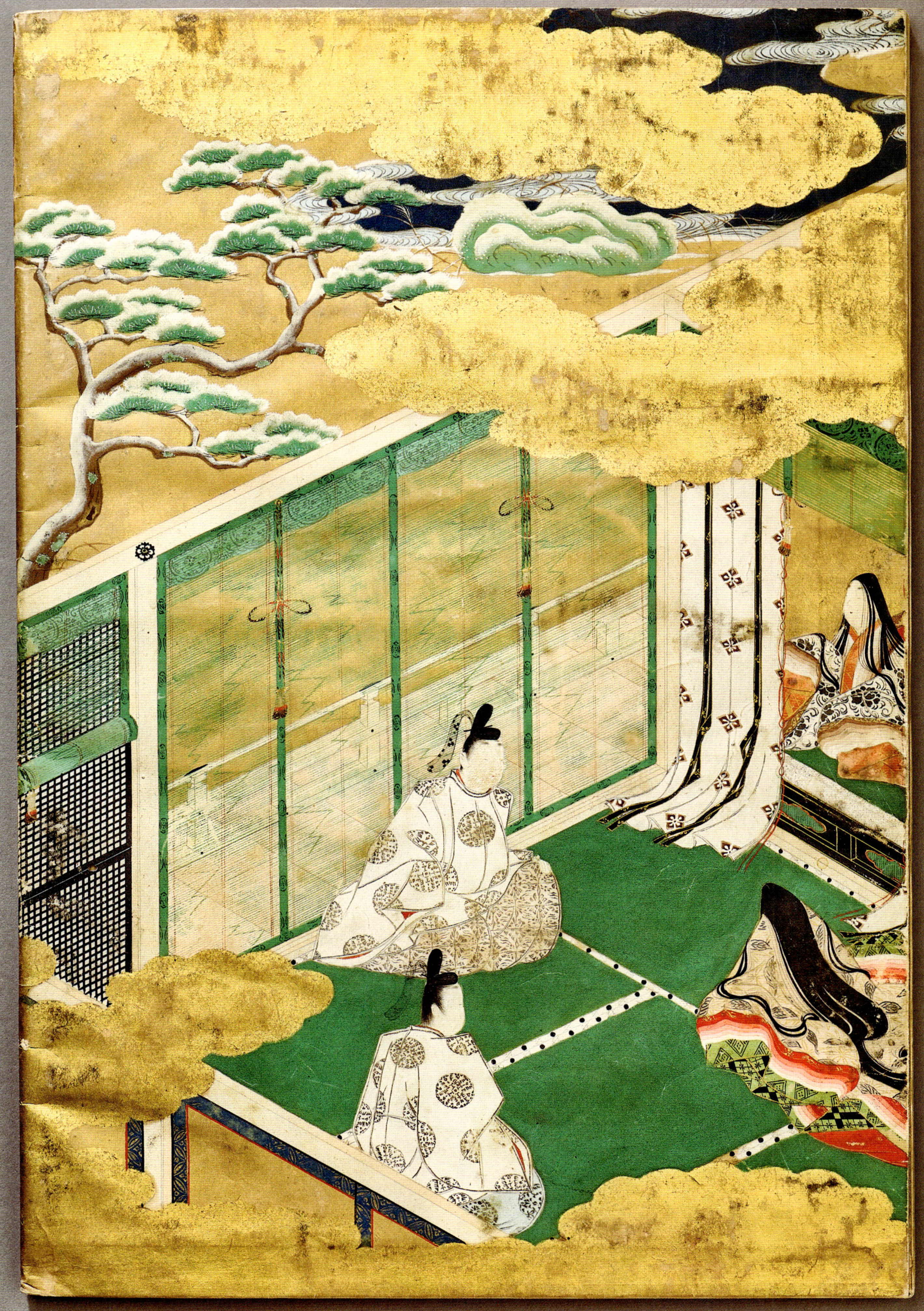

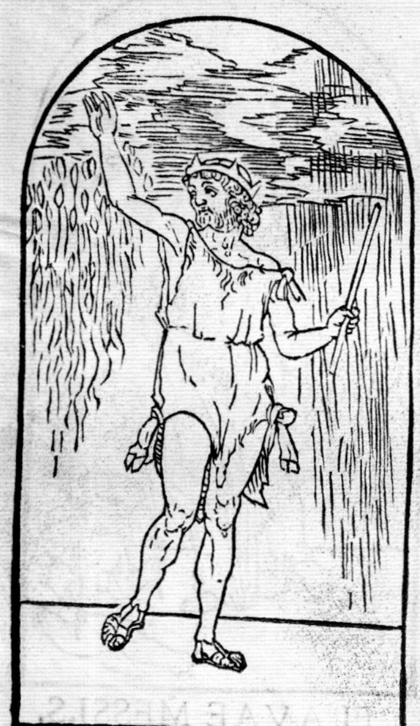

HYEMI AEOLIAE.S.

Ad questo nobile figmento el præstante artifice, electo solertemente el marmoro hauea, che oltra la candidecia sua era uenato (al requisito loco) de nigro, ad exprimere el tenebroso aere illumino, & nebuloso cum cadente grandine. Sopra la plana della dicta ueneranda, Ara rigidamente rigoroso ꝓmineua el rude simulachro del hortulano custode, cum tutti gli sui decenti & propriati insignii. Laquale mysteriosa Ara tegeua uno cupulato umbraculo, sopra quatro pali nel solo infixi affirmato & substentato. Gli quali pali diligētemente erano inuestiti di fructea, & florea frondatura, Et el culmo tutto intecto de multiplici fiori, & tra ciascuno palo nel lymbo dellapertura, o uero hiato del umbraculo affixo pendeua una ardente lampada, & in circuito ornatamente bractee doro dalle fresche & uerifere aure inconstante uexate, & cum metallei crepituli sonante, nelquale simulachro, cum maxima religionē & prisco rito rurale & pastorale alcune amole, o uero ampulle uitree cū spumāte cruore del immolato Asello, & cum caldo lacte & scintillante Mero spargendo rumpeuano, & cum fructi. fiori. fronde. festa, & gioie libauano, Hora drieto a questo glorioso Triumpho, conduceuano, cum antiqua & siluatica cerimonia illaqueato el seniculo Iano, de reste & trece intorte di multiplici fiori, cantanti carmini ruralmēte Talassii, Hymænei, & Fescennii, & istrumenti rurestricum suprema lætitia & gloria, celebremente exultanti, & cum solenni plausi saltanti, & uoce fœmelle altisone, Per laquale cosa nō manco piacere & dilecto cum stupore quiui tali solenni riti & celebre feste me inuase, che la admiratione degli præcedenti triumphi.

*

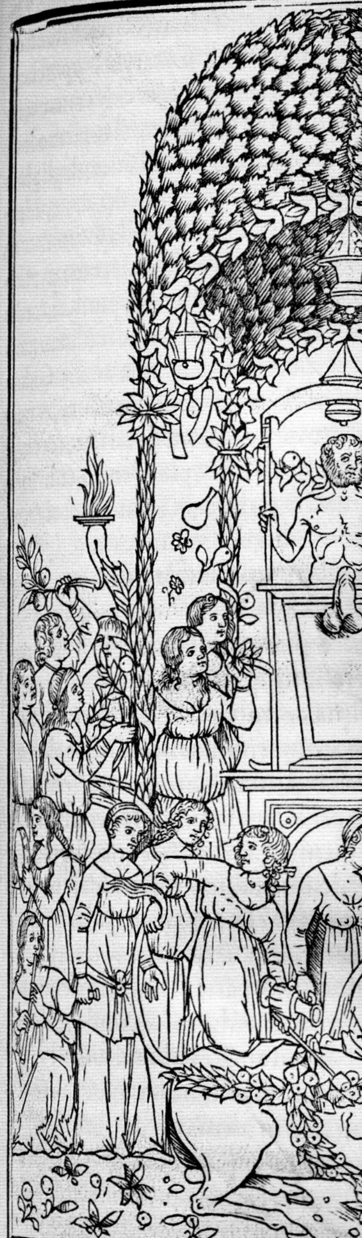

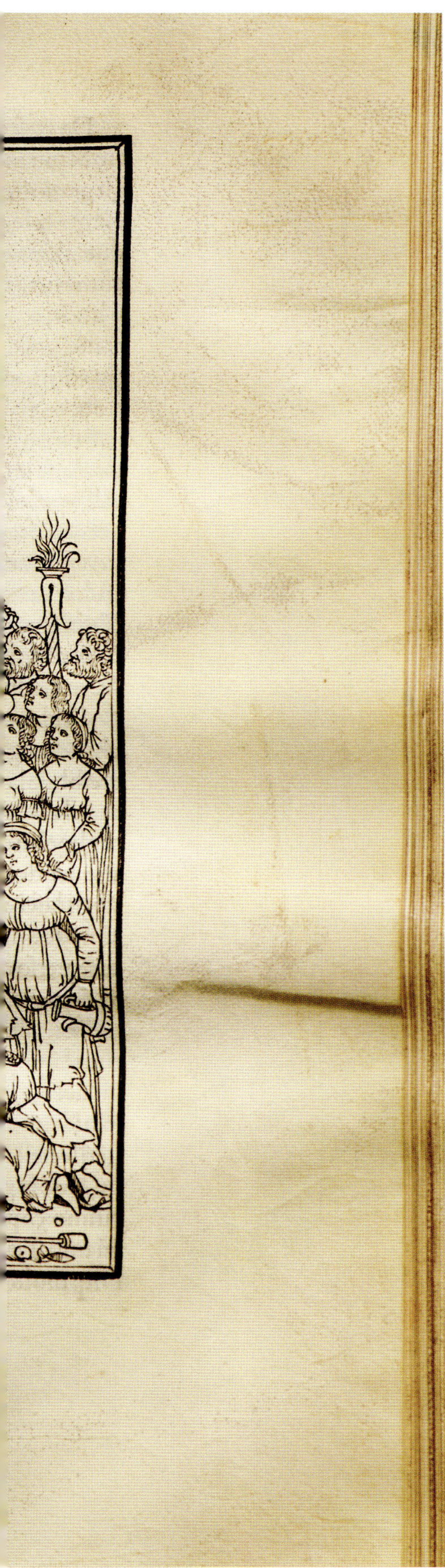

Francesco Colonna (ca. 1453–1517)
Hypnerotomachia Poliphili
Venice: Aldus Manutius, 1499
The Miriam and Ira D. Wallach Division of Art, Prints and Photographs, Spencer Collection

The only illustrated book produced by the famed Aldine Press in Venice, *Hypnerotomachia Poliphili* (meaning, roughly, "Poliphilus's Strife of Love in a Dream") has been described as one of the most beautiful books ever made. The novel's enigmatic narrative follows Poliphilus's search for his beloved, Polia, which brings the protagonist into contact with landscapes filled with perplexing ruins, fragments of epigraphy, and mysterious elements inspired by the art of classical antiquity. Aldus Manutius's Aldine Press specialized in printing Greek and Roman classics in economical pocket-book formats. Illustrated with 168 woodcuts, the *Hypnerotomachia* was both considerably larger and more expensive than Manutius's usual output. More lavish still is the volume shown here. One of only three such deluxe impressions, the Spencer Collection's copy is printed on the finest Italian vellum and can be studied in conjunction with a second paper-printed copy held in the Library's Rare Book Division.

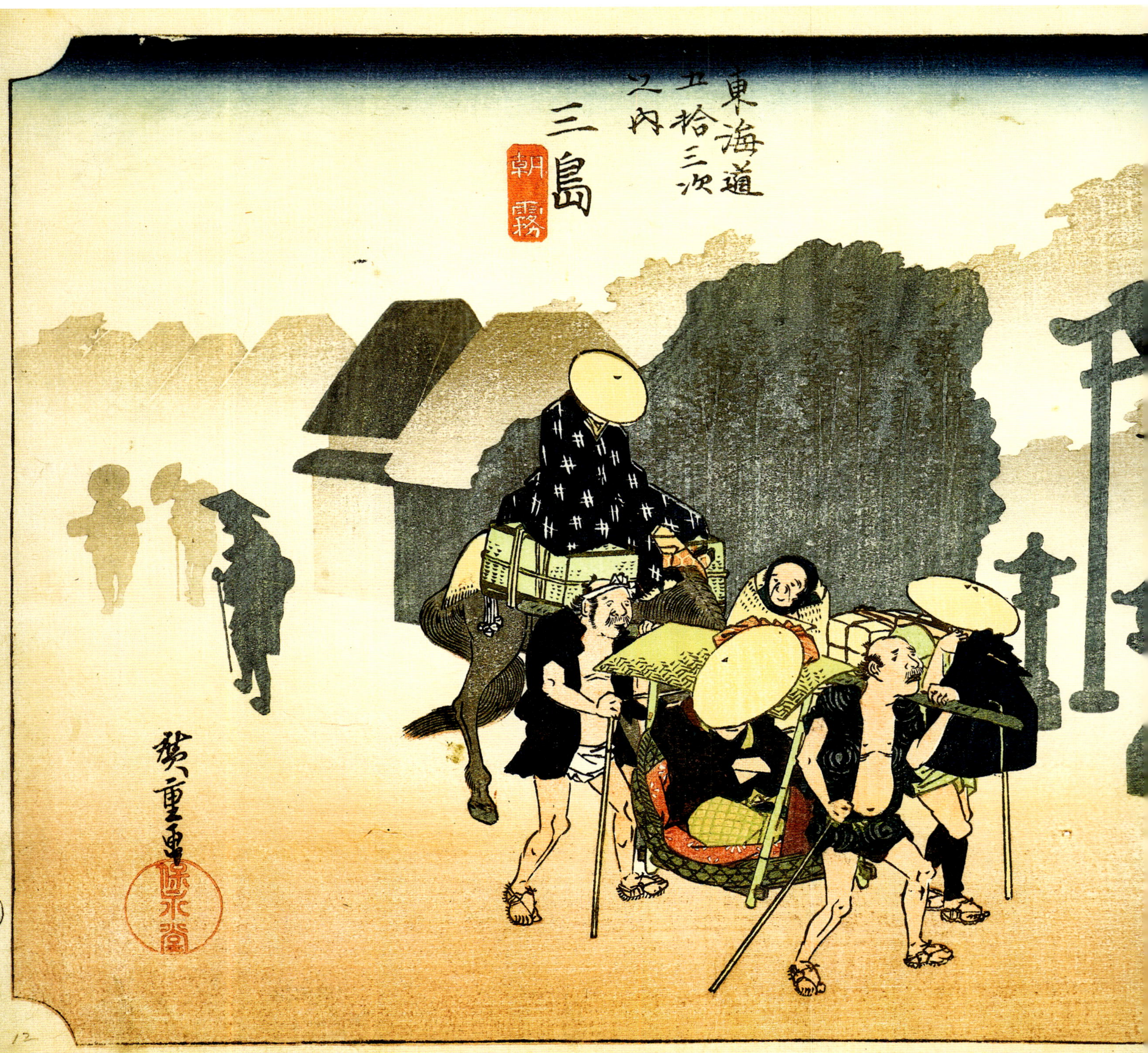
東海道
五拾三次
之内
三島
朝霧
廣重画
保永堂

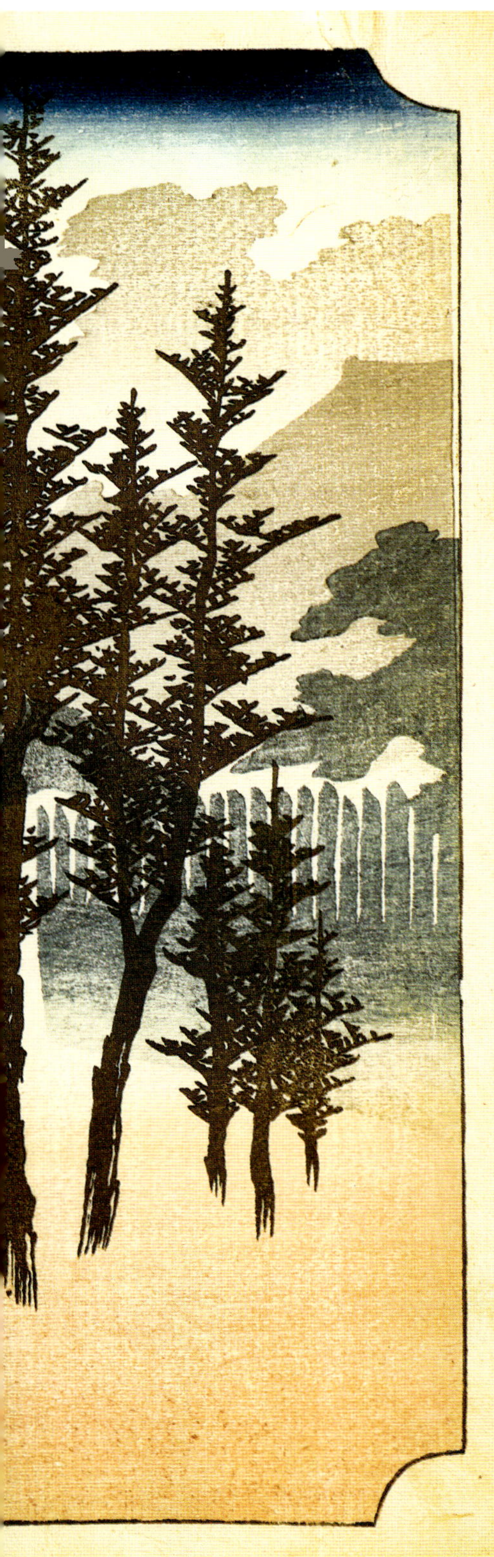

Andō Hiroshige (1797–1858)
Mishima: Morning Mist* from *The Fifty-Three Stations of the Tōkaidō
Woodcut, 1832
The Miriam and Ira D. Wallach Division of Art, Prints and Photographs, Print Collection

The Japanese artist Andō Hiroshige achieved widespread recognition in the West as soon as artists and collectors in the 19th century began discovering Japan's rich and varied woodcut tradition (also referred to as Ukiyo-e prints). One of the printmaker's most impressive and important series, *The Fifty-Three Stations of the Tōkaidō*, documents the trip the artist undertook from Edo to Kyoto in 1832. Hiroshige made numerous sketches on his journey as part of an official delegation transporting horses to the Imperial Court. Stirred by the beauty of the landscapes, changing weather patterns, and the physical challenges of travel, Hiroshige captured qualities that earned him the appellation "artist of rain and snow." The Library purchased a rare first-edition impression of *Tōkaidō Road* in 1955 from the well-known scholar and collector Ernest Fenollosa. It has an important place among the Print Collection's Ukiyo-e prints and augments the Spencer Collection's Ehon volumes (Japanese illustrated books).

Kitagawa Utamaro (1753–1806)
Gifts of the Ebb Tide
Woodblock printed book with mica and gold leaf on paper, ca. 1789
The Miriam and Ira D. Wallach Division of Art, Prints and Photographs, Spencer Collection

Gifts of the Ebb Tide pairs poems about seashells with exquisite images of them. The book memorializes a visit to the seaside in 1789, telling us that the renowned poet Akera Kankō (1740–1800) and six companions journeyed across Japan's Shinagawa Bay to spend time gathering seaweed and seashells. After some heavy drinking, he and the other poets began seeking different sorts of shells, an activity that inspired each to compose a poem. Kankō's friend Tsutaya Jūzaburō offered to publish the book after the group's return to Edo, while the young Japanese artist Kitagawa Utamaro agreed to create the accompanying Ukiyo-e woodcut illustrations. Utamaro rendered the shells mentioned in each poem in full color, embellishing them with sprinkled mica, gold paint, and pipette-blown pigment, and further enhancing their lifelike quality with embossing that conveys their dimpled and coiled exteriors. This is one of two copies of this dazzling volume in the Library's Spencer Collection.

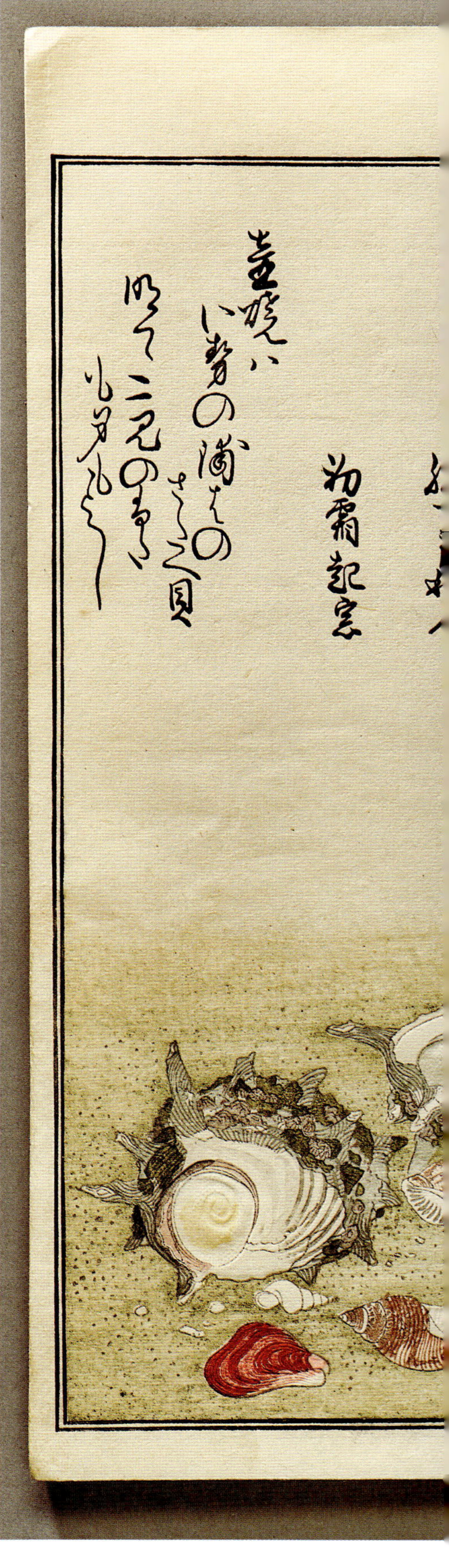

志ろくもや
ゐきり晴る
しら
なみの
うへ
きのふ
より
ちるらむの
色

小蒙茭成

大屋裏住

うつ川の水のそこ切程乃
しら玉の
なかれよりいつれ
蔦紫
ゆかりの貝

打よする浪の涙ハ
音羽の草紙にて
寐しい月をまする
枕貝

臺所力方

市谷の花にも紫
緋縮緬も波に志衣ず
恋の名婦唐ちの里
花乃色貝

長松娥娥

九重の紅入て

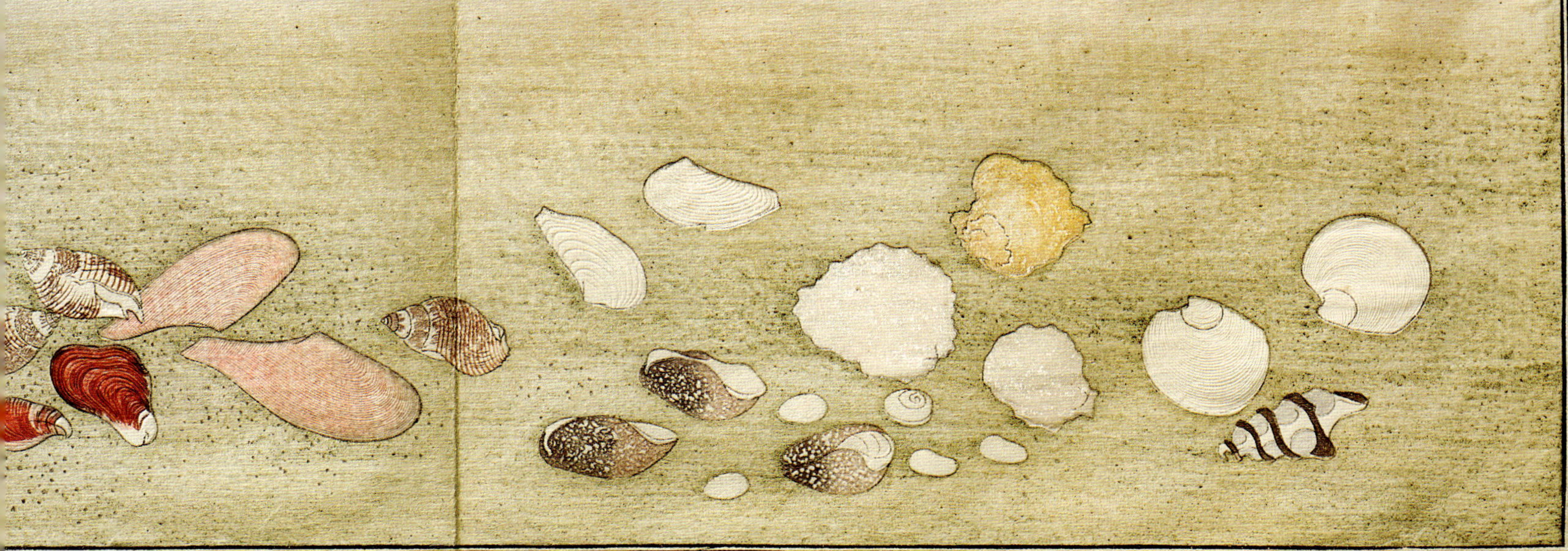

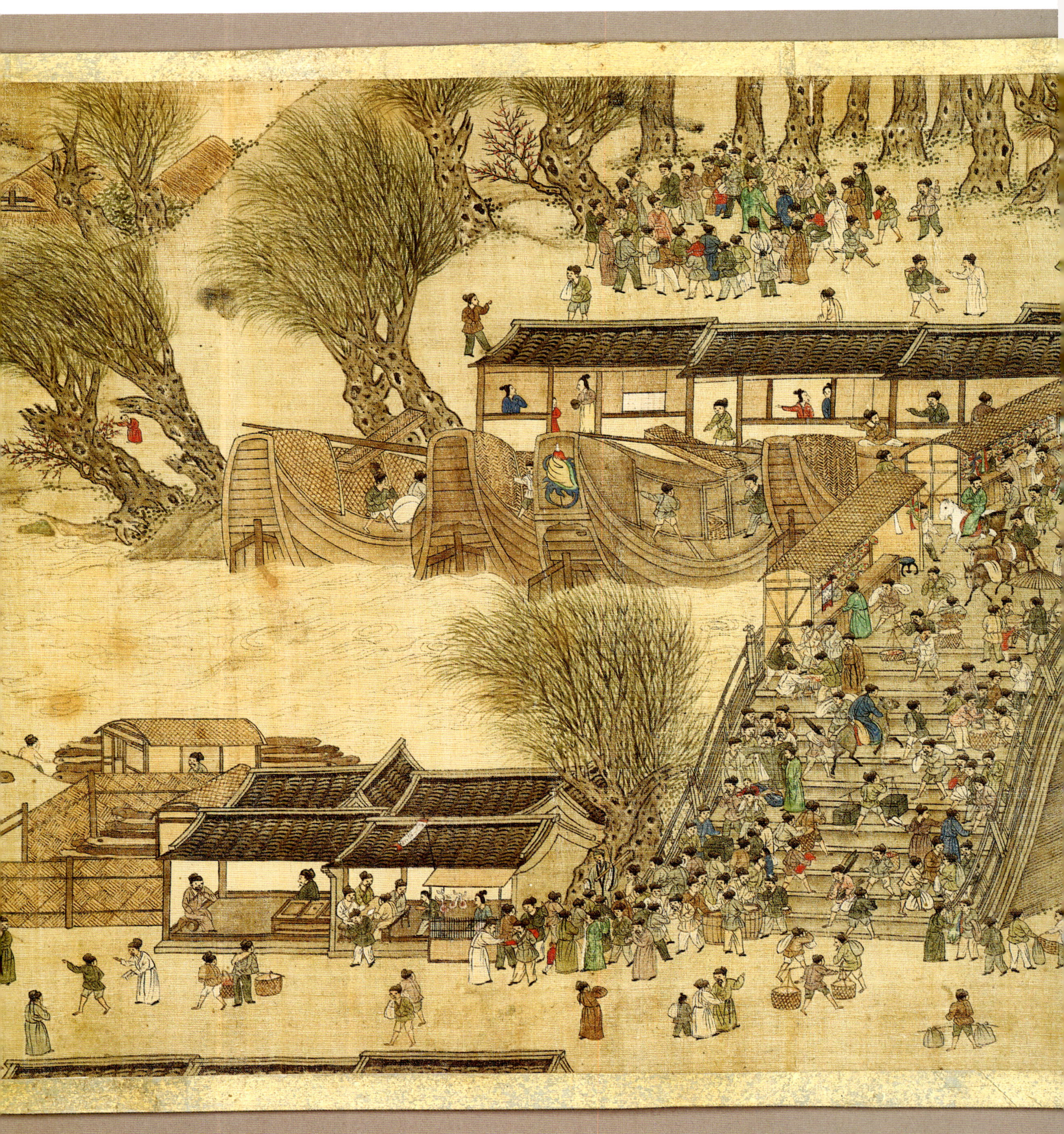

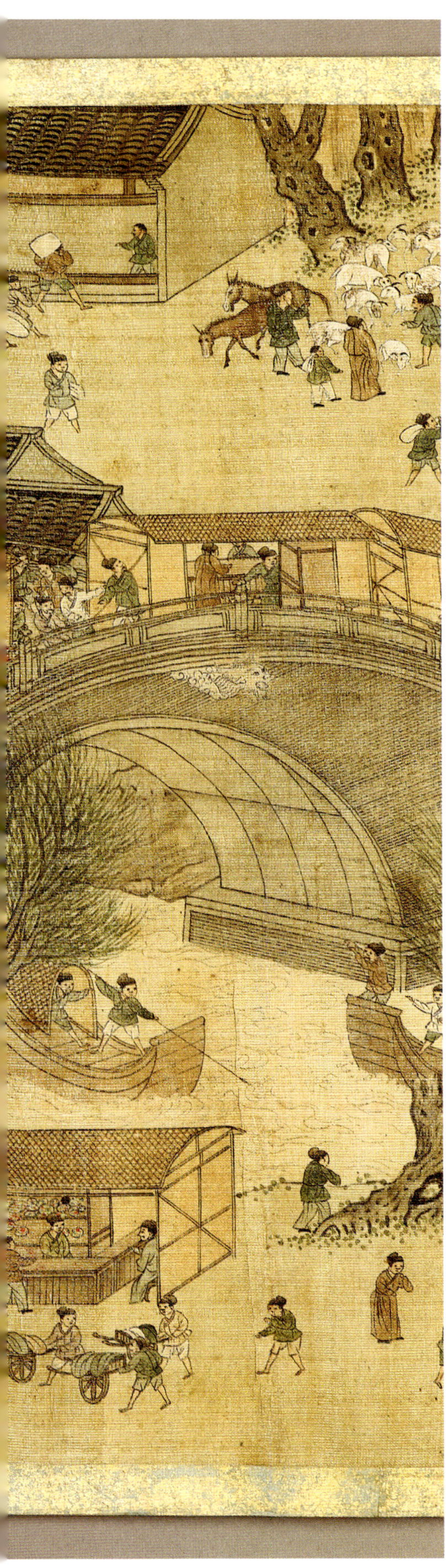

Anonymous, after Zhang Zeduan (fl. 12th century)
***Along the River During the Qingming Festival* scroll**
Pigment on silk, 17th century
The Miriam and Ira D. Wallach Division of Art, Prints and Photographs,
Spencer Collection

This 17th-century copy of the celebrated 12th-century Qingming scroll (Palace Museum, Beijing) depicts the celebrations associated with the so-called tomb sweeping, or Qingming, festival. The event has been observed in China for more than 2,500 years and is a cornerstone of traditional Chinese ancestor worship. Rather than focusing on the holiday's prayers and rituals, however, the scroll is famous for its vivid portrayal of the festivities associated with the day, as well as for its lively depiction of scenes of everyday 12th-century life. Attributed to the artist Zhang Zeduan, the original scroll is one of the most famous works of Chinese art and consequently much imitated; the National Palace Museum in Taipei alone has eight versions. The Library's copy forms part of the Spencer Collection's rich and varied holdings of Asian scrolls, which offer numerous opportunities for comparative study.

Albrecht Dürer (1471–1528)

Fortuna

Engraving, 1501–1502

The Miriam and Ira D. Wallach Division of Art, Prints and Photographs, Print Collection

Among Albrecht Dürer's most ambitious large-format engravings, *Fortuna* reflects knowledge that the artist put into practice after his first visit to Italy in 1494: the work's subject derives from a poem by the Italian humanist poet Angelo Poliziano, and the ideal figural proportions of the nude female protagonist are based on those recommended by the classical architect Vitruvius. Inspired by the famous map of Venice that Jacopo de Barbari had created two years earlier, the winged figure surmounting a globe hovers over a bird's-eye view of an Alpine village, a symbol of the inconstancy of fortune. Centuries before satellite photography or hot-air balloon rides, Dürer rendered the hill town from a vantage point that involved a flight of the imagination. *Fortuna* is one of more than 400 original prints and illustrated books by the German artist in the Wallach Division's Print and Spencer Collections, and additional works by Dürer can be found in the Rare Book Division.

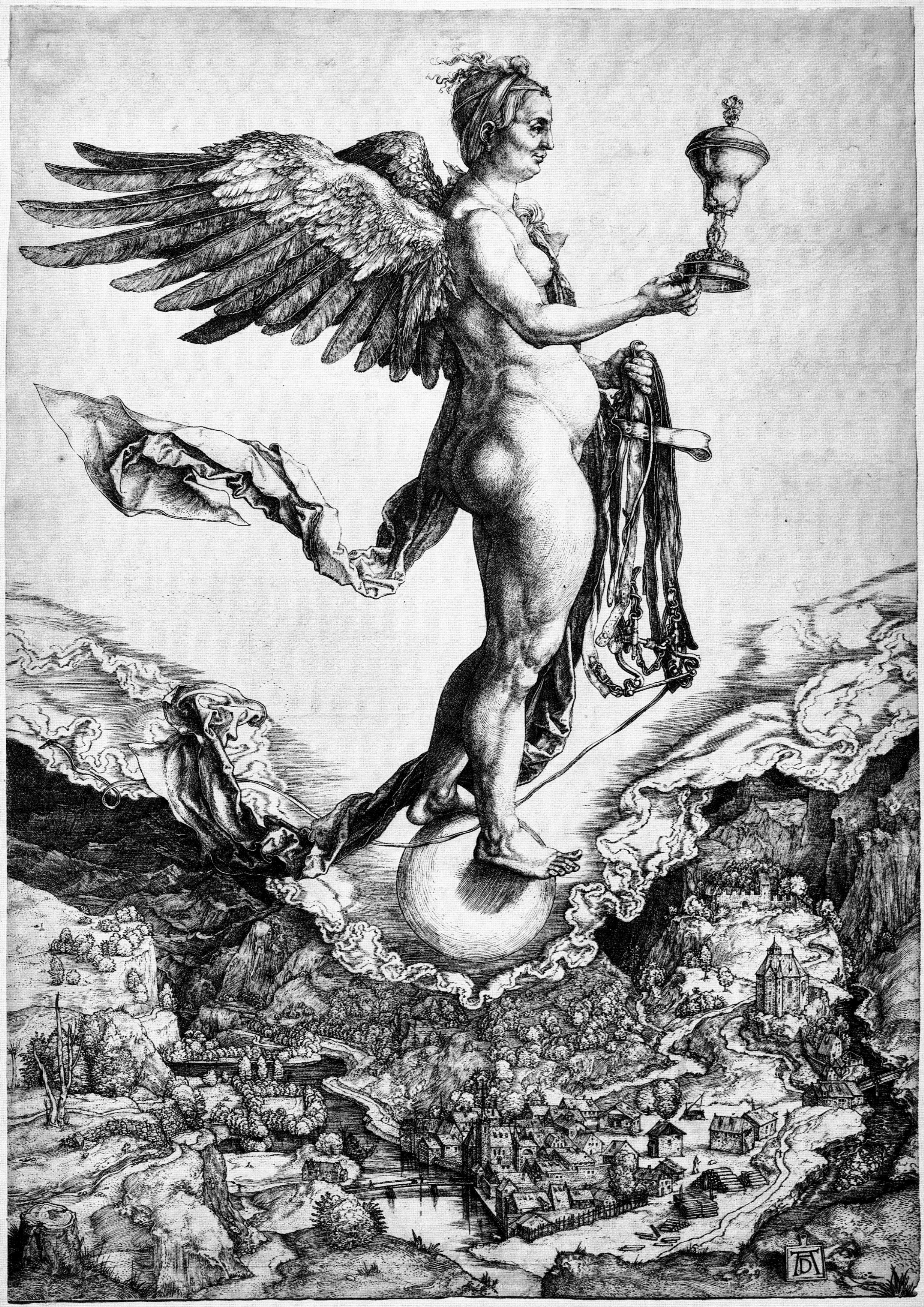

diuiditur. Ante pedes eius est quaedam Corona stel-
lis effecta: de qua prius diximus. Hic praeceps occidit: Exoritur directus. Hab& autem in capite
stellas duas: in arcu duas: in sagitta unam: in dex-
tro cubito unam: in manu priore unam: in uentre
scapulo unam: inter scapillio duas: in cauda unam: in priore genu unam: in pede unam: in inferiore ge-
nu unam: in poplite unam. Omnino est stellarum pollice
quindecim. Corona autem centauri est stellarum
septem.

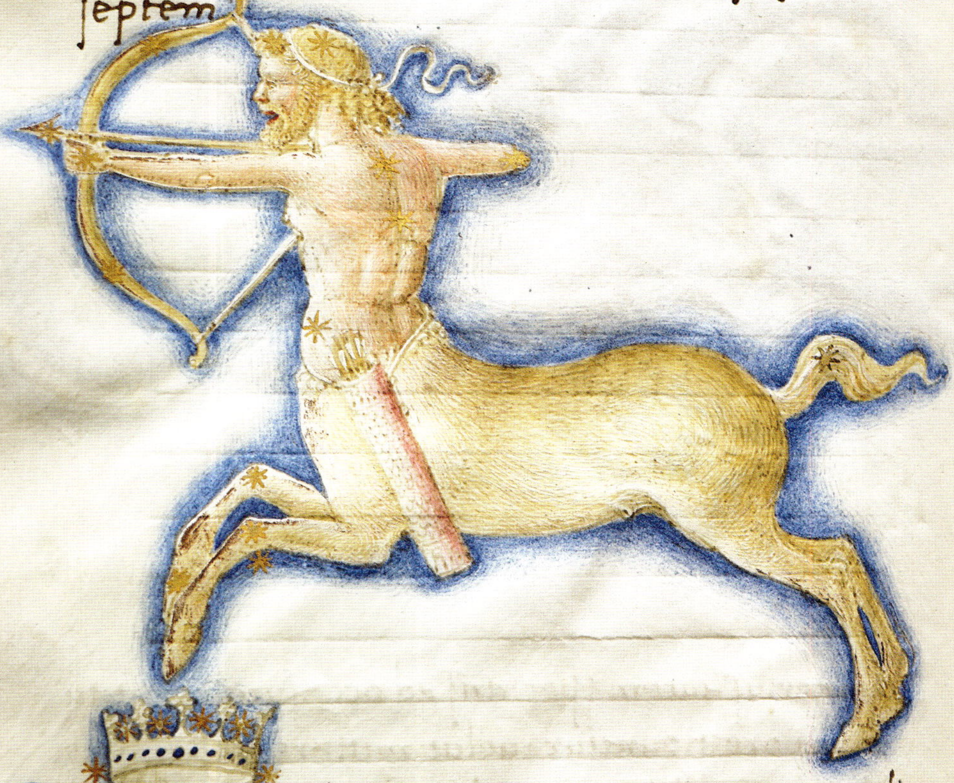

Capricornus ad occasum spectans: & totus in Zodi-
aco circulo deformatus: cauda & toto corpore me-
dius diuiditur ab hyemali circulo suppositus aqua-
rij manu sinistrae. Occidit autem praeceps: & ex

oritur ante directu
Infra ceruicem una
pede unam: in pri
scapulo pillio hab& stellas
cauda duas: & ita
+xxvi. uigintiunus.

Aquarius hab& pe
manum autem si
rigens tergum. de
tingens: spectat ad
natus necesse est,
to uideri. Effusio
qui solutarius figur
Sed aquarius & oc
usq reliquis men

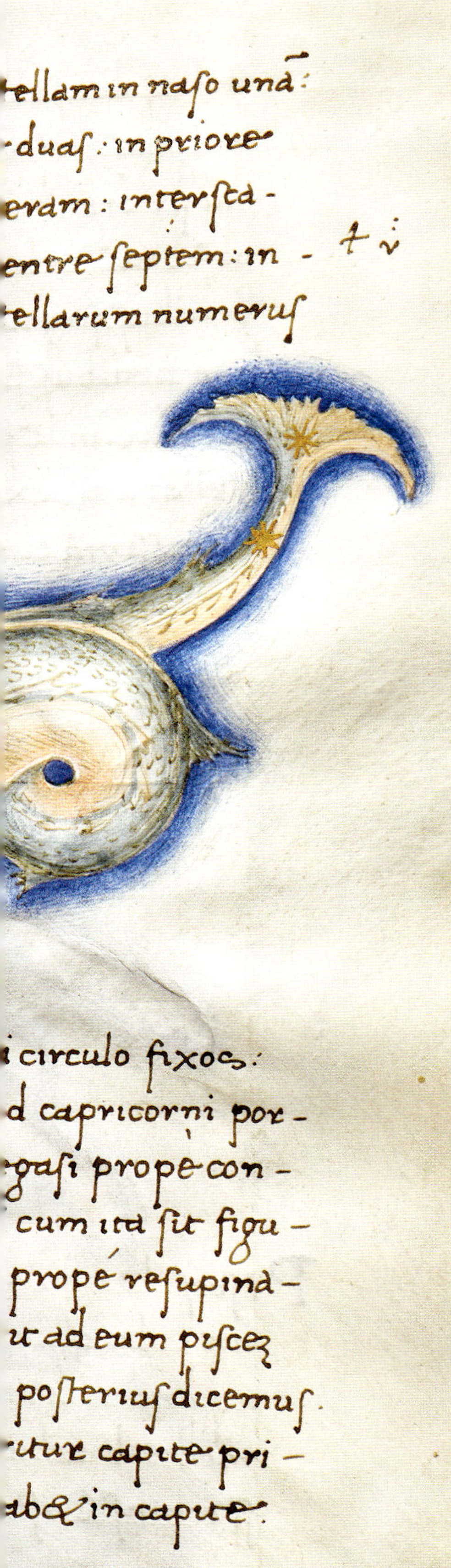

Gaius Julius Hyginus (fl. 1st century CE)
De astronomia
Illuminated manuscript, 1475–1480
The Miriam and Ira D. Wallach Division of Art, Prints and Photographs, Spencer Collection

The New York Public Library possesses one of the largest and finest collections of medieval and Renaissance illuminated manuscripts in North America. This exquisite manuscript is a Latin astrological poem by the 1st-century CE astronomer Hyginus. It is decorated with thirty-eight illustrations of the constellations in their traditional anthropomorphic or zoomorphic forms by at least two, and perhaps three, different artists. One of these artists is Gabriele Vendramin, a student of the famed Renaissance artist Mantegna. Three of the other illuminations are attributed to another artist known as "the Douce Master" (named after the collection of illuminated manuscripts assembled by the antiquary and collector Francis Douce). The celestial miniatures are placed between sections of text in an elegant humanist script that has been recognized as the hand of Francesco Buzzaccarini.

Hyginus, believing in occult correspondences between earthly and heavenly bodies, based his poem largely on the Hellenistic writer Aratus. He, in turn, relied for his knowledge on the 4th-century BCE Greek mathematician Eudoxios of Cnidos. This 15th-century manuscript may have been produced in Padua, at that time one of the main centers in Europe for the study of astrology.

Hartmann Schedel (1440–1514)
Liber chronicarum*, also known as the *Nuremberg Chronicle
Nuremberg: Anton Koberger, 1493
Rare Book Division

The *Liber chronicarum*—also known as the *Nuremberg Chronicle*, after its place of printing—is a universal history of the Christian world from its creation to the 1490s. The work was published in 1493 by Anton Koberger, the most successful German printer of the era, and holds the distinction of being the most heavily illustrated book of the 15th century: its 600 pages are graced with more than 1,800 woodcuts depicting various historical events and personages, along with numerous topographical views. Interestingly, however, these lavish illustrations were rendered with only around 650 wooden blocks, resulting in certain images appearing more than once for differing purposes.

Today, histories such as the *Liber chronicarum* are valued by researchers investigating early modern Europe. The New York Public Library is honored to hold in trust eight copies of this important work.

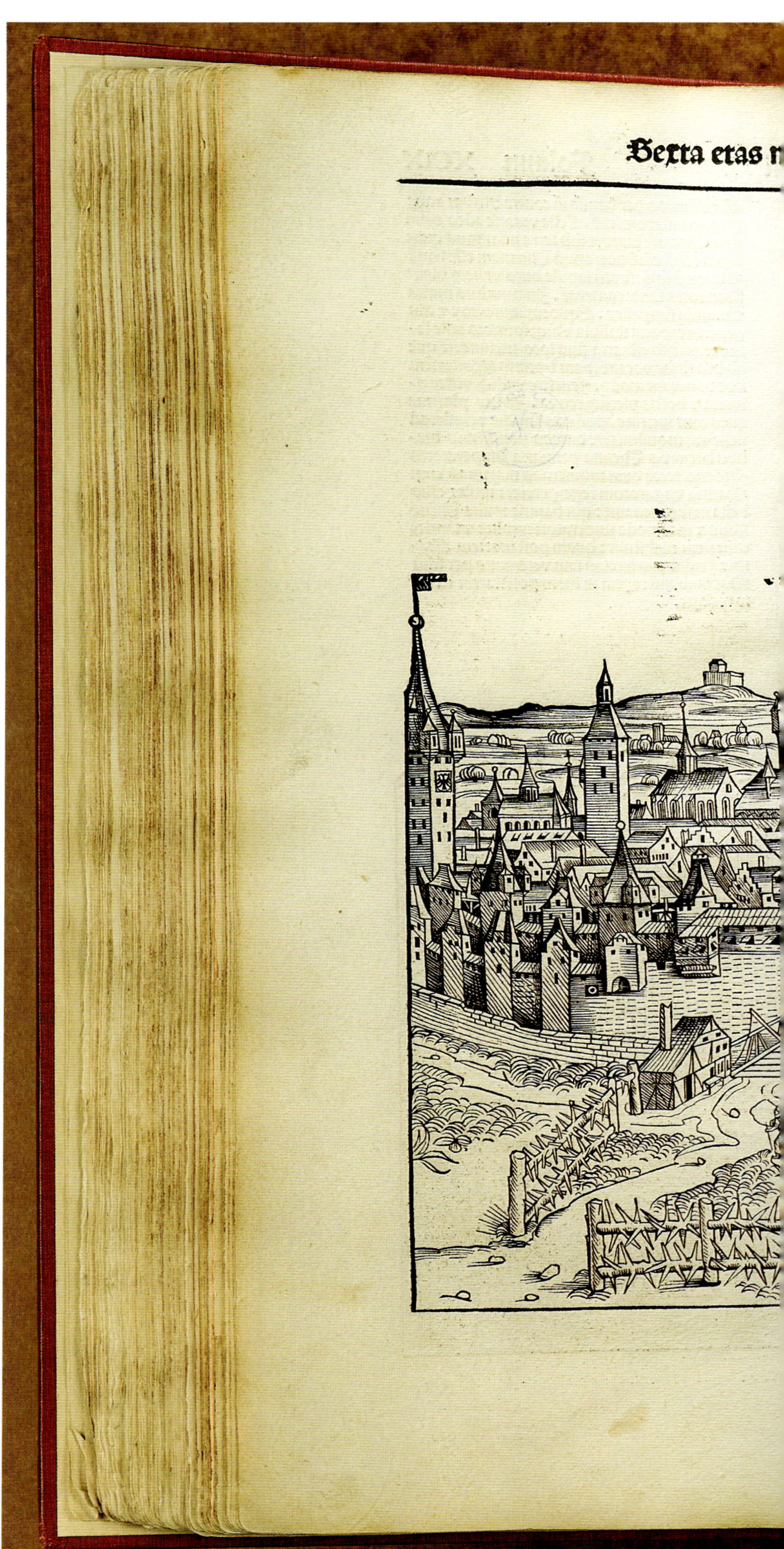

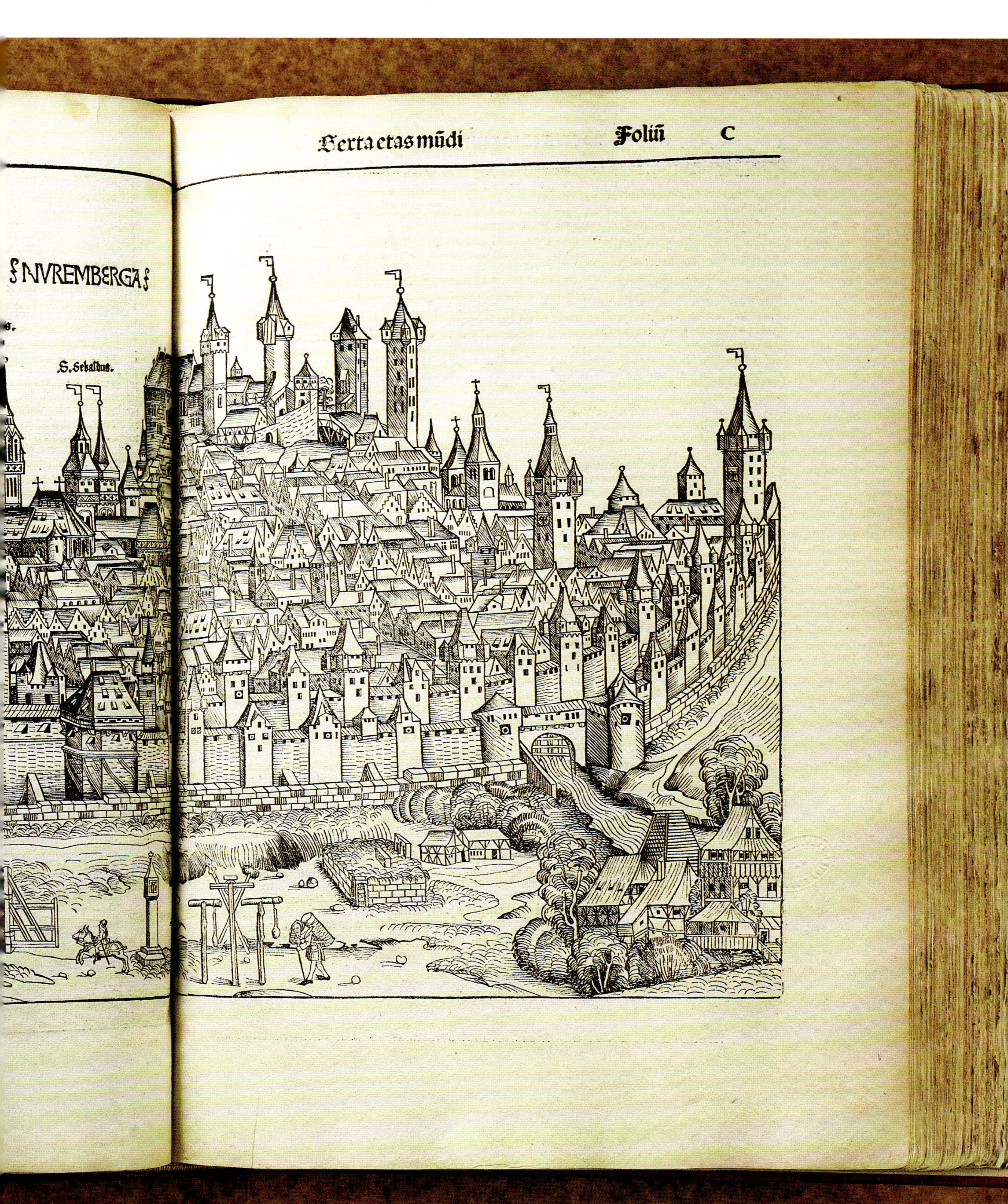

Sexta etas mūdi
Foliū
C
NVREMBERGA
S. Sebaldus.

Der diser bestien want vnd der endkrist bezaichnet vnd Im ist gegeben ein mund ze sprechen grosse plasphemierung von Im selb vnd spricht er sey gottes son vnd er ist also gut versprechen vnd Im ist gegeben xlij monat zu thon grosse zaichen also das er in den werden dar sich alles volck solt vndertanig machen an ein wenig dye do werden behalten

Vnd das volck hat an gepet die bestia vnd haben gesagt wer ist geleich diser bestien oder wer mag wider sie fechten

Vnd der drach hat vff gethan den mund in versprechung zu dem herren vnd sein zu verlaugnen das er got sey vnd sich zw ver nichten got vnd sein tabernackl vnd auch der dy do wonen in dem hymel vnd im ist gegeben ein streyt mit den heiligen gotz vnd sie zu überwinden vnd Im ist gegeben die macht in allem volck Vnd sie haben In angebett all die da wonnen auff der erden der name nit geschriben stendt In dem puch des lebens das lambes das da getöt ist von anbegyn der werlt welich oren hab der höre Vnd wer da In gefencknuss kompt der muss dar In beleiben Vnd wer da mit dem swert töttet der muss mit dem swert gericht werden das Ist die gedult vnd der glaube der heyligen vnnsers herren etc

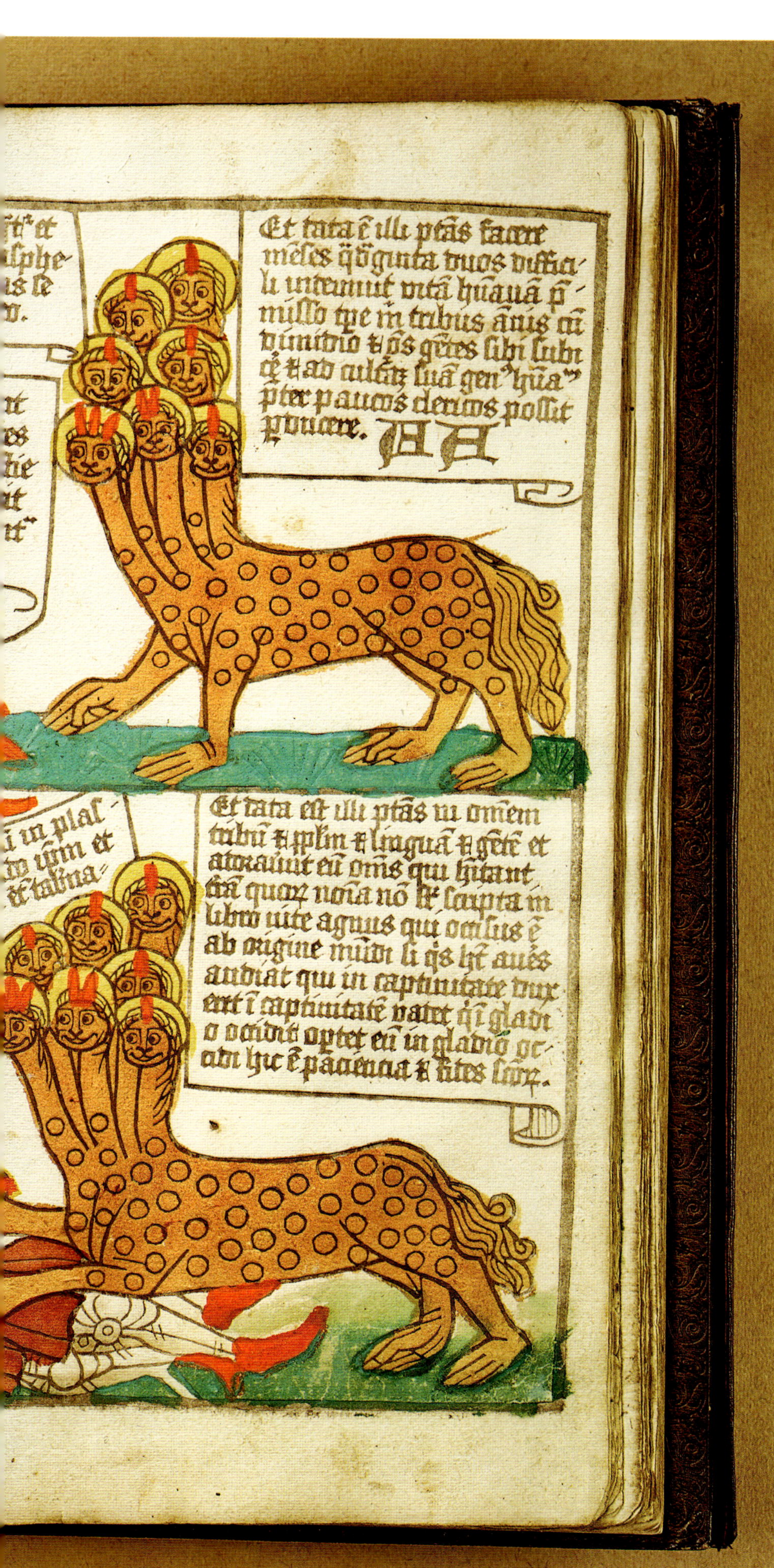

Apocalypsis Sancti Johannis
ca. 1470
Rare Book Division

This example of a block book, or xylographica, combines striking images with an abbreviated text from the Book of Revelation, or Apocalypse. Volumes like this were most likely intended for use by illiterate individuals under the guidance of an educated person who could read the condensed text to explain the pictures.

Woodcut printing persisted alongside the use of a mechanical printing press in the mid-15th century. The printer would lay a leaf of paper over an inked, relief-cut block, and rub the back of the sheet to transfer the ink. The page's reverse is often blank, because the now-indented paper does not permit a satisfactory double-sided impression. Though undoubtedly produced in some numbers, block books are today of the utmost rarity, with some surviving only in fragmentary copies.

Shunkichi Kikuchi (1916–1990)

Photographs taken in Hiroshima for the Special Committee for the Investigation of A-bomb Damage

Gelatin silver prints mounted to album pages, October 1–22, 1945

The Miriam and Ira D. Wallach Division of Art, Prints and Photographs, Photography Collection

In the weeks following the atomic bombings of Hiroshima on August 6, 1945, and Nagasaki three days later, the Japanese Ministry of Education formed a special committee of doctors and scientists to survey the aftermath of the attacks. The committee commissioned the creation of a documentary film, for which it hired photographers Shunkichi Kikuchi and Shigeo Hayashi to shoot stills. Kikuchi accompanied the medical team to triage centers in Hiroshima during the first three weeks of October 1945 and produced more than 700 negatives—among them, the earliest comprehensive visual documentation of the *hibakusha* (atomic bomb survivors) and the devastated cityscape. The pages of this period binder contain contact prints as well as contemporaneous notes—part of an archive related to the production of the film—that offer a graphic account of countless grim scenes that were censored during the Allied occupation of Japan.

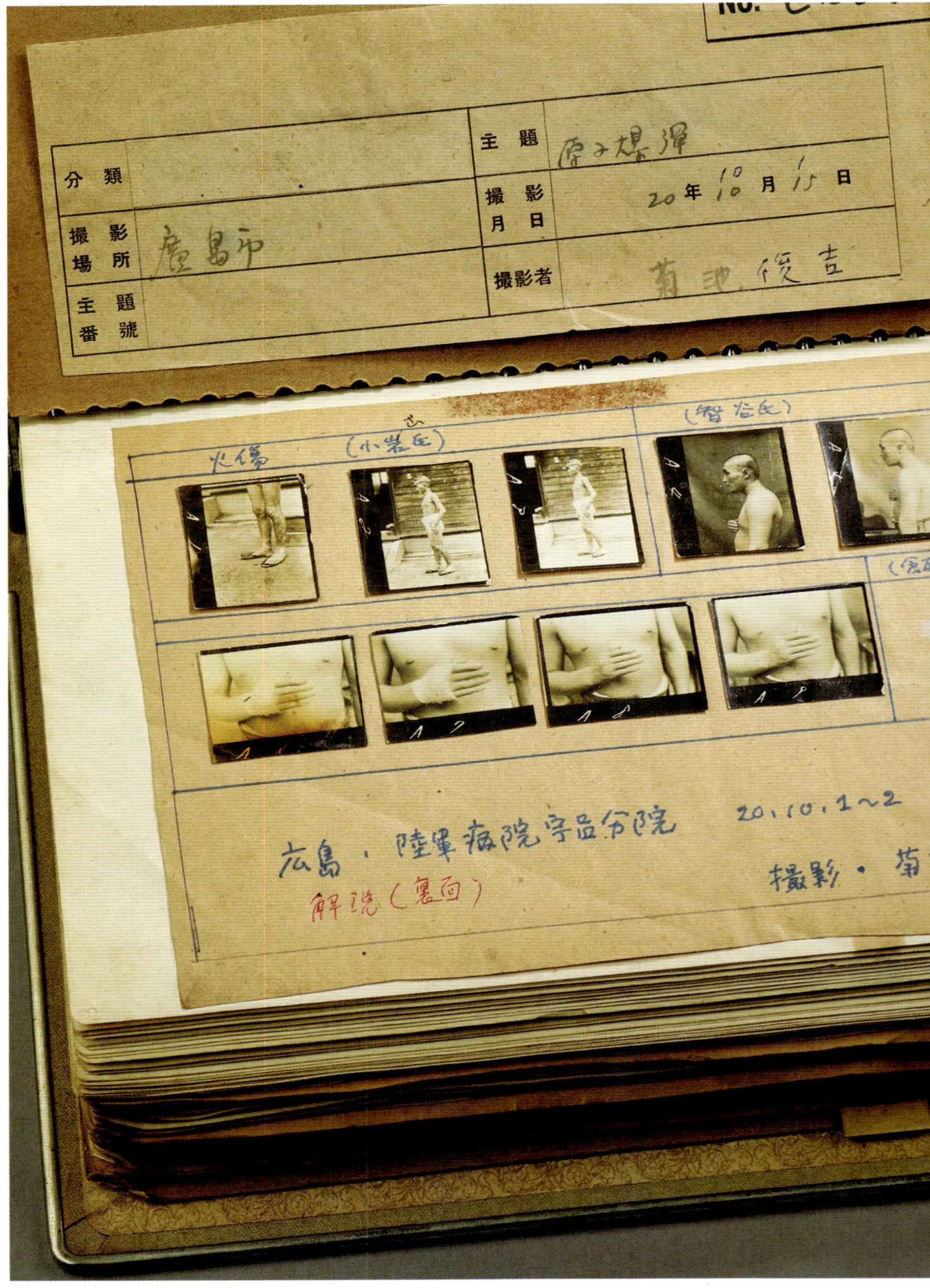

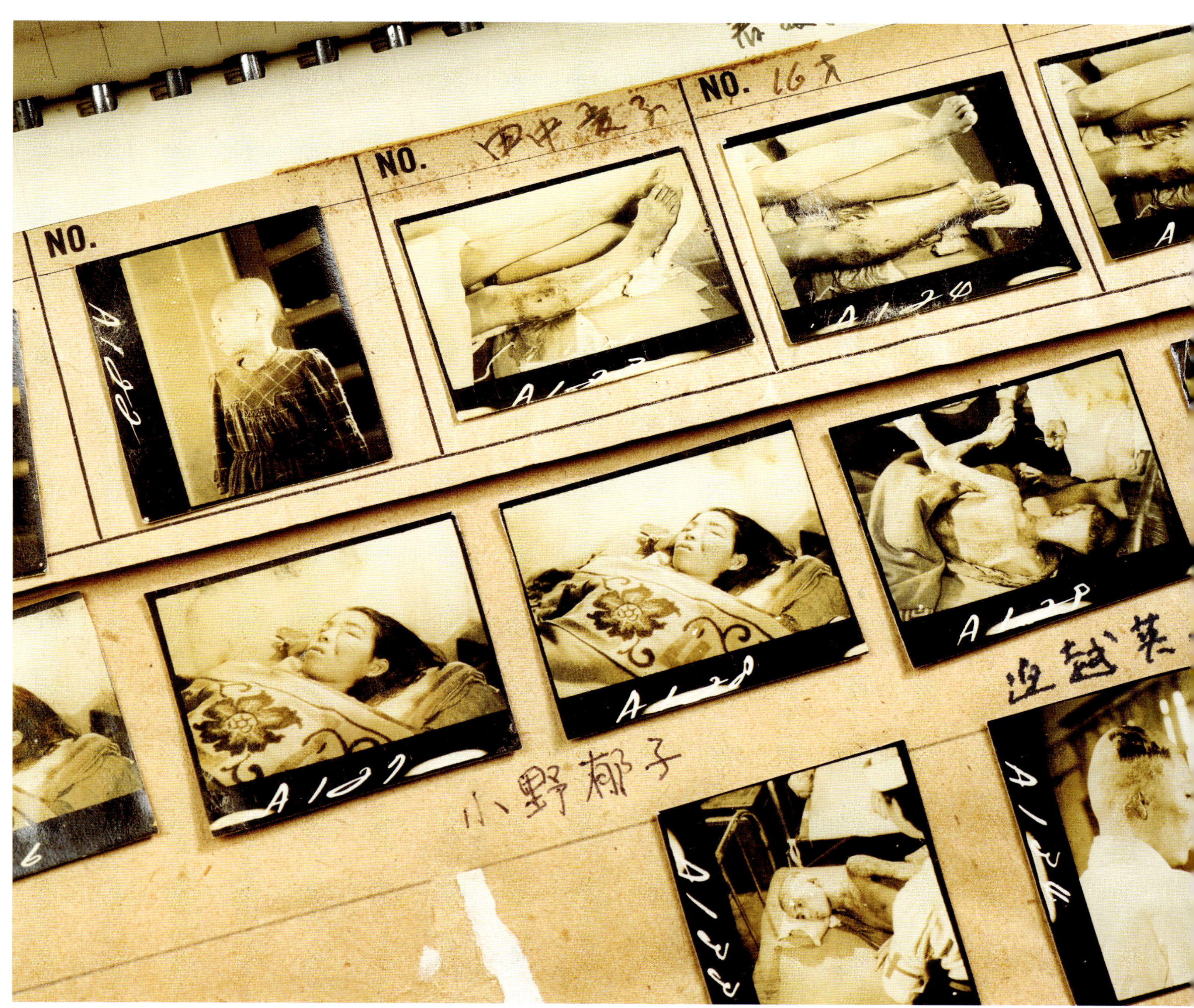

NO.
NO.
NO.

Delteil 272
Loga 723

Expresivo doble fuerza
Idea y litogª por Goya

Francisco Goya (1746–1828)
***Espresivo doble fuerza* (*Expressive of double force*)**
Transfer lithograph, 1819
The Miriam and Ira D. Wallach Division of Art, Prints and Photographs, Print Collection

While Aloys Senefelder's invention of lithography in Munich between 1796 and 1799 soon found application in cities throughout Europe, it was only in 1819, when the printmaker José Maria Cardano founded Madrid's first lithographic workshop, that the technology arrived in Spain. At age seventy-three, Francisco Goya was no longer a youngster, but he was game to try his hand at the new medium, resulting in the creation of ten rare trial proofs. Printed on the verso of one of Cardano's discarded prints, the Library's lithograph is evidence of the spirit of experimentation in which Goya entered the project. Titled *Espresivo doble fuerza*, the lithograph shows a couple seated on the ground, apparently fighting or pushing each other. The work belonged to Samuel Putnam Avery's important collection of close to 18,000 prints, which he bequeathed to the Library in 1900, and which formed the impetus for the Library to start its print collection.

William Blake (1757–1827)
Milton: a Poem in 2 Books
London, ca. 1804–1811
Rare Book Division

The visionary English poet and artist William Blake explored the relationship between text and image in illustrated works such as *Milton: a Poem in 2 Books*. The volume's exquisite illustrations and vibrant coloring, which seem to flow from and wrap around the text itself, become yet another element to be read. The overall effect is at once dramatic and sublime, highlighting intense religious themes of the verse while guiding readers' eyes across the page.

Blake printed *Milton*, along with his other books, using an uncommon relief-etching process. He also hand-colored the volumes, so each of the four known copies of *Milton* is distinct. Today, in addition to being esteemed for their rarity and beauty, Blake's creations are regarded as important milestones in the history of printing, being forebears of modern-day private press and artists' book productions.

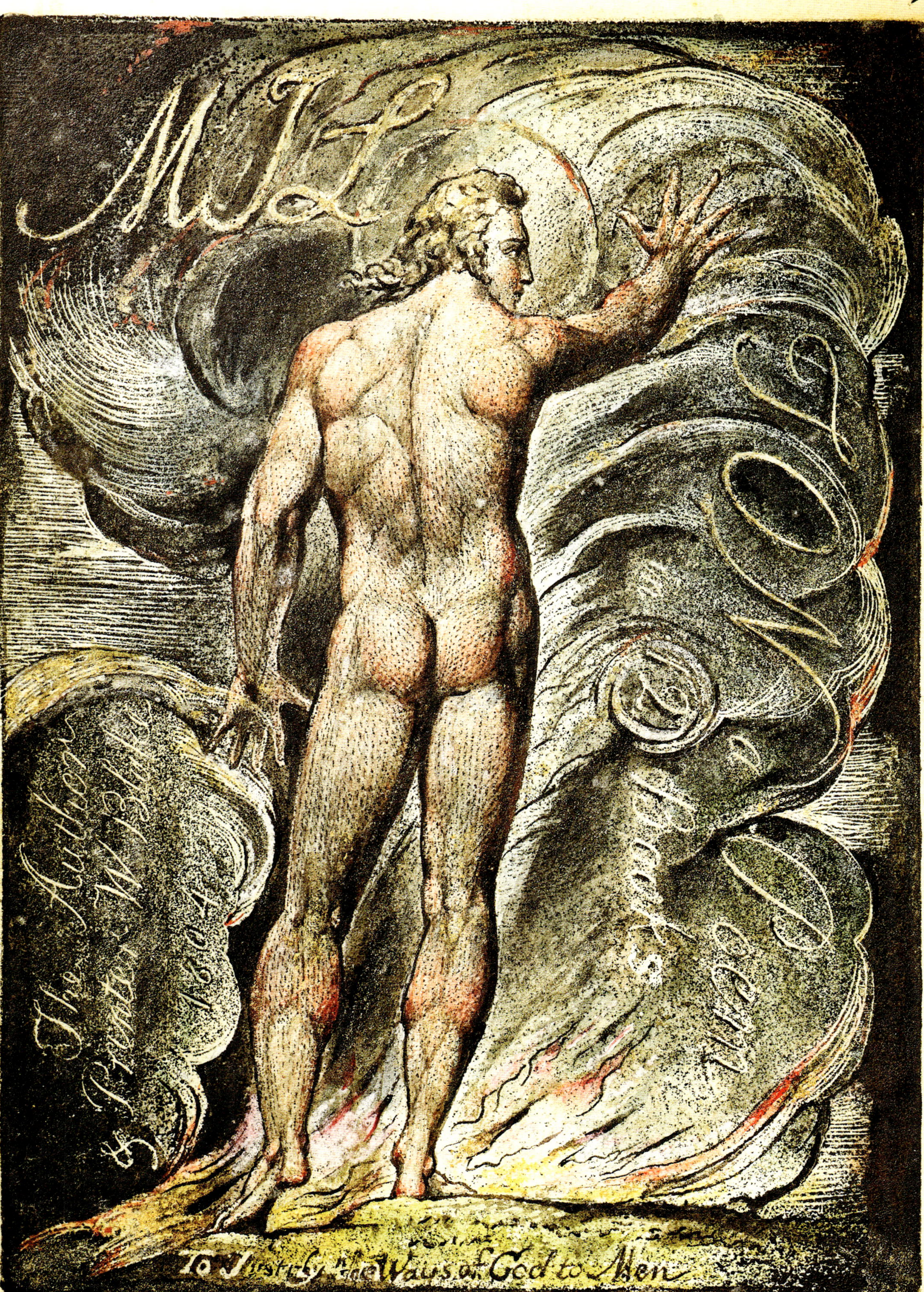
1
MIL
TON
a Poem in 2 Books
The Author & Printer W Blake 1804
To Justify the Ways of God to Men

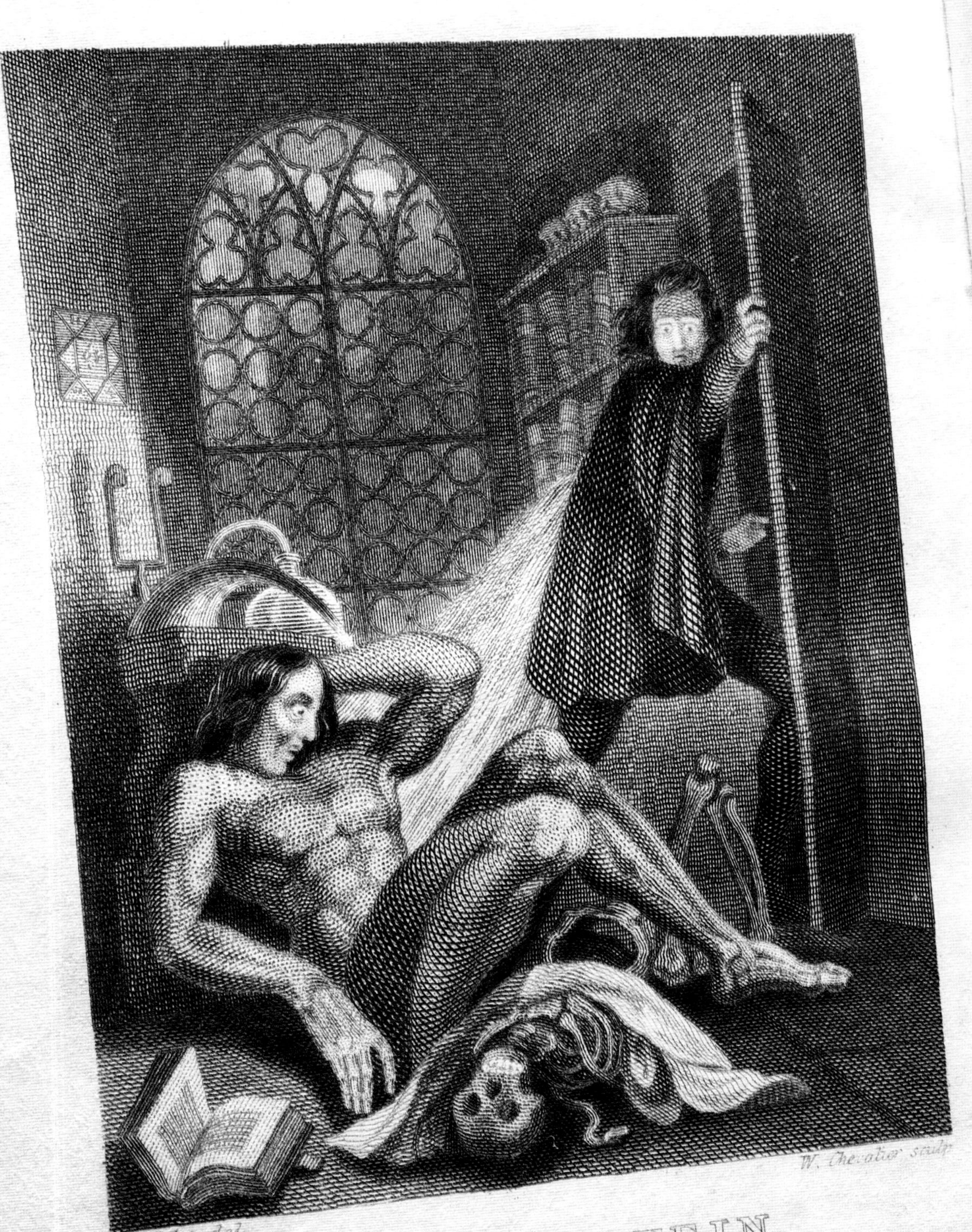

FRANKENSTEIN.

"By the glimmer of the half-extinguished light, I saw the dull, yellow eye of the creature open; it breathed hard, and a convulsive motion agitated its limbs.
** * * I rushed out of the room."*

Page 43.

London: Published by H. Colburn and R. Bentley, 1831.

Mary Wollstonecraft Shelley (1797–1851)
Frankenstein, or the Modern Prometheus
London: Richard Bentley, 1836
The Carl H. Pforzheimer Collection of Shelley and His Circle

Frankenstein was anonymously published in 1818 when its author was twenty years old, and the story of a chemistry student who creates a living, speaking creature from corpses has captivated readers ever since. Mary Shelley's introduction to the revised 1831 edition—the first to be illustrated—describes the tale's origins in a contest held at Lord Byron's villa on Lake Geneva ("'We will each write a ghost story,' said Lord Byron.") Here we see the creature awakening while his terrified creator flees. This monster is nothing like Boris Karloff's famous rendition; rather, he resembles Thomas Potter Cooke's portrayal. The creator of the stage role in 1823, Cooke danced across the stage in a toga, his skin painted blue. The theatrical version of *Frankenstein* was a hit, ensuring the continued success of the novel.

Letter from John Milton (1608–1674) to Carlo Dati (1619–1675)

April 20, 1647

Manuscripts and Archives Division

John Milton, the English poet who composed sonnets and wrote epic poetry—including *Paradise Lost*—also penned tracts concerning political and social issues. Although praised as one of the preeminent writers in the English language, Milton also wrote in Latin, Greek, and Italian. This letter to Carlo Roberto Dati bears testament to a friendship that transcended linguistic and national borders in the early modern period. Milton met Dati, a Florentine nobleman nearly ten years his junior, during his trip to Florence, Italy, in 1638. Milton wrote to Dati expressing his great sadness at leaving Florence and reflecting on the friendships he had established in the city. A line from Milton greets visitors to the Main Reading Room of The New York Public Library: "A good Book is the pretious life-blood of a master spirit, imbalm'd and treasur'd up on purpose to a life beyond life."

Carolo Dato Patricio Florentino
Joannes Miltonius Londinensis
S. P. D.

Perlatis inopinato literis ad me tuis, mi Carole, quanta et quam nova sim vo-
luptate perfusus, quandoquidem non est ut pro re satis queam dicere, volo ex
dolore saltem, sine quo vix ulla magna hominibus delectatio concessa est, id
aliqua [illegible] intelligas. Dum enim illa tua prima percurro, in quibus Elegantia cum
[illegible] sane contendit, merum illud quidem gaudium esse dixerim: prae-
sertim [illegible], ubi vincat Amicitia, operam te dare videam. [illegible] vero cum incido
[illegible] scribis, [illegible] te [illegible] ad [illegible], quas [illegible] perisse scio, tum
[illegible] est laetitia. Mox
etiam gravius quiddam sentit [illegible] persaepe soleo,
[illegible] forte vicinia, aut aliquo [illegible] usus necessitudo [illegible] sive casu
sive lege [illegible] re alia commendabiles, assidere quotidie,
obtundere, enecare etiam mehercule, quoties collibitum erit; [illegible] os mores,
ingenium, studia tam belle conciliaverant, illos jam [illegible] aut morte,
aut iniquissima locorum distantia [illegible] mihi [illegible] et ita confestim e
conspectu plerumque tolli, ut in perpetua fere solitudine versari mihi necesse
sit. Te quod ais, ex quo Florentia discessi, mea de salute solicitum, semper
mei memorem fuisse, gratulor mihi sane par illud utrinque et mutuum acci-
disse, quod ego me solum sensisse meo fortasse merito arbitrabar. Gravis
admodum, ne te celem, discessus ille et mihi quoque fuit, eosque meo animo
aculeos infixit qui etiam nunc altius inhaerent; quoties mecum cogito
tot simul sodales atque amicos tam bonos, tamque commodos una in urbe
longinqua illa quidem, sed tamen charissima invitum me et plane divul-
sum reliquisse. Testor illum mihi semper sacrum et solenne futurum Damonis
tumulum: in cujus funere ornando cum luctu et moerore oppressus ad ea,
quae potui, solatia confugere, et respirare paulisper cupiebam, non aliud mihi
quicquam jucundius occurrit, quam vestrum omnium gratissimam mihi
memoriam, tuique nominatim in mentem revocasse. Id quod ipse jam diu
legisse debes, siquidem ad vos carmen illud pervenit, quod ex te nunc primum
audio. Mittendum ego sane sedulo curaveram, ut esset ingenii quantulum-
cunque, amoris autem adversum vos mei vel illis paucis versiculis, emble-
matis ad morem inclusis testimonium haudquaquam obscurum. Existima-
bam etiam fore hoc modo, ut vel te vel alium ad scribendum in Angliam
allicerem; mihi enim, si prior scriberem, necesse erat, ut vel ad omnes, vel
si quem aliis praetulissem, verebar ne in caeterorum, qui id rescissent, offen-
sionem caderem; cum permultos adhuc superesse illic sperem, qui hoc a me
officium vendicare certe potuerint. Nunc tu omnium primus insperato hoc
tuo literas invitante, ne dicam priorum illarum jactura debitas jam tibi
a me respondendi vices reliquorum expostulatione liberasti. Quanquam
fateor accessisse ad illam silentii causam turbulentissimum illum, ex quo do-
mum reversus sum, Britanniae nostrae statum, qui animum meum paulo post
ab studiis excolendis ad vitam et fortunas quoquo modo tuendas necessario
convertit. Ecquem tu inter tot civium commissa praelia, caedes, fugas, bo-
norum direptiones recessum otio literario alicubi tutum dari putes posse?
Nos tamen etiam inter haec mala (quoniam de studiis meis certior fieri postulas)
sermone patrio haud pauca in lucem dedimus: quae nisi essent Anglice scripta,
libens ad vos mitterem, quorum judiciis plurimum tribuo. Poëmatum quidem,
quae pars Latina est, quoniam expetis, brevi mittam. Atque id sponte jampridem
fecissem, nisi quod, propter ea quae in Pontificem Romanum aliquot paginis
asperius dicta sunt, suspicabar vestris auribus fore minus grata. Nunc abs te
peto, ut, quam veniam, non dico Aligerio, et Petrarchae vestro [illegible]
sed mea, ut scis, olim apud vos loquendi libertati, singulari cum humanitate
dare consuevistis, eandem impetres (nam de te mihi persuasum est) ab caeteris
amicis, quoties de vestris ritibus nostro more loquendum erit. Exequias,
Ludo[illegible]

δεινὸν γὰρ πόντου μετὰ κύμασι πήματι κύρσαι.

δεινὸν δ' εἴ κ' ἐπ' ἄμαξαν ὑπέρβιον ἄχθος ἀείρας,

ἄξονα καυάξαις τὰ δὲ φορτία μαυρωθείη.

μέτρα φυλάσσεσθαι· καιρὸς δ' ἐπὶ πᾶσιν ἄριστος.

ὡραῖος δὲ γυναῖκα τεὸν ποτὶ οἶκον ἄγεσθαι.

μήτε τριηκόντων ἐτέων μάλα πόλλ' ἀπολείπων,

μήτ' ἐπιθεὶς μάλα πολλά· γάμος δέ τοι ὥριος οὗτος.

ἡ δὲ γυνή, τέτορ' ἡβώη, πέμπτῳ δὲ γαμοῖτο.

παρθενικὴν δὲ γαμεῖν, ὥς κ' ἤθεα κεδνὰ διδάξῃς.

τὴν δὲ μάλιστα γαμεῖν, ἥτις σέθεν ἐγγύθι ναίει

πάντα μάλ' ἀμφὶς ἰδών· μὴ γείτοσι χάρματα γήμῃς.

οὐ μὲν γάρ τι γυναικὸς ἀνὴρ ληίζετ' ἄμεινον,

Hesiod (fl. ca. 700 BCE)
"The Golden Age," from *Works and Days*
ca. 1300
Manuscripts and Archives Division

Faith in progress, like trust in technological advance, is a relatively recent phenomenon. Much older is the myth of a Golden Age, present in nearly every culture. Unlike the peoples of the Silver, Bronze, and Iron Ages, the lucky inhabitants of this earlier, imaginary era lived without toil or distress, did not suffer the ravages of time, and submitted to death in the form of sleep. Hesiod records one of the earliest poetic treatments of the Golden Age in his *Works and Days*, where, ironically, hope exists only at the bottom of the legendary Pandora's jar, or box. This spread of a Renaissance manuscript copy of the Greek original discloses how Golden Agers "had all good things; the grain-giving field bore crops of its own accord, much and unstinting, and they themselves, willing, mild-mannered, shared out the fruits of their labors together with many good things, wealthy in sheep, dear to the blessed gods."

Charles Darwin (1809–1882)
On the Origin of Species by Means of Natural Selection
London: W. Clowes and Sons for John Murray, 1859
Rare Book Division

Charles Darwin's seminal work is widely considered the most influential scientific treatise of the 19th century. Darwin presents the theory that populations evolve over time through natural selection—the process whereby organisms that are better adapted to their environment tend to survive and therefore produce more offspring, which then often inherit those advantageous characteristics. It also put forward the theory of common descent, which proposed that biological diversity was the result of a branching pattern of evolution from a common ancestor.

Darwin's theory has long excited controversy and, at times, outright hostility, but it has nevertheless prevailed within the scientific establishment and is foundational to the field of evolutionary biology. Thinkers and writers in other fields have co-opted many of Darwin's ideas, using them to justify arguments for or against colonialism, free-market economics, and creationism, among other practices and ideas.

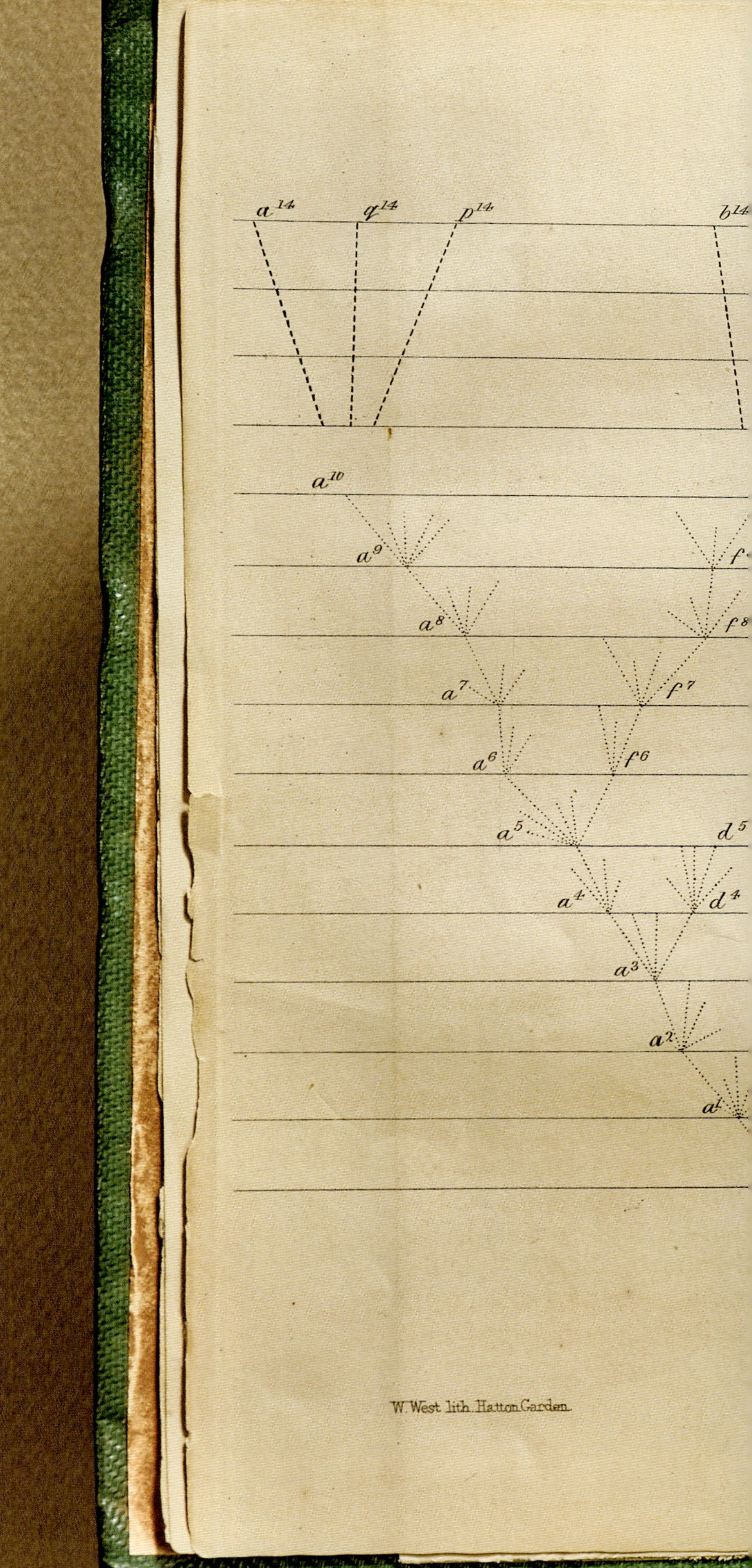

ON

THE ORIGIN OF SPECIES

BY MEANS OF NATURAL SELECTION,

OR THE

PRESERVATION OF FAVOURED RACES IN THE STRUGGLE FOR LIFE.

By CHARLES DARWIN, M.A.,

FELLOW OF THE ROYAL, GEOLOGICAL, LINNÆAN, ETC., SOCIETIES;
AUTHOR OF 'JOURNAL OF RESEARCHES DURING H. M. S. BEAGLE'S VOYAGE ROUND THE WORLD.'

LONDON:
JOHN MURRAY, ALBEMARLE STREET.
1859.

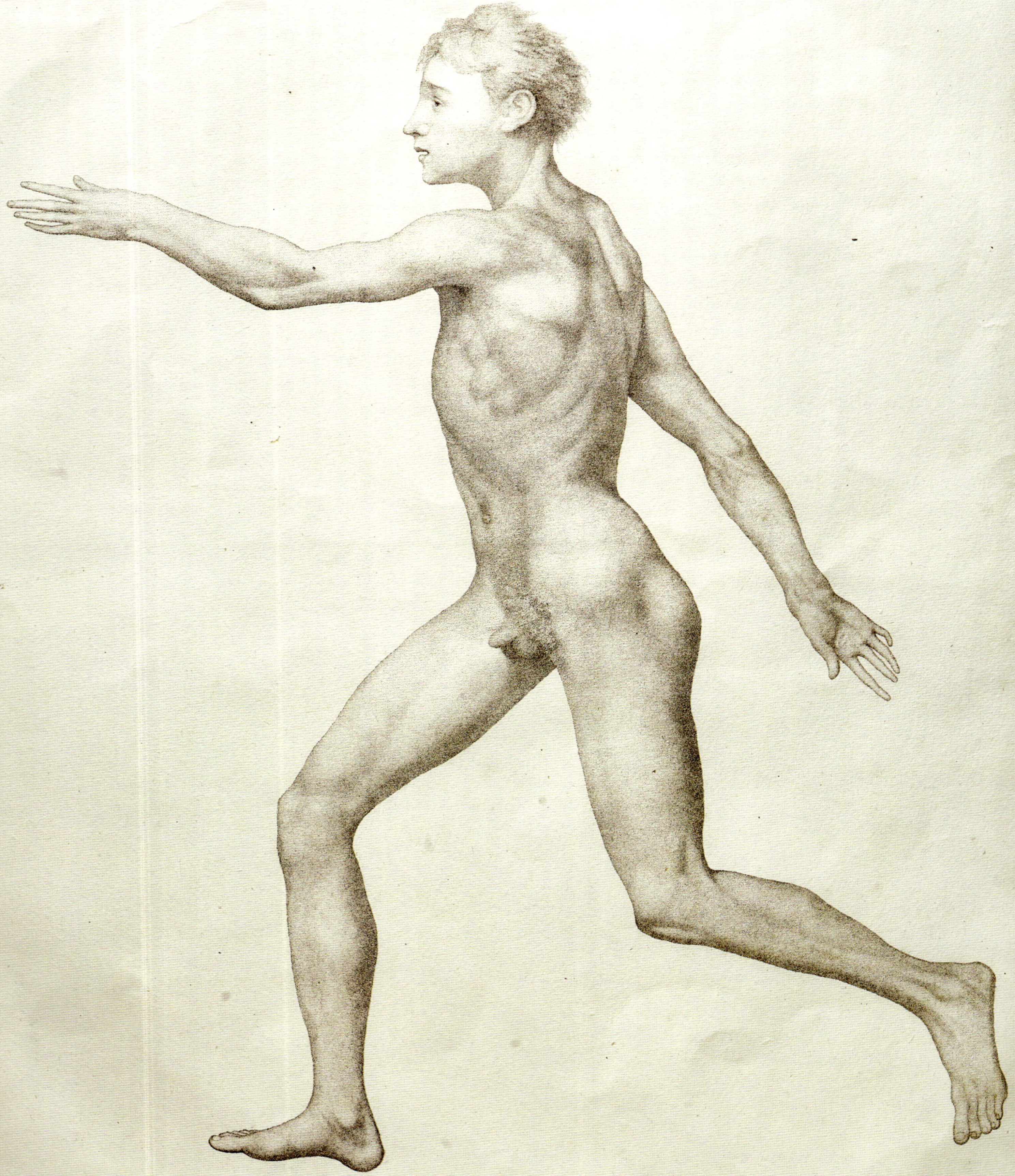

TAB. VIII.

George Stubbs (1724–1806)

Of a Comparative Anatomical Exposition of the Structure of the Human Body, with that of a Tiger and Common Fowl

London: Printed for the author, by W. and C. Spilsbury, Snowhill; and sold by J. White, Fleet-Street, and Longman and Rees, Paternoster-Row, 1803–1806

The Miriam and Ira D. Wallach Division of Art, Prints and Photographs, Spencer Collection

Well known for his paintings of horses, George Stubbs is not generally remembered as one of England's great natural scientists. This is a work of uncommon ambition and great rarity, begun when the artist was already seventy-one years of age and continued for the last decade of his life. Pursuing the idea that the anatomies of creatures could be compared with one another, the artist relates the external form and muscular structure of the human body, the tiger, and the common fowl to one another. The idea may seem peculiar now, but it is indebted to other 19th-century studies regarding the shared structure of all living creatures. The prints constitute extraordinarily fine and vivid examples of stipple engraving, a method that uses dots of various density to model form without line. The Library acquired the two volumes in 2016, purchased from the Estate of the Seventh Earl of Clarendon, whose family had owned the work continuously since acquiring it directly from Stubbs.

Eadweard James Muybridge (1830–1904)

Racking (pacing); saddle; brown horse, Pronto* from the series *Animal Locomotion. An Electro-Photographic Investigation of Consecutive Phases of Animal Movements

Collotype, 1884–1887

The Miriam and Ira D. Wallach Division of Art, Prints and Photographs, Photography Collection

Eadweard Muybridge first started photographing horses in 1872, when Leland Stanford, the railroad magnate and founder of Stanford University, encouraged him to prove whether all four hooves leave the ground at once during a gallop. (They do.) The challenge led Muybridge to invent a system by which the horse's movement tripped wires that then released the camera's shutters. He succeeded in his experiments by 1878, leading him to publish *Animal Locomotion* with the backing of the University of Pennsylvania. This magnum opus included 781 collotypes—photomechanical prints—that appear to sequentially show how horses and other animals, including humans, move. While some of the plates are more scientific and have gridlines in the background, others—such as his photograph of a woman in semitransparent drapery carrying a teacup up the stairs—are decidedly more artistic. Because of the nudes included in the series, the Library originally cataloged the whole set with other materials having to do with sex.

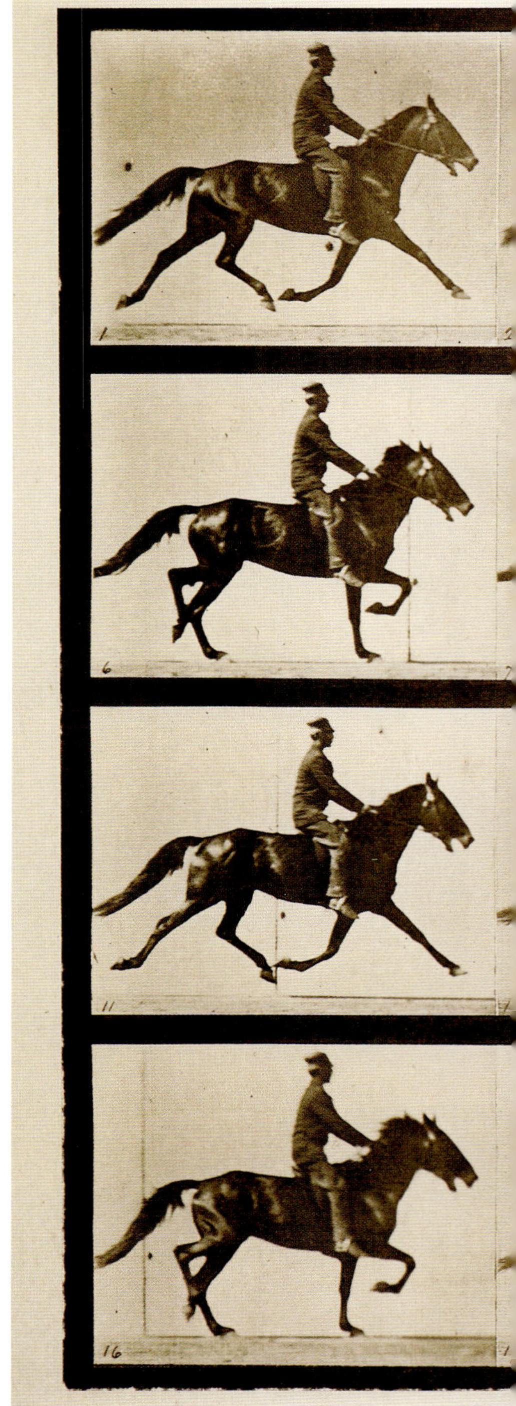

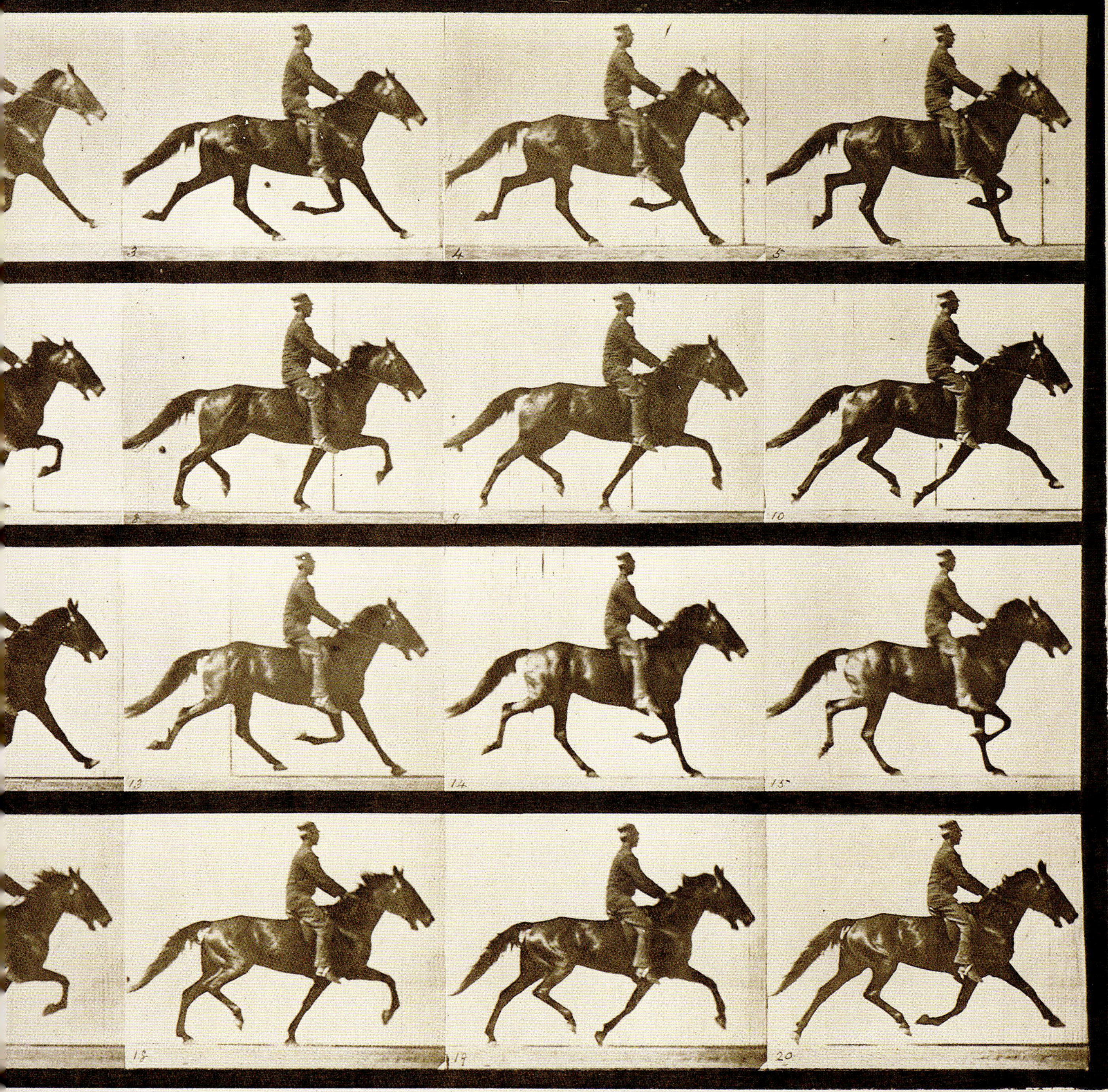

PHILOSOPHIÆ NATURALIS PRINCIPIA MATHEMATICA

Autore *JS. NEWTON*, *Trin. Coll. Cantab. Soc.* Matheseos Professore *Lucasiano*, & Societatis Regalis Sodali.

IMPRIMATUR.
S. PEPYS, *Reg. Soc.* PRÆSES.
Julii 5. 1686.

LONDINI,

Jussu *Societatis Regiæ* ac Typis *Josephi Streater*. Prostat apud plures Bibliopolas. *Anno* MDCLXXXVII.

Isaac Newton (1642–1727)
Philosophiae naturalis principia mathematica
London: Joseph Streater for the Royal Society, 1687
Rare Book Division

First published in 1687, Sir Isaac Newton's *Philosophae naturalis principia mathematica* set out the principles of the laws of universal gravitation and motion. The *Principia* formed the dominant scientific viewpoint until the 20th century, when Einstein's theory of relativity superseded it. In this work, Newton uses his mathematical description of gravity to explain laws of planetary motion as well as to account for tides, the trajectories of comets, the precession of the equinoxes, and other natural phenomena.

While he has long been esteemed as one of history's greatest scientific minds, Newton himself was more reserved when assessing his achievements. Writing to his colleague and rival Robert Hooke in 1676, he once remarked, "If I have seen further, it is by standing on the shoulders of giants."

Euclid (fl. ca. 300 BCE)

Elementa Geometriae

Venice: Erhard Ratdolt, 1482

Rare Book Division

Euclid's *Elementa Geometriae*, first published in Venice in 1482, is the oldest mathematical work still in general use and is historically considered to be the most-read book besides the Bible. It is known to have influenced Galileo Galilei, Abraham Lincoln, Edna St. Vincent Millay, Albert Einstein, and countless others. The text of the initial edition, pictured here, derives from Abelard of Bath's 12th-century translation of an Arabic-language version of the original Greek text, produced around 300 BCE.

In his preface to the book, the printer Erhard Ratdolt attributes the prevailing dearth of mathematical works to the difficulties involved in illustrating geometrical figures—but he notes with marketing savvy that he himself has discovered a method for printing them. Although he does not share the secret of his success, it involved the use of type-metal rules that, having been bent into the desired shape, could be printed alongside the letterpress text and woodcut figures.

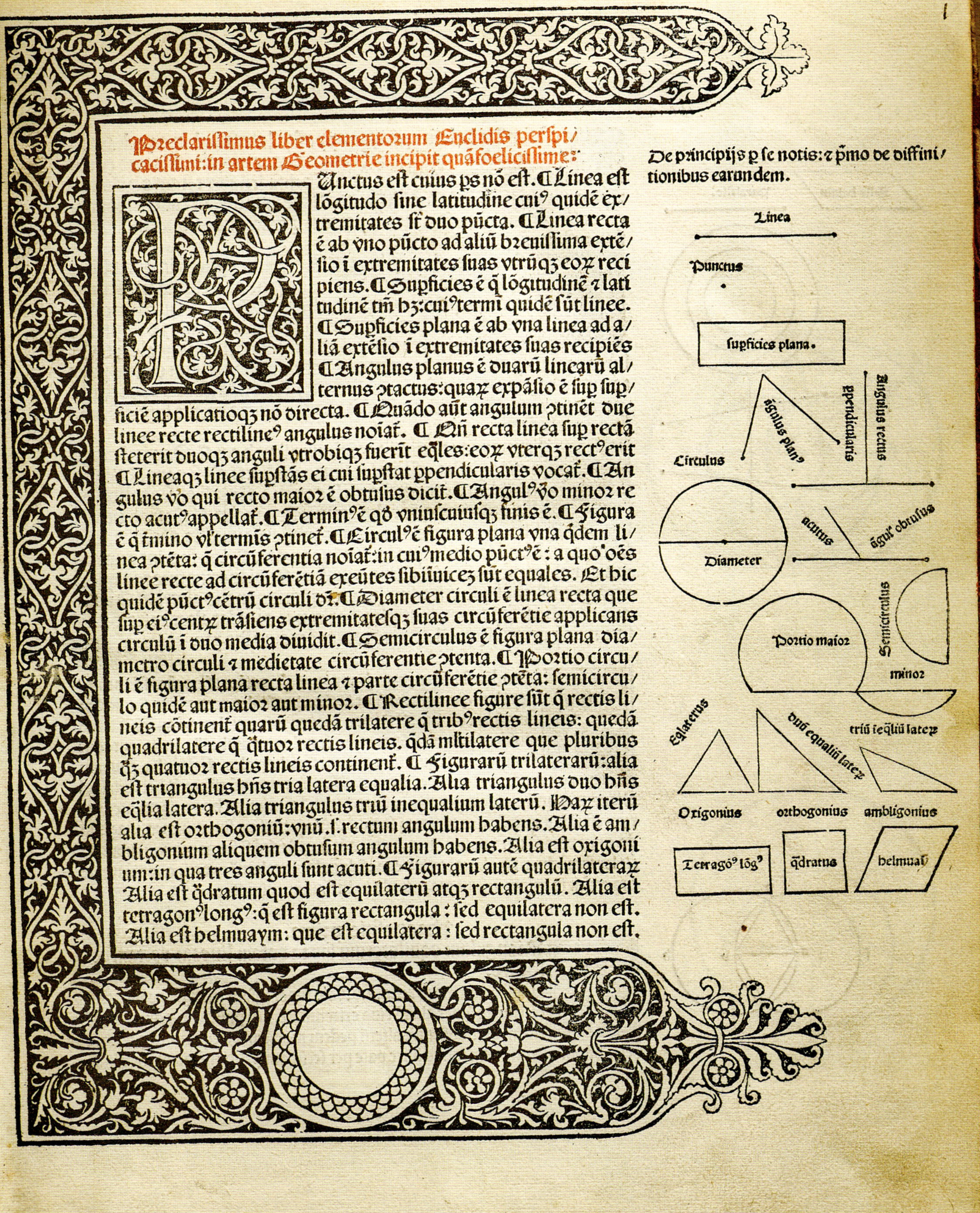

Preclarissimus liber elementorum Euclidis perspi/
cacissimi: in artem Geometrie incipit quā foelicissime:

De principijs p se notis: ꝛ pmo de diffini/
tionibus earundem.

Punctus est cuius ps nō est. ¶ Linea est
lōgitudo sine latitudine cuiꝰ quidē ex/
tremitates sᷓt duo pūcta. ¶ Linea recta
ē ab vno pūcto ad aliū breuissima extē/
sio i extremitates suas vtrūqꝫ eoꝝ reci
piens. ¶ Supficies ē q̄ lōgitudinē ꝛ lati
tudinē tm̄ hꝫ: cuiꝰ termi quidē sūt linee.
¶ Supficies plana ē ab vna linea ad a/
liā extēsio i extremitates suas recipiēs
¶ Angulus planus ē duarū linearū al/
ternus ꝯtactus: quaꝝ expāsio ē sup sup/
ficiē applicatioqꝫ nō directa. ¶ Quādo aūt angulum ꝯtinēt due
linee recte rectilineꝰ angulus noiat̄. ¶ Qn̄ recta linea sup rectā
steterit duoqꝫ anguli vtrobiqꝫ fuerit eq̄les: eoꝝ vterqꝫ rectꝰ erit
¶ Lineaqꝫ linee supstās ei cui supstat ppendicularis vocat̄. ¶ An
gulus vō qui recto maior ē obtusus dicit̄. ¶ Angulꝰ vō minor re
cto acutꝰ appellat̄. ¶ Terminꝰ ē qd̄ vniuscuiusqꝫ finis ē. ¶ Figura
ē q̄ tmino vł termīs ꝯtinet̄. ¶ Circulꝰ ē figura plana vna q̄dem li/
nea ꝯtēta: q̄ circūferentia noiat̄: in cuiꝰ medio pūctꝰ ē: a quo oēs
linee recte ad circūferētiā exeūtes sibiīuicē sūt equales. Et hic
quidē pūctꝰ cētrū circuli dr̄. ¶ Diameter circuli ē linea recta que
sup eiꝰ centꝝ trāsiens extremitatesqꝫ suas circūferētie applicans
circulū i duo media diuidit. ¶ Semicirculus ē figura plana dia/
metro circuli ꝛ medietate circūferentie ꝯtenta. ¶ Portio circu/
li ē figura plana recta linea ꝛ parte circūferētie ꝯtēta: semicircu/
lo quidē aut maior aut minor. ¶ Rectilinee figure sūt q̄ rectis li/
neis cōtinent̄ quarū quedā trilatere q̄ tribꝰ rectis lineis: quedā
quadrilatere q̄ q̄tuor rectis lineis. q̄dā młtilatere que pluribus
q̄ꝫ quatuor rectis lineis continent̄. ¶ Figurarū trilaterarū: alia
est triangulus hn̄s tria latera equalia. Alia triangulus duo hn̄s
eq̄lia latera. Alia triangulus triū inequalium laterū. Haꝝ iterū
alia est orthogoniū: vnū .s. rectum angulum habens. Alia ē am/
bligonium aliquem obtusum angulum habens. Alia est oxigoni
um: in qua tres anguli sunt acuti. ¶ Figurarū autē quadrilateraꝝ
Alia est q̄dratum quod est equilaterū atqꝫ rectangulū. Alia est
tetragonꝰ longꝰ: q̄ est figura rectangula: sed equilatera non est.
Alia est helmuaym: que est equilatera: sed rectangula non est.

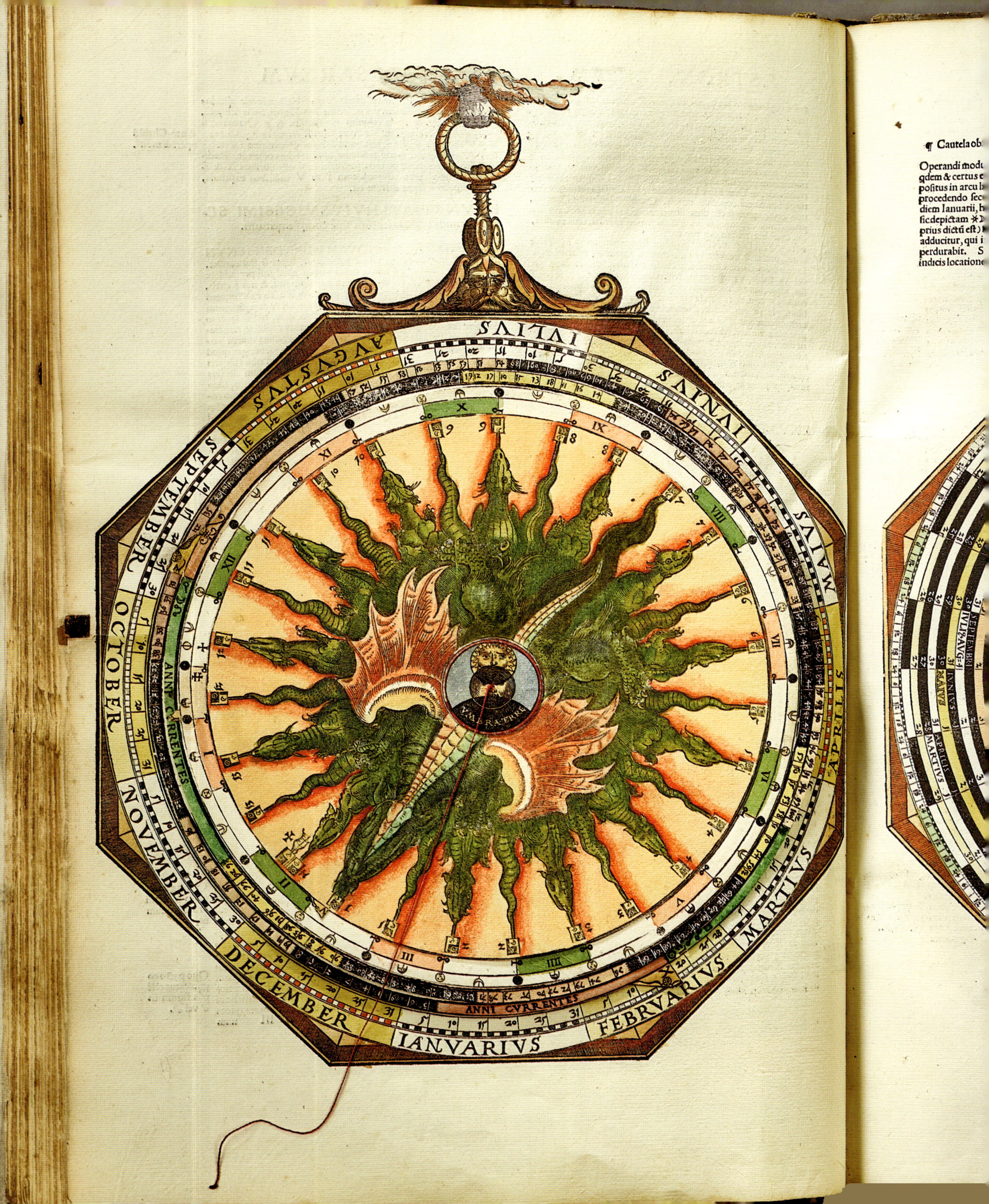
IVLIVS
IVNIVS
MAIVS
APRILIS
MARTIVS
FEBRVARIVS
IANVARIVS
DECEMBER
NOVEMBER
OCTOBER
SEPTEMBER
AVGVSTVS
ANNI CVRRENTES
ANNI CVRRENTES
¶ Cautela ob
Operandi modu
gdem & certus e
positus in arcu la
procedendo sec
diem Ianuarii, h
sic depictam
prius dictũ est)
adducitur, qui i
perdurabit. S
indicis locatione

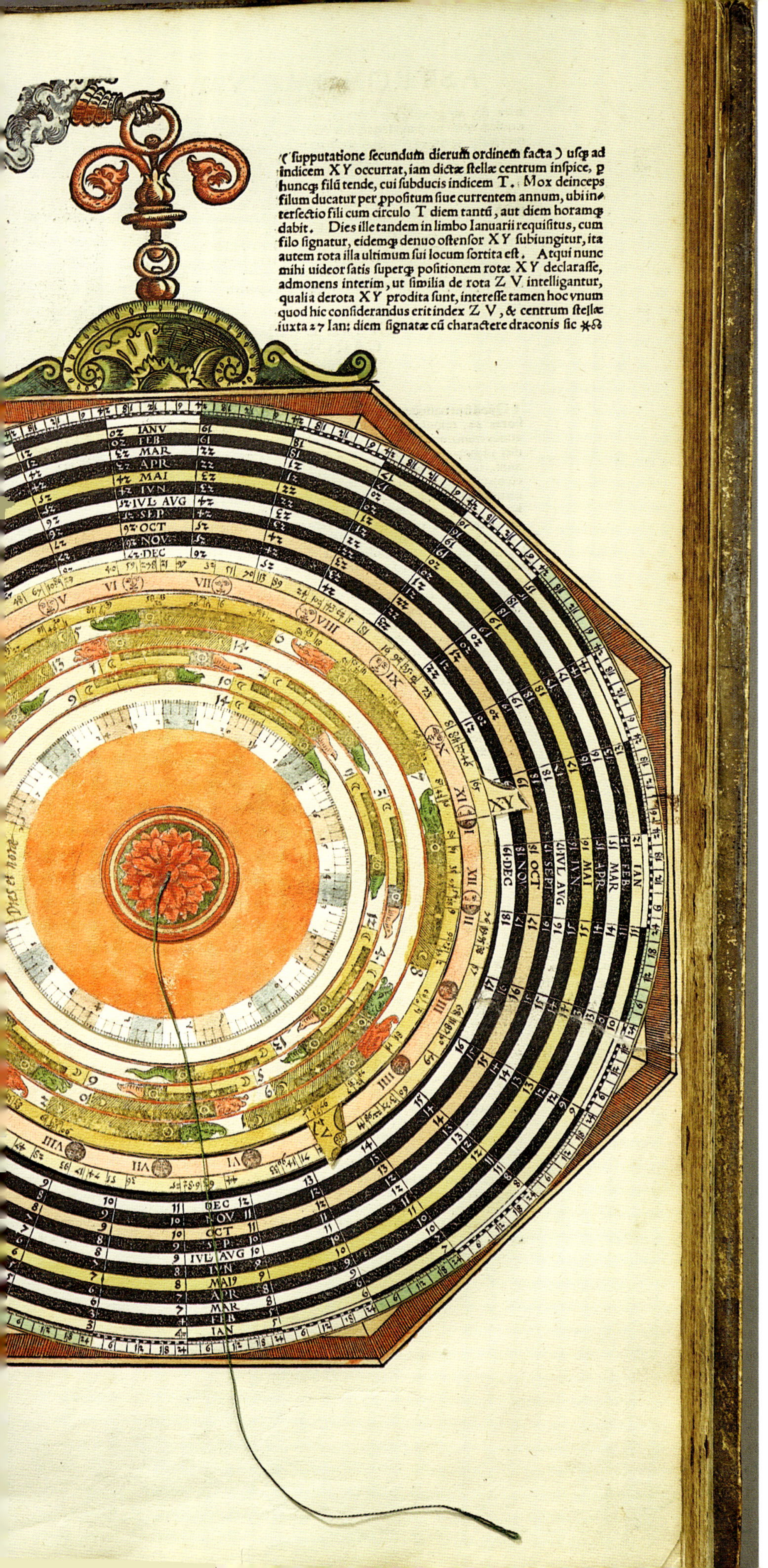

Peter Apian (1495–1552)
Michael Ostendorfer
(ca. 1490–1549), artist
Astronomicum caesareum
Ingolstadt, 1540
Rare Book Division

This work is considered to be one of the most beautiful and spectacular contributions to the art of 16th-century book making. *Astronomicum caesareum* was published by Petrus Apianus (Peter Apian), one of the foremost mathematicians, astronomers, and cartographers of the 16th century. The book's title translates to "Imperial Astronomy" and is a direct reference to its two dedicatees, Emperor Charles V and King Ferdinand I of Spain.

This particularly vibrant, pristine copy of *Astronomicum caesareum* is perhaps Apian's most notable published work. The book features more than twenty elaborately decorated rotating discs, called volvelles, which, when manipulated, represent the functions of the astrolabe and other astronomical instruments used to calculate the positions of stars and planets. As one might imagine, over time and with use, these moving paper elements do not often survive intact.

Nicolaus Copernicus (1473–1543)
De revolutionibus orbium coelestium
Nuremberg: Johannes Petreius, 1543
Rare Book Division

Perhaps the most famous—and disruptive—illustration in all of Western science, this image in the astronomer Nicolaus Copernicus's *De revolutionibus orbium coelestium* depicts the sun at the center of our solar system, a revolutionary proposition that countered centuries of geocentric-based theories and principles. Indeed, by placing the sun at the center, Copernicus could explain observed phenomena in a simpler and more elegant manner, accounting for the movement of heavenly bodies.

Copernicus suffered a stroke in late 1542 and died just as his book was being published, and thus he did not witness the furor his then-radical argument caused. While his heliocentric theory would be debated for years to come, and *De revolutionibus* itself would be subject to censorship by religious authorities, Copernicus's ideas did, in time, achieve widespread acceptance. His work accelerated the Scientific Revolution and forms the basis for modern astronomy.

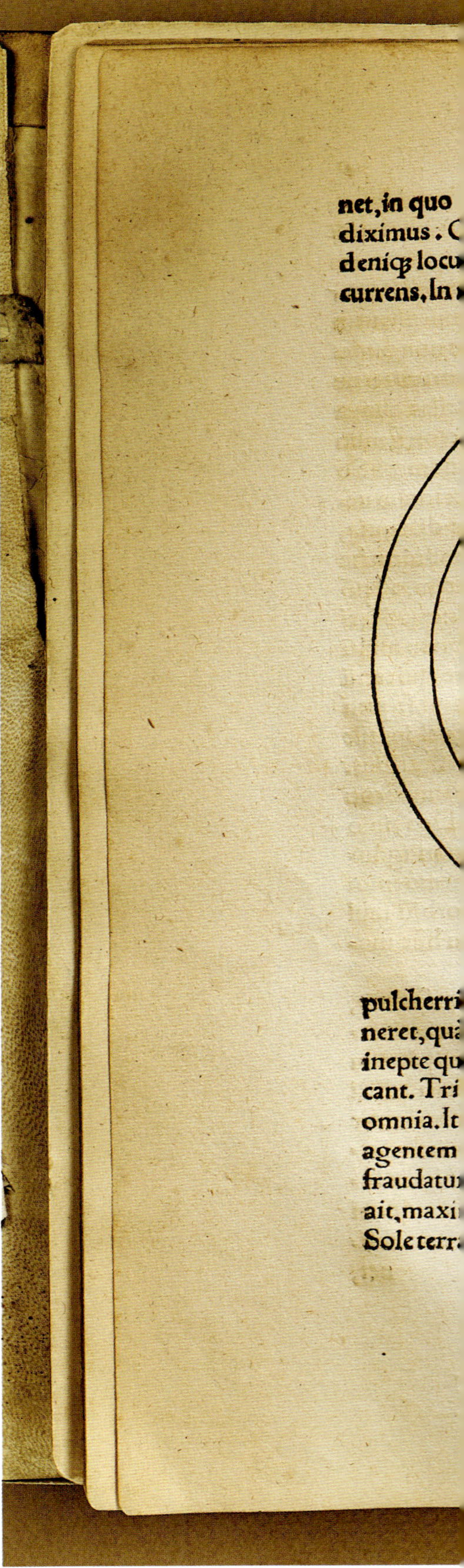

ari tanquam epicyclo contineri
nono menſe reducitur. Sextum
octuaginta dierum ſpacio circū
. reſidet Sol. Quis enim in hoc

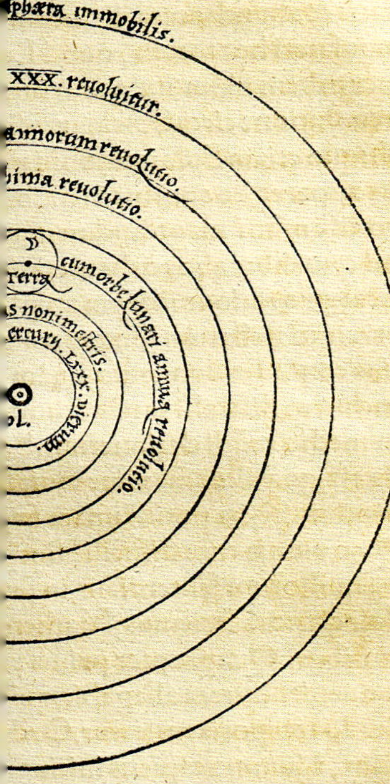

n hanc in alio uel meliori loco po
poſsit illuminare? Siquidem non
di, alij mentem, alij rectorem uo-
Deum, Sophoclis Electra intuentē
n ſolio regali Sol reſidens circum
familiam. Tellus quoq; minime
ſed ut Ariſtoteles de animalibus
natione habet. Concipit interea à
nnuo partu. Inuenimus igitur ſub
hac

hac ordinatione admirandam mundi ſymmetriam, ac certū harmoniæ nexum motus & magnitudinis orbium: qualis alio modo reperiri non poteſt. Hic enim licet animaduertere, nõ ſegniter contemplanti, cur maior in Ioue progreſſus & regreſſus appareat, quàm in Saturno, & minor quàm in Marte: ac rurſus maior in Venere quàm in Mercurio. Quodq; frequentior appareat in Saturno talis reciprocatio, quàm in Ioue: rarior adhuc in Marte, & in Venere, quàm in Mercurio. Præterea quòd Saturnus, Iupiter, & Mars acronycti propinquiores ſint terræ, quàm circa eorū occultationem & apparitionem. Maxime uero Mars pernox factus magnitudine Iouem æquare uidetur, colore duntaxat rutilo diſcretus: illic autem uix inter ſecundæ magnitudinis ſtellas inuenitur, ſedula obſeruatione ſectantibus cognitus. Quæ omnia ex eadem cauſa procedunt, quæ in telluris eſt motu. Quòd autem nihil eorum apparet in fixis, immenſam illorū arguit celſitudinem, quæ faciat etiam annui motus orbem ſiue eius imaginem ab oculis euaneſcere. Quoniā omne uiſibile longitudinem diſtantiæ habet aliquam, ultra quam non amplius ſpectatur, ut demonſtratur in Opticis. Quòd enim à ſupremo errantium Saturno ad fixarum ſphæram adhuc plurimum interſit, ſcintillantia illorum lumina demõſtrant. Quo indicio maxime diſcernuntur à planetis, quodq; inter mota & non mota, maximam oportebat eſſe differentiam. Tanta nimirum eſt diuina hæc Opt. Max. fabrica.

De triplici motu telluris demonſtratio. Cap. XI.

VM igitur mobilitati terrenę tot tantaq; errantium ſyderum conſentiant teſtimonia, iam ipſum motum in ſumma exponemus, quatenus apparentia per ipſum tanquã hypoteſim demonſtrentur, quę triplicē omnino oportet admittere. Primum quem diximus νυχθήμερινον à Græcis uocari, diei noctisq; circuitum proprium, circa axem telluris, ab occaſu in ortum uergentem, prout in diuerſum mundus ferri putatur, æquinoctialem circulum deſcribendo, quem nonnulli æquidialem dicunt, imitantes ſignificationem Græcorum,

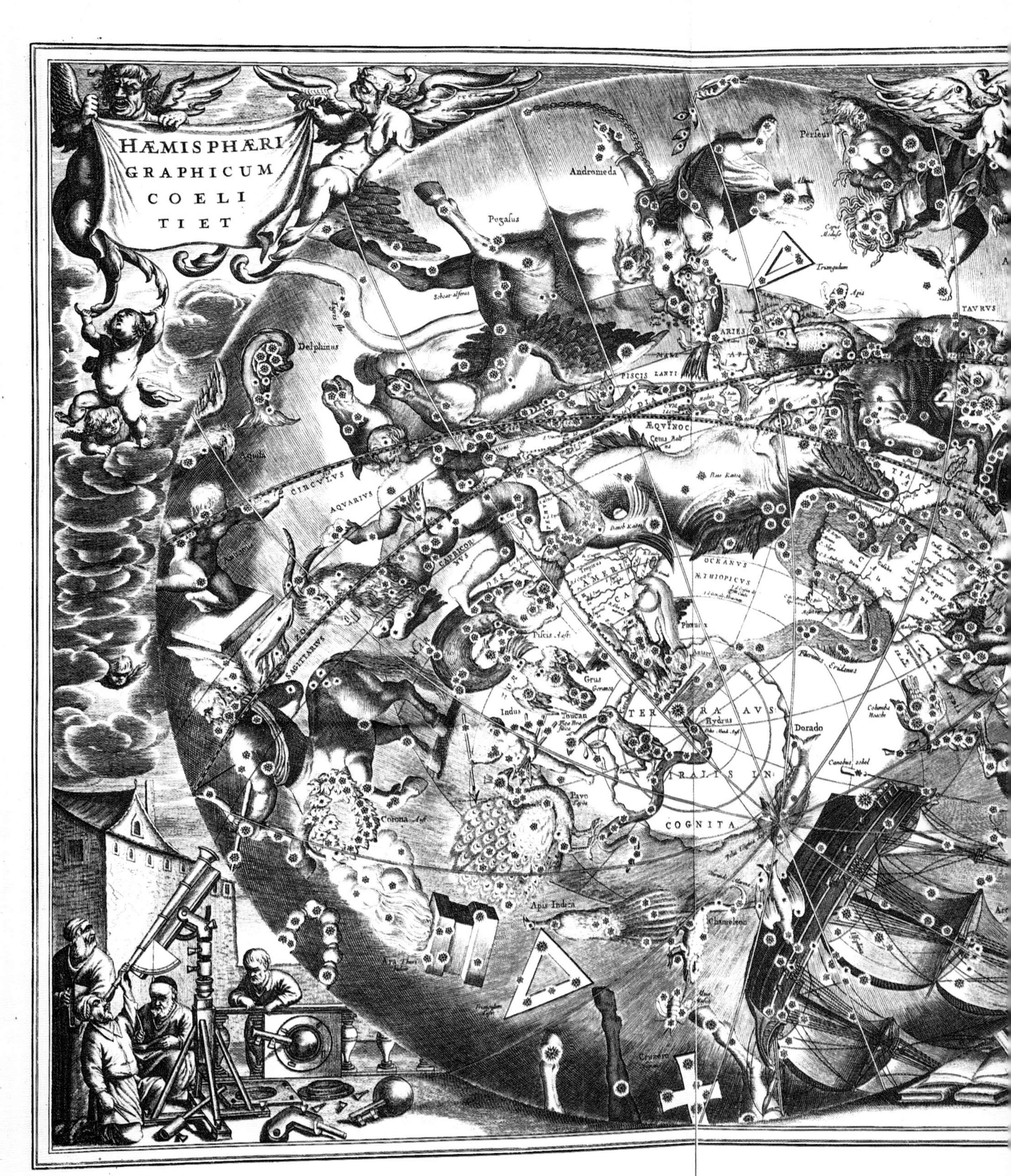
HÆMISPHÆRI
GRAPHICUM
COELI
TIET
Andromeda
Perseus
Pegasus
Triangulum
Apis
TAURUS
ARIES
Delphinus
Aquila
CIRCULUS
AQUARIUS
ÆQUINOC
OCEANUS
ÆTHIOPICUS
Phœnix
Piscis Aust.
Grus
Indus
Toucan
Hydrus
Dorado
TER
RA AUS
COGNITA
Pavo
Corona Aust.
Apis Indica
Chamæleon

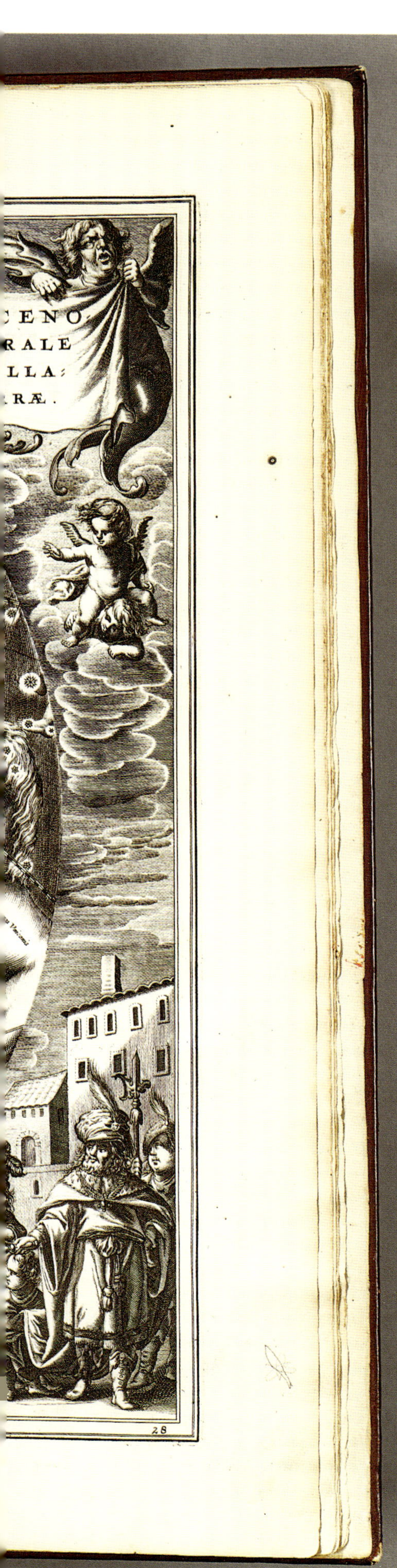

Andreas Cellarius (ca. 1596–1665)
Harmonia Macrocosmica
Amsterdam: Johannes Janssonius, 1661
Lionel Pincus and Princess Firyal Map Division

This most celebrated of early celestial atlases is also the only one published in the Netherlands during the golden age of Dutch cartography. *Harmonia Macrocosmica* completes the multivolume history of all creation first conceived by Gerardus Mercator in 1569. It consists of twenty-nine charts depicting the competing worldviews of Claudius Ptolemy, Martianus Capella, Nicolaus Copernicus, and Tycho Brahe. Engraved plates in the Baroque style illustrate more than 400 pages of text and depict the motions of the sun, moon, and planets, as well as delineations of classical and biblical constellations. In the preface, Cellarius mentions his intention to create a second volume to address the new astronomical observations made available by the invention of the telescope. Unfortunately, this was never realized, due to his death in 1665.

Johannes Kepler (1571–1630)
***Harmonices mundi* (*Harmony of the Worlds*)**
Lincii, Austriæ: sumptibus Godofredi Tampachii excudebat Ioannes Plancvs, 1619
Music Division, The New York Public Library for the Performing Arts, Dorothy and Lewis B. Cullman Center

The "music of the spheres" was a literary conceit given new meaning by Johannes Kepler, the first astronomer to correctly identify the elliptical orbits of planets around the sun. His 1619 edition of *Harmonices mundi* argued that the geometric ratios found in harmonious relationships between musical pitches were based on the same ratios exemplified by the planets as they orbited the sun. The significance of Kepler's approach—both for astronomy and for music theory—was in its emphasis on the mathematical relationships between physical objects, as opposed to the mathematical properties of objects in and of themselves. "The movements of the heavens," Kepler wrote, "are nothing except a certain everlasting polyphony." Or, as the poet John Keats wrote two centuries later, "Heard melodies are sweet but those unheard are sweeter."

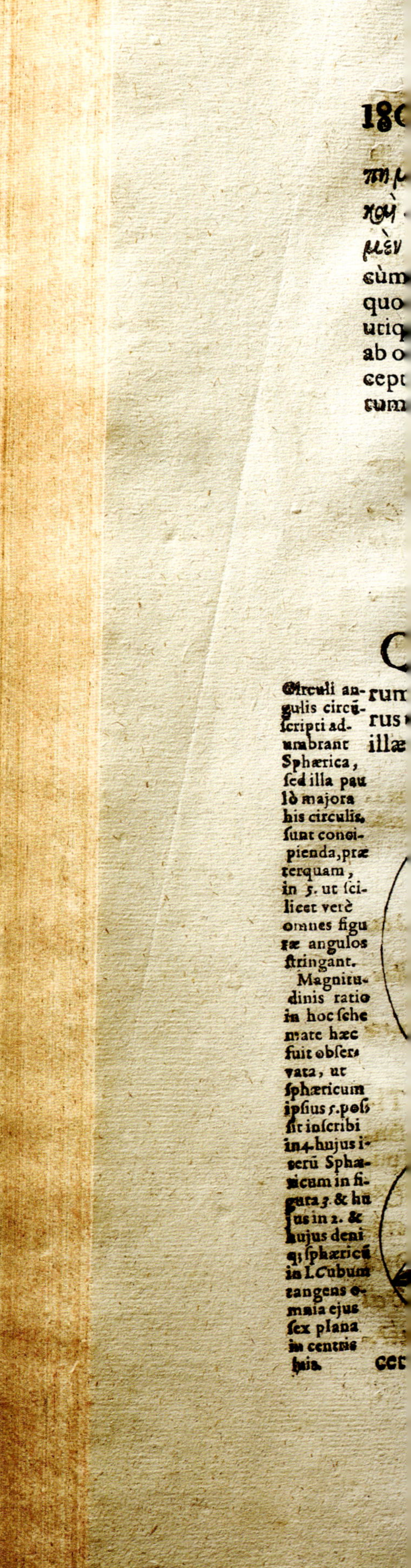
Circuli angulis circũscripti adumbrant Sphærica, sed illa paulò majora his circulis, sunt concipienda, præterquam in 5. ut scilicet verè omnes figuræ angulos stringant.
Magnitudinis ratio in hoc schemate hæc fuit observata, ut sphæricum ipsius 5. possit inscribi in 4. hujus iterũ Sphæricum in figura 3. & hujus in 2. & hujus deniq; sphæricũ in I. Cubum tangens omnia ejus sex plana in centris suis.

ν ἅπασι παραλλάξομεν, ἀνάγκη θεοὺς τε νας εὔχεσθαι πάντας, κατὰ νοῦν ἐκείνοις ις δὲ ὑμῖν εἰπεῖν. Enimvero Socrates, imum Mentis habent, quoties negocium aliud aggrediuntur, Deum semper invocent: Nos n universitate differere animus est, nisi planè erramus, necesse est, Deos Deasque votis con, ut talia dicamus, quæ primùm ipsis maximè grata & accepta.

CAPUT I.

que Figuris solidis regularibus.

ræ planæ regulares congruerent ad, dictum est libro secundo: de quinque nimiras) propter planas ibi locuti sumus. Numearius ibi demonstratus fuit; additumque, cur icis denominatæ, & cui quælibet Elemento, quamque ob proprietatem, comparata sit. Jam in hujus libri vestibulo rursum de his figuris, ob seipsas, non ob planas, agendum erit; quantum quidem sufficit ad Harmoniam Cœlorum: cætera reperiet lector in Epitomes Astronomiæ parte alterâ, libro quarto.

Igitur ex Mysterio Cosmographico hic breviter inculco Ordinem quinque figurarum in Mundo, quarum tres primariæ, duæ secundariæ. Cubus enim 1. extimus & amplissimus, quia primigenius, & rationem habens *Totius*, ipsâ generationis suæ formâ. Sequitur Tetraëdron 2. tanquam *Pars* sectione Cubi cõstituta, primaria tamen & ipsa, angulo solido trilineari, ut Cubus. Intra Tetraëdron est Dodecaëdron 3. Ultima primariarum, similis scilicet partibus, Tetraëdri similibus, id est, ex Tetraëdris

ëdris irregularibus, quibus tegitur Cubus intus. Huic succedit Icosaëdron 4. ob similitudinem, ultima secundariarum, angulo solido plurilineari utentium. Intimum est Octoëdron 5. Cubi simile, & prima figura secundariarum, cui ideò primus locus interiorum debetur, quippe inscriptili; uti cubo circumscriptili primus exteriorum.

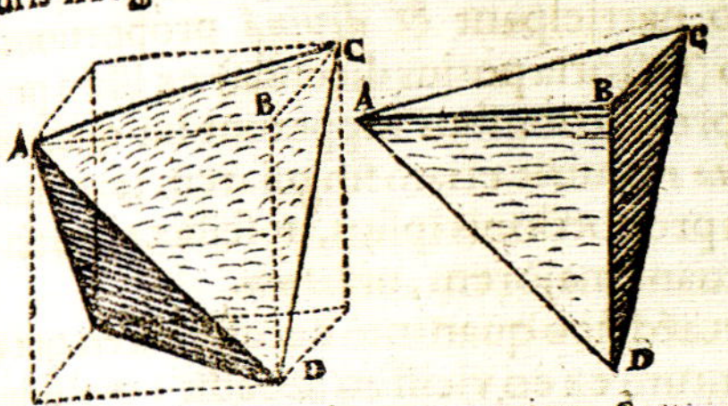

In priori figurá apparet Tetraedron ACDF latens in Cubo; sic ut quodlibet Tetraedri planum ut ACD, tegatur ab uno cubi angulo ACDB In secunda figura apparet Cubus AED latens intus in Dodecaedro, sic ut quodlibet Cubi planum, ut AED, tegatur à duob⁹ Dodecaedri angulis seu Pẽtaedro ABCDE quod est sectile in tria Tetraedra dissimilia per duo plana, DCA, & ABD.

Sunt autem notabilia duo veluti conjugia harum figurarum, ex diversis combinata classibus: Mares, Cubus & Dodecaëdron ex primarijs; fœminæ, Octoëdron & Icosiëdron ex secundarijs; quibus accedit una veluti cœlebs aut Androgynos, Tetraëdron; quia sibi ipsi inscribitur, ut illæ fœmellæ maribus inscribuntur & veluti subjiciuntur, & signa sexus fœminina masculinis opposita habent, angulos scilicet planiciebus.

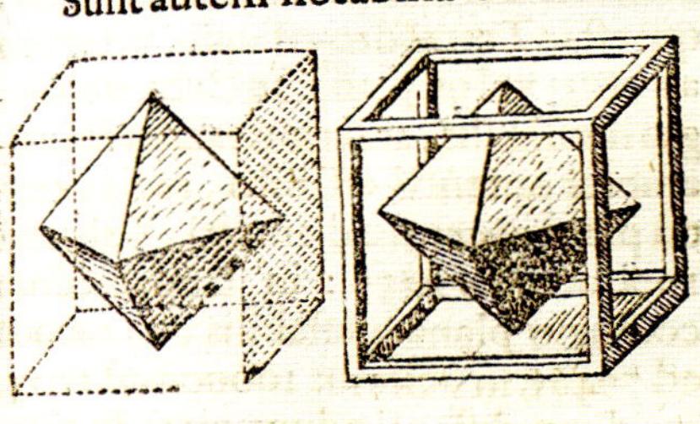

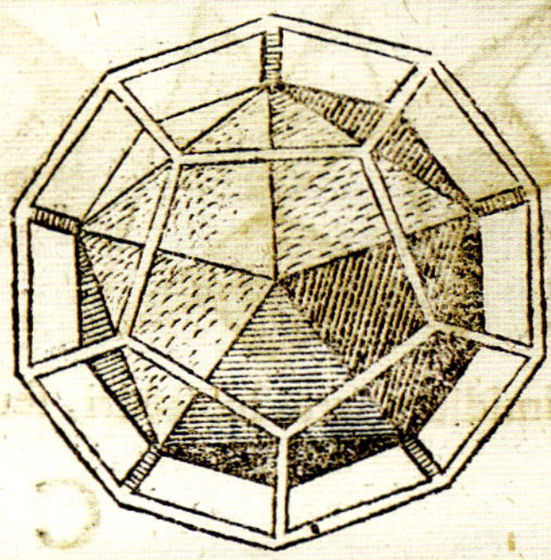

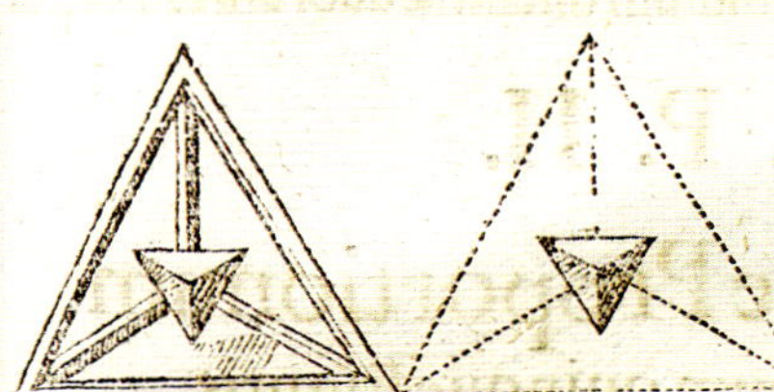

Hic vides Octaedron inscriptum Cubo; Icosiedron Dodecaedro, Tetraedron Tetraedro.

Prætereà ut Tetraëdron est elementum, viscera & veluti costa Cubi Maris; sic Octaëdron fœmina, est elementum & pars Tetraëdri, aliâ ratione: ita mediat Tetraëdron in hoc conjugio.

Præcipua connubiorum seu familiarum differentia in hoc consistit: quòd Cubicæ quidem *Effabilis* est proportio; nam Tetraëdron est Triens de corpore Cubico, Octaëdron semissis de Tetraëdrico, sexta pars Cubi: Dodecaëdrici verò conjugij proportio est *Ineffabilis* quidem, sed *Divina*.

Harum duarum vocum copulatio jubet cavere Lectori, de earum significatu. Vox enim *Ineffabilis* hic non denotat per se nobilitatem aliquam, ut aliàs in Theologia & rebus divinis; sed denotat conditio-

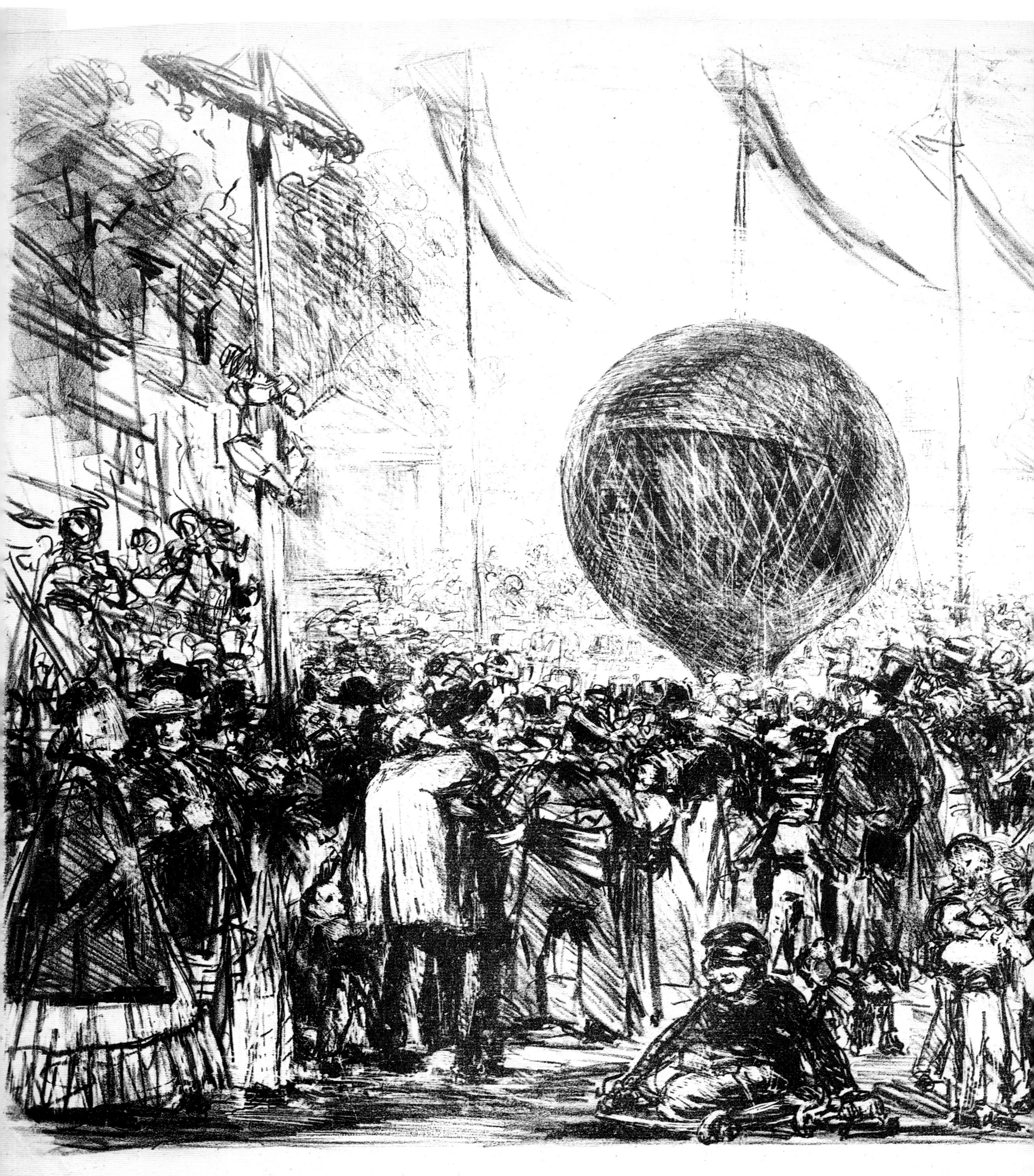

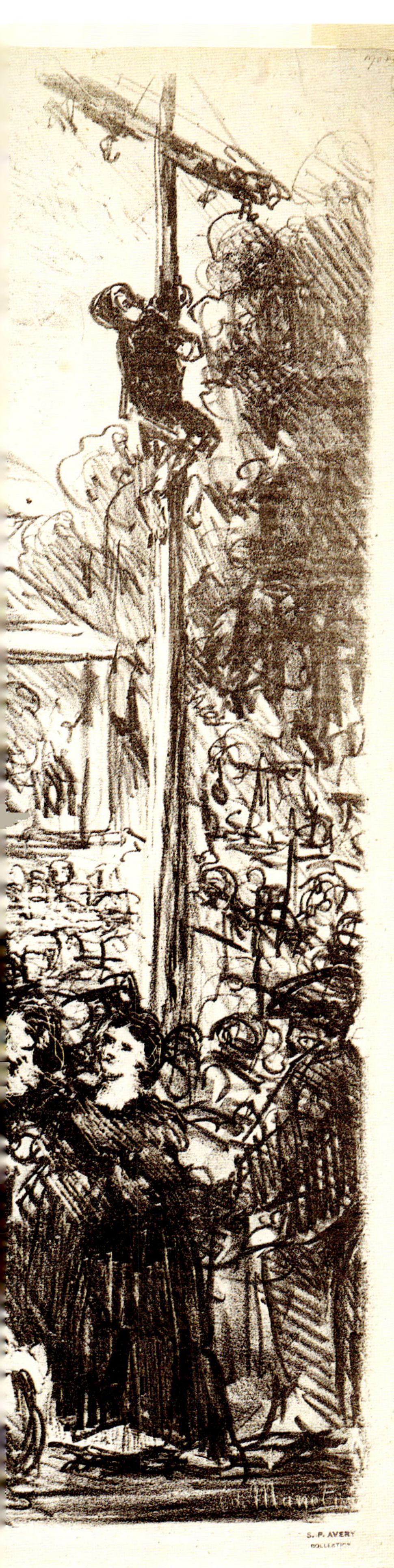

Édouard Manet (1832–1883)
Le Ballon (The Balloon)
Lithograph, 1862
The Miriam and Ira D. Wallach Division of Art, Prints and Photographs, Print Collection

Édouard Manet's *Le Ballon* is both rare and profoundly ahead of its time. The publisher Alfred Cadart invited Manet to create a lithograph for a portfolio he hoped would launch a lithography revival. The artist chose as his subject the Fête de L'Empereur, a summer festival held each year to commemorate Napoleon I's birthday, on August 15. Large crowds of Parisians gathered to watch balloon rides and engage in other popular entertainments on the Esplanade des Invalides. Manet rendered the scene with thick, forceful strokes of the lithographic crayon, creating a poetic interpretation that verges at times on abstraction. Too radical for its time, the work was not considered worthy of reproduction, and Cadart jettisoned his project. This is one of only five impressions of the print. Thanks to a gift from Samuel Putnam Avery, the Library's Print Department has one of the most important collections of Manet prints in the world.

Étienne Léopold Trouvelot (1827–1895)

Saturn* from the series *The Trouvelot Astronomical Drawings

New York: Charles Scribner's Sons, 1881–1882

Rare Book Division

In 1872, Étienne Léopold Trouvelot, a French-American artist and amateur astronomer, joined the staff of the Harvard College Observatory. There—and, later, at the United States Naval Observatory and the Paris Observatory—he produced thousands of sketches of astronomical phenomena, some of which he exhibited at the 1876 Centennial Exposition in Philadelphia to great acclaim.

Encouraged by the public's positive response to his artwork, Trouvelot resolved to publish a selection of his best images. In 1882, Charles Scribner's Sons of New York issued *The Trouvelot Astronomical Drawings*, a suite of fifteen chromolithographic prints depicting various celestial wonders and comprising one of the most impressive American color plate books. While this work was produced in an edition of perhaps 300 copies, most were broken up over the years. The Library's Rare Book Division preserves one of four known complete sets of Trouvelot's *Drawings*, which still hauntingly evoke the mystery and beauty of the cosmos.

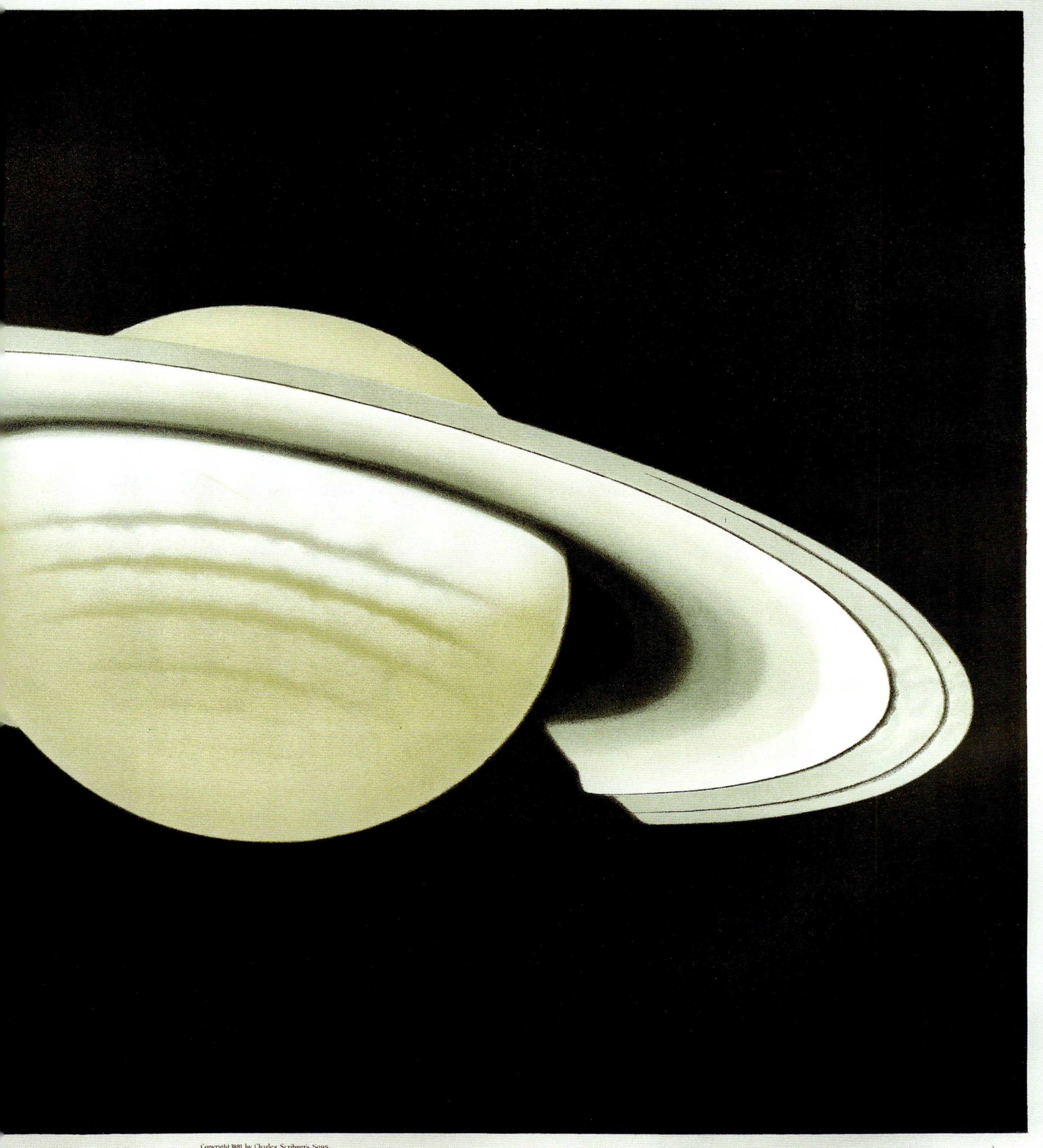

THE PLANET SATURN.

Observed on November 30. 1874, at 5 h. 50 M.P.M.

E. L. Trouvelot

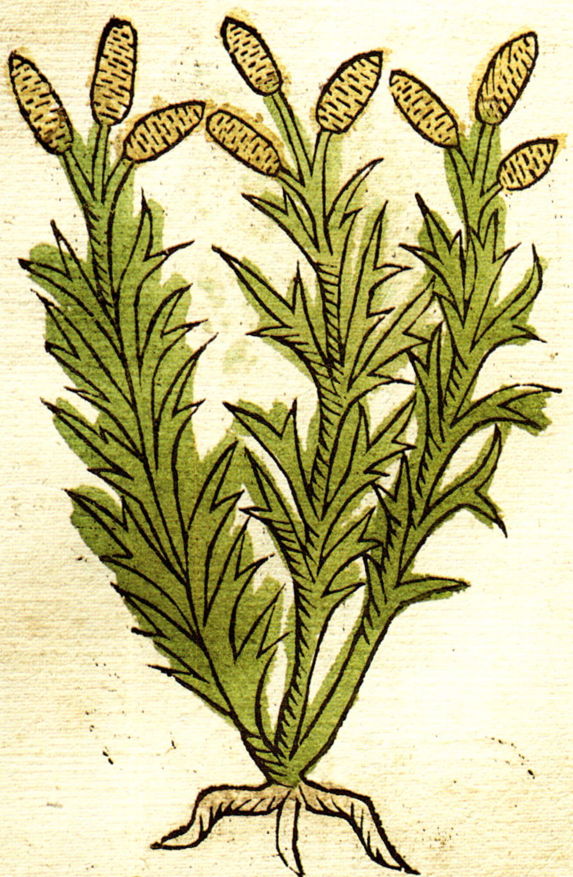

Ain safft allso genannt. Capitulum. .ccxlvi.

Jcium latine. Grece liceos. Arabice hadahh. ¶ Serapio in dem bůch Aggregatoris in dem capitel hadahh id est licium. beschreibt vns vnd spricht das diser safft komme von ainem baum gienset dẽ mör. Diser baum ist dornit vnd bringt frucht die geleichet dẽ langẽ pfffer. Diser safft der wirt allso gemacht. Die pletter stost man vnd prest den safft daraus. disen safft seüdet man das er als dick wirt als honig. darnach trücknet man den in der sunnen. Den solt du allso probiren. zünde den an mit ainẽ prinnenden liecht. vñ wenn er ain schaum gibt so er verlischt so ist er gerecht. ¶ Liciũ wirt zů zeitten gefelscht mit wermůtsafft vñ ochssen gallen. ¶ Circa instans. Liciũ ist haiß an dẽ ersten grad vñ trucken an dẽ andern. ¶ Diser safft soll gesamelt werden in dẽ mayen. vñ wert. v. iar vnuersert an seiner krafft. ¶ Für die flecken in den augen. Nym diß saffts. vñ misch den mit rosen wasser. vñ thů das in die augen. sie werdent klar. ¶ Diser safft gestrichẽ an den hals. benimbt ain geschwer darinne squinantia genannt. ¶ Von disem safft liß Pandecta das. cccxix. capitel. do findestu vil tugent von disem safft.

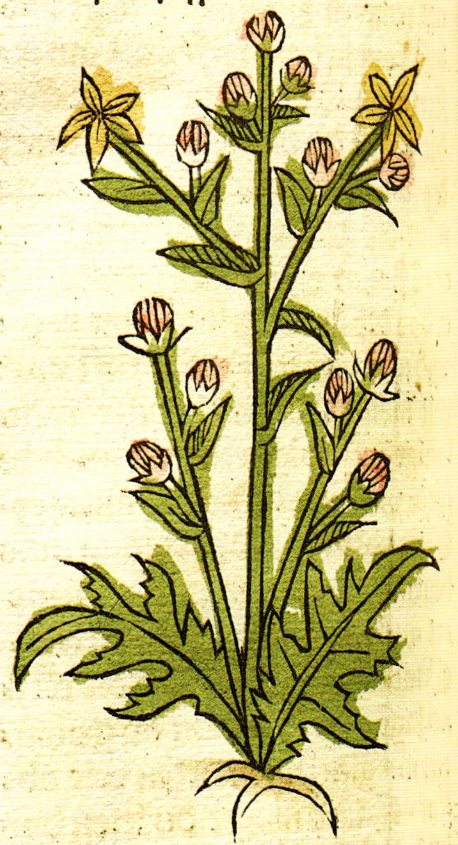

Ain gumi allso genannt Capitulum. .ccxlvii.

Acta latine. Grece anchusa. Arabice aec. ¶ Pandecta capitulo. ij. steet geschriben das diß sei ain gumi gienset dẽ

mör. ¶ Mit disem gumi
das tůch rott. ¶ Sera
bůch Aggregatoris in d
aec spricht das diser ba
sent vil in arabia. das
von ist genannt lacta.
et an der gestalt dem mi
auch an dẽ rauch. ¶ P
ta ist hayß vnd truckn
¶ Auicenna. Lacta is
pleüreticis=das ist ain
vmb die prust. des ein
mit ainem syropel von
cht. des gleichen asmat
die vast keichent. allso
¶ Lacta thůt auff alle
ung der lebern vnd des
eingenomen mit ayren
gen ützet. benimbt es
sucht.

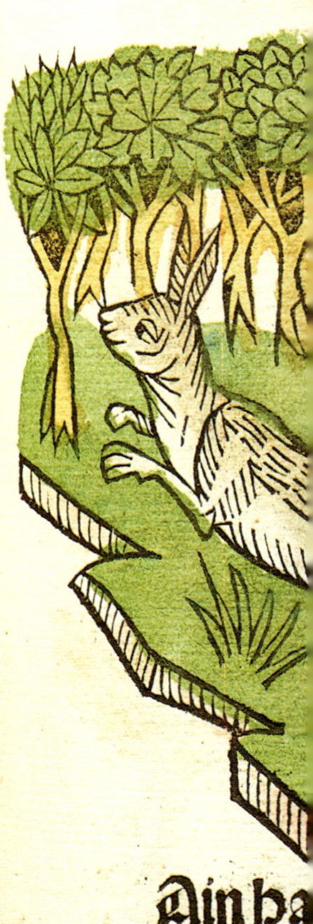

Ain ha

apitulum · ccxlviii ·
Epus latine · Grece leges ·
Arabice arnaben · ¶ Der
mayster almansor spricht ·
as vnder allen tieren kain flaisch
s vil melancolei mach als hasen
aisch · ¶ Das hirn von dē hasen
ebraten vñ geessen · benimbt das
tern am leib · als dañ gar dick ge
hicht nach ainer krankeit · ¶ Die
allen der hasen benemen vergifft
ie mit essig eingenomen · ¶ Item
ertzhasen allso lebend gebrant ·
epuluer · dienet vast wol für den
tain · das eingenomen mit wein ·
¶ Mit dem hasen hirn der iungen
inde wenglin geschmiret · macht
eichtlich vnd on schmertzen zeen
wachssen · ¶ Item von disem thie
e lisz pandecta das · lvj · capitel · do
findest du sein tugent ·

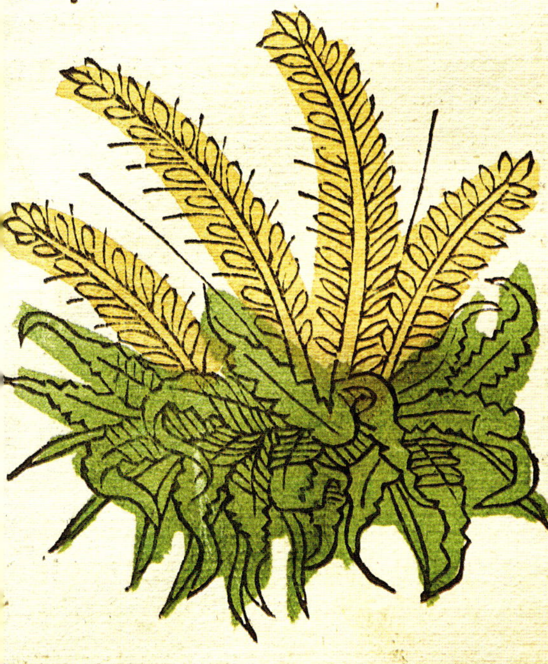

wilderklee ·

c iiij

Johannes von Wonnecke Caub
(1430–1503/04)
Gart der Gesundheit
Ulm: Konrad Dinckmut, 1487
Rare Book Division

Johannes von Wonnecke Caub's *Gart der Gesundheit* was one of the most important botanical works of the 15th century. Its 435 chapters, written in a southern German dialect, address the medicinal values and uses of 368 plants and eleven animal substances. A woodcut illustration accompanies nearly every entry, making the work one of the more heavily illustrated printed books of the 1400s.

Gart der Gesundheit was a popular book, appearing in fourteen separate editions between 1485 and 1501. This edition in the Library's Rare Book Division is extremely rare; it is one of only three known complete copies, and the only complete copy in the Americas.

Magical Prayers Against Demons
1813
Manuscripts and Archives Division

Syriac, the language of ancient Syria, was a western dialect of Aramaic and is the language in which many important early Christian texts are preserved. This text reflects folk beliefs of the East Syriac community, who lived in the neighboring plains of Azerbaijan, in northwestern Iran, and in the mountainous region of eastern Turkey. The community used the texts to cure diseases and thought that they protected believers from dangers. The colophon of this manuscript from Kurdistan reveals it was completed in 1813. It was created in the time of Mar Yūḥannānm, the bishop of the monastery of Mar Ḥazqiyel, located near Rustāqā in Syria. Wilberforce Eames, who had joined the staff of the Lenox Library in New York City in 1885, acquired this manuscript for the Library.

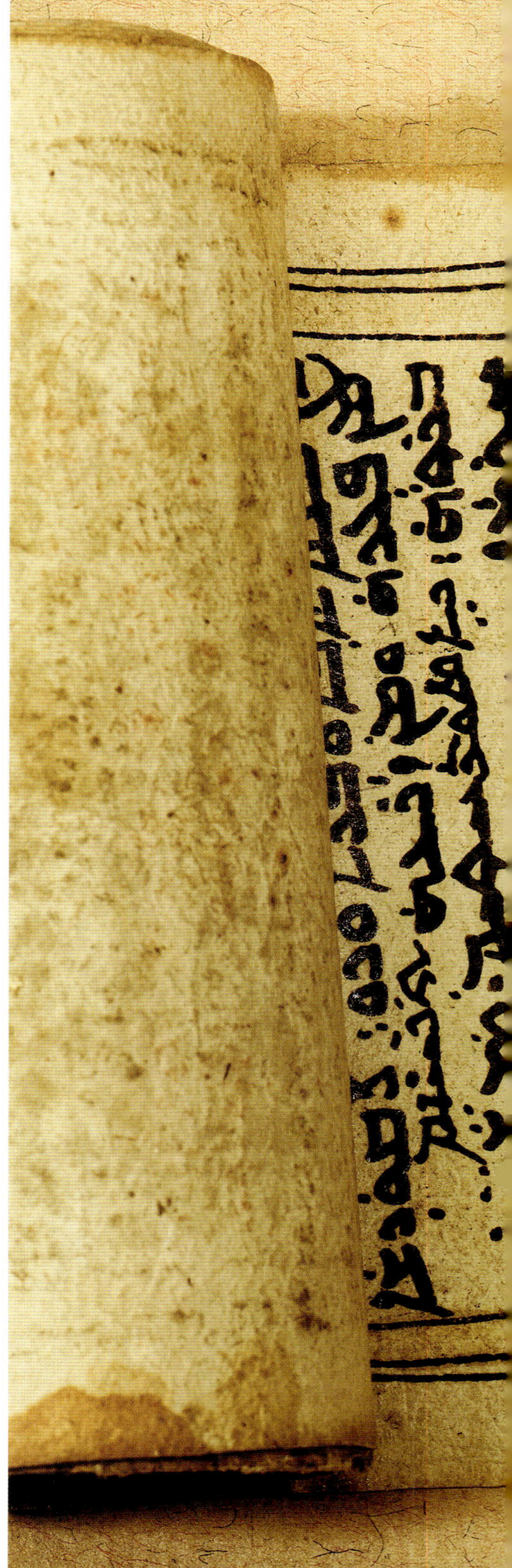

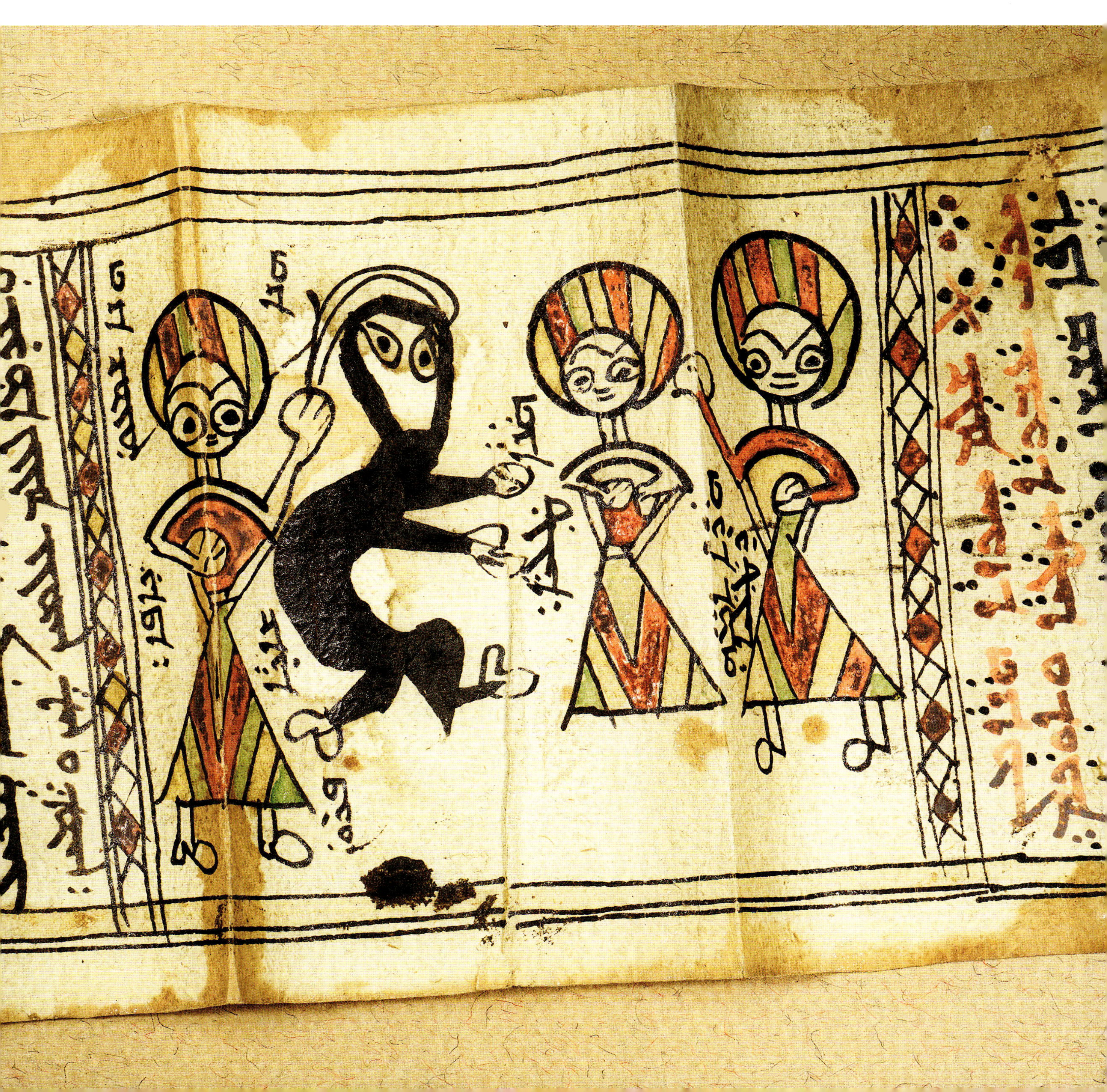

128

A COVNTER-BLASTE TO Tobacco.

Supposed to be written by the K. or by the Erle of Northampton.

This is undoubtedly King James's Tract: For, it was published in the Collection of his works in 1616, by the Bishop of Winchester.

¶ Imprinted at London
by R. B.
Anno 1604.

James I, King of England (1566–1625)
A Counterblaste to Tobacco
London: Robert Barker, 1604
George Arents Collection

A Counterblaste to Tobacco, written by King James I of Great Britain, stands as one of the earliest pieces of anti-tobacco literature. In his treatise, the monarch argues against the recreational use of the plant, seeing the practice as both a social and health concern. Smoking, in particular, draws his ire; he calls it "a custome loathsome to the eye, hatefull to the Nose, harmefull to the braine, [and] dangerous to the lungs." Though he did not ban tobacco's use, James did impose a 4,000 percent tax on its sale. When this measure failed to decrease demand, the king adopted a more pragmatic approach: nationalizing the entire tobacco trade, which enabled the Crown to profit directly, and handsomely, through the crop's ever-growing popularity.

This first-edition copy of James's *Counterblaste* is held by the Library's George Arents Collection, which documents the history, culture, and lore of tobacco.

Anna Atkins (1799–1871)

Alaria esculenta* from Part XII of *Photographs of British Algae: Cyanotype Impressions

Cyanotype, ca. 1849

The Miriam and Ira D. Wallach Division of Art, Prints and Photographs, Spencer Collection

Encouraged by her father, a prominent member of the British scientific community, Anna Atkins (née Children) began in the early 1840s to experiment with the new art of photography, making her among the earliest women to do so. That distinction would not be her most significant legacy, however. Privy to Sir John Herschel's accidental invention of the cyanotype, Atkins applied that photographic process—and the deep field of Prussian blue it yields—to the problem of how to make multiple prints that conveyed precise information about her growing collection of British seaweed specimens.

With great skill and determination, she coated, arranged, exposed, and developed photograms of more than 400 unique specimens, issuing them to her "botanical friends" as plates of a self-published book. The first installment appeared in October 1843, making hers the very first photographically illustrated book in history. This stellar example, which demonstrates Atkins's compositional flair, was produced several years into her decade-long project.

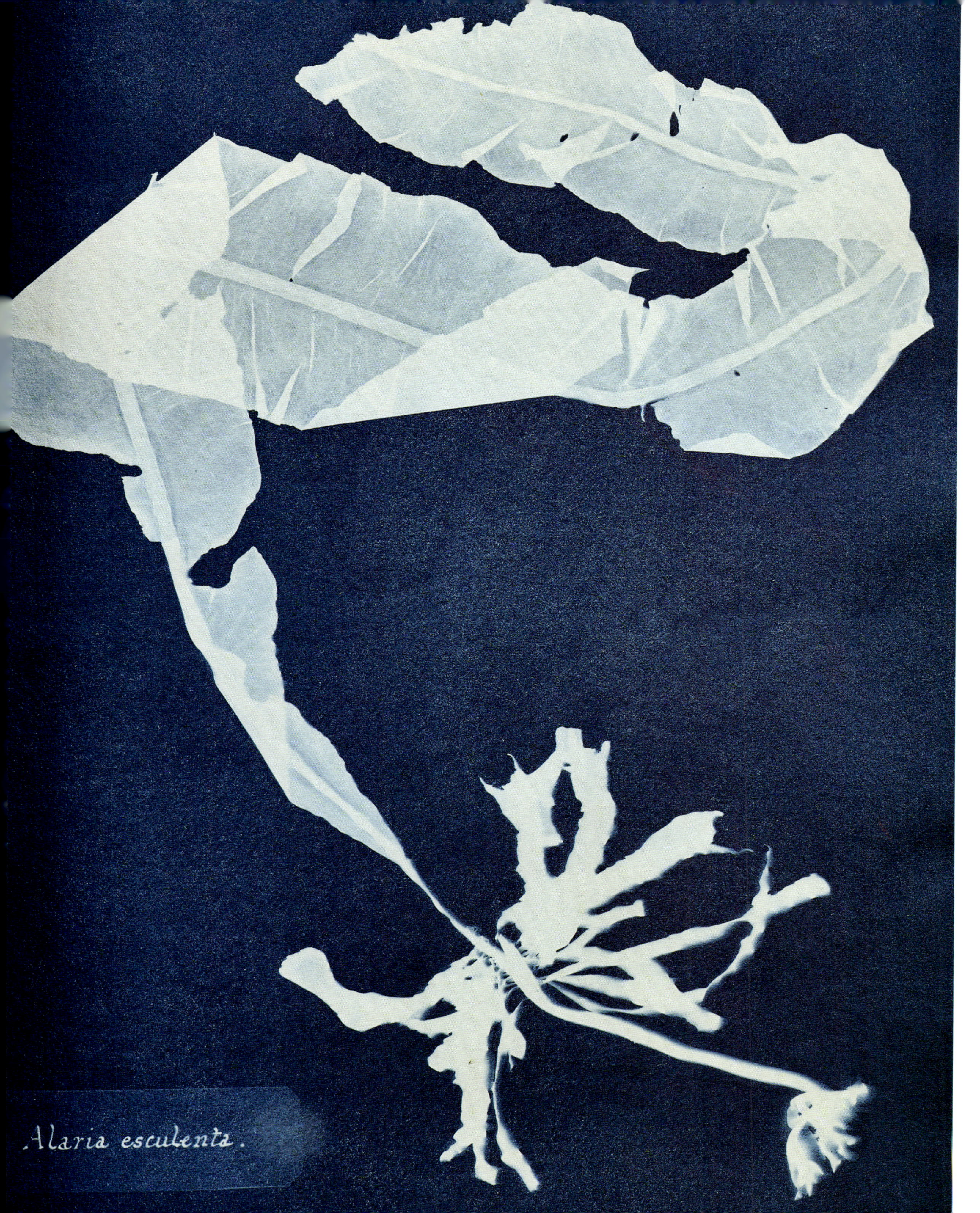
Alaria esculenta.

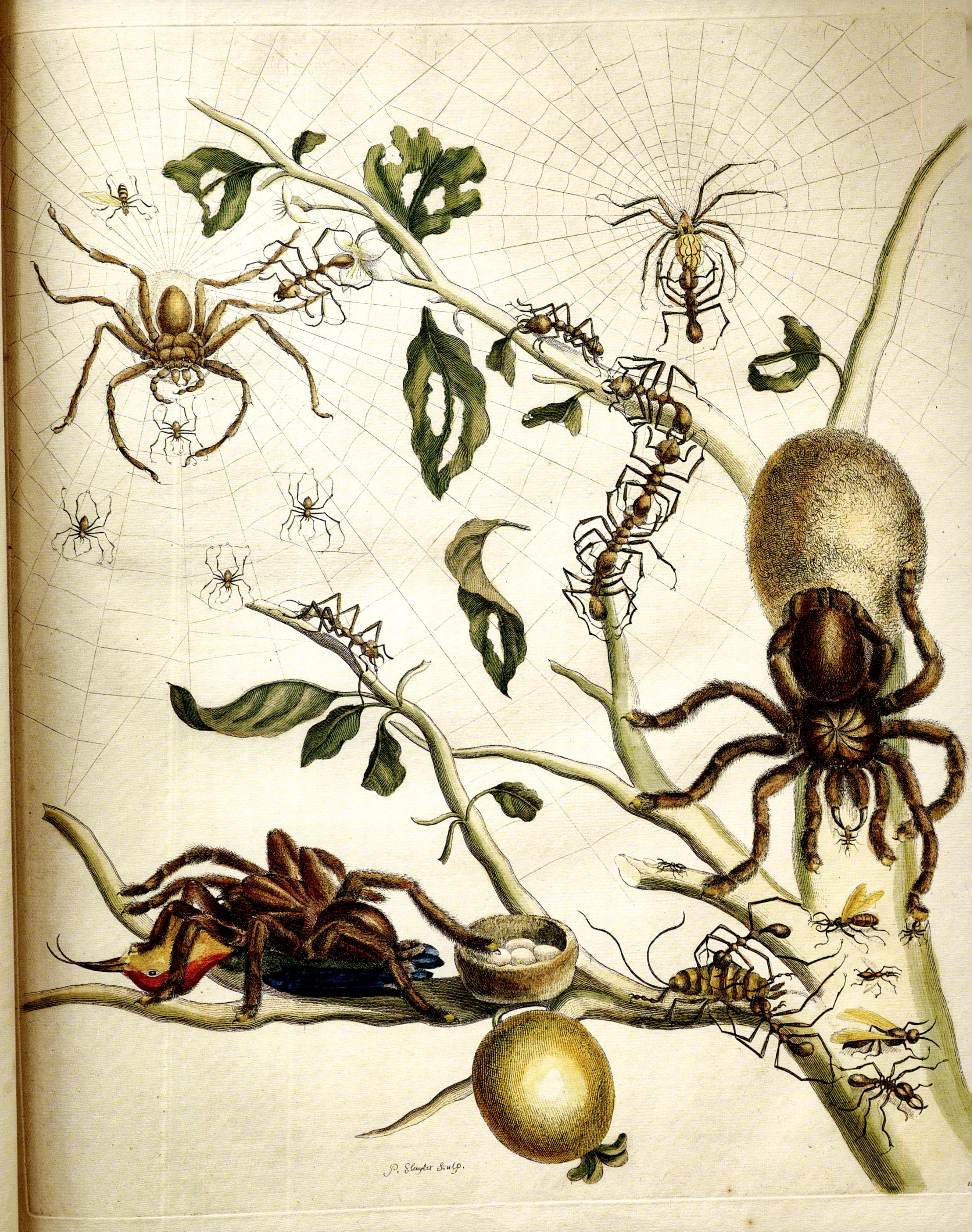
P. Sluyter Sculp.

Maria Sibylla Merian (1647–1717)

Dissertation sur la generation et les transformations des insectes de Surinam . . .

The Hauge: Pierre Gosse, 1726

Rare Book Division

In 1699, the German-born illustrator and naturalist Maria Sibylla Merian sailed with her daughter from the Netherlands to South America to study the insects of Suriname, which was then a Dutch colony. She spent several years carefully recording the behavior and life cycles of butterflies, beetles, ants, spiders, and other creatures, becoming one of the first naturalists to directly observe insects in their own habitat.

On her return to Europe, Merian published, at her own expense, *Metamorphosis insectorum Surinamensium* (1705). This pioneering book—the first to depict insects in their natural settings—was viewed as an advance in the field of entomology, and it is still revered today for its scientific accuracy and beauty. This copy, printed in 1726 and given a slightly different title, is drawn from the Rare Book Division's outstanding holdings of early works in the field of natural history.

Franz Kafka (1883–1924)
A.L. Lloyd (1908–1982), translator
Copy of *The Metamorphosis* owned and annotated by Vladimir Nabokov (1899–1977)
New York: Vanguard Press, 1946
Henry W. and Albert A. Berg Collection of English and American Literature

The Library acquired the archive of Vladimir Nabokov in 1991. Among this enormous collection of manuscripts, diaries (spanning the years 1941 through 1977), notebooks, correspondence (comprising nearly fifty linear feet), portraits, working drafts, and galley proofs of his work, there are several heavily annotated copies of the books that Nabokov used when teaching classes in Russian and European literature at Cornell University between 1948 and 1959. Nabokov's teaching copies of *Mansfield Park*, *Swann's Way*, and *Ulysses* provide unparalleled insights into the novelist as reader and teacher. His copy of A.L. Lloyd's English translation of Kafka's *Metamorphosis*, which Nabokov dismissed as "idiotic," contains copious annotations, marginal scorings, drawings, and English translation enhancements so voluminous that they constitute almost a retranslation of the text. Shown here are Nabokov's entomological notes written to address his question, "What is the 'vermin' into which poor Gregor is transformed?" as well as his sketch of the beetle on the facing page.

What is the "vermin" into which poor Gregor is transformed?

It obviously belongs to the phylum Arthropoda but does this arthropod belong to the class "insect" or to that of "spiderlike creatures" or "centipedes" or even "crustaceans"? (see 78)

Critics have assumed it to be a cockroach but this is an insect of flattened form (i.e. not with a round back and a tremendous, convex belly as Gregor has) and with six comparatively large legs (not the "numerous little legs" of Gregor). The "numerous" if meaning more than six would put it into another class of arthropods — not insects. However, six may seem numerous to a transformed man. Wing cases? It is brown. He had mandibles (p. 27) The old charwoman calls him "dung beetle" (not "cockroach" as in this idiotic translation). About 3 feet long

He never found out that there were wings under the hard covering of his back (the "wing cases" under which a beetle's flimsy little wings are concealed.

as

gregor samsa

use space at bottom of pages for your notes.

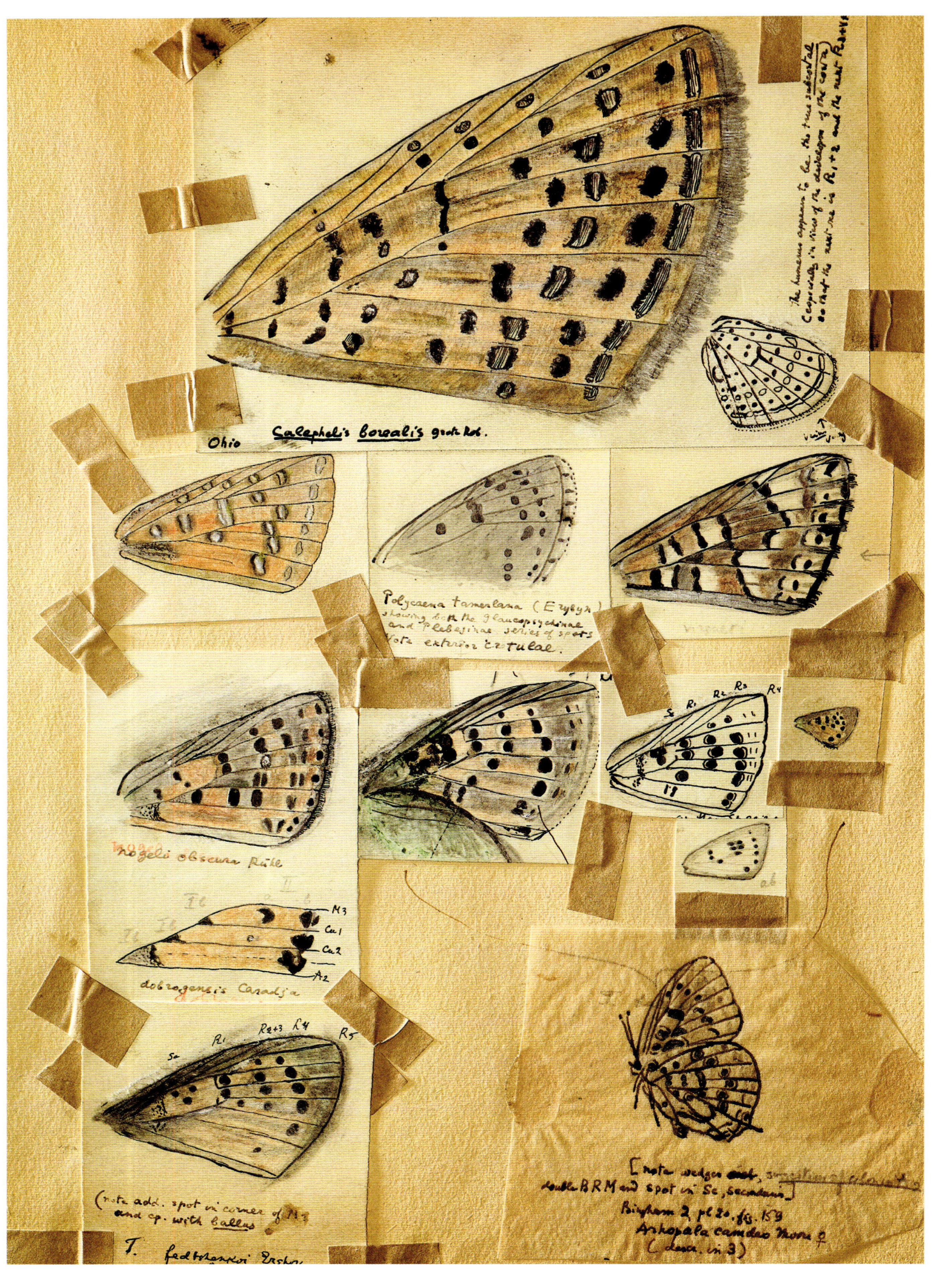

Vladimir Nabokov (1899–1977)
Page from scrapbook containing hand-drawn diagrams and manuscript notes
ca. 1946
Vladimir Nabokov Papers, Henry W. and Albert A. Berg Collection of English and American Literature

"My pleasures are the most intense known to man: writing and butterfly hunting," Nabokov said in 1962. His passion for butterflies emerged at an early age: he started collecting specimens when he was seven and over time filled thousands of index cards with notes on the subject. Fifteen years before he published *Lolita* (1955), Nabokov immigrated to the United States, where he taught comparative literature at Wellesley College and Cornell University. He continued his study of butterflies and, in the mid-1940s, was a research fellow for lepidoptery at Harvard's Museum of Comparative Zoology. There, he compiled scrapbooks filled with detailed drawings of the genitalia of blue butterflies of the subspecies *Lycaeides*, along with wing patterns for several other types of butterfly. Nabokov also discovered a new species, the Karner blue, in upstate New York in 1944.

John James Audubon (1785–1851)
The birds of America; from original drawings by John James Audubon
London: Pub. by the author, 1827–1838
Rare Book Division

The naturalist and artist John James Audubon traveled extensively throughout the United States during the 1820s and 1830s, endeavoring to record and paint all of the country's indigenous bird species. This monumental task culminated in 1827 with the publication of his *Birds of America*. Issued serially in installments over a period of twelve years, *Birds of America* stands not only as one of the most beautiful books ever created, but also as an important contribution to the ornithological field: of the 435 birds illustrated in the work's four volumes, twenty-five were previously undocumented, and six are now extinct.

The hand-colored illustration shown here—which is rendered through a combination of etching, engraving, and aquatint print processes—depicts the Carolina Parakeet, a once-common but now extinct species. It serves as a dramatic yet representative example of Audubon's art, which combines subtle detail and sheer dynamism to portray its subjects in a realistic, life-sized fashion.

No. 6 PLATE XXVI.

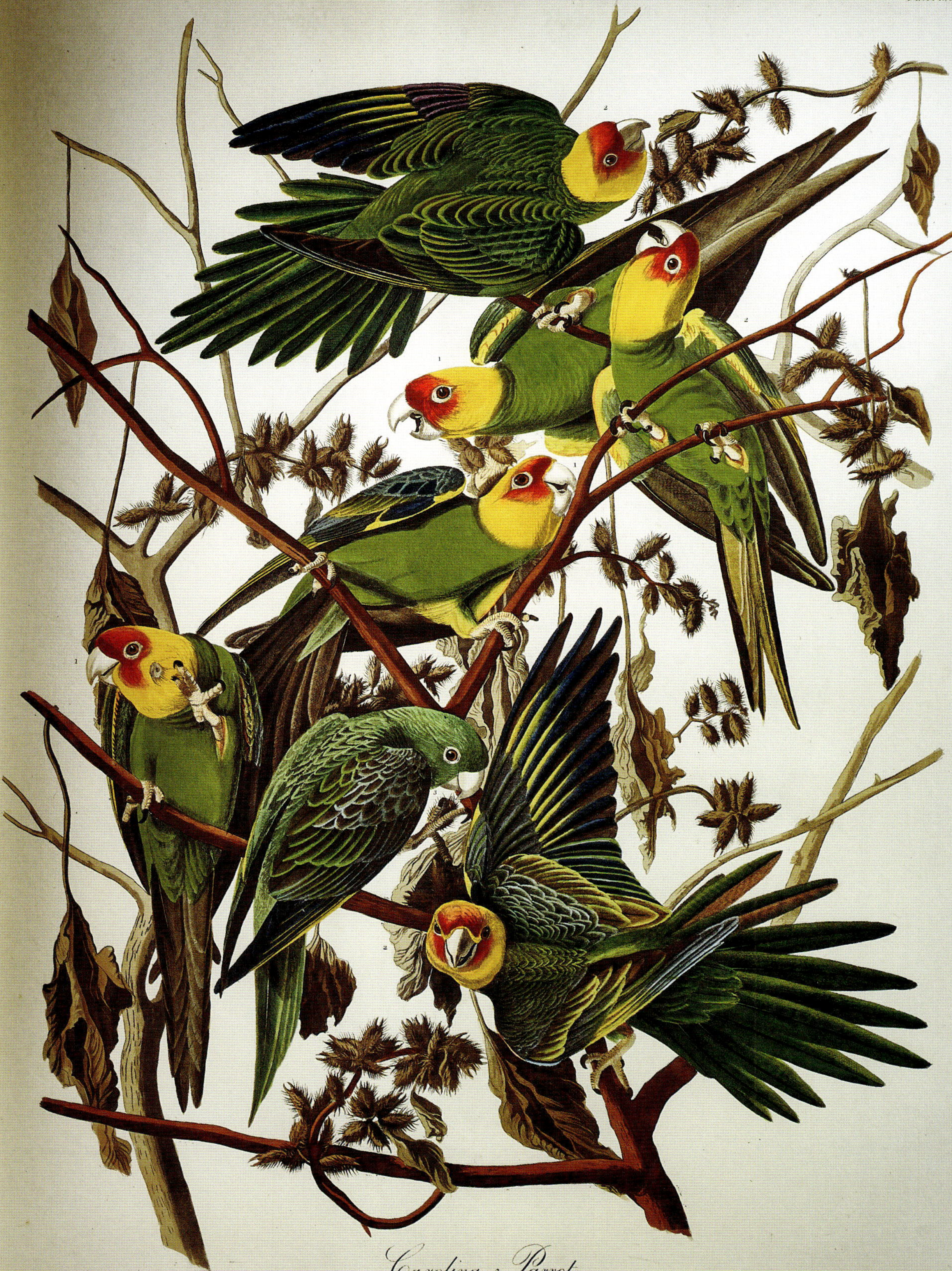

Carolina Parrot.

PSITTACUS CAROLINENSIS. Linn.

Males 1. Females 2. Young 3.

Cockle-bur. Xanthium strumarium.

Drawn from Nature & Published by John J. Audubon, F.R.S.E.L.S.

Engraved, Printed, & Coloured by R. Havell.

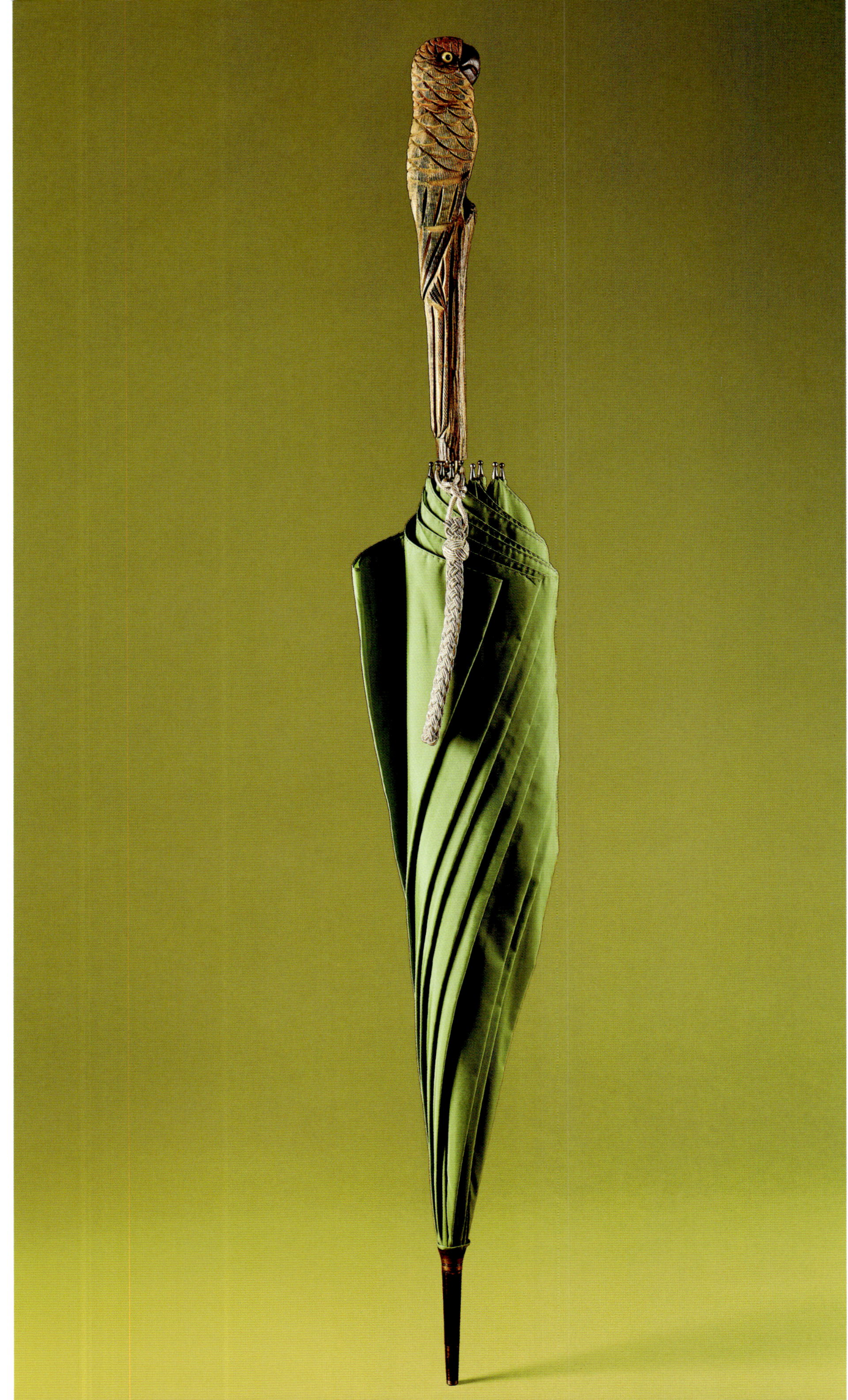

Umbrella belonging to P.L. Travers (1899–1996)
Rare Book Division

This fanciful umbrella belonged to the author of *Mary Poppins* and resembles the one that allowed the title character to fly. Pamela Lyndon (P.L.) Travers's American editor presented the umbrella to The New York Public Library in May 1972; at the same time, Travers herself donated a small collection of artifacts associated with her well-loved storybook series.

Umbrellas of this design, widely available during Travers's lifetime, had powerful childhood associations for the author. As a girl growing up in Australia, she had greatly admired a similar umbrella that a family maid considered her pride and joy. Travers began to save her pennies to purchase one of her own, only to hear her coolly sophisticated parents ridicule the servant's—and by implication, her own—idea of finery.

Ancient cookery manuscript
15th century
Manuscripts and Archives Division

This manuscript is a collection of medieval English recipes formulated by the Master Cooks of King Richard II in 14th-century England. The first printed edition, published in 1780, bore the title *The Forme of Cury.* The compiled recipes include meat and vegetable dishes that show connections with Arabic cooking, as well as Mediterranean influences from Portugal and Spain. It is among the oldest sources of English cookery, and the first to mention recipes with olive oil and spices such as cardamom, ginger, nutmeg, and cloves. The manuscript, a bequest of Helen Hay Whitney, is also the oldest manuscript written in English held in The Library's collections.

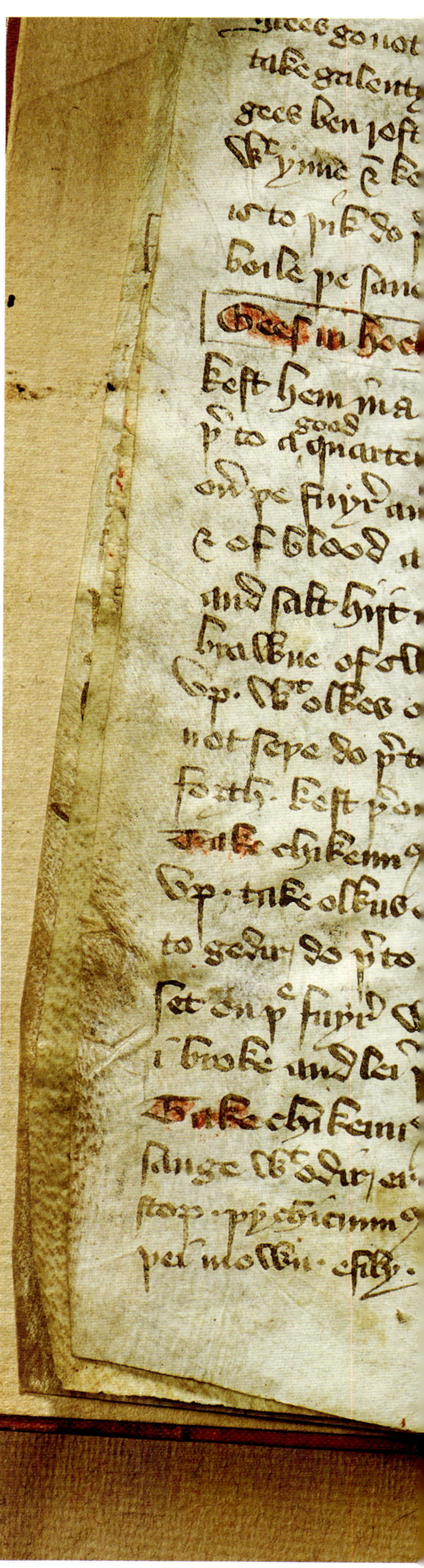

d fille þe gees þ w. sowe þe hole
welle and kepe þe grees þat falles
& do hit in a posnette. and whan
d smyt hym yn peces. & take
et and putte þynne wyne & if
galyngale & pond of donce & salt
s in disshes & ley þe sawce abo
gees & smyt hem on peces an
half wyne half water
and erbes and seþe hem in a p
fast and make a colour of bre
w and do þto ponder of f
forþ. Gernelle de pork
oile hit grynd small and lye
n þe fuyre w w grees let
nd ponder fort and messe hit
nce. Chikenes in caude
m yn good broþ take hem
s and þe broþ and alie
sug ynolh. saffren & s
ng seþ þe chikenys hole
ne. Chikenus in brocy
m. Take p[er]sely and
le garlec and grapes
m in good broþ & p
ynne messe hym and

ponder donce. Ffor to make feyssalkines. partrich. rysens.
tak good broþ and do þrynne feyssalkins partrich. &
and do þerto hol pepir and floure of canell. a good quantite
and let hit seþe þ w and messe hit forþ. & cast þon ponder
donce. Blank maung. tak capons and seþ hem. take þe
broþ. take alemand y blanched. grynd hem & lei hem up w þe broþ
cast þe mylke yn a potte. wasch rys and do þ to & lete seþe
take þe brawnes of þe capons and tese hit small. and kest
þ to. tak fair white grees. sug salt and kest þ ynne and
let hit seþe messe hit forþ and florich it w anneys in confit
red w alemand fryed in oile. Brawn desir. Take alem bla
che. hem. grynd hem and tempre hem up w white wyn
on flesh day w good broþ. cast þerynne flo of rys. oþer
amydon and lei hit þ w. take brawnes of capons y grind
small. sug & salt and cast þ to and florisch w annys w.
take a vessell y heelet and put yn saffren. Morre. take
alemand unblanchet. wasch hem. grynde hem up w red
wyne and alie hem w floure of rys. do þ to pynes y
fryed and colour hit w saunderus. do þ to pond fort
and pond donce. do þynne salt and boile hit. messe
hit forþ. flerissh hit w whit anys in confit
Charlet. take pork and seþ hit welle and hewe hit
small. cast hit in a panne and breke eyren þ to & stirye
hit welle togedir. do þ to cow mylke and saffroune.

en premier lieu jeusse la demande comme une
chose impossible pour mon d'accepter et
puis vous dirois que une entrevue serviroit
le mieulx a propos pour parachever la
cause qui mostreroit une grande
absurdite Mais me asseurant que
Monsieur la Motte vous satisfera
assez bien me purgent de tel crime
comme de qui nullement suis coulpable
Je ne feray ceste plus longue synon pour
vous rendre mes trescordielles graces
pour les continuelz honneurs que me faictes
et vous supplier que Monsieur la Motte
reçoit de nos mains quelq' faveur pour
avoir si sagement manie ceste cause
et pour s'y estre tant sagement porte
Aussi me estre tresaffectiussement recommande
a vostre bonne grace de prieray
le Seigneur Dieu vous garder de
tout mall et vous donner bonne vie
et longue. De Kelingworth
ce 22 iour d'Aoust

Vostre tresassuree bonne Seur
et Cousine

Elizabeth R

Letter from Queen Elizabeth I (r. 1588–1603) to King Charles IX (r. 1560–1574)
August 22, 1572
George Arents Collection

Among the many suitors of Queen Elizabeth I was Francis, Duke of Anjou and Alençon, the brother of King Charles IX of France. Charles hoped that an arranged marriage between his brother and Elizabeth would help forge an alliance between the two countries. In this letter, written during the summer of 1572, Elizabeth explains to the French king that, while she holds both him and his brother in the highest esteem, she nevertheless considers the marriage offer "a thing impossible for me to accept," principally due to their age difference: at the time, Elizabeth was thirty-eight years old, twenty-one years Francis's senior.

William Shakespeare (1564–1616)
Mr. William Shakespeares Comedies, Histories, & Tragedies. Published according to the True Originall Copies
London: Isaac Jaggard and Edward Blount, 1623
Rare Book Division

Mr. William Shakespeares Comedies, Histories, & Tragedies, commonly referred to as the First Folio, is the first true collected printing of William Shakespeare's plays, and arguably the most important book in all of English literature. Of the thirty-six plays contained in the volume, eighteen appeared in print for the first time in this edition—including such works as *The Tempest*, *Macbeth*, and *Henry VIII*. Without this printing, these Shakespearean classics may not have been preserved for posterity. Martin Droeshout the Younger, a Flemish-born artist working in London during the period, engraved the iconic frontispiece, one of two contemporary likenesses of the playwright.

Mr. WILLIAM
SHAKESPEARES
COMEDIES, HISTORIES, & TRAGEDIES.

Publiſhed according to the True Originall Copies.

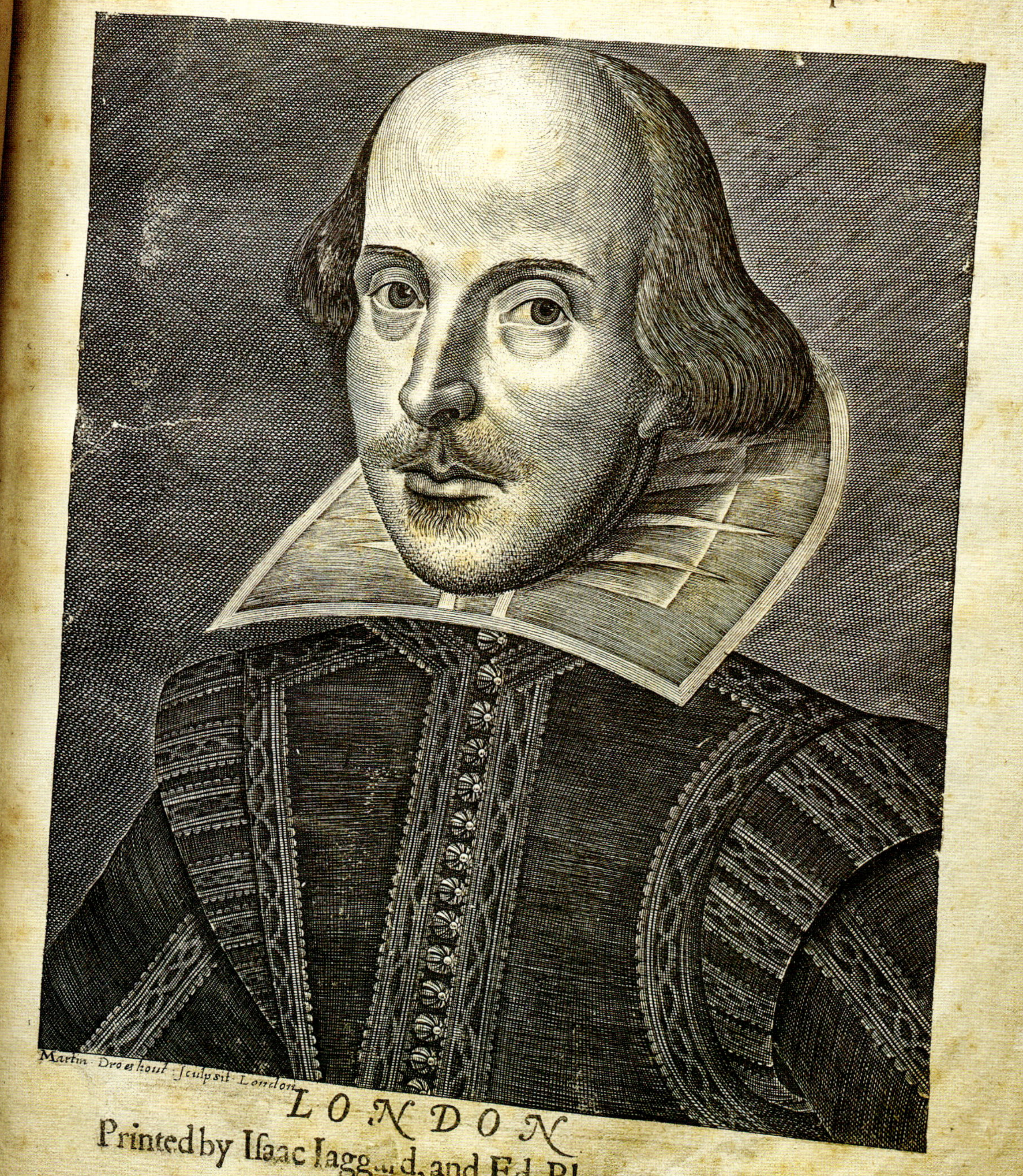

LONDON
Printed by Iſaac Iaggard, and Ed. Blount. 1623

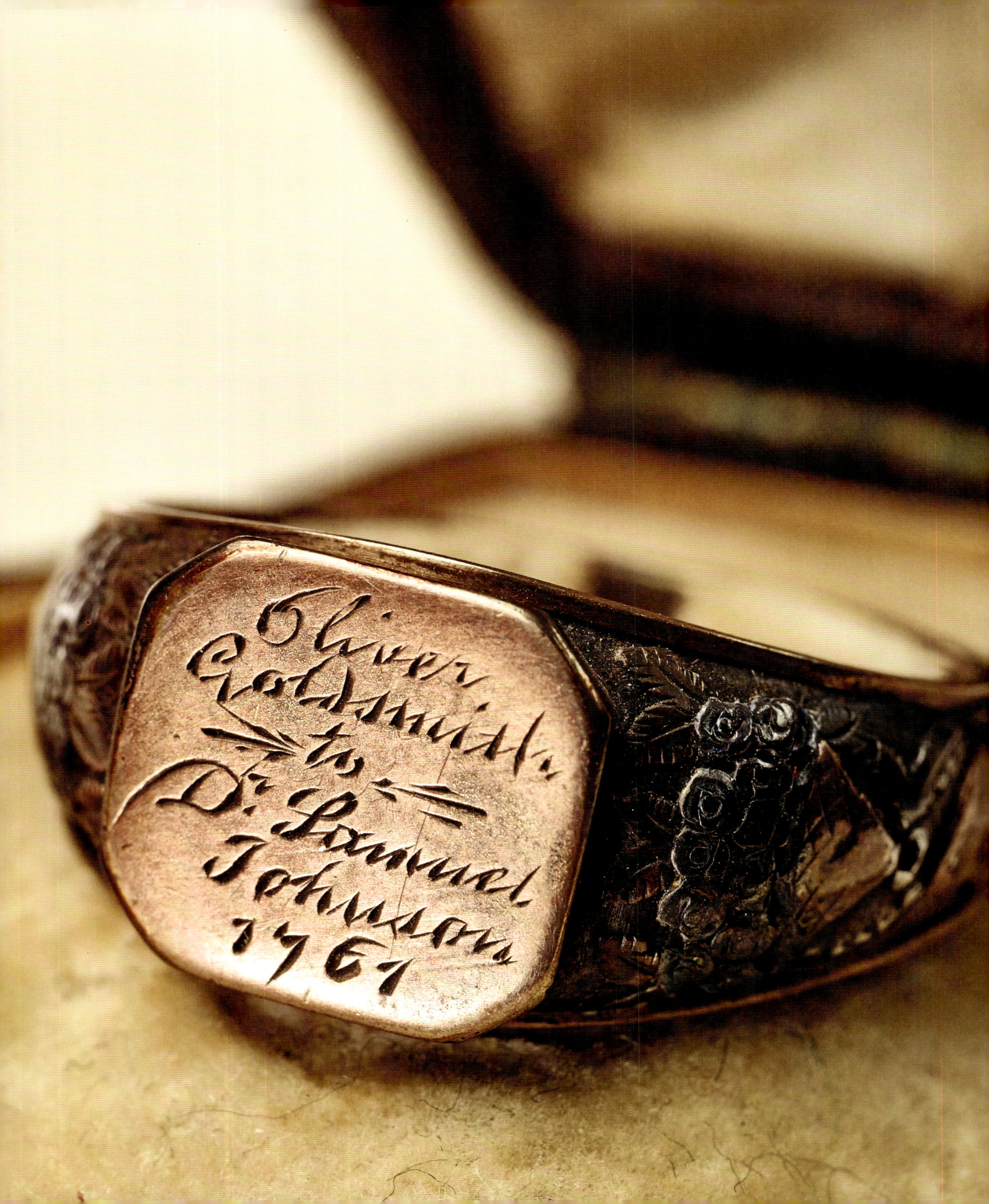
Oliver
Goldsmith
to
Dr. Samuel
Johnson
1761

A gift for the "Great Cham of Literature"

Silver and gilt, chased with flowers on black enamel, ca. 1761

Henry W. and Albert A. Berg Collection of English and American Literature

The great lexicographer Samuel Johnson once said of his friend Oliver Goldsmith: "No man was more foolish when he had not a pen in his hand, or more wise when he had." The Irish playwright, novelist, and poet first met Johnson on May 31, 1761. In this year, according to one Goldsmith biographer, "work and money began to pour in upon him. . . . He was fond of giving suppers; he was developing a taste for fine clothes, peach-coloured velvets, magnificent rings." Goldsmith may have given Johnson (titled the "Great Cham of Literature" by his biographer James Boswell) this friendship ring in 1761 or at a later date—Johnson did not receive his first honorary doctorate, from Trinity College Dublin, until 1765. Biographies of Johnson and Goldsmith are silent about the gift of this ring, which was sold as lot 18 in the auction of the property of Bertram, 5th Earl of Ashburnham, on June 28, 1921. The Library acquired the ring when the Owen D. Young Collection was incorporated into the Berg Collection in 1941.

Ellen, or, the Naughty Girl Reclaimed

London, 1811

The Carl H. Pforzheimer Collection of Shelley and His Circle

Ellen is one of a series of paper dolls published at the Temple of Fancy, a London stationer specializing in beautiful watercolored materials like this. Her companions include *Hubert, the Cottage Youth*, and *Little Fanny.* These appealing dolls were individually sold in a cardboard holder with several outfits, including hats, and a book recounting the child protagonist's adventures—each requiring a change of clothes. For Ellen, these changes tell the story of her redemption. Beginning as "a stubborn, naughty child," Ellen spoils her clothes (change to her extravagantly muddy coat), throws a book in her teacher's face (dunce's cap goes on), and runs away, only to be stripped and kidnapped by gypsies (change to rags). Abandoned in a forest, she is rescued by an old woman and employed selling apples on street corners (change to a costermonger's cloak). Discovered at last by her parents, Ellen's final change shows her repentant, diligent—and clean.

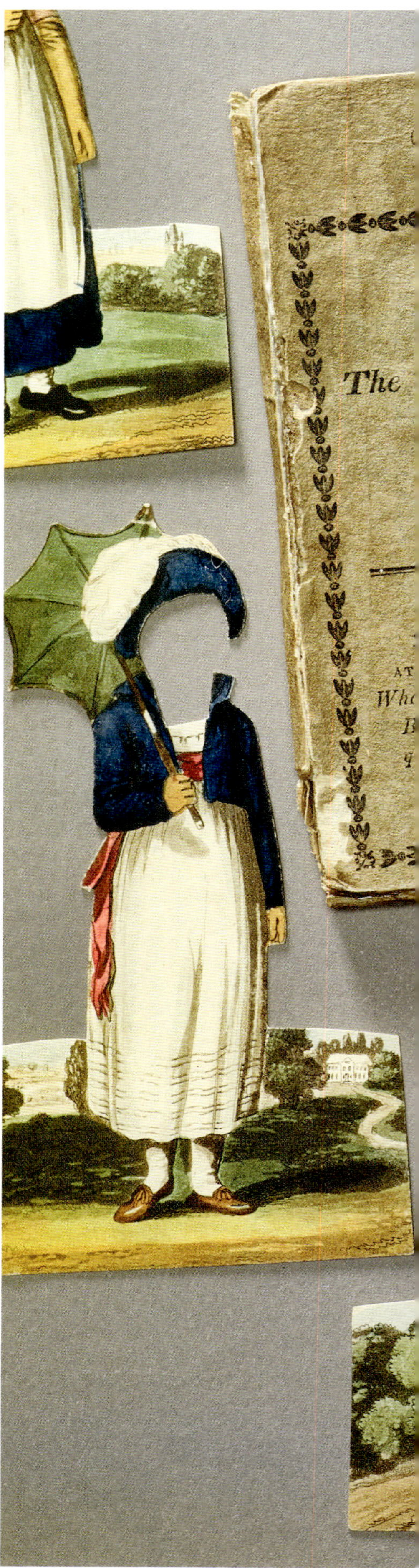

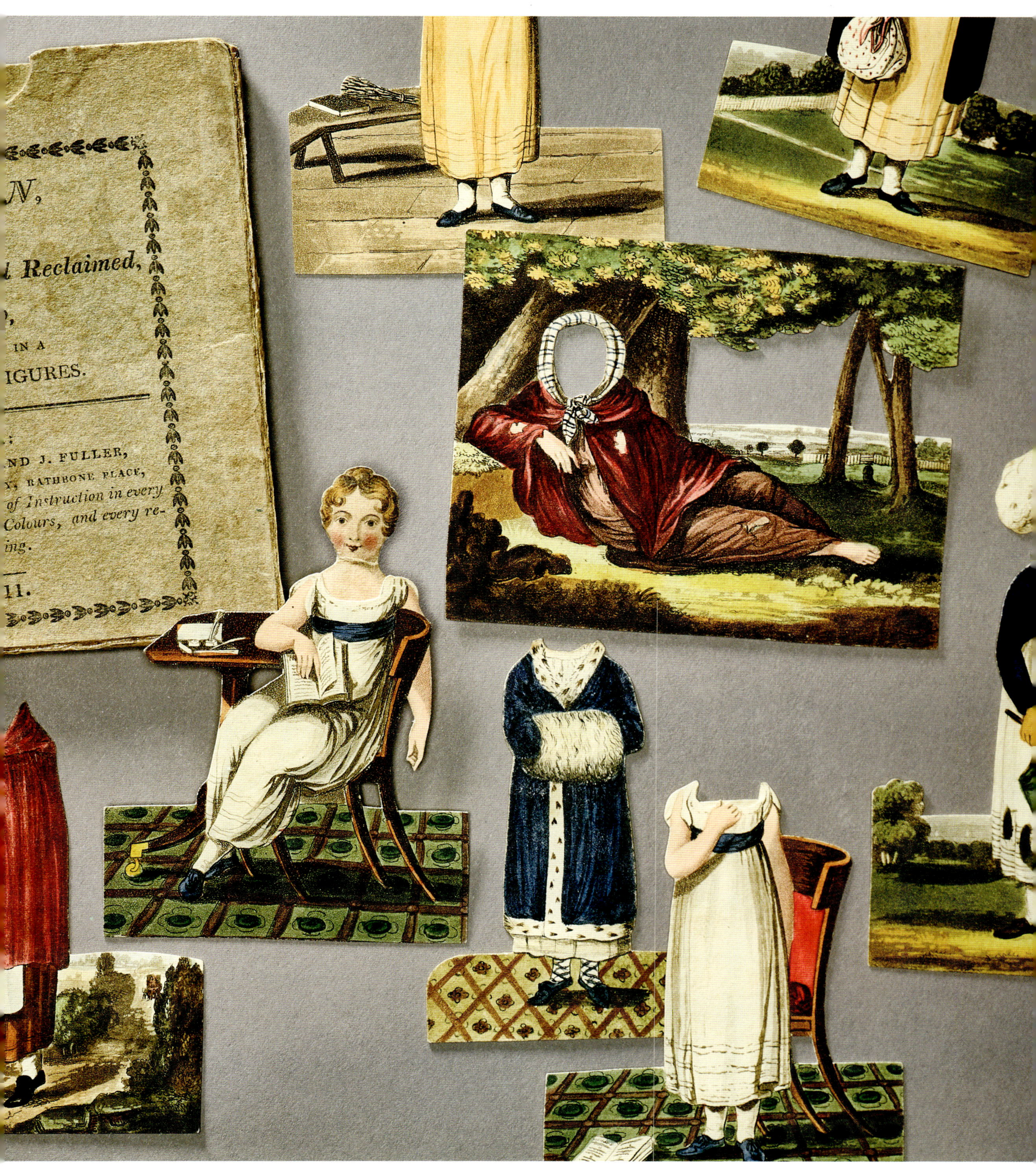
Reclaimed,
IN A
IGURES.
ND J. FULLER,
BATHBONE PLACE,
of Instruction in every
Colours, and every re-
ing.
11.

When Winchester races first took thier beginning
It is said the good people forgot thier old Saint
Not applying at all for the leave of Saint Swithin
And that William of Wykehams approval was faint.

The races however were fixed and determined
The company came and the Weather was charming
The Lords and the Ladies were satined & ermined
And nobody saw any future alarming.—

But when the old Saint was informed of these doings
He made but one Spring from his Shrine to the Roof
Of the Palace which now lies so sadly in ruins
And then he addressed them all standing aloof.

Oh! subjects rebellious! Oh Venta depraved
When once we are buried you think we are gone
But behold me immortal! By vice you're enslaved

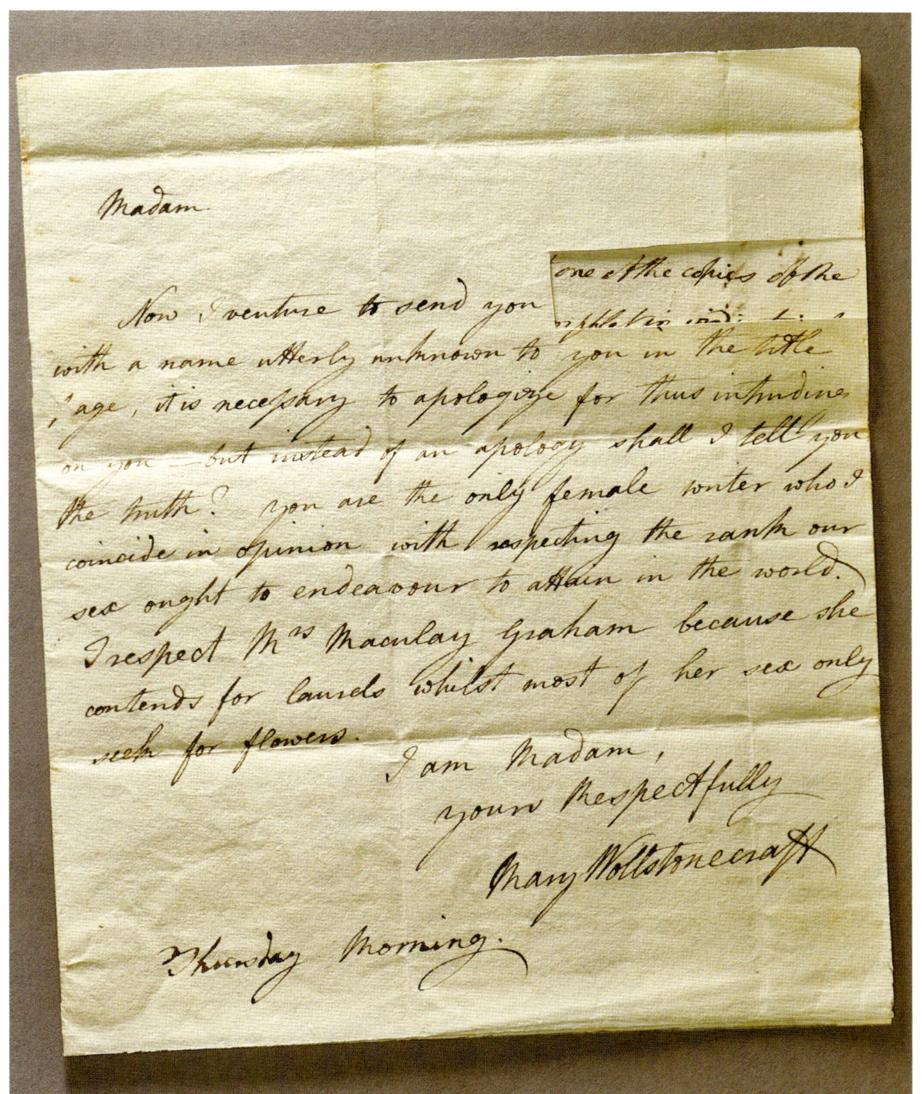

Madam

Now I venture to send you one of the copies of the [illegible] with a name utterly unknown to you in the title page, it is necessary to apologize for thus intruding on you — but instead of an apology shall I tell you the truth? you are the only female writer who I coincide in opinion with respecting the rank our sex ought to endeavour to attain in the world. I respect Mrs Macaulay Graham because she contends for laurels whilst most of her sex only seek for flowers.

I am Madam,
yours Respectfully
Mary Wollstonecraft

Thursday Morning.

Letter from Mary Wollstonecraft (1759–1797) to Catharine Macaulay (1731–1791)
December 30, 1790
The Carl H. Pforzheimer Collection of Shelley and His Circle

“I respect Mrs Macaulay Graham because she contends for the laurels, whilst most of her sex only seek for the flowers.” Thus Mary Wollstonecraft wrote in December 1790 to the historian Catharine Macaulay, responding to Macaulay’s intervention in the “pamphlet war” provoked in the United Kingdom by the French Revolution, and sending a pamphlet of her own. Still two years away from her pioneering *A Vindication of the Rights of Woman*, Wollstonecraft was already a cogent feminist writer. She greeted Macaulay as a fellow contender in a struggle that is still far from won.

Percy Bysshe Shelley (1792–1822)

Manuscript draft of *A Philosophical View of Reform*

1819

The Carl H. Pforzheimer Collection of Shelley and His Circle

Writing in Florence in late 1819, Percy Bysshe Shelley—an important English Romantic poet, and the husband of Mary Wollstonecraft Shelley—drafted his most mature work promoting British political reform in this vellum notebook. In those days, few but landowners could vote in Britain and Shelley's response, while complex, was aimed at the common reader and rings out clear: "If the Houses of Parliament obstinately & perpetually refuse to concede any reform to the people, my vote is for universal suffrage and equal representation," he wrote. The treatise went unpublished in his lifetime and for long after. Carl H. Pforzheimer purchased it at Sotheby's in 1921 and immediately made it available to scholars, lending it to one of them over the summer of 1923. This is no longer the practice of the collection, but we welcome researchers to study the manuscript in the Library's reading room.

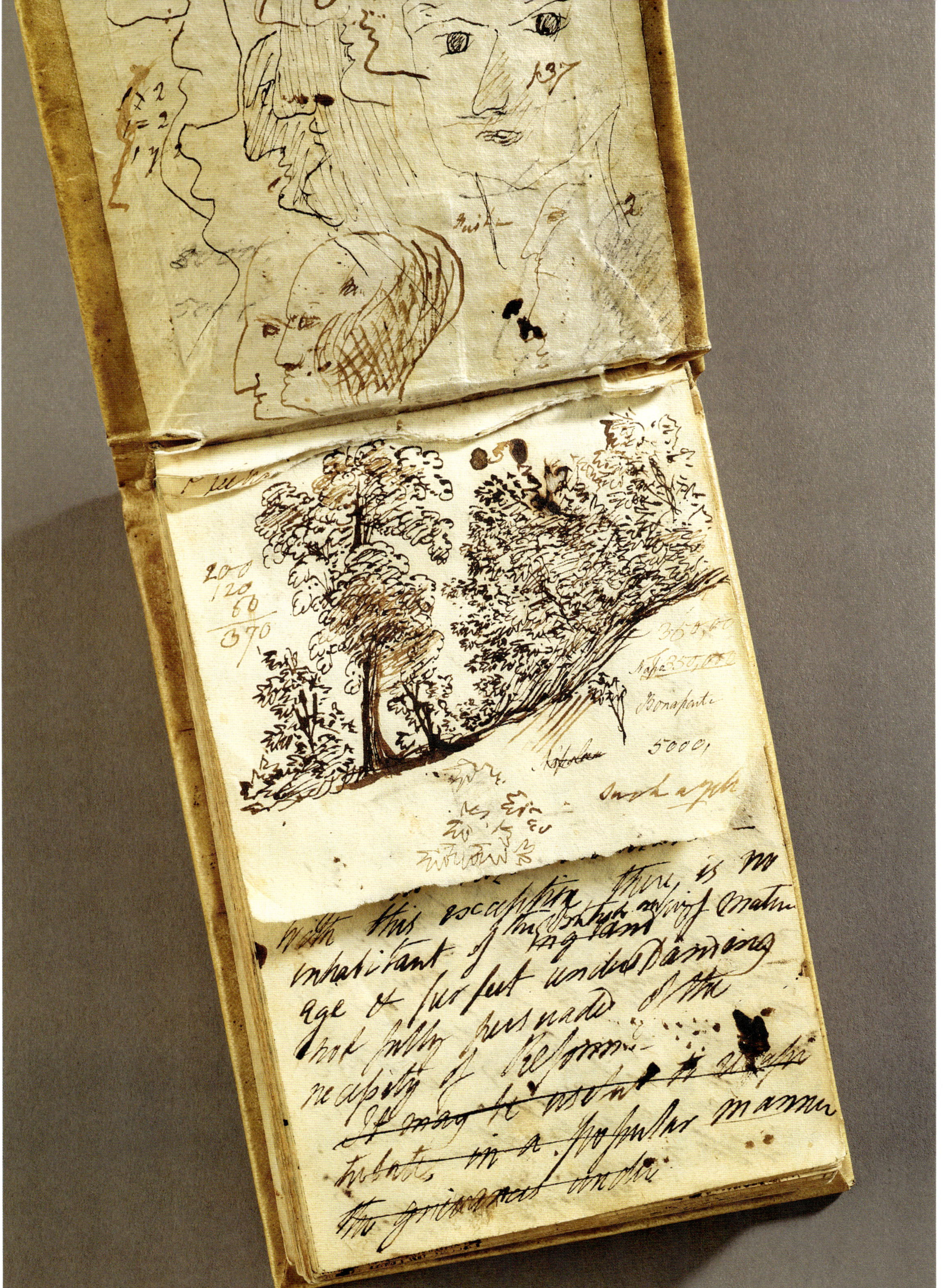
Bonaparte
5000
With this exception there is no
inhabitant of England of mature
age & perfect understanding
not fully persuaded of the
necessity of Reform
in a popular manner
under

The Keep of the Bridge

This Keep or round tower is celebrated in tradition as being the abode of the fairy Ebon it is situated on a small aclivity before it flows a broad stream of water & behind it there is a large wood or rather forest which covers a very high hill said to be the identical hill on which the magician of the sea lost his life for presuming to release Gambia from the horrible dungeon in which the fairy had confined him when I saw the keep it was night & the moon was shedding her mild glory on all around illuminating the topmost branches of the gloomy forest whose shade was to dense for the light to penetrate farther & gilding the ivy which clung to the grey walls of the Keep so as to make them appear as if they were embroidered with silver while in the clear still waters of the river the whole arch of the firmament with the bright moon hanging in the midst & the sparkling stars spangling the sky were reflected so truly as to seem almost as magnificent as the glorious original after contemplating this beautiful prospect for some time I entred the tower & passing throug the dreary Hall lighted only by a ray of moon light which found its way through an arched & grated window I opened the massive iron door which leads to Gambia's dungeon & then descending the long narrow stairs I reached the dreadful apartment & dreadful indeed it was there was still burning the torch of the magician which cast a bloody unearthly light around the place & as I entred the huge door closed after me though no living creature appeared I was alone it was night — I could not open the door though I tried with all my strength — I thought how dreadful it would be to die in such a place yet this I knew must be the inevitable consequence of my temerity I threw myself on the ground in despair & remained motionless & stupid with horror for some time at last I saw a thin misty form rise out of the earth it beckoned to me I arose the door opened I found myself outside the castle & imediatly quitted the haunted tower & returned to it no more.

CB July 13 1832

Charlotte Brontë (1816–1855)

Manuscript draft of "The Keep of the Bridge"

July 13, 1829

Henry W. and Albert A. Berg Collection of English and American Literature

Measuring just three and one-half inches high, this folded piece of paper was used by Charlotte Brontë to record one of her earliest attempts at writing fiction. Shortly after she turned thirteen, Brontë penned "The Keep of the Bridge," a short story that leans toward gothic melodrama, in a minuscule copperplate hand intended to resemble printed type. On the back, she sketched a stone bridge with a round Norman keep, or tower, to accompany the story. Making miniature manuscripts and model books was a common pastime in the Brontë family: Charlotte, her younger brother, Branwell, and sisters Emily and Anne began collaborating on plays, stories, and poems in 1827. The siblings explored fantastical, magical worlds in their collective writing, and the melodramatic tone that appears in Brontë's "The Keep of the Bridge" would later return, far more subtly, in *Jane Eyre* (1847).

William Morris (1834–1896), printer and publisher
Edward Burne-Jones (1833–1898), illustrator
***The Works of Geoffrey Chaucer.* Printed by me William Morris at the Kelmscott Press, Upper Mall, Hammersmith, in the country of Middlesex, Finished on the 8th day of May, 1896.**
The Miriam and Ira D. Wallach Division of Art, Prints and Photographs, Spencer Collection

William Morris was a pioneer in the book arts, though he is perhaps better known today as a textile and furniture designer. Dismayed by the industrial processes used to mass-produce books in the late 19th century, Morris sought to re-create the look of books published four centuries earlier. He acquired a printing press similar to that of Johannes Gutenberg, and from 1891 until 1898, published fifty-three titles under the imprint of the Kelmscott Press. Morris designed *The Works of Geoffrey Chaucer* together with his close friend, the renowned Pre-Raphaelite painter Edward Burne-Jones. Four years in the making, it was one of Morris's last publications—and is also considered one of his best. To re-create the feel of a Renaissance book, Morris developed his own type, created his own paper, and printed the entire project by hand. He produced only 424 copies of the book, including this one in the Library's Spencer Collection.

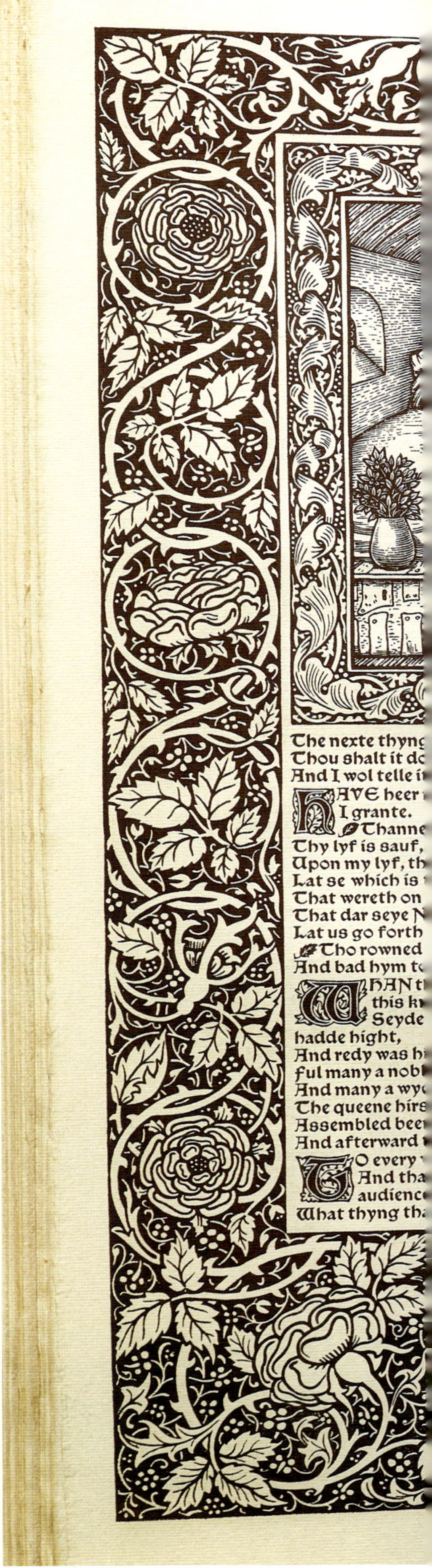

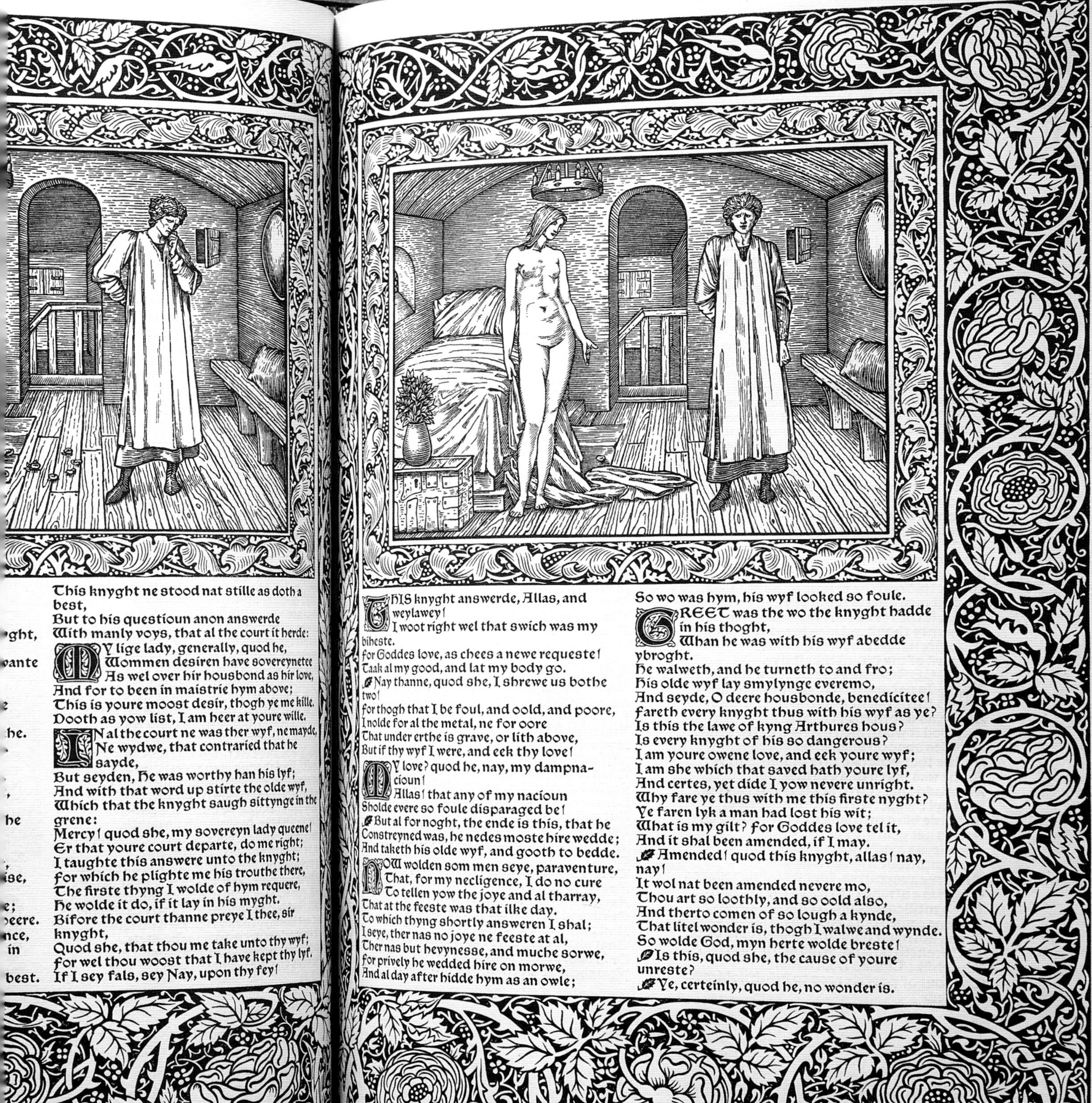

This knyght ne stood nat stille as doth a best,
But to his questioun anon answerde
With manly voys, that al the court it herde:
MY lige lady, generally, quod he,
Wommen desiren have sovereynetee
As wel over hir housbond as hir love,
And for to been in maistrie hym above;
This is youre moost desir, thogh ye me kille.
Dooth as yow list, I am heer at youre wille.
IN al the court ne was ther wyf, ne mayde,
Ne wydwe, that contraried that he sayde,
But seyden, He was worthy han his lyf;
And with that word up stirte the olde wyf,
Which that the knyght saugh sittynge in the grene:
Mercy! quod she, my sovereyn lady queene!
Er that youre court departe, do me right;
I taughte this answere unto the knyght;
For which he plighte me his trouthe there,
The firste thyng I wolde of hym requere,
He wolde it do, if it lay in his myght.
Bifore the court thanne preye I thee, sir knyght,
Quod she, that thou me take unto thy wyf;
For wel thou woost that I have kept thy lyf.
If I sey fals, sey Nay, upon thy fey!

THIS knyght answerde, Allas, and weylawey!
I woot right wel that swich was my biheste.
For Goddes love, as chees a newe requeste!
Taak al my good, and lat my body go.
Nay thanne, quod she, I shrewe us bothe two!
For thogh that I be foul, and oold, and poore,
I nolde for al the metal, ne for oore
That under erthe is grave, or lith above,
But if thy wyf I were, and eek thy love!
MY love? quod he, nay, my dampnacioun!
Allas! that any of my nacioun
Sholde evere so foule disparaged be!
But al for noght, the ende is this, that he
Constreyned was, he nedes moste hire wedde;
And taketh his olde wyf, and gooth to bedde.
NOW wolden som men seye, paraventure,
That, for my necligence, I do no cure
To tellen yow the joye and al tharray,
That at the feeste was that ilke day.
To which thyng shortly answeren I shal;
I seye, ther nas no joye ne feeste at al,
Ther nas but hevynesse, and muche sorwe,
For prively he wedded hire on morwe,
And al day after hidde hym as an owle;
So wo was hym, his wyf looked so foule.
GREET was the wo the knyght hadde in his thoght,
Whan he was with his wyf abedde ybroght.
He walweth, and he turneth to and fro;
His olde wyf lay smylynge everemo,
And seyde, O deere housbonde, benedicitee!
Fareth every knyght thus with his wyf as ye?
Is this the lawe of kyng Arthures hous?
Is every knyght of his so dangerous?
I am youre owene love, and eek youre wyf;
I am she which that saved hath youre lyf,
And certes, yet dide I yow nevere unright.
Why fare ye thus with me this firste nyght?
Ye faren lyk a man had lost his wit;
What is my gilt? For Goddes love tel it,
And it shal been amended, if I may.
Amended! quod this knyght, allas! nay, nay!
It wol nat been amended nevere mo,
Thou art so loothly, and so oold also,
And therto comen of so lough a kynde,
That litel wonder is, thogh I walwe and wynde.
So wolde God, myn herte wolde breste!
Is this, quod she, the cause of youre unreste?
Ye, certeinly, quod he, no wonder is.

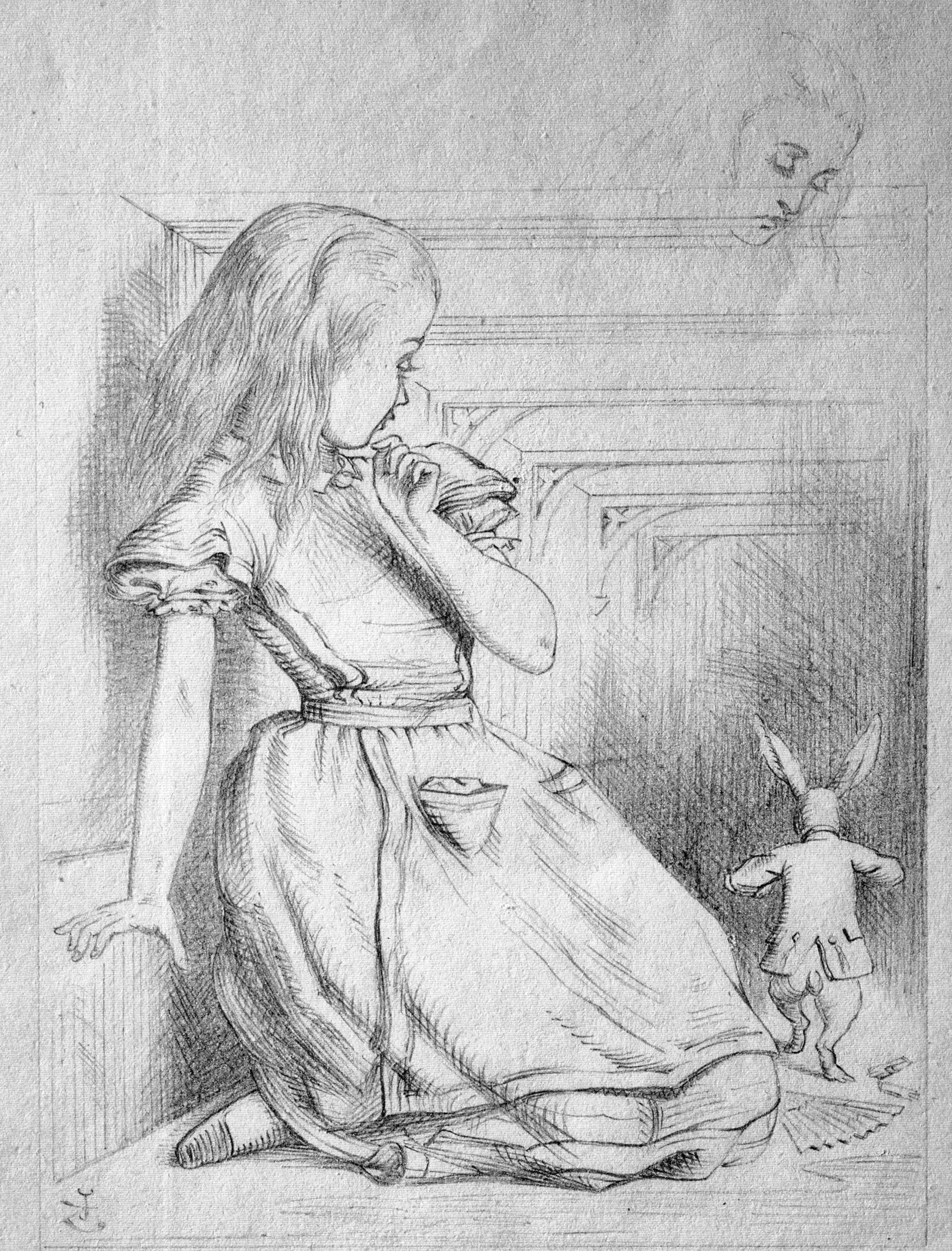

John Tenniel (1820–1914)

"The Rabbit . . . scurried away into the darkness"

Graphite on paper, 1865 or later

Henry W. and Albert A. Berg Collection of English and American Literature

Lewis Carroll published *Alice's Adventures in Wonderland* in 1865, but the story originated three years earlier on an afternoon picnic with ten-year-old Alice Liddell, her two sisters, and another family friend. The children asked for a story, and Carroll sent his heroine "straight down a rabbit-hole, to begin with, without the least idea what was to happen afterwards." Carroll later wrote down the tale, filling the manuscript with his own drawings. After deciding to publish, Carroll commissioned John Tenniel—one of the top illustrators of the day—to make new pictures. Tenniel's designs are now synonymous with the tale. In the decades following the book's immediate success, collectors frequently asked Tenniel to make drawings of his own illustrations. This fine example includes a study of Alice's face in profile in the upper margin.

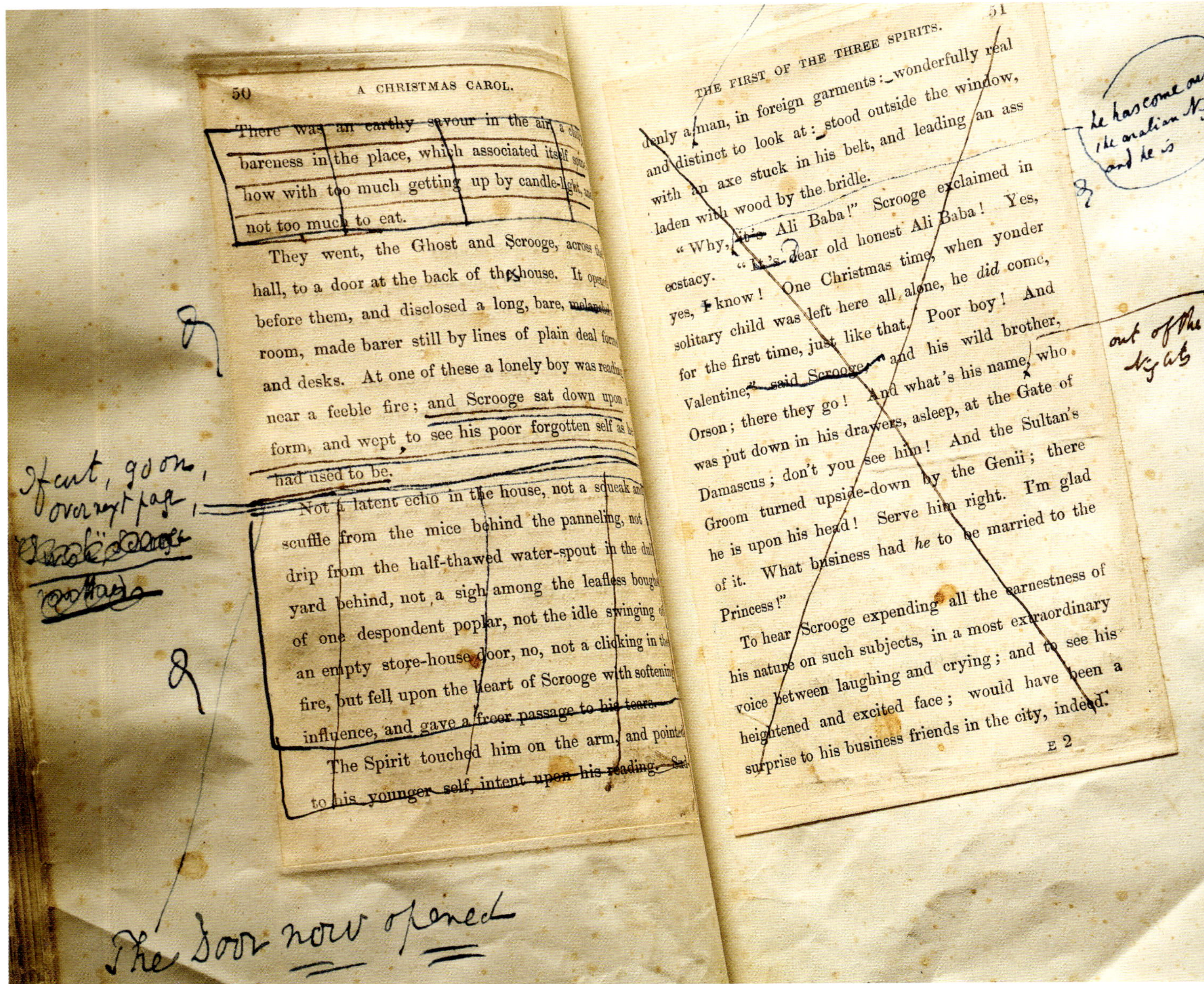

50 A CHRISTMAS CAROL.

There was an earthy savour in the air, a chilly bareness in the place, which associated itself somehow with too much getting up by candle-light, and not too much to eat.

They went, the Ghost and Scrooge, across the hall, to a door at the back of the house. It opened before them, and disclosed a long, bare, melancholy room, made barer still by lines of plain deal forms and desks. At one of these a lonely boy was reading near a feeble fire; and Scrooge sat down upon a form, and wept to see his poor forgotten self as he had used to be.

Not a latent echo in the house, not a squeak and scuffle from the mice behind the panneling, not a drip from the half-thawed water-spout in the dull yard behind, not a sigh among the leafless boughs of one despondent poplar, not the idle swinging of an empty store-house door, no, not a clicking in the fire, but fell upon the heart of Scrooge with softening influence, and gave a freer passage to his tears.

The Spirit touched him on the arm, and pointed to his younger self, intent upon his reading. Sud-

THE FIRST OF THE THREE SPIRITS. 51

denly a man, in foreign garments: wonderfully real and distinct to look at: stood outside the window, with an axe stuck in his belt, and leading an ass laden with wood by the bridle.

"Why, it's Ali Baba!" Scrooge exclaimed in ecstacy. "It's dear old honest Ali Baba! Yes, yes, I know! One Christmas time, when yonder solitary child was left here all alone, he *did* come, for the first time, just like that. Poor boy! And Valentine," said Scrooge, "and his wild brother, Orson; there they go! And what's his name, who was put down in his drawers, asleep, at the Gate of Damascus; don't you see him! And the Sultan's Groom turned upside-down by the Genii; there he is upon his head! Serve him right. I'm glad of it. What business had *he* to be married to the Princess!"

To hear Scrooge expending all the earnestness of his nature on such subjects, in a most extraordinary voice between laughing and crying; and to see his heightened and excited face; would have been a surprise to his business friends in the city, indeed.

E 2

Charles Dickens (1812–1870)

Dickens's reading copy of *A Christmas carol in prose: Being a ghost story of Christmas*

London: Bradbury and Evans, 1849

Henry W. and Albert A. Berg Collection of English and American Literature

Dickens was a world-renowned literary celebrity when he began giving public readings in December 1853. For his first performances, he chose *A Christmas Carol*, which was seasonally appropriate, one of his most popular books, and among the shortest. But though he reduced the text dramatically, the first readings (which approximately 6,000 people attended) lasted more than three hours. This prompt copy—Dickens's own, which he used on stage—attests to the edits he made to the performance over the next sixteen years. He deleted or severely abridged large portions of text, as seen here. Dickens employed a different voice and style for each of his characters—from a "sulky growl" for Scrooge to a "childish treble" for Tiny Tim and "cold, haughty voices" for the spirits of Christmas Past, Present, and Future—and thus added notes to remind himself of what tone and emphasis to use.

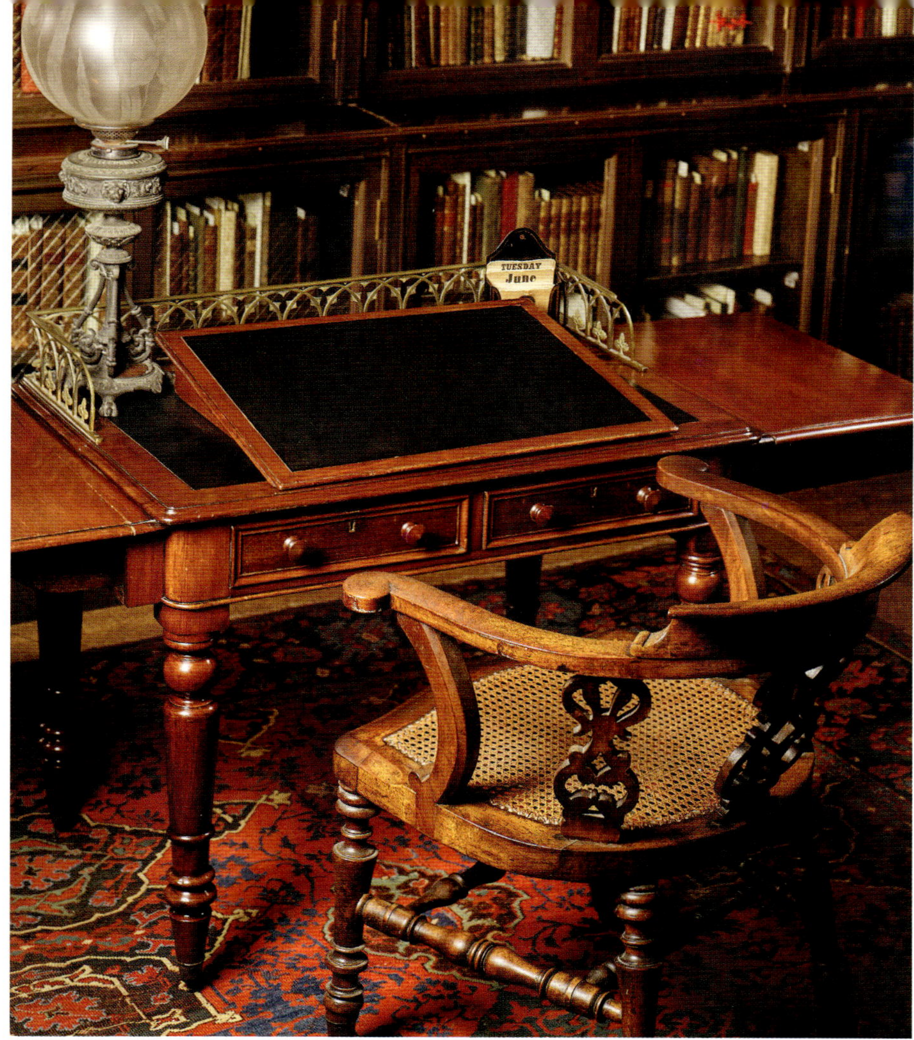

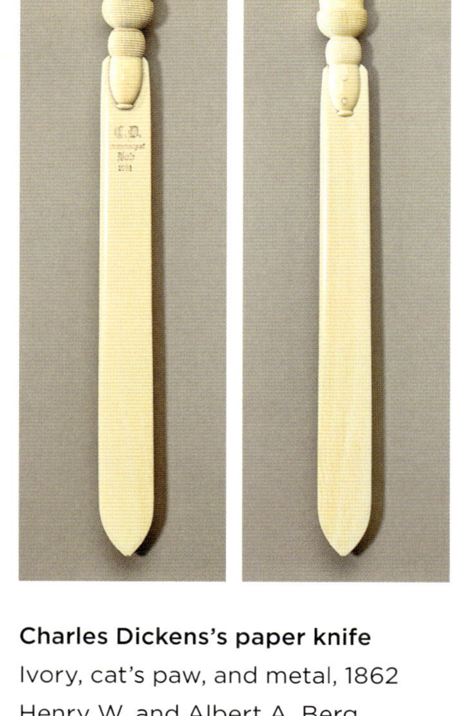

Charles Dickens's paper knife
Ivory, cat's paw, and metal, 1862
Henry W. and Albert A. Berg Collection of English and American Literature

Charles Dickens's desk, writing slope, lamp, calendar, and chair
Desk: Mahogany and leather, on metal castors, before 1870
Writing slope: Wood and leather, before 1870
Lamp: Metal and frosted glass with ceramic knob, before 1870
Desk calendar: tinned iron, paint, and paper, before 1870
Chair: Wood and cane, on metal castors, before 1859
The Henry W. and Albert A. Berg Collection of English and American Literature

Charles Dickens likely drafted part of his novel *Hard Times* (1854) while seated in this cane-bottom chair, and he may have written chapters of *Great Expectations* (1860–1861) at this small mahogany writing desk while bathed in the light of this oil lamp. Dickens almost certainly penned some of his more than 15,000 letters on this writing slope; leather-covered and neatly angled, it would have provided a comfortable surface for his fast-flowing pen. The chair originally decorated Dickens's office at *Household Words*, the weekly magazine he edited in the 1850s, but it was moved to his home sometime in the years following. This ensemble, including the small desk calendar tucked behind the writing slope, all came from Gad's Hill Place, Dickens's primary residence for the last decade of his life.

Charles Dickens was a dog lover, but his daughter Mamie persuaded him to let her keep a white kitten, Williamina, that she received as a gift. Williamina gave birth to a litter of kittens; all but one—Bob—were given away. Mamie related that "the master's cat," so called by the household servants for his devotion to Dickens, would "follow him about the garden like a dog, and sit with him while he wrote," and even snuff out candles with his paw in a bid for attention from Dickens. After Bob died, his paw was fashioned into this paper knife, engraved "C.D. / In memory of Bob / 1862." It is likely that the paper knife was not actively used, and that it was regarded as a decorative tribute to a beloved pet.

Winnie-the-Pooh and Friends
ca. 1921
Rare Book Division

On his first birthday, in 1921, Christopher Robin Milne received a small teddy bear that had been purchased at Harrods department store in London. Christened Winnie-the-Pooh, the bear was joined in due course by several now-familiar companions: Eeyore, Piglet, Kanga, Tigger, and Roo. (Roo was eventually lost in an apple orchard.) Together, these stuffed animals came to serve not only as Christopher's playmates but also as the inspiration for several classic works such as *Winnie-the-Pooh* (1926) and *The House at Pooh Corner* (1928), all written by his father, A.A. Milne.

Brought to the United States in 1947, the toys remained with Milne's American publisher, E.P. Dutton, until 1987, when they were donated to The New York Public Library. Today, they stand as a beloved centerpiece of the Library's renowned collection of children's literature, continuing to delight and inspire both the young and young at heart.

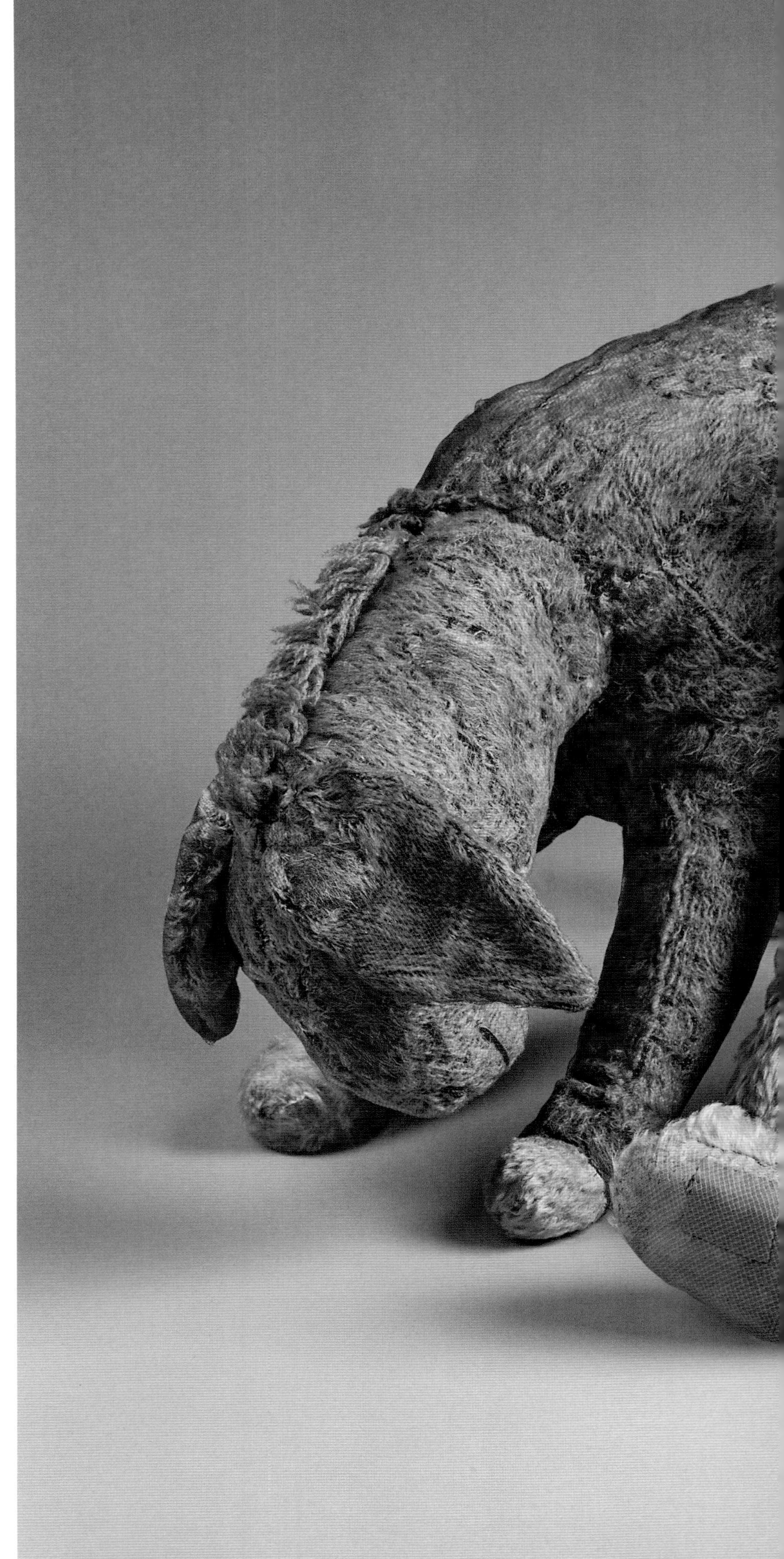

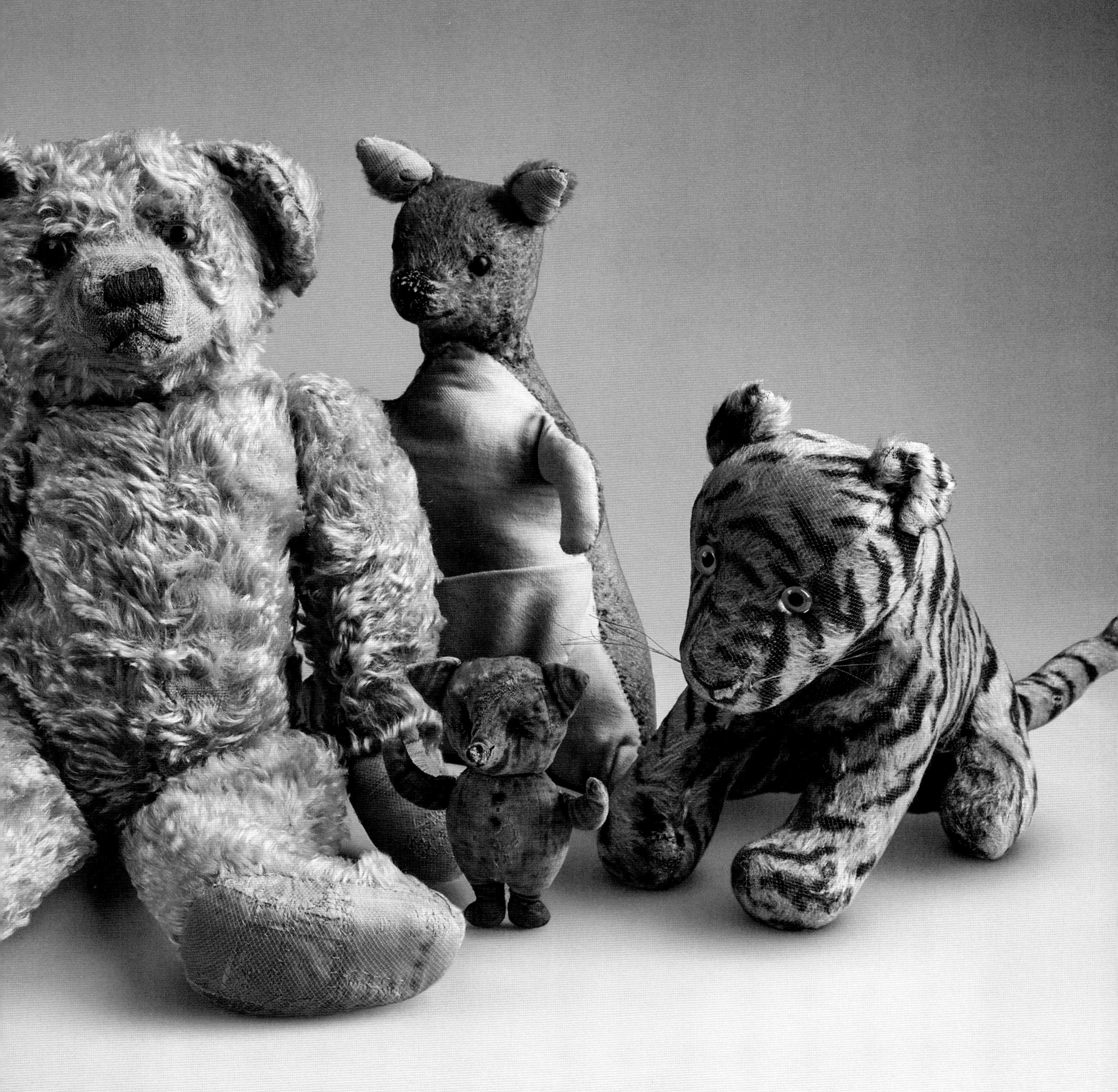

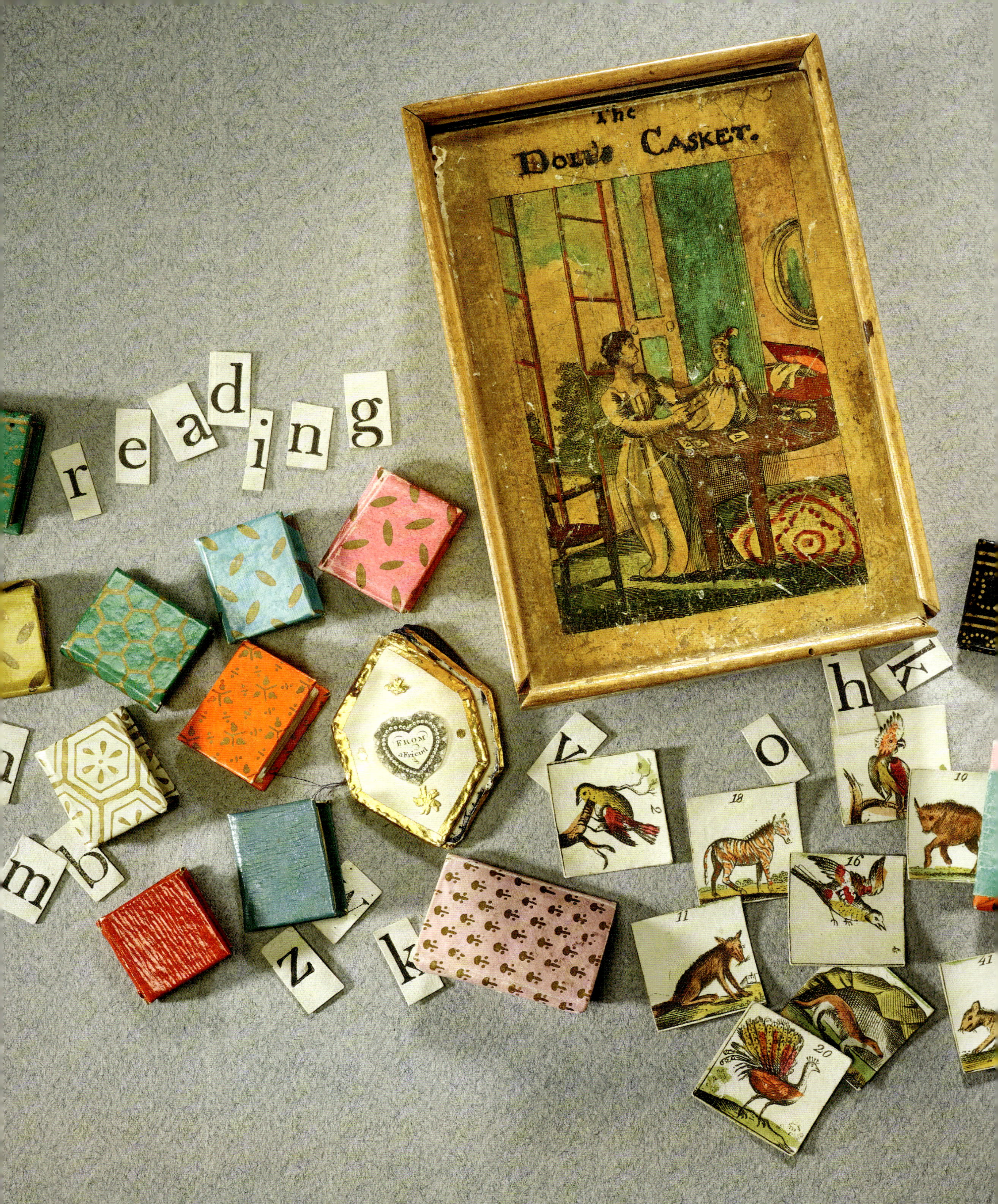
The
DOLL'S CASKET.
reading
FROM
a friend

The Doll's Casket

London: John Marshall, ca. 1810

George Arents Collection

The name of this very rare treasure implies nothing morbid: "casket" is simply an old-fashioned word for a chest or box. This is, in fact, a miniature library containing twelve tiny picture books, each featuring full-page illustrations, engraved and hand-colored. The little library also holds two battledores, or small paddles; packets of paper beasts, birds, and objects; a portfolio of landscapes; a bag of letters to make words with; "a Curious Map of the world"; and a pincushion with twelve pins, six black and six white. An accompanying sheet addressed to the "Doll's Mamma" describes a game: If the doll behaves badly, the owner should stick it with a black pin; if well, with a white one. On achieving all white pins, the doll earns a reward from her casket, and "Thus in time clearly . . . she will become a good doll." While common during the 18th and 19th centuries, most miniature toy chests like this have not survived, with their many pieces having long since been mislaid or destroyed.

Virginia Woolf (1882–1941)
Manuscript draft of
Mrs. Dalloway
October 6, 1922
Virginia Woolf collection of papers, Henry W. and Albert A. Berg Collection of English and American Literature

Mrs. Dalloway (1925) was a groundbreaking achievement for Virginia Woolf. "I might become one of the interesting—I will not say great—but interesting novelists," she wrote in her diary shortly before its publication. Now considered an essential work of modernist literature, the novel—which unfolds on a single summer's day around a shell-shocked war veteran and, separately, a London society matron preparing to host a party—explores consciousness and life after World War I. The origins of *Mrs. Dalloway* are to be found in this notebook. Here, amid the final chapters for her novel *Jacob's Room* (1922) and several book reviews, Woolf penned (with many revisions) "The Prime Minister." This eighteen-page story, along with a single-page outline and some notes on possible revisions, would form the core of Woolf's masterpiece, *Mrs. Dalloway.*

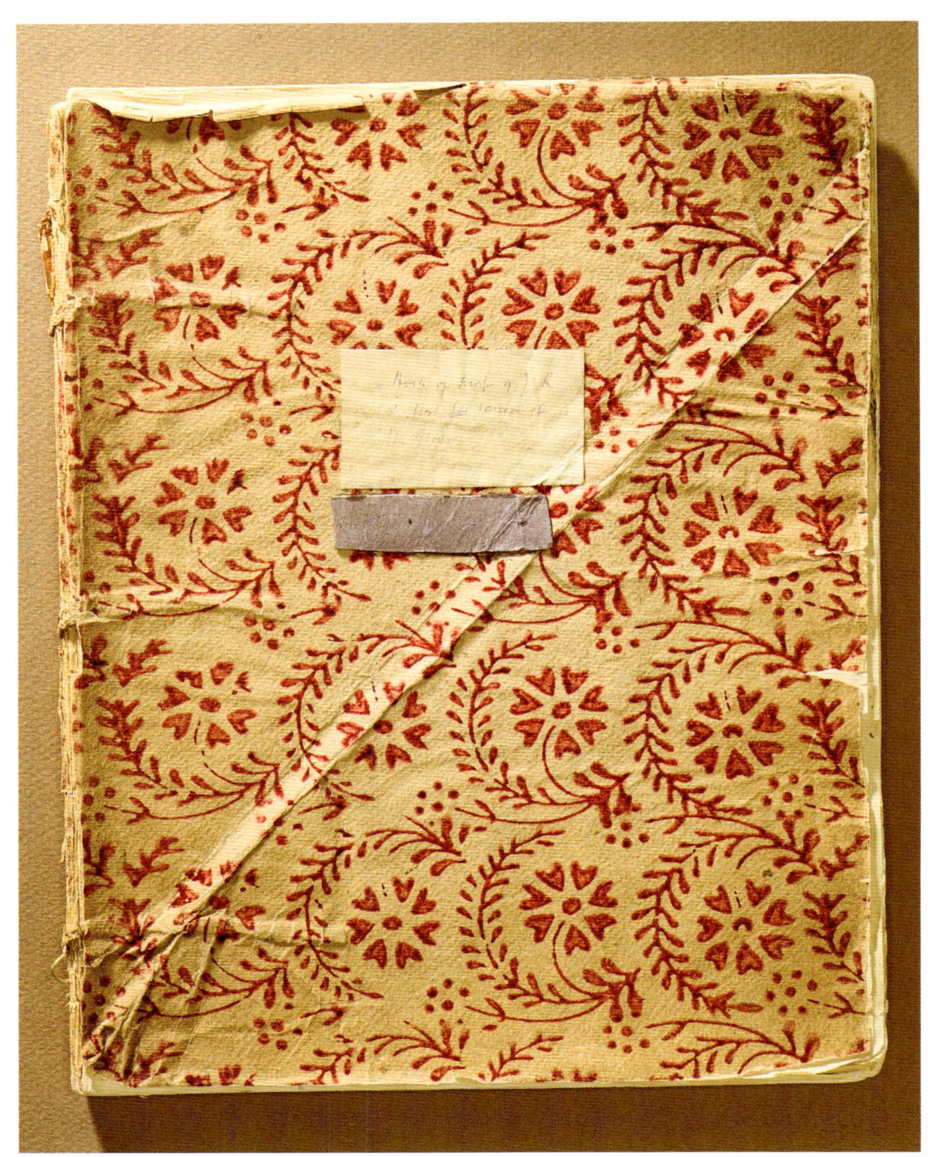

Jacobs Room

March 12th. (added chapter IX a)

Abide with me,
Fast falls the eventide,
The shadows deepen,
Lord with me abide —

"At my place we used to have ~~a hymn~~

Gulls rode gently swaying in ~~litter~~ ~~fo~~ groups of two or three quite near the boat; the cormorant ~~skimmed~~, as if following his long strained neck, skimmed from bay to bay, for the coast was folded into little bays, where the waves break for ever unseen, though the drone of the tide in the caves comes across the water, low, monotonous, like the voice of some one talking to himself.

in eternal pursuit

Rock of ages cleft for me,
Let me hide myself in thee

Public school boys have the old testament almost by heart; nothing pleases them better than to cap quotations; ~~as the~~ loosen the bands which as little boys ~~were~~ ~~tightly~~ tied of them tight: now they are men. They can dare the gods:

Like the ~~tw~~ blunt tooth of some monster a rock broke the surface; brown; overflown with perpetual waterfalls; ~~It~~

Rock of ages.

Jacob sang, lying on his back, ~~with his~~ looking up into the sky at midday; from which every shred of cloud had been withdrawn. It was ~~immaculate~~, eternal, ~~as if~~ like something permanent, with the displayed

Virginia Woolf's walking stick

Wood, before 1941

Henry W. and Albert A. Berg Collection of English and American Literature

In early 1941, wartime rationing and isolation exacerbated Virginia Woolf's depression, and she began to feel she had "lost all power over words." In the late morning of March 28, Woolf put on her fur coat, took her walking stick, and left suicide notes for her husband, Leonard, and sister, Vanessa. "I want to tell you that you have given me complete happiness . . . But I know that I shall never get over this: & I am wasting your life. It is this madness," she wrote Leonard. She then walked to the nearby river Ouse, put a large stone in her pocket, and either walked or leapt into the water. Leonard found her walking stick that afternoon, but her body was not recovered until three weeks later.

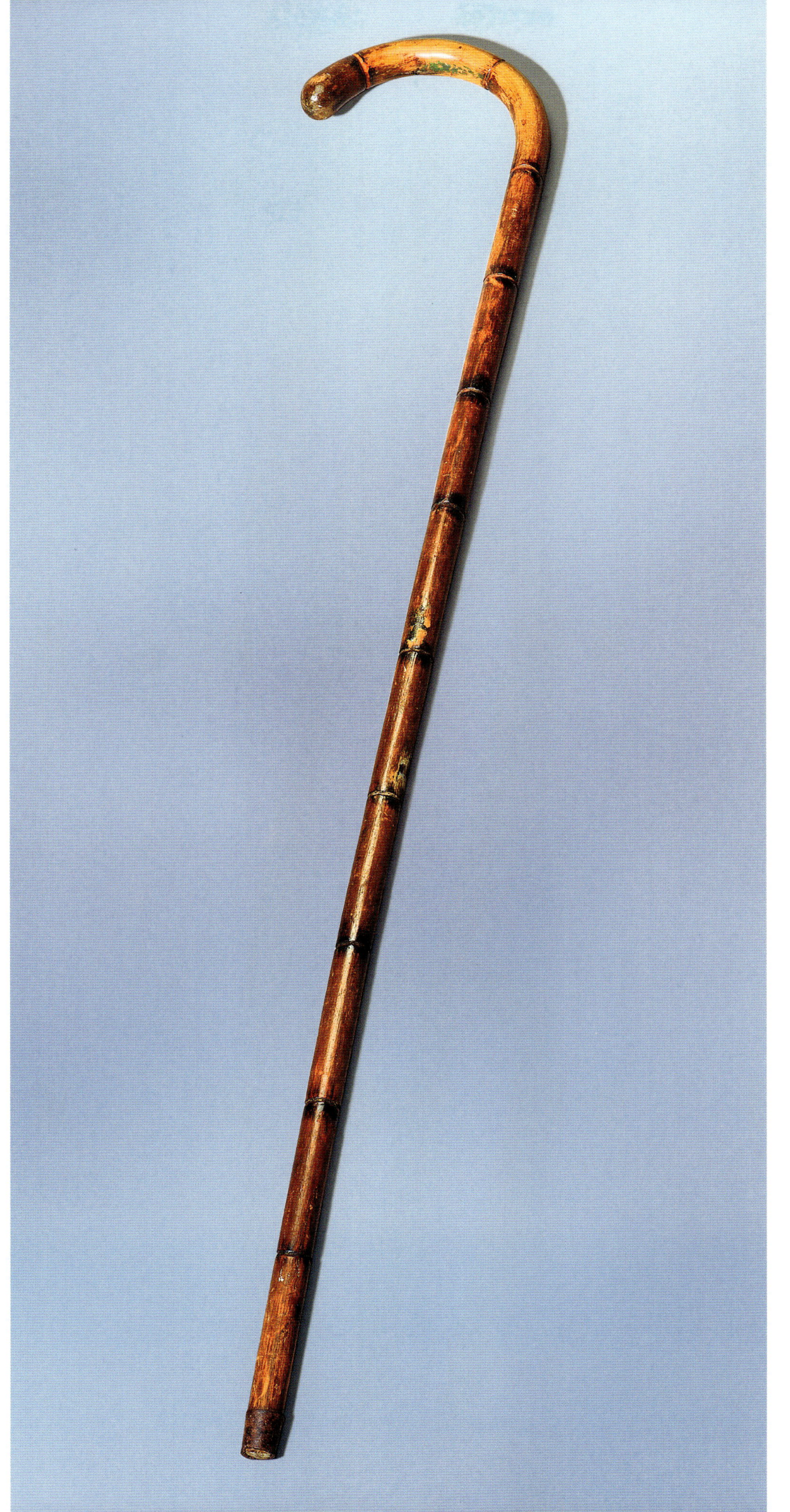

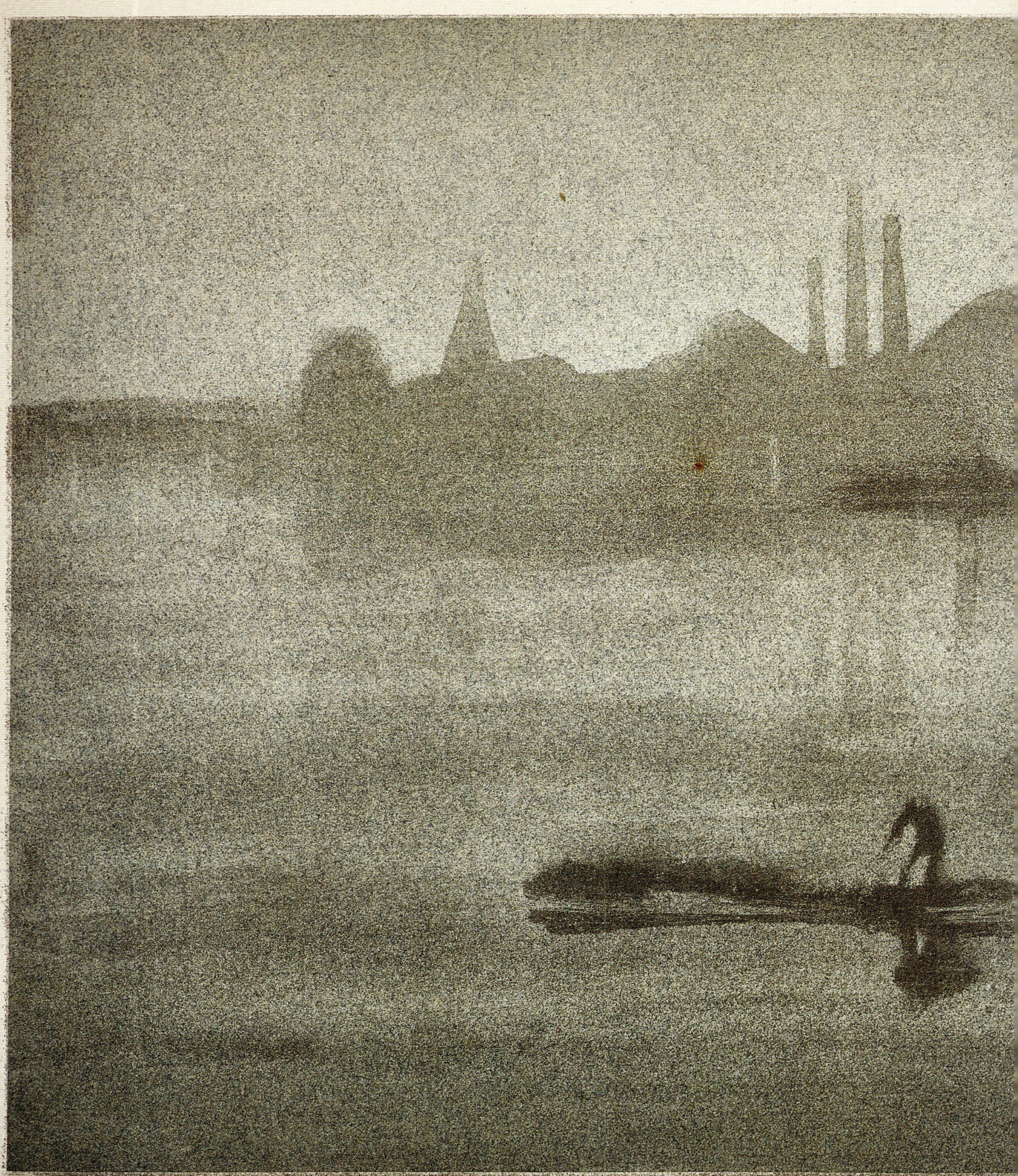

James Abbott McNeill Whistler (1834–1903)
Nocturne
Lithotint on blue chine, 1878
The Miriam and Ira D. Wallach Division of Art, Prints and Photographs, Print Collection

American-born James Abbott McNeill Whistler studied art in Paris and then moved to London, where he pursued printmaking with the same seriousness as painting. Fascinated by turns with the lagoons of Venice and the Thames of London, Whistler strove to capture the moody qualities of the fog, mist, and veils of humidity around these great bodies of water. Using washes applied directly to the lithography stone, and manipulating them with additions of crayon and abrasions that created highlights, Whistler simulated in print the atmospheric nuances that he achieved in his paintings. Initially, Whistler called his images of the river at nighttime "moonlights," but he later adopted the term "nocturne," which he liked because of its association with a form of abstraction linked to music. With the gift of the Library's Avery Collection, the Wallach Division inherited one of the world's most distinguished holdings of Whistler prints.

Sean O'Casey and George Bernard Shaw at the opening night of O'Casey's *Within the Gates*, Royalty Theatre, London

1934

Henry W. and Albert A. Berg Collection of English and American Literature

The playwrights Sean O'Casey and George Bernard Shaw enjoyed a twenty-four-year friendship. Although quite different in temperament, they were alike in their Protestant backgrounds, socialist politics, and fierce renunciation of their native Ireland—at the time this photograph was taken, they were expatriates living in London. Both were prolific: Shaw wrote more than fifty plays and O'Casey, more than twenty, plus six volumes of autobiography. Eileen O'Casey, the playwright's widow, recalled that "their sense of humor—and it was a cruel sense of humor, to be sure—was so close they seemed to be reading each other's minds." Despite their enduring friendship, Shaw and O'Casey were rarely photographed together; this is one of only two known images of the dramatists in each other's company. The Berg Collection has the largest collection of O'Casey manuscript materials in the world, as well as a major Shaw archive.

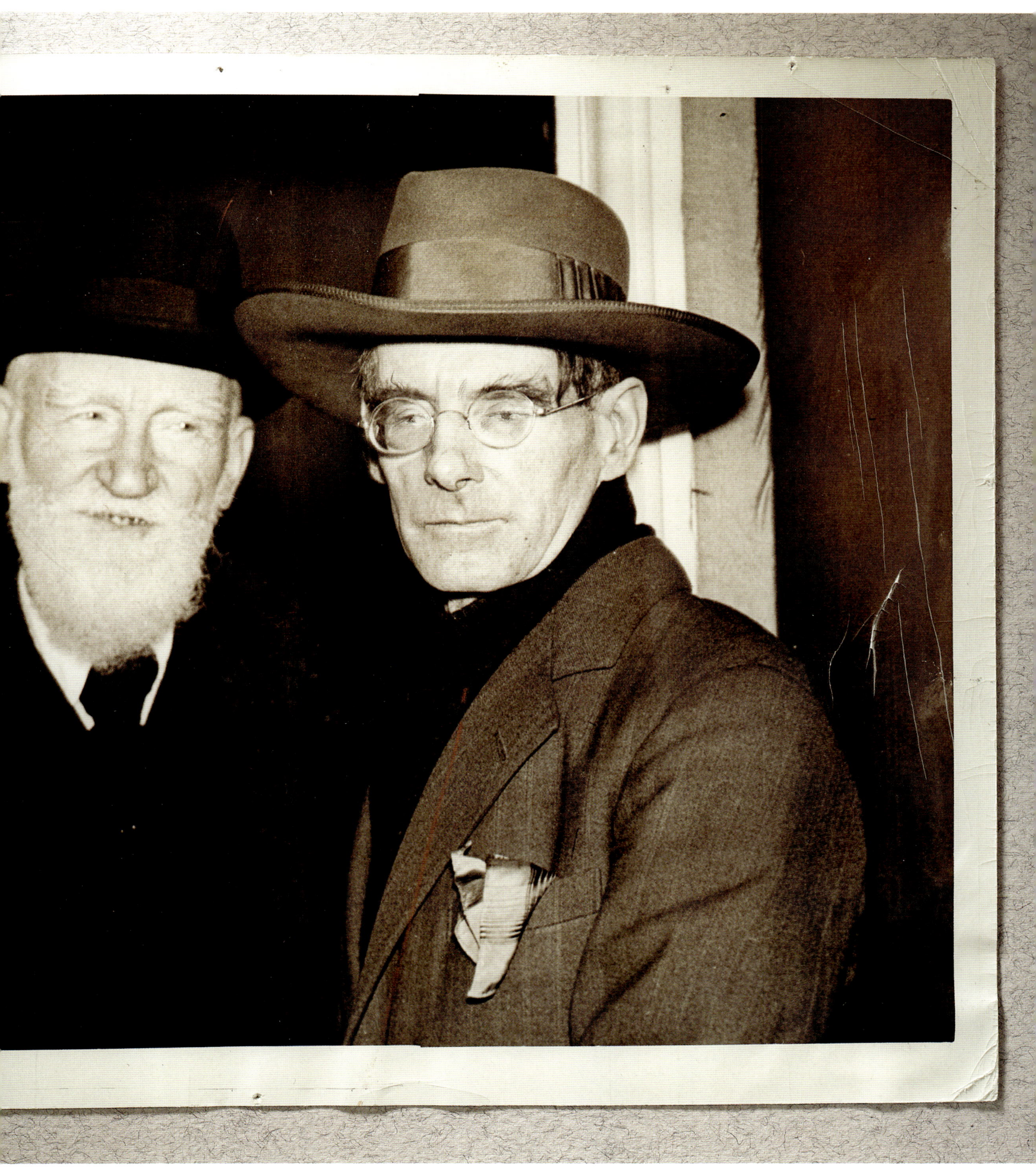

The Wild Swans at Coole

I

The trees are in their autumn beauty,
The woodland paths are dry,
Under the October twilight the water
Mirrors a still sky;
Upon the brimming water among the stones
Are nine & fifty swans

II

The nineteenth autumn has come upon me
Since I first made my count;
I saw, before I had well finished,
All suddenly mount
And scatter wheeling in great broken rings
Upon their clamorous wings

III

I have looked upon those brilliant creatures
And now my heart is sore,
All's changed since I, hearing at twilight
The first time on this shore,
The bell-beat of their wings above my head
Trod with a lighter tread.

~~III~~ IV

Unwearied now, lovers by lovers,
They paddle in the cold
Companionable streams or climb the air;
Their hearts have not grown old;
Passion or conquest wander where they will
Attend upon them still.

William Butler Yeats (1865–1939)

Manuscript of "The Wild Swans at Coole"

1917

Henry W. and Albert A. Berg Collection of English and American Literature

When John Butler Yeats, the portrait painter and father of William Butler Yeats, visited New York in 1907, he refused to return to his native Ireland. Instead, he spent the remaining fifteen years of his life in the city under the patronage of his friend John Quinn, a corporate lawyer and prodigious collector of art and manuscripts. Through an informal arrangement with W.B. Yeats, Quinn paid John Butler Yeats's bills in return for original manuscripts of the poet's work. In July 1919, W.B. Yeats sent Quinn a package containing a mixture of working drafts and fair copies of all of the poems that make up the volume *The Wild Swans at Coole*. Shown here is the fair copy of the title poem. John Quinn's papers are held in the Library's Manuscripts and Archives Division, and Augustus John's 1909 portrait of Quinn hangs on the east wall of the Edna Barnes Salomon Room.

Gisèle Freund (1908–2000)
Photograph of James Joyce chatting with Sylvia Beach, the owner of Shakespeare and Company, and Adrienne Monnier
1938
Henry W. and Albert A. Berg Collection of English and American Literature

Sylvia Beach published James Joyce's *Ulysses* in 1922 under the imprint of her bookshop, Shakespeare and Company, 12 rue de l'Odeon, Paris. In 1938, Beach's longtime partner, Adrienne Monnier, suggested that Gisèle Freund photograph Joyce in advance of the publication of his subsequent novel, *Finnegans Wake*. This is one of a series of photographs that Freund, who had become Monnier's partner in 1936, took of Joyce, Beach, and Monnier in conversation at Shakespeare and Company, which by then had become a famous center of literary modernism. Joyce, who was notoriously averse to having his photograph taken, became comfortable enough with Freund to invite her to photograph him at home, and her portraits are considered to be the most intimate images of the author. One of Freund's portraits of Joyce appeared on the cover of *Time* magazine on May 8, 1939.

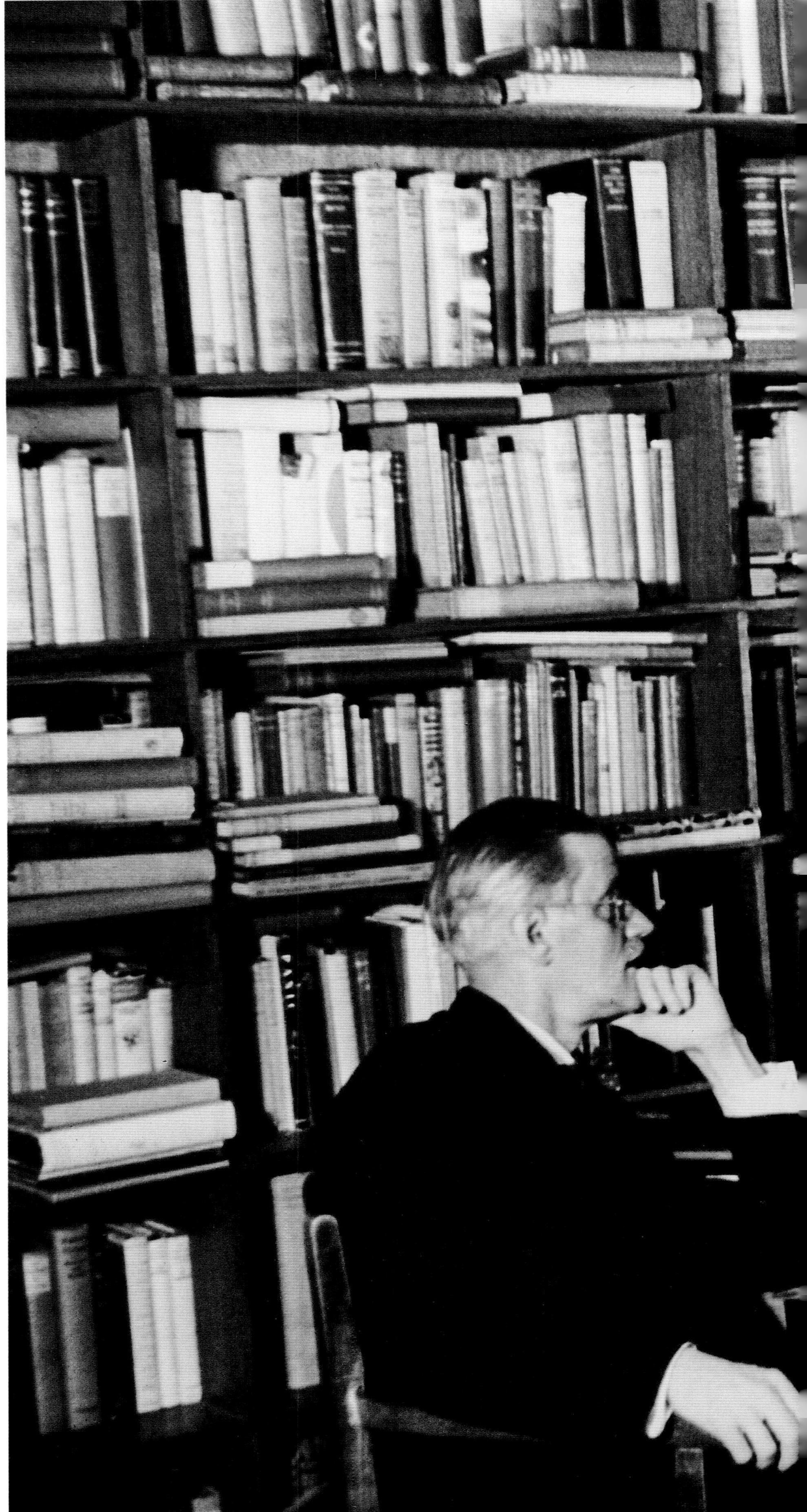

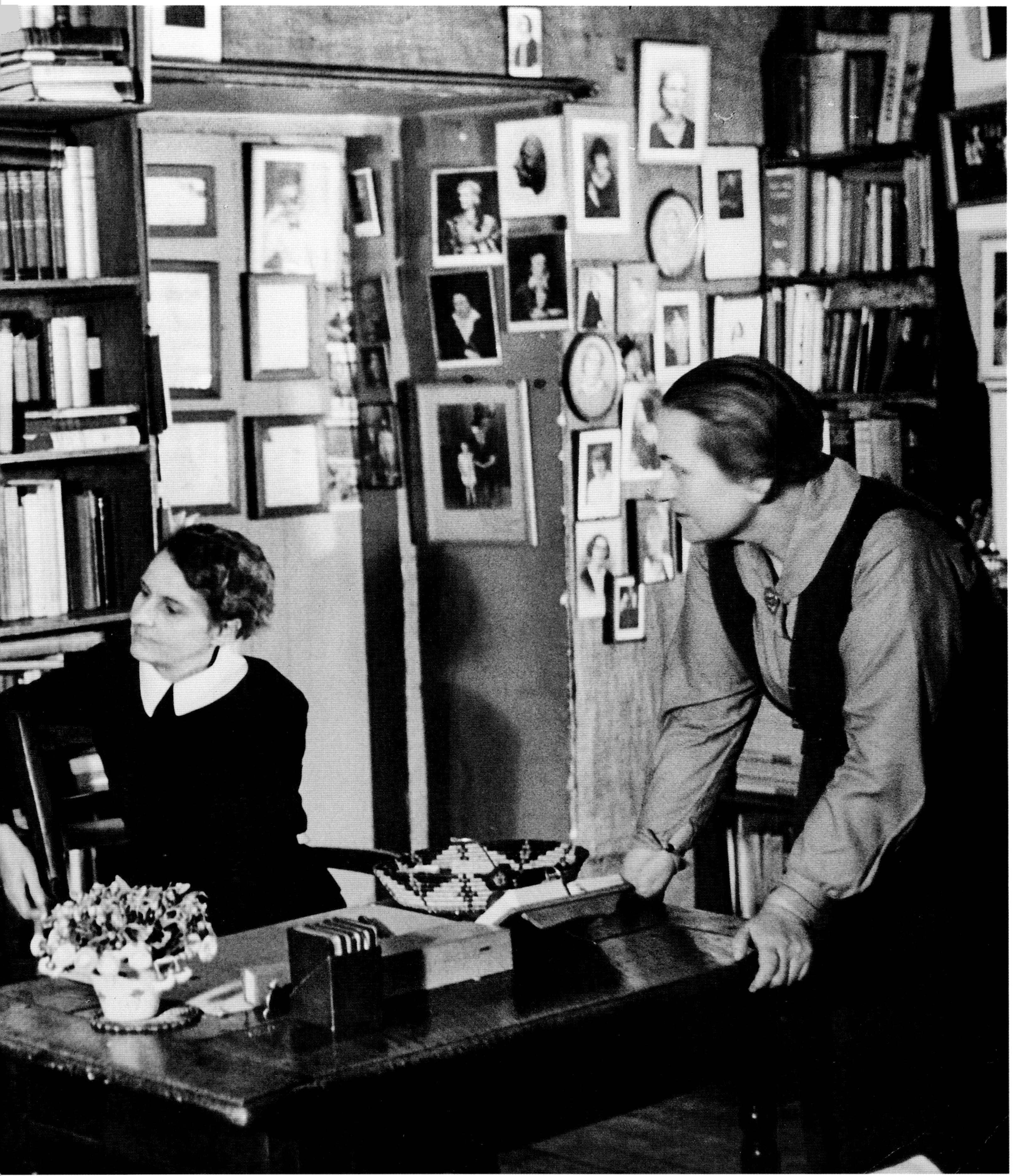

Fisher King
~~King Fishing~~

Here is the man with three staves, and here the Wheel,
And here is the one-eyed merchant, and this card,
Which is blank, is something he carries on his back,
Which I am forbidden to see. I look in vain
For the Hanged Man. Fear death by water.
I see crowds of people, walking round in a ring.
(I John saw these things, and heard them).
Thank you. If you see dear Mrs. Equitone,
Tell her I bring the horoscope myself,
One must be so careful these days.

Unreal
~~Terrible~~ City, I have sometimes seen and see
Under the brown fog of your winter dawn
A crowd flow over London Bridge, so many,
I had not thought death had undone so many.
Sighs, short and infrequent, were ~~expired~~, ~~exhaled~~ ~~expired~~ exhaled.
And each ~~one~~ ~~kept~~ his eyes before his feet. (~~held~~ fixed; man)
Flowed up the hill and down King William Street,
~~To where Saint Mary Woolnoth kept the time~~
~~With a dead sound on the final stroke of nine.~~
There I saw one I knew, and stopped him, crying: "Stetson!
"You who were with me in the ships at Mylae!
"That corpse you planted last year in your garden,
"Has it begun to sprout? Will it bloom this year?"
"Or has the sudden frost disturbed its bed?
"Oh keep the Dog far hence, that's ~~foe~~ to men,
"Or with his nails he'll dig it up again!
"You! hypocrite lecteur, - mon semblable, - mon frere!"

Blake. Too often used

J.J.

yet?

T.S. Eliot (1888–1965)

Manuscript draft of *The Waste Land*

1914–1922

Henry W. and Albert A. Berg Collection of English and American Literature

The Waste Land—one of the most important poems of the 20th century—began as a "hoard of fragments." Eliot commenced working on the long poem in 1914 and closely guarded this, the only draft, for the next eight years he devoted to it. Only his first wife, Vivienne, and fellow poet Ezra Pound—both of whom left comments and revisions in the margins of the text—were privy to the minutiae of Eliot's process. Eliot drafted the poem in the hours he could find outside of his five-and-a-half-day workweek as a clerk at Lloyd's Bank in London (the "Unreal City" of Eliot's masterpiece), and it was eventually published in 1922. The following year, Virginia Woolf set the type for the first book edition of the poem, which was published by her Hogarth Press. "I think he believes in 'living phrases' & their difference from dead ones," she recorded in her diary after their first meeting.

***The Champion of England at the Coronation of His Majesty George IV* panorama**

Hand-painted etching and wood, 1821

The Carl H. Pforzheimer Collection of Shelley and His Circle

This rolled panorama could be described as a prototype moving picture, although it moves very slowly. As viewers pulled the paper scroll from its boxwood drum, they saw unfurl not just the "Champion of England" on his white horse but the whole procession of courtiers, musical instruments, and attendants at the coronation of George IV. They include the king's herb woman and six maids, the high constable and dean's beadle of Westminster, fifes, drums, drum major, eight trumpets, kettle drum, six clerks in Chancery, the King's chaplains—and on it goes, for more than nine feet of hand-painted etching. The panorama is as orderly as George's youth had been unrestrained—though both are quite colorful.

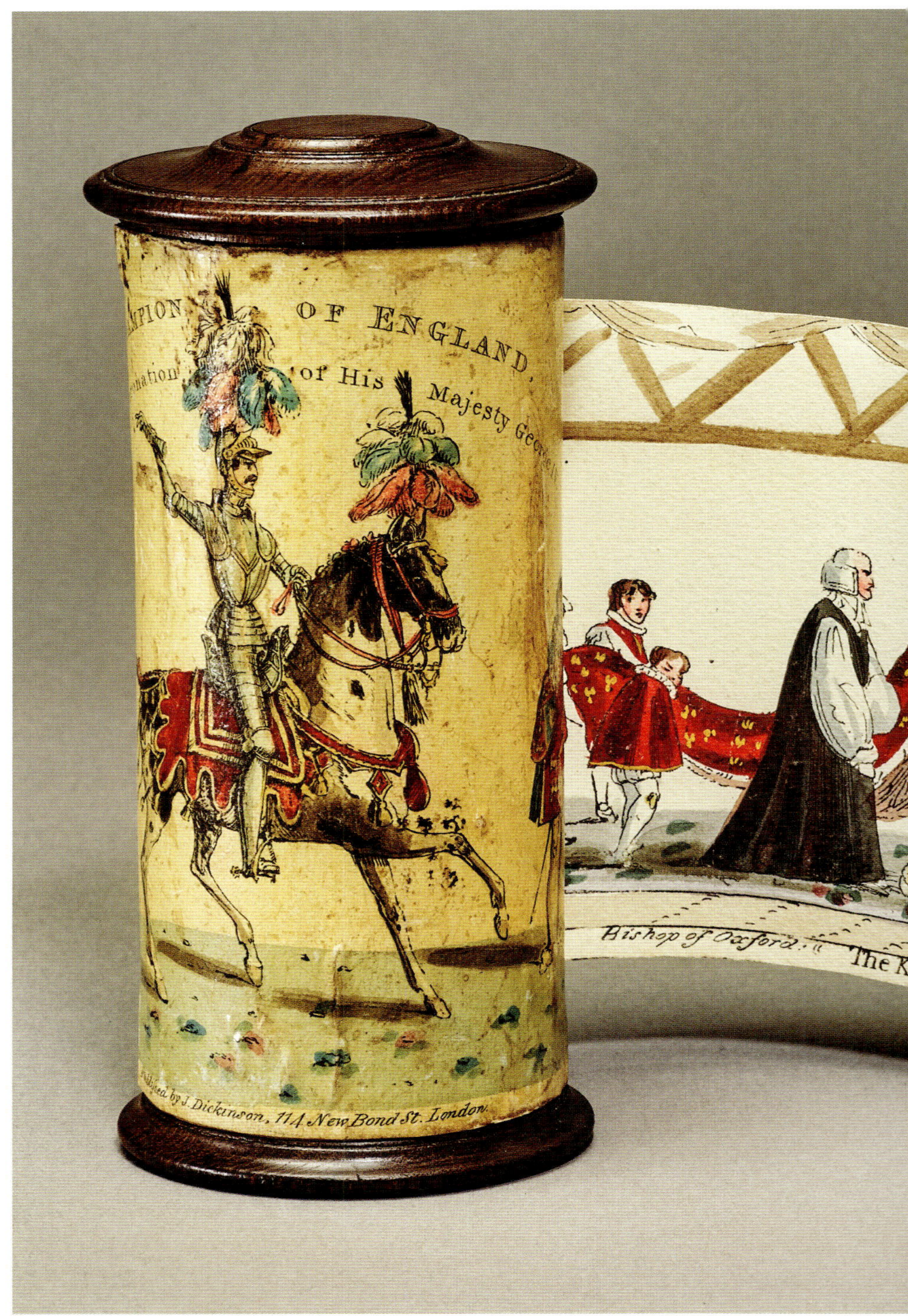

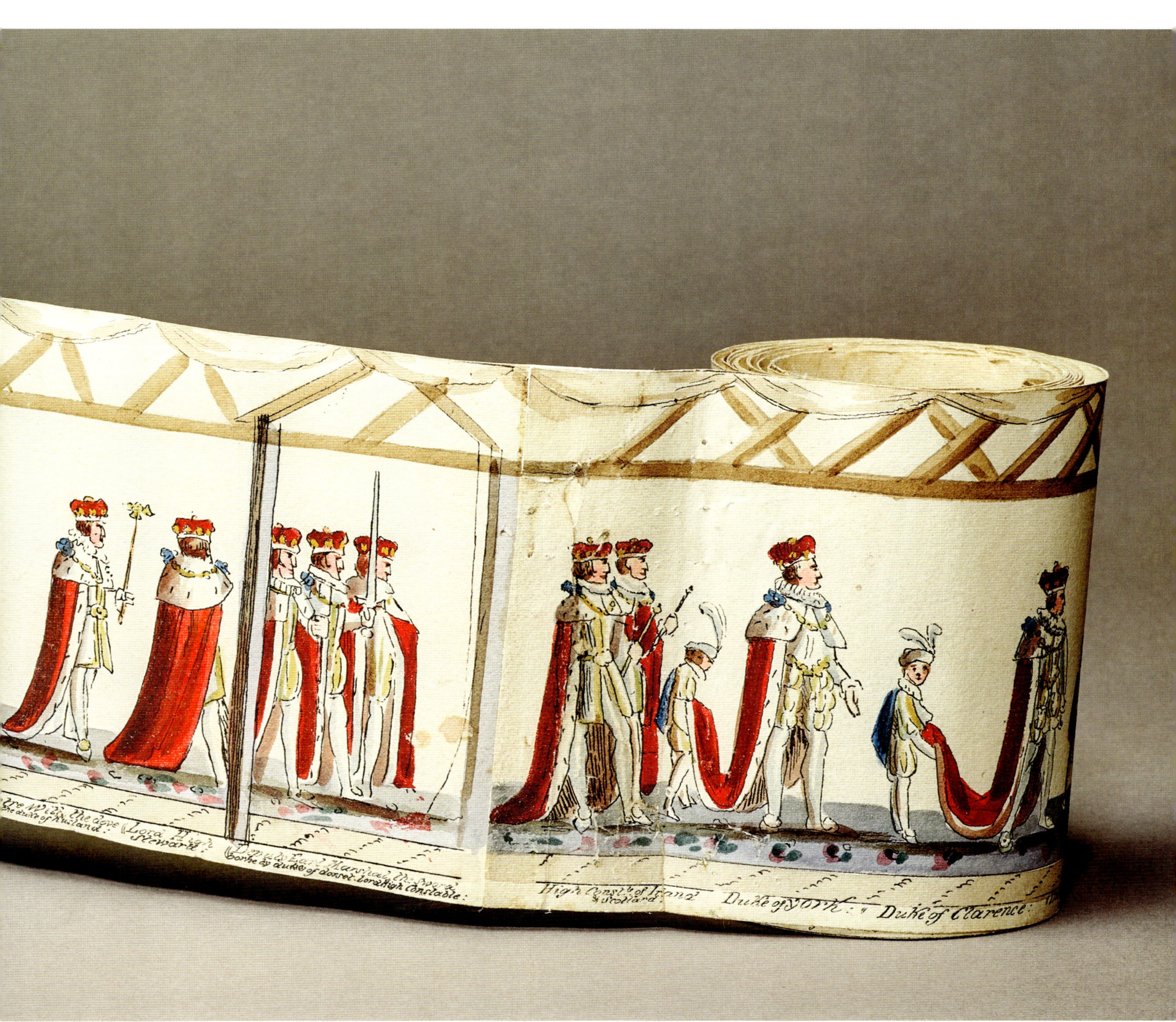

Lord High Steward
Borne by Duke of Dorset. Lord High Constable
Duke of York
Duke of Clarence

Mark Twain (1835–1910)

Manuscript of *A Connecticut Yankee in King Arthur's Court*

1887

Henry W. and Albert A. Berg Collection of English and American Literature

Shown here are three pages from the autograph manuscript of *A Connecticut Yankee in King Arthur's Court,* published in 1889, which Mark Twain characterized as "one vast sardonic laugh at the trivialities, the servilities of our poor human race." The novel is a satiric fable about the inevitable defeat of progress by human nature, an attack on feudalism and monarchy, and a celebration of democratic values. The 932-page manuscript contains numerous revisions and many passages that were suppressed from the first edition. One change indicates that Twain may have originally intended to locate the action in "Astolat" rather than Camelot. The moment in the novel in which Hank Morgan, its central character, discovers that he is in Camelot and not Bridgeport is memorialized on a Library Way plaque (on New York City's 41st Street, between Fifth and Park Avenues). The Berg Collection has 49 portraits of Twain, more than 80 of his autograph and typed manuscripts, a diary, notebook, and nearly 500 of his letters.

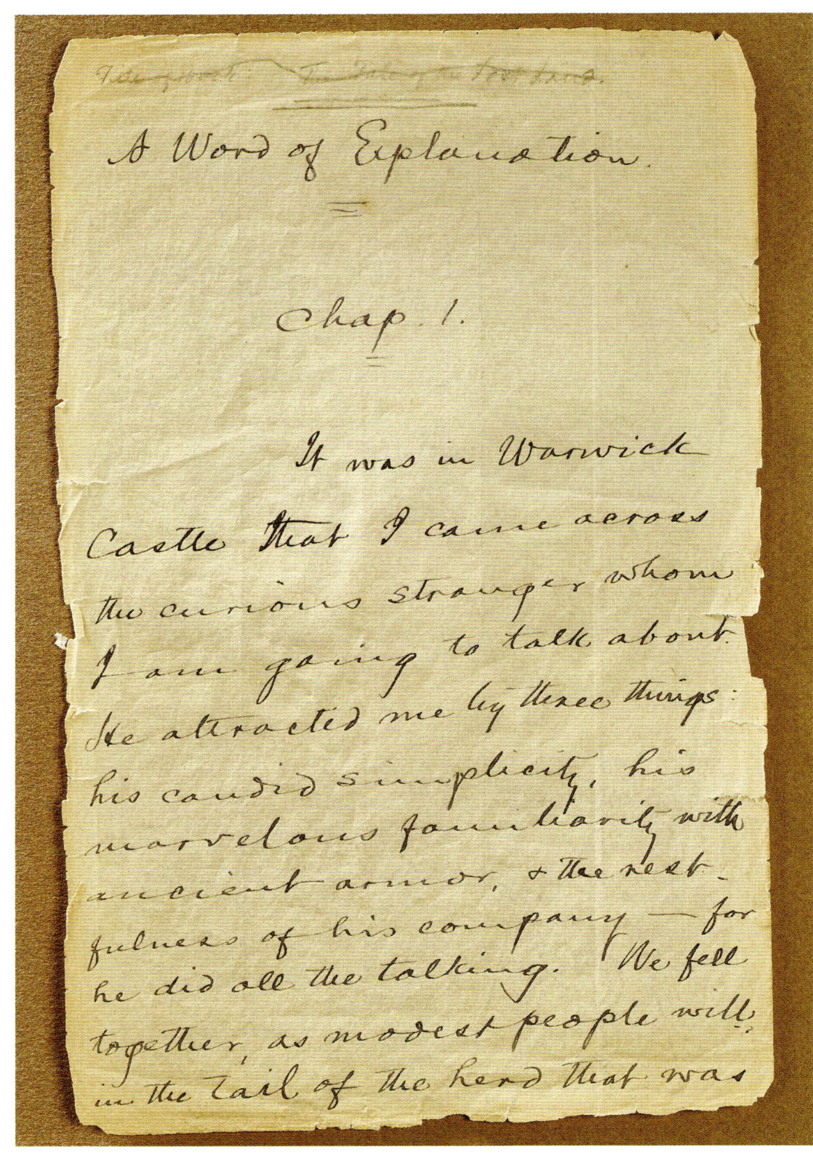

A Word of Explanation.

Chap. 1.

It was in Warwick Castle that I came across the curious stranger whom I am going to talk about. He attracted me by three things: his candid simplicity, his marvelous familiarity with ancient armor, & the restfulness of his company — for he did all the talking. We fell together, as modest people will, in the tail of the herd that was

5

"Wit ye well, I saw it done." Then, after a pause, added: "I did it myself."

~~When I~~

By the time I had recovered from the ~~electric~~ surprise of this remark, he was gone.

All that evening I sat by my fire at the Warwick Arms, steeped in a dream of the olden time, while the rain beat upon the windows & the wind roared about the eaves & corners. From time to time I dipped into old Sir Thomas Mallory's enchanting book, & fed at its rich feast of prodigies & adventures, ~~rolled its sweet marvels under my tongue~~, breathed-in the fragrance of its obsolete names, & dreamed again. Midnight being come at length, I read three ~~one~~ more

18

we never came to any asylum — so I was up a stump, as you may say. I asked him how far we were from Hartford. He said he had never heard of the place; which I took to be a lie. At the end of an hour we saw a far-away town sleeping in a valley by a winding river; & beyond it, on a hill, a vast gray fortress, with towers & turrets, the first I had ever seen, out of a picture.

"Bridgeport?" said I, pointing. "Camelot," ~~"Astolat,"~~ said he. 4

~~Next p. is p. 2 of Notes~~

~~Go to page 2 of "NOTES."~~

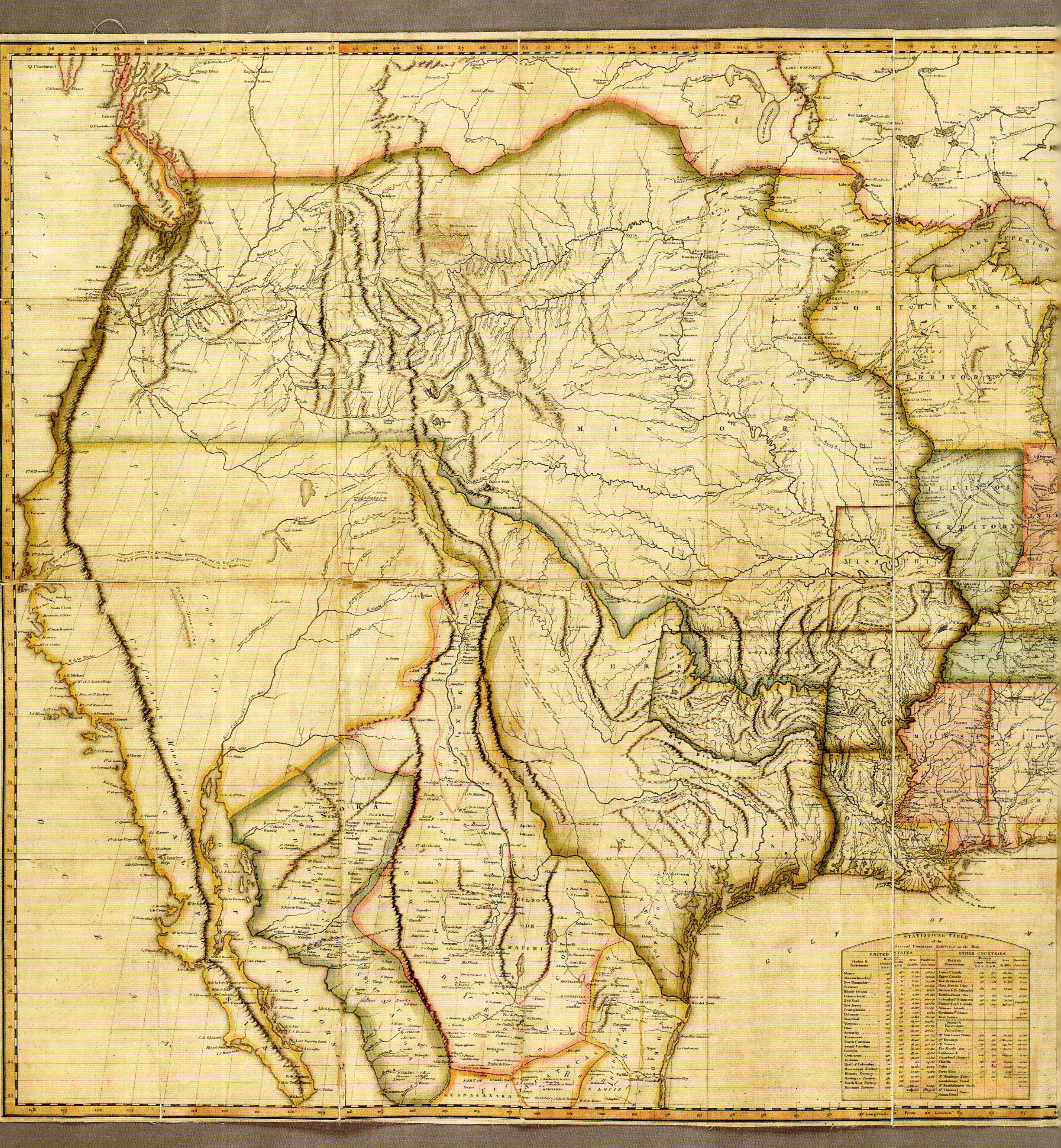

LAKE SUPERIOR
NORTH WEST
TERRITORY
ILLINOIS
TERRITORY
GULF
STATISTICAL TABLE

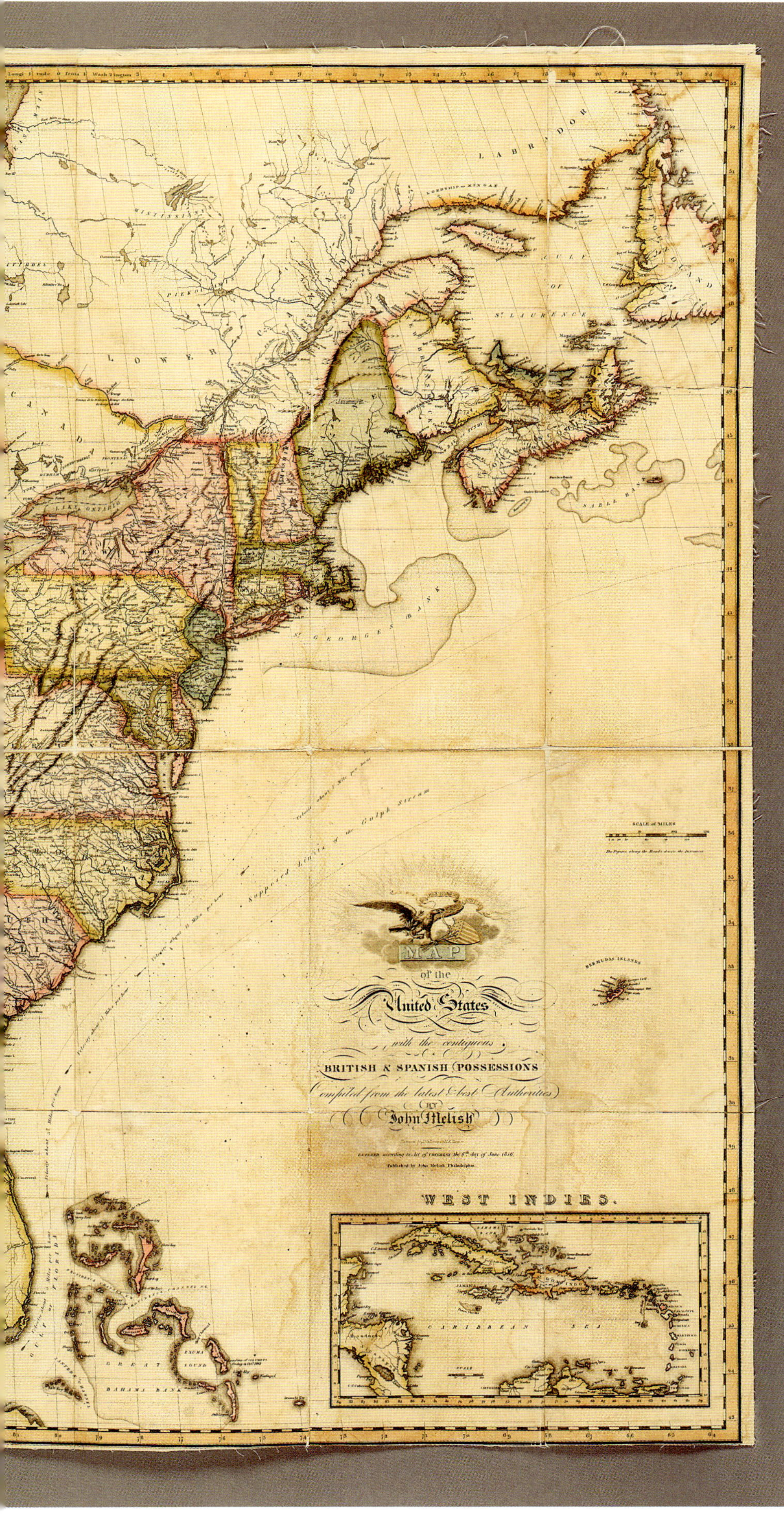

John Melish (1771–1822)
Map of the United States with the contiguous British & Spanish possessions
1816 (2nd state)
Lionel Pincus and Princess Firyal Map Division

John Melish's map is regarded as the single most important and influential map of America published in the 19th century, notable not only for its extraordinary geographic accuracy but also for its powerful visual representations of what would later be termed Manifest Destiny. In the expansionist spirit brought on by victory in the War of 1812, Melish dramatically broadened the geographical frame of the republic, extending the nascent country to the Pacific Coast and embracing areas then recognized as Spanish or British dominions. Thomas Jefferson and James Madison celebrated the map's grandeur. Melish's vision proved prophetic: a later edition of this map was used to finalize the borders of the United States and New Spain under the Adams–Onís Treaty of 1819. The Library's copy contains manuscript annotations and coloring that update the map to show the admissions of Alabama (1819) and Missouri (1821) to the Union.

George Catlin (1796–1872)
North American Indian Portfolio. Hunting Scenes and Amusements of the Rocky Mountains and Prairies of America
London: C. & J. Adlard for George Catlin, 1844
Rare Book Division

Beginning in 1830, the artist George Catlin spent eight years traveling among the indigenous peoples of the Great Plains, observing and painting their way of life. On his return to the East, he exhibited his work in major cities such as Pittsburgh, Cincinnati, and New York, while also delivering public lectures that drew on his western experiences. These endeavors were well attended but failed to turn a profit, and Catlin soon found himself in debt.

In the hopes of improving his financial situation, Catlin traveled to Great Britain and had a selection of his paintings reproduced as hand-colored lithographs. He planned to sell this suite of prints, titled the *North American Indian Portfolio*, to well-heeled English subscribers. The plan did little to alleviate his monetary woes, however, as the project failed to elicit the anticipated interest. Nonetheless, in spite of Catlin's business failings, his artwork remains prized today for its vivid depiction of Native American culture.

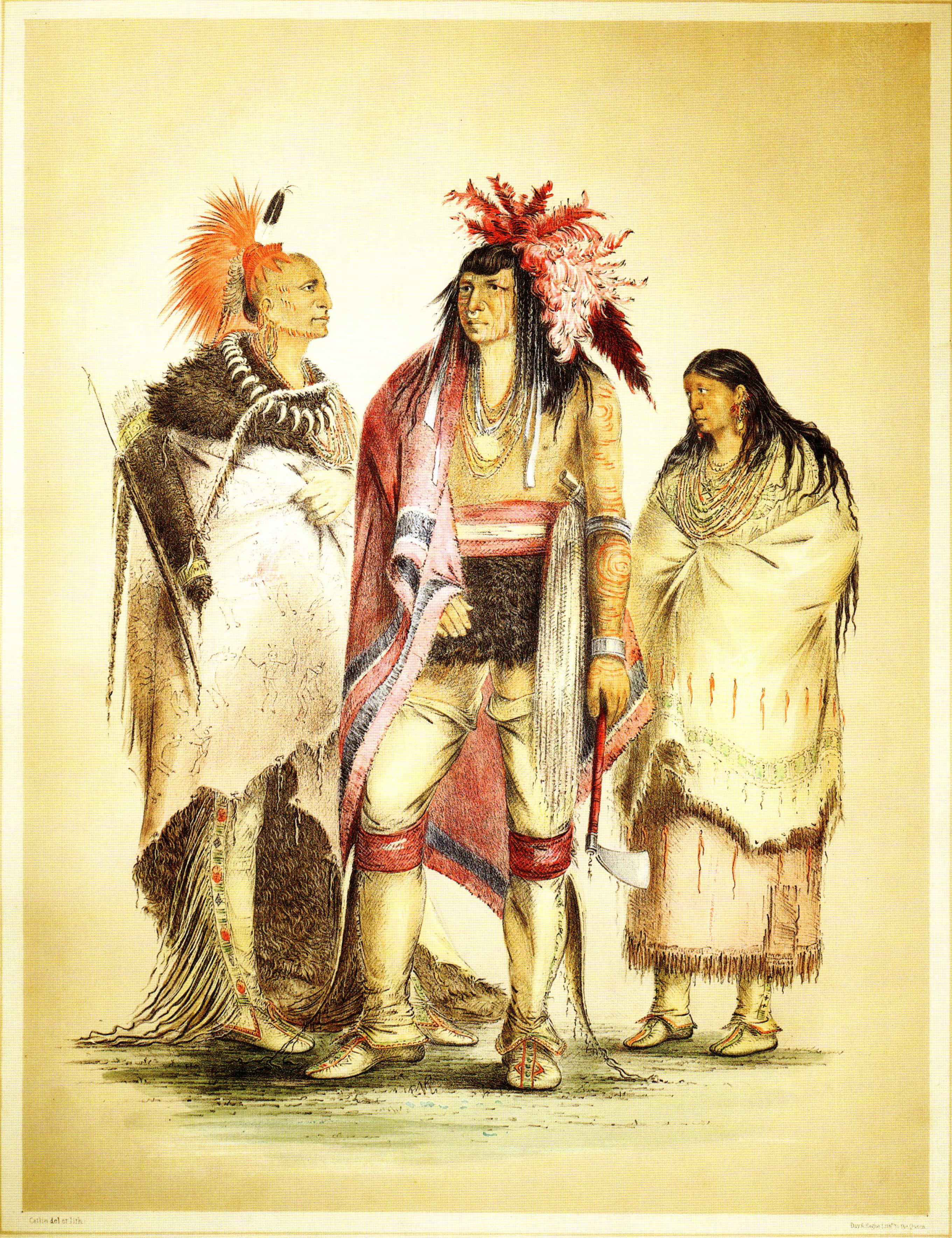
Catlin del et lith.
Day & Haghe Lithrs to the Queen
No 1.

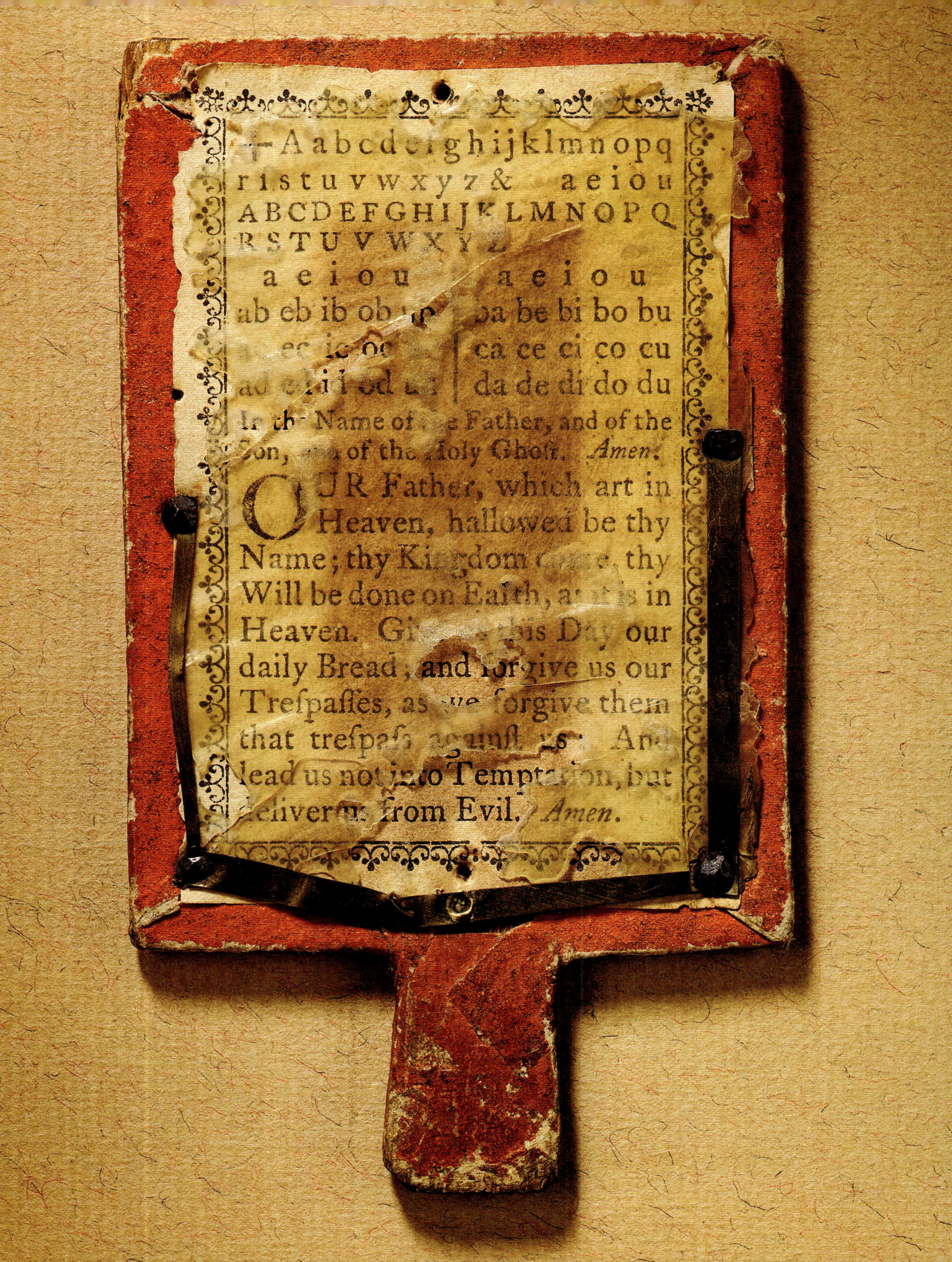
Aabcdefghijklmnopq
ristuvwxyz& aeiou
ABCDEFGHIJ LMNOPQ
RSTUVWXY
aeiou aeiou
ab eb ib ob
ba be bi bo bu
ca ce ci co cu
da de di do du
Name of Father, and of the
of the Amen.
OUR Father, which art in
Heaven, hallowed be thy
Name; thy Kingdom thy
Will be done on Earth, in
Heaven. Day our
daily Bread; and forgive us our
Trefpaffes, as forgive them
that trefpafs
lead us not into Temptation, but
from Evil. Amen.

Hornbook
18th century
Rare Book Division

Hornbooks, a form of children's primer, were common in America and England from the late 16th to the late 18th centuries. These small works consisted of a paddle-shaped wooden frame on which was mounted a single sheet of paper or vellum (calfskin) featuring the alphabet and Lord's Prayer. The object's name itself derived from the thin, transparent piece of cow's horn that served to overlay and protect the text.

Like many childhood possessions, hornbooks lived a hard life. Typically hung from a youth's neck or waist and subjected to regular use, they did not often withstand the rigors of childhood, and this example represents a rare survival.

The New-England primer enlarged. For the more easy attaining the true reading of English. To which is added, the Assembly of divines catechism

Boston: S. Kneeland, & T. Green, 1727

Rare Book Division

The New-England Primer was first printed in Boston around 1690. It became one of the most successful children's textbooks published in America during the 18th and early 19th centuries. Although the content of this small, pocket-size volume varied slightly from one edition to the next, it typically contained a mix of secular and religious subjects—reading instruction coupled with moral lessons and Christian catechism. This amalgam of the spiritual and earthly reflected the staunch faith from which it sprang, as the Puritans of New England believed the act of reading the Bible to be a central tenet of achieving salvation.

The millions of copies of the primer sold often fell victim to heavy use, and relatively few survive. This 1727 printing held by the Rare Book Division is the earliest known dated example.

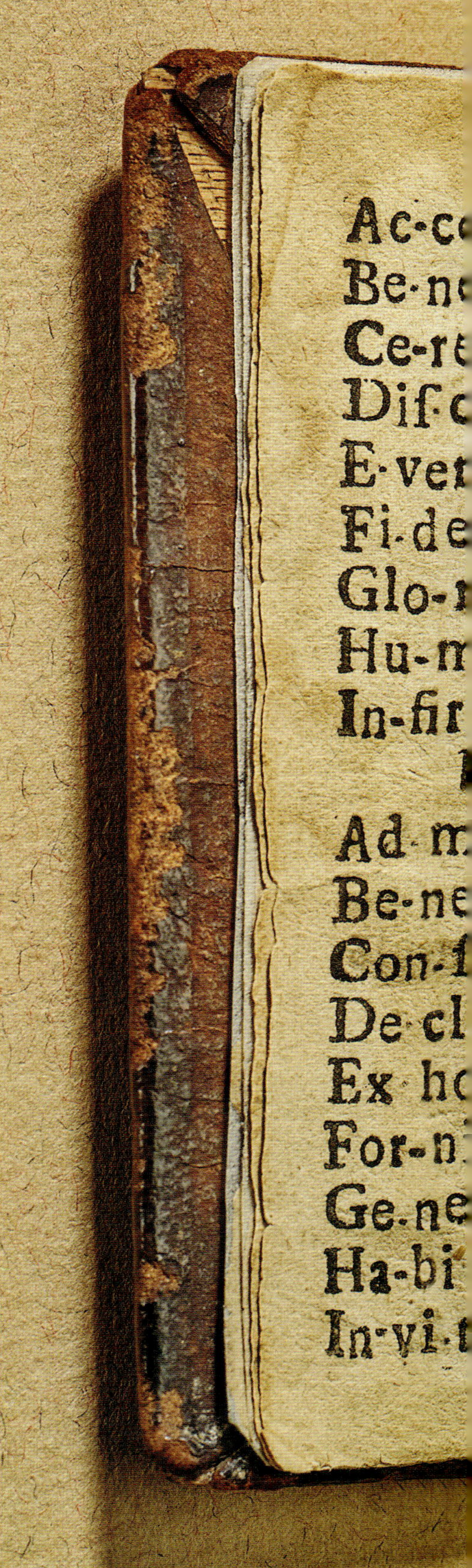

four Syllables.

Accompany
Benevolence
Ceremony
d Diſcontented
Everlaſting
Fidelity
Glorifying
Humility
Infirmity.

five Syllables.

Admiration
Beneficial
Conſolation
Declaration
Exhortation
Fornication
Generation
Habitation
Invitation

A — In *Adam's* Fall
We Sinned all.

B — Thy Life to Mend
This *Book* Attend.

C — The *Cat* doth play
And after ſlay.

D — A *Dog* will bite
A Thief at night.

E — An *Eagles* flight
Is out of ſight.

F — The Idle *Fool*
Is whipt at School.

A Declaration by the Representatives of the UNITED STATES OF AMERICA in General Congress assembled.

When in the course of human events it becomes necessary for one people to dissolve the political bands which have connected them with another, and to assume among the powers of the earth the separate and equal station to which the laws of nature & of nature's god entitle them, a decent respect to the opinions of mankind requires that they should declare the causes which impel them to the separation.

We hold these truths to be self evident; that all men are created equal; that they are endowed by their Creator with inherent & inalienable rights; that among these are life, liberty, & the pursuit of happiness; that to secure these rights, governments are instituted among men, deriving their just powers from the consent of the governed; that whenever any form of government becomes destructive of these ends, it is the right of the people to alter or to abolish it, and to institute new government, laying it's foundation on such principles & organising it's powers in such form as to them shall seem most likely to effect their safety & happiness. prudence indeed will dictate that governments long established should not be changed for light & transient causes. and accordingly all experience hath shewn that mankind are more disposed to suffer while evils are sufferable, [illegible] themselves by abolishing the forms [illegible] they are accustomed. but when a long train of abuses & usurpations, begun at a distinguished period, & pursuing invariably the same object, evinces a design to reduce them under absolute despotism, it is their right, it is their duty, to throw off such government & to provide new guards for their future security. such has been the patient sufferance of these colonies; & such is now the necessity which constrains them to expunge their former systems of government. the history of the present king of Great Britain, is a history of unremitting injuries & usurpations, among which appears no solitary fact to contradict the uniform tenor of the rest; but all have in direct object the establishment of an absolute tyranny over these states. to prove this let facts be submitted to a candid world, for the truth of which we pledge a faith yet unsullied by falsehood.

He has refused his assent to laws the most wholesome & necessary for the public good:

he has forbidden his governors to pass laws of immediate & pressing importance, unless suspended in their operation till his assent should be obtained; & when so suspended, he has neglected utterly to attend to them.

he has refused to pass other laws for the accomodation of large districts of people, unless those people would relinquish the right of representation in the legislature, a right inestimable to them & formidable to tyrants only:

Thomas Jefferson (1743–1826)

Jefferson's handwritten copy of the Declaration of Independence

1776

Manuscripts and Archives Division

On June 11, 1776, the Second Continental Congress appointed a committee in Philadelphia to draft a statement announcing the complete and utter breaking away of the thirteen American colonies from the British government. Thomas Jefferson quickly assumed the role of primary author; the other four members, John Adams, Benjamin Franklin, Roger Sherman, and Robert R. Livingston, made minor verbal suggestions. The text underwent a number of changes and deletions before Congress ratified the document on the fourth of July. In the following days, Jefferson made several copies—reinstating the excised text—and sent them to five or six friends. In the Library's copy, Jefferson underlined the restored passages, including one that castigates King George III for "obtruding" slavery and the slave trade (an "execrable commerce") on the colonies. Jefferson was himself a slave owner.

John S. Kennedy, a Library trustee, donated this manuscript along with a copy of the Bill of Rights and other items he purchased in 1896 from Dr. Thomas Addis Emmet, a collector of Americana. Both of these documents are unique to the Library.

Dorothea Lange (1895–1965)
Destitute pea pickers in California, Mother of seven children. Age thirty-two. Nipomo, California
Gelatin silver print, 1936
The Miriam and Ira D. Wallach Division of Art, Prints and Photographs, Photography Collection

In 1935, Dorothea Lange accepted an invitation to join a small corps of documentary photographers employed by the Resettlement Administration, a New Deal government agency established to aid farmers whose lives and livelihoods were ravaged by the Dust Bowl and Great Depression. Charged with raising awareness of the dire need for such aid, Lange portrayed her subjects in a manner that was at once unflinchingly factual and deeply humanizing. Perhaps no single photograph more memorably or effectively galvanized public support to address the growing humanitarian crisis than this picture of a young mother huddled with her children in a pea pickers' camp in rural California. Within a day of its first appearance in the newspaper, relief was delivered to migrant camps in Nipomo. The Library owns four prints of this iconic image, which later became known as "Migrant Mother." At least one of these initially circulated as part of the Picture Collection of The Miriam and Ira D. Wallach Division of Art, Prints and Photographs.

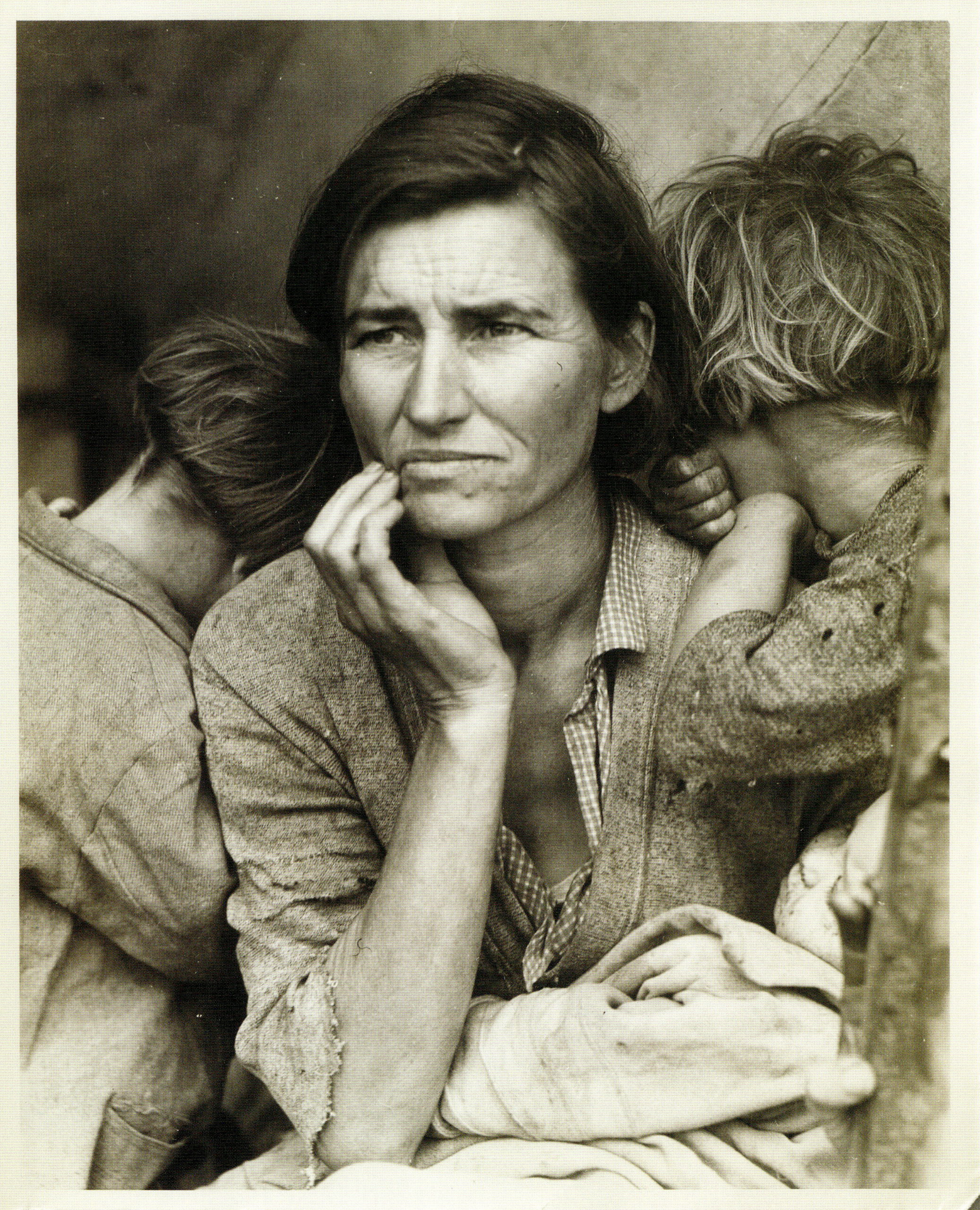

The Pennsylvania Packet, *and Daily Advertiser.*

[Price Four-Pence.] WEDNESDAY, September 19, 1787. [No. 2690.]

WE, the People of the United States, in order to form a more perfect Union, establish Justice, insure domestic Tranquility, provide for the common Defence, promote the General Welfare, and secure the Blessings of Liberty to Ourselves and our Posterity, do ordain and establish this Constitution for the United States of America.

ARTICLE I.

Sect. 1. ALL legislative powers herein granted shall be vested in a Congress of the United States, which shall consist of a Senate and House of Representatives.

Sect. 2. The House of Representatives shall be composed of members chosen every second year by the people of the several states, and the electors in each state shall have the qualifications requisite for electors of the most numerous branch of the state legislature.

No person shall be a representative who shall not have attained to the age of twenty-five years, and been seven years a citizen of the United States, and who shall not, when elected, be an inhabitant of that state in which he shall be chosen.

Representatives and direct taxes shall be apportioned among the several states which may be included within this Union, according to their respective numbers, which shall be determined by adding to the whole number of free persons, including those bound to service for a term of years, and excluding Indians not taxed, three-fifths of all other persons. The actual enumeration shall be made within three years after the first meeting of the Congress of the United States, and within every subsequent term of ten years, in such manner as they shall by law direct. The number of representatives shall not exceed one for every thirty thousand, but each state shall have at least one representative; and until such enumeration shall be made, the state of New-Hampshire shall be entitled to chuse three, Massachusetts eight, Rhode-Island and Providence Plantations one, Connecticut five, New-York six, New-Jersey four, Pennsylvania eight, Delaware one, Maryland six, Virginia ten, North-Carolina five, South-Carolina five, and Georgia three.

When vacancies happen in the representation from any state, the Executive authority thereof shall issue writs of election to fill such vacancies.

The House of Representatives shall chuse their Speaker and other officers; and shall have the sole power of impeachment.

Sect. 3. The Senate of the United States shall be composed of two senators from each state, chosen by the legislature thereof, for six years; and each senator shall have one vote.

Immediately after they shall be assembled in consequence of the first election, they shall be divided as equally as may be into three classes. The seats of the senators of the first class shall be vacated at the expiration of the second year, of the second class at the expiration of the fourth year, and of the third class at the expiration of the sixth year, so that one-third may be chosen every second year; and if vacancies happen by resignation, or otherwise, during the recess of the Legislature of any state, the Executive thereof may make temporary appointments until the next meeting of the Legislature, which shall then fill such vacancies.

No person shall be a senator who shall not have attained to the age of thirty years, and been nine years a citizen of the United States, and who shall not, when elected, be an inhabitant of that state for which he shall be chosen.

The Vice-President of the United States shall be President of the senate, but shall have no vote, unless they be equally divided.

The Senate shall chuse their other officers, and also a President pro tempore, in the absence of the Vice-President, or when he shall exercise the office of President of the United States.

The Senate shall have the sole power to try all impeachments. When sitting for that purpose, they shall be on oath or affirmation. When the President of the United States is tried, the Chief Justice shall preside: And no person shall be convicted without the concurrence of two-thirds of the members present.

Judgment in cases of impeachment shall not extend further than to removal from office, and disqualification to hold and enjoy any office of honor, trust or profit under the United States; but the party convicted shall nevertheless be liable and subject to indictment, trial, judgment and punishment, according to law.

Sect. 4. The times, places and manner of holding elections for senators and representatives, shall be prescribed in each state by the legislature thereof; but the Congress may at any time by law make or alter such regulations, except as to the places of chusing Senators.

The Congress shall assemble at least once in every year, and such meeting shall be on the first Monday in December, unless they shall by law appoint a different day.

Sect. 5. Each house shall be the judge of the elections, returns and qualifications of its own members, and a majority of each shall constitute a quorum to do business; but a smaller number may adjourn from day to day, and may be authorised to compel the attendance of absent members, in such manner, and under such penalties as each house may provide.

Each house may determine the rules of its proceedings, punish its members for disorderly behaviour, and, with the concurrence of two-thirds, expel a member.

Each house shall keep a journal of its proceedings, and from time to time publish the same, excepting such parts as may in their judgment require secrecy; and the yeas and nays of the members of either house on any question shall, at the desire of one-fifth of those present, be entered on the journal.

Neither house, during the session of Congress, shall, without the consent of the other, adjourn for more than three days, nor to any other place than that in which the two houses shall be sitting.

Sect. 6. The senators and representatives shall receive a compensation for their services, to be ascertained by law, and paid out of the treasury of the United States. They shall in all cases, except treason, felony and breach of the peace, be privileged from arrest during their attendance at the session of their respective houses, and in going to and returning from the same; and for any speech or debate in either house, they shall not be questioned in any other place.

No senator or representative shall, during the time for which he was elected, be appointed to any civil office under the authority of the United States, which shall have been created, or the emoluments whereof shall have been encreased during such time; and no person holding any office under the United States, shall be a member of either house during his continuance in office.

Sect. 7. All bills for raising revenue shall originate in the house of representatives; but the senate may propose or concur with amendments as on other bills.

Every bill which shall have passed the house of representatives and the senate, shall, before it become a law, be presented to the president of the United States; if he approve he shall sign it, but if not he shall return it, with his objections to that house in which it shall have originated, who shall enter the objections at large on their journal, and proceed to reconsider it. If after such reconsideration two-thirds of that house shall agree to pass the bill, it shall be sent, together with the objections, to the other house, by which it shall likewise be reconsidered, and if approved by two-thirds of that house, it shall become a law. But in all such cases the votes of both houses shall

First printing of the Constitution of the United States of America, published in *The Pennsylvania Packet, and Daily Advertiser*
Philadelphia: J. Dunlap and D.C. Claypoole, September 19, 1787
Rare Book Division

Throughout the summer of 1787, delegates to the Constitutional Convention in Philadelphia grappled with the question of how best to remedy the shortcomings of the Articles of Confederation (the first U.S. Constitution) in order to create a stronger, more centralized government. Among the chief points of contention was the composition of the proposed United States Senate, and how these representatives, along with the nation's chief executive, should be elected. Matters related to taxation, commerce, national defense, and the institution of slavery further divided the attendees, threatening at times to derail the proceedings altogether.

Nevertheless, through successive compromises and revisions to the text, a workable draft of the document gradually emerged. On September 17, the new Constitution of the United States was at last approved and signed by the delegates. Two days later, the initial public printing of the United States Constitution appeared in Philadelphia's *The Pennsylvania Packet, and Daily Advertiser*, the first successful daily newspaper published in the United States. The New York Public Library preserves a copy of this historic printing, which allowed Americans to read this document for the first time.

Lewis Wickes Hine (1874–1940)

Jennie is 51 inches in height and has been in the mill one year. When asked how old she was, she hesitated, then said, "I don't remember." Then, confidentially, "I'm not old enough to work, but I do just the same." She earns forty-eight cents a day. She works some at night. Out of fifty employees, ten were children about her size.

Gelatin silver print, 1908

The Miriam and Ira D. Wallach Division of Art, Prints and Photographs, Photography Collection

Sociologist Lewis Hine's photographs of children working helped to change American labor laws. Hine had taught at the Ethical Culture School in New York City and photographed immigrants arriving at Ellis Island before he started working for the National Child Labor Committee. He photographed throughout the southern and eastern United States, documenting child labor in the fields, mills, factories, streets, and mines. Hine's work was not easy to accomplish, and he encountered much resistance from the managers of the workplaces he photographed. Nevertheless, he was able to create a substantial body of work that transformed public opinion and labor laws. This particular photograph came to the Library with hundreds of others through the Russell Sage Foundation, which sponsored Hine's photographic work.

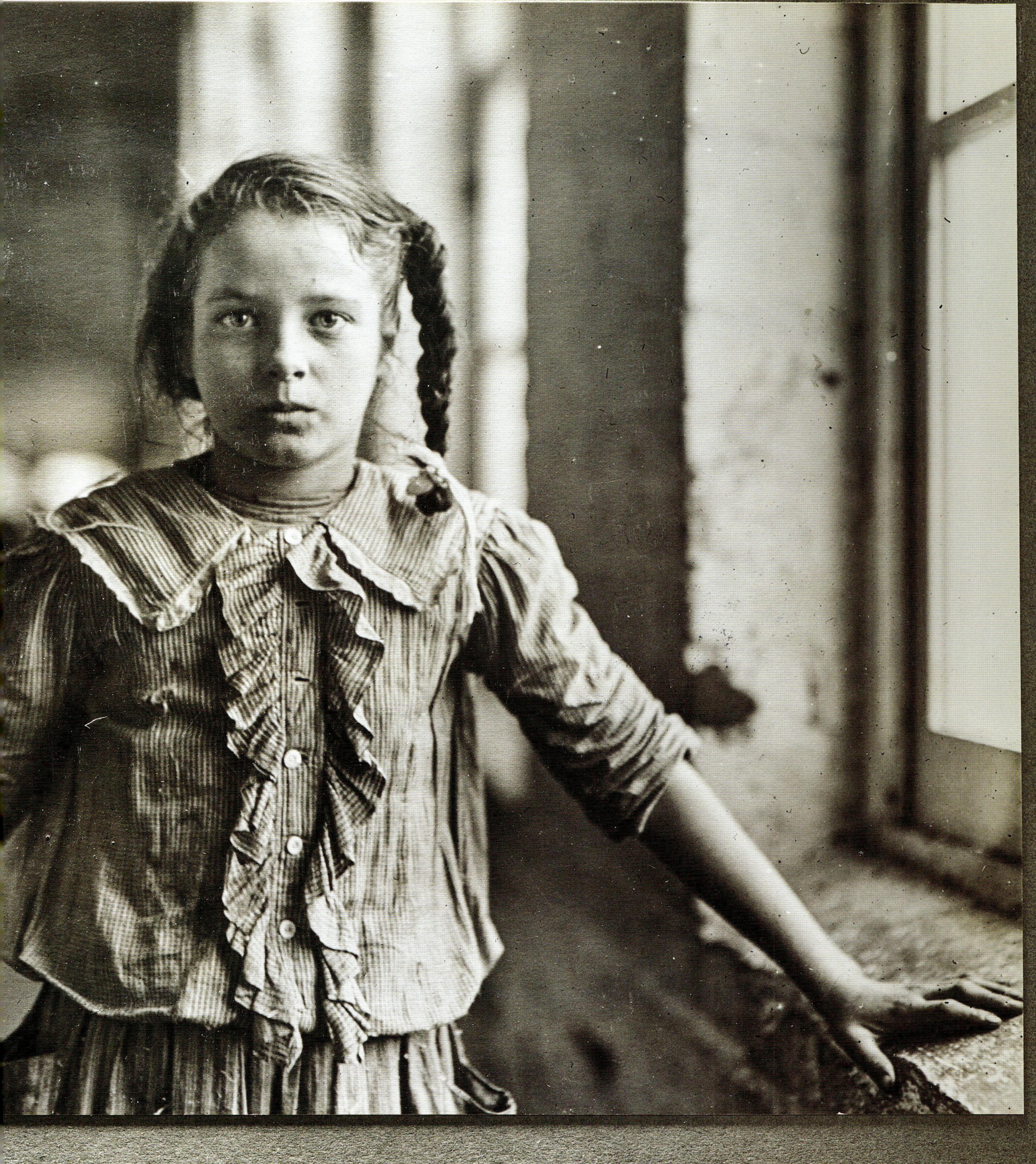

Friends, & Fellow-Citizens

The period for a new election of a citizen, to administer the Executive government of the United States, being not far distant, and the time actually arrived, when your thoughts must be employed in designating the person, who is to be cloathed with that important trust, it appears to me proper, especially as it may conduce to a more distinct expression of the public voice, that I should now apprise you of the resolution I have formed, to decline being considered among the number of those, out of whom a choice is to be made.—

I beg you, at the same time, to do me the justice to be assured, that this resolution has not been taken, without a strict regard to all the considerations appertaining to the relation, which binds a dutiful citizen to his country—and that, in withdrawing the tender of service which silence in my situation might imply, I am influenced by no diminution of zeal for your future interest, no deficiency of grateful respect for your past kindness; but am supported by a full conviction

George Washington (1732–1799)

Washington's handwritten Farewell Address

1796

Manuscripts and Archives Division

George Washington's Farewell Address marked the end of his second term as president and was based on drafts, like this one written in Washington's own hand, in which he collaborated with both James Madison and Alexander Hamilton to articulate his hopes and concerns for the future of the United States. The address first appeared in a Philadelphia newspaper in 1796 and was frequently reprinted. Washington attempted to chart a course of action for the country to follow after he left office, stressing the importance of national unity over political party and wishing for the country to stay neutral in foreign affairs, avoiding "the necessity of those overgrown military establishments which . . . are inauspicious to liberty." James Lenox, one of the Library's founding donors, purchased this manuscript at auction in 1848.

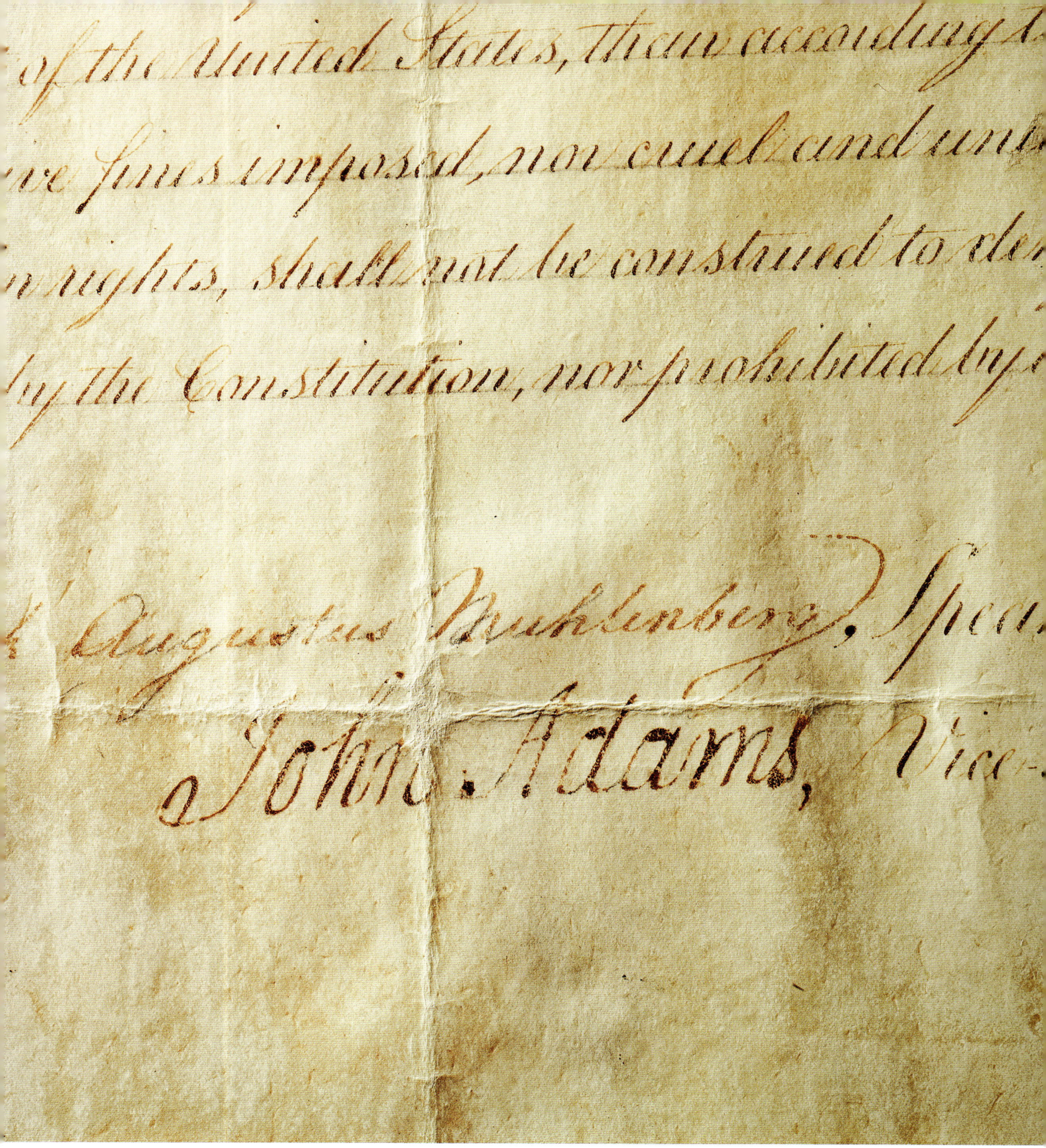

of the United States, than according t

ive fines imposed, nor cruel and unu

n rights, shall not be construed to den

by the Constitution, nor prohibited by

Augustus Muhlenberg, Spea

John Adams, Vice-

Bill of Rights
1789
Manuscripts and Archives Division

Following the ratification of the United States Constitution in 1788, the new federal government of the United States began operating on March 4, 1789. The first Congress convened in New York City roughly one month before George Washington was elected the first president. James Madison introduced for Congress's consideration the first draft of the Bill of Rights, intended to address issues omitted from the U.S. Constitution. After several months of deliberation, Congress adopted ten of the proposed twelve amendments to the U.S. Constitution—including protections guaranteeing free speech and religion—and sent them to the states for ratification. Like all of America's founding documents, the Bill of Rights tacitly accepts human slavery, but it does begin the ongoing process of attaining what the Constitution calls "a more perfect union." George Washington requested that handwritten copies of the Bill of Rights be made, one for Congress and one for each of the original thirteen states. The New York Public Library holds one of these fourteen original copies, acquired along with a draft of the Declaration of Independence through a donation from Library Trustee John S. Kennedy.

Joseph-Siffred Duplessis
(1725–1802)
Portrait of Benjamin Franklin (1706–1790)
Pastel, 1783
No Division

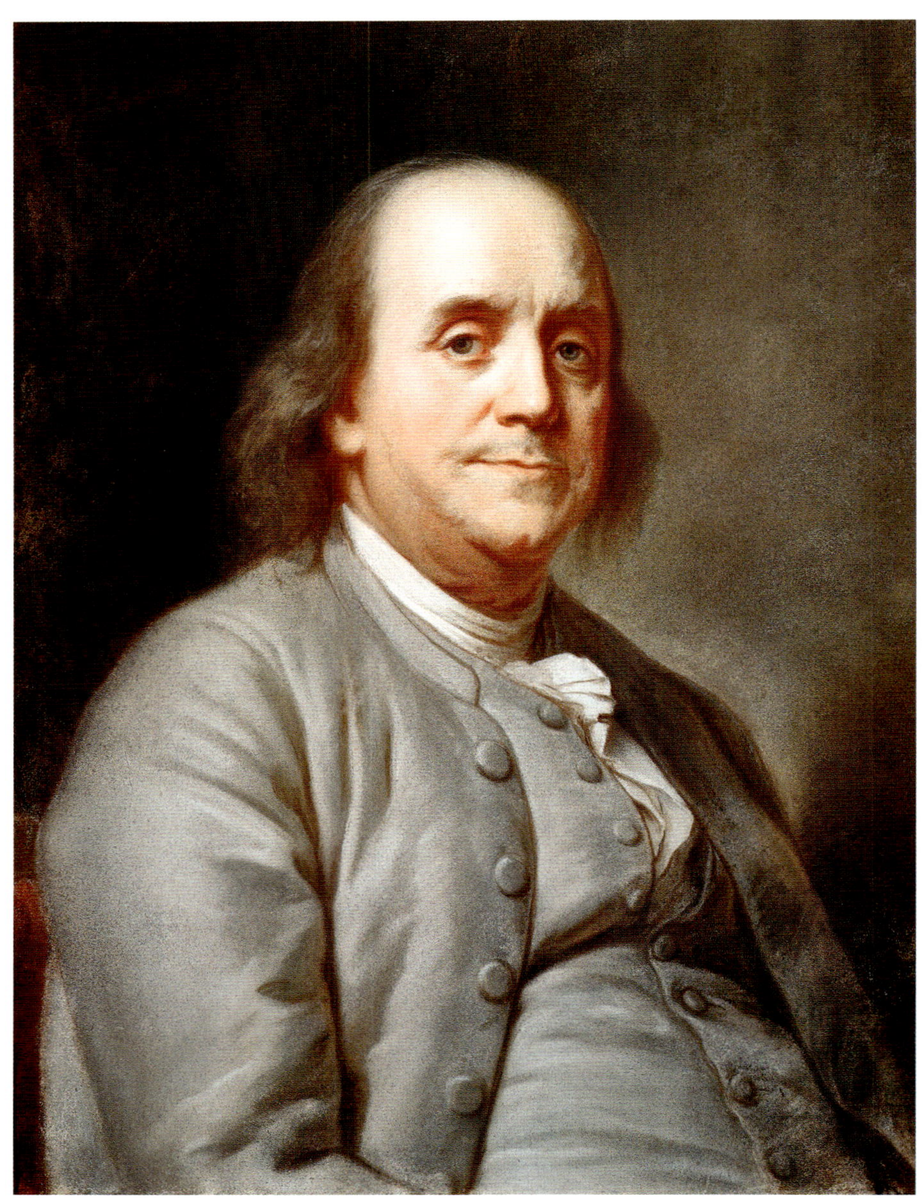

On October 26, 1776, Benjamin Franklin set sail from Philadelphia for Paris to raise support for the American War of Independence, hoping to negotiate a formal alliance between France and the rebellious British colonies. Paris's literary and scientific circles admired his intellect and unpretentious self-presentation, and the elderly statesman quickly became a fixture in high society. Multiple portraits of Franklin were created after his arrival in Paris, including this pastel by Joseph-Siffred Duplessis, King Louis XVI's official portraitist. Recent scholarship shows that the portrait, once thought to have been made after Duplessis created his oil painting of Franklin (now in the Metropolitan Museum of Art's collection), in fact preceded and inspired that canvas. Pastel allowed Duplessis to execute this portrait from life at Franklin's home in Passy. The work, donated in 1896, was among the earliest gifts to the Library.

Marcus Tullius Cicero
(106–43 BCE)
M.T. Cicero's Cato Major, or His Discourse of Old-Age
Philadelphia: B. Franklin, 1744
Rare Book Division

Benjamin Franklin enjoyed a long, successful career as a printer, an avocation noteworthy among a lifetime full of professional and intellectual accomplishments: he is considered to have been the foremost printer in the British colonies. While often celebrated as the author and publisher of *Poor Richard's Almanack*, Franklin's own favorite production was this edition of Cicero's *Cato Major*, which was one of the first works of classical literature to be translated and issued in North America.

Franklin took great care in the preparation of this volume: he selected an elegant Caslon typeface that was large enough for people with poor eyesight to read, and he worked to achieve a harmonious balance of text and blank space on the page. As a result, many consider the book to be Franklin's most handsome work. This copy of *Cato Major* was formerly owned by the noted designer, writer, and printer William Morris.

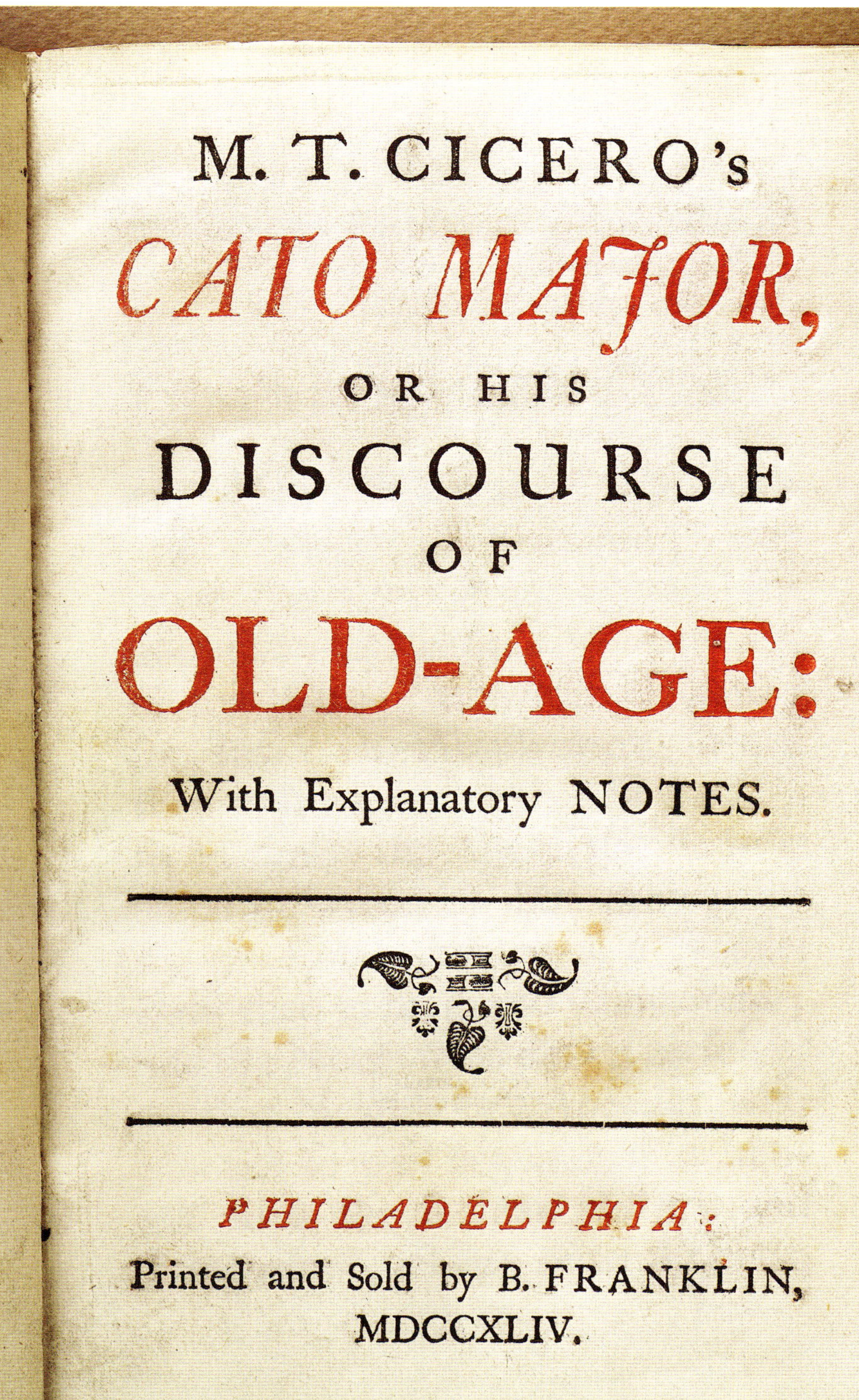

M. T. CICERO's
CATO MAJOR,
OR HIS
DISCOURSE
OF
OLD-AGE:
With Explanatory NOTES.

PHILADELPHIA:
Printed and Sold by B. FRANKLIN,
MDCCXLIV.

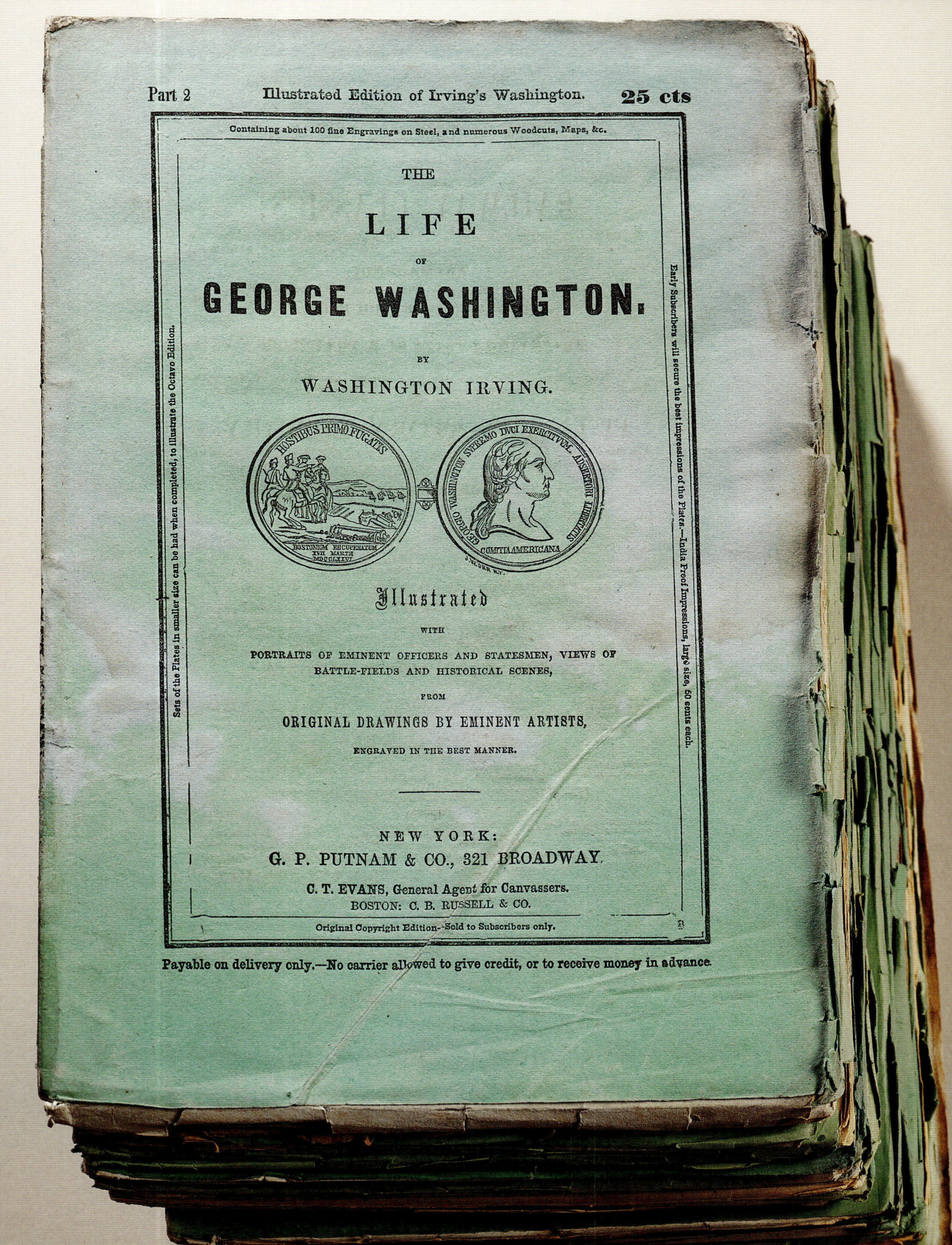

Part 2
Illustrated Edition of Irving's Washington.
25 cts
Containing about 100 fine Engravings on Steel, and numerous Woodcuts, Maps, &c.
THE
LIFE
OF
GEORGE WASHINGTON.
BY
WASHINGTON IRVING.
HOSTIBUS PRIMO FUGATIS
COMITIA AMERICANA
Illustrated
WITH
PORTRAITS OF EMINENT OFFICERS AND STATESMEN, VIEWS OF BATTLE-FIELDS AND HISTORICAL SCENES,
FROM
ORIGINAL DRAWINGS BY EMINENT ARTISTS,
ENGRAVED IN THE BEST MANNER.
NEW YORK:
G. P. PUTNAM & CO., 321 BROADWAY.
C. T. EVANS, General Agent for Canvassers.
BOSTON: C. B. RUSSELL & CO.
Original Copyright Edition—Sold to Subscribers only.
Sets of the Plates in smaller size can be had when completed, to illustrate the Octavo Edition.
Early Subscribers will secure the best impressions of the Plates.—India Proof Impressions, large size, 50 cents each.
Payable on delivery only.—No carrier allowed to give credit, or to receive money in advance.

Washington Irving (1783–1859)

Life of George Washington

New York: G.P. Putnam & Co., 1855–1859

George Arents Collection

Though he is best remembered today for his short fiction—especially the stories "Rip Van Winkle" and "The Legend of Sleepy Hollow"—the American writer Washington Irving believed that his monumental *Life of George Washington* would be the "crowning achievement" of his literary career. Irving began working on the biography in earnest in 1847, undertaking a great deal of preliminary research, and he spent most of the remaining years of his life completing it. The first volume of the book appeared in 1855, and the remaining four installments were published over the next four years. This copy in the George Arents Collection shows the work as it initially appeared, serially in parts—a first edition of an important account of America's first president by its first great literary celebrity.

Phillis Wheatley (1753–1784)
Poems on Various Subjects, Religious and Moral
London: Printed for A. Bell, 1773
Manuscripts, Archives and Rare Books Division, Schomburg Center for Research in Black Culture

A prominent poet in her own time and now a key figure in the American literary canon, Phillis Wheatley was born free in Africa, then enslaved and later manumitted in the United States in the 18th century. Her *Poems on Various Subjects, Religious and Moral* is the first known book of poetry published by a black woman, and was a literary sensation when initially released in London in 1773. The volume testified to the intelligence and creativity that many Americans believed Africans to lack, and as such, Wheatley's work served the abolitionist cause. In the 19th century, titles like this inspired Arturo Alfonso Schomburg's collecting, as it represented the "vindicating evidences" of black history and culture that he sought to accumulate and make available. He included this book in the collection that he sold to The New York Public Library in 1926, the "seed library" from which today's collection in the Schomburg Center has grown.

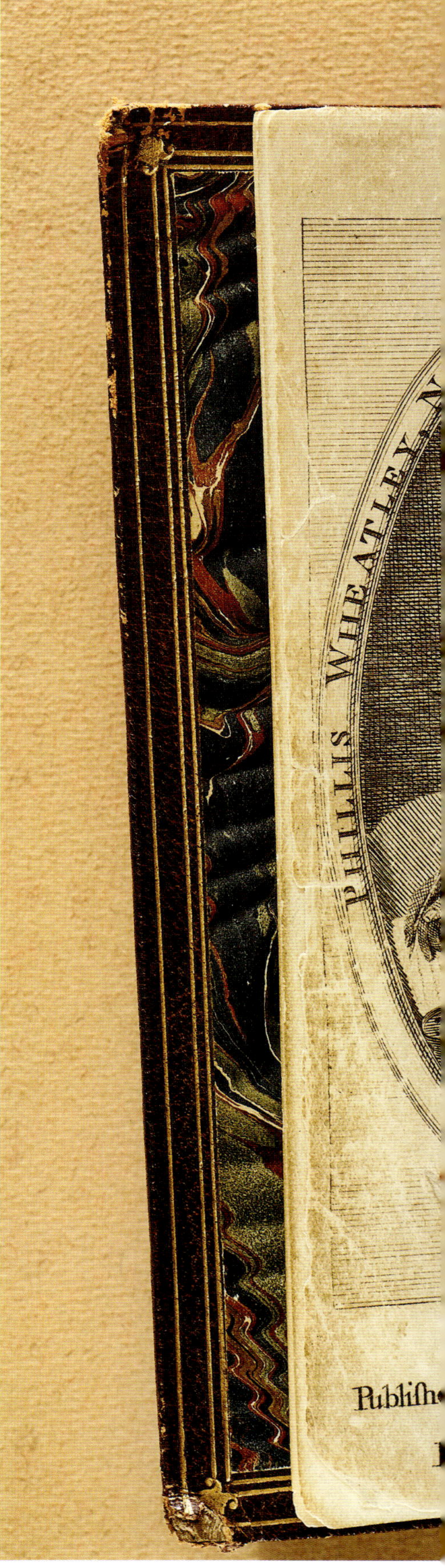

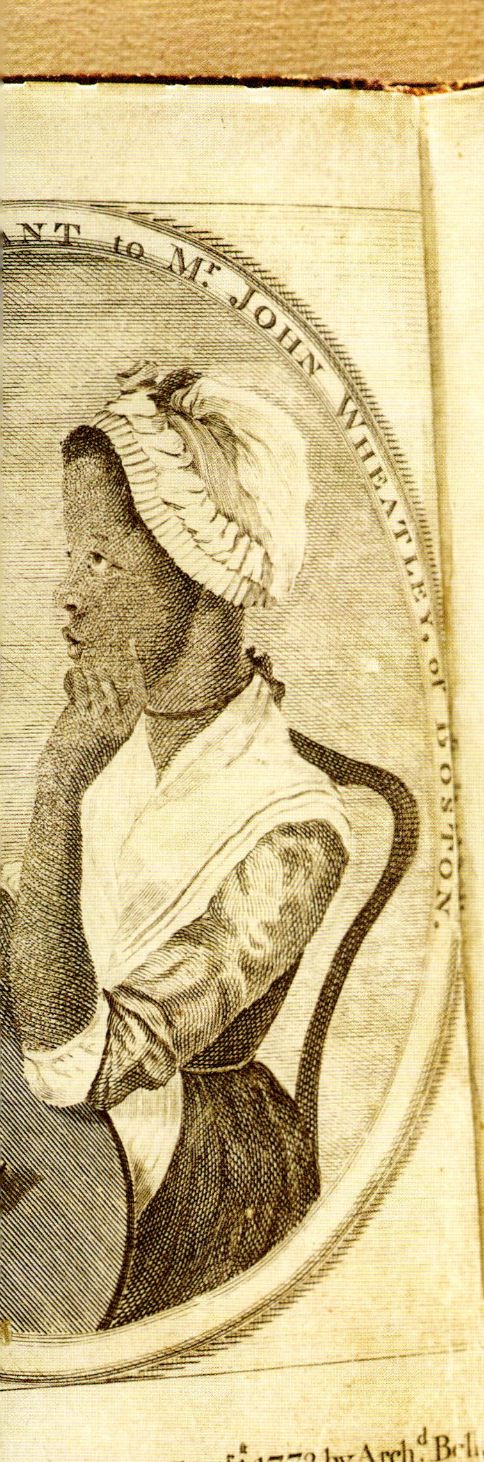

P O E M S

O N

VARIOUS SUBJECTS,

RELIGIOUS AND MORAL.

B Y

PHILLIS WHEATLEY,

NEGRO SERVANT to Mr. JOHN WHEATLEY,
of BOSTON, in NEW ENGLAND.

L O N D O N:
Printed for A. BELL, Bookseller, Aldgate; and sold b
Messrs. COX and BERRY, King-Street, BOSTON.
MDCCLXXIII.

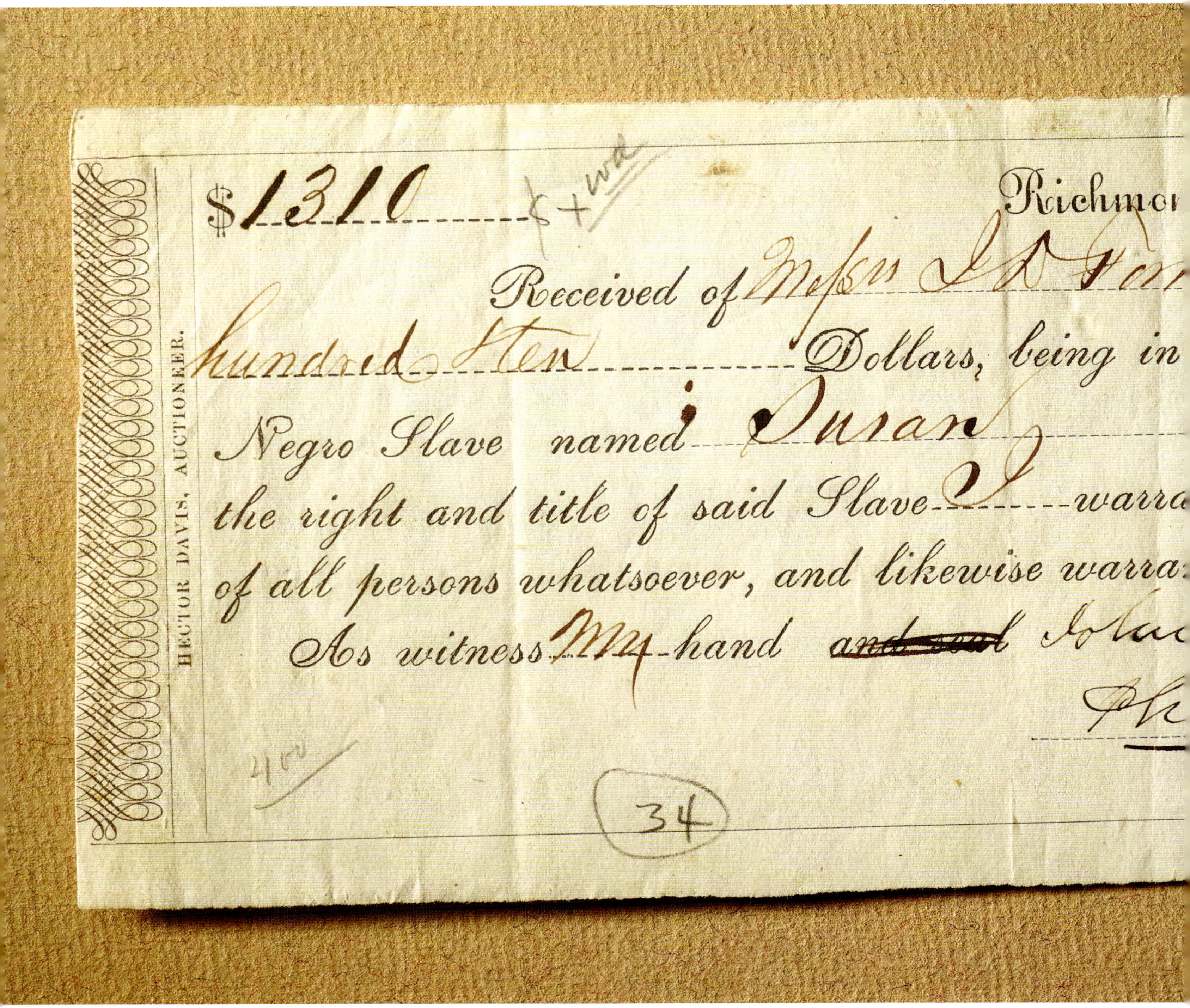

$1310 ________ 8 + wa

Richmon

Received of Messrs I D Far

hundred & ten ________ Dollars, being in

Negro Slave named ______ Susan

the right and title of said Slave ______ warra

of all persons whatsoever, and likewise warra

As witness my hand ~~and seal~~

HECTOR DAVIS, AUCTIONEER.

400

34

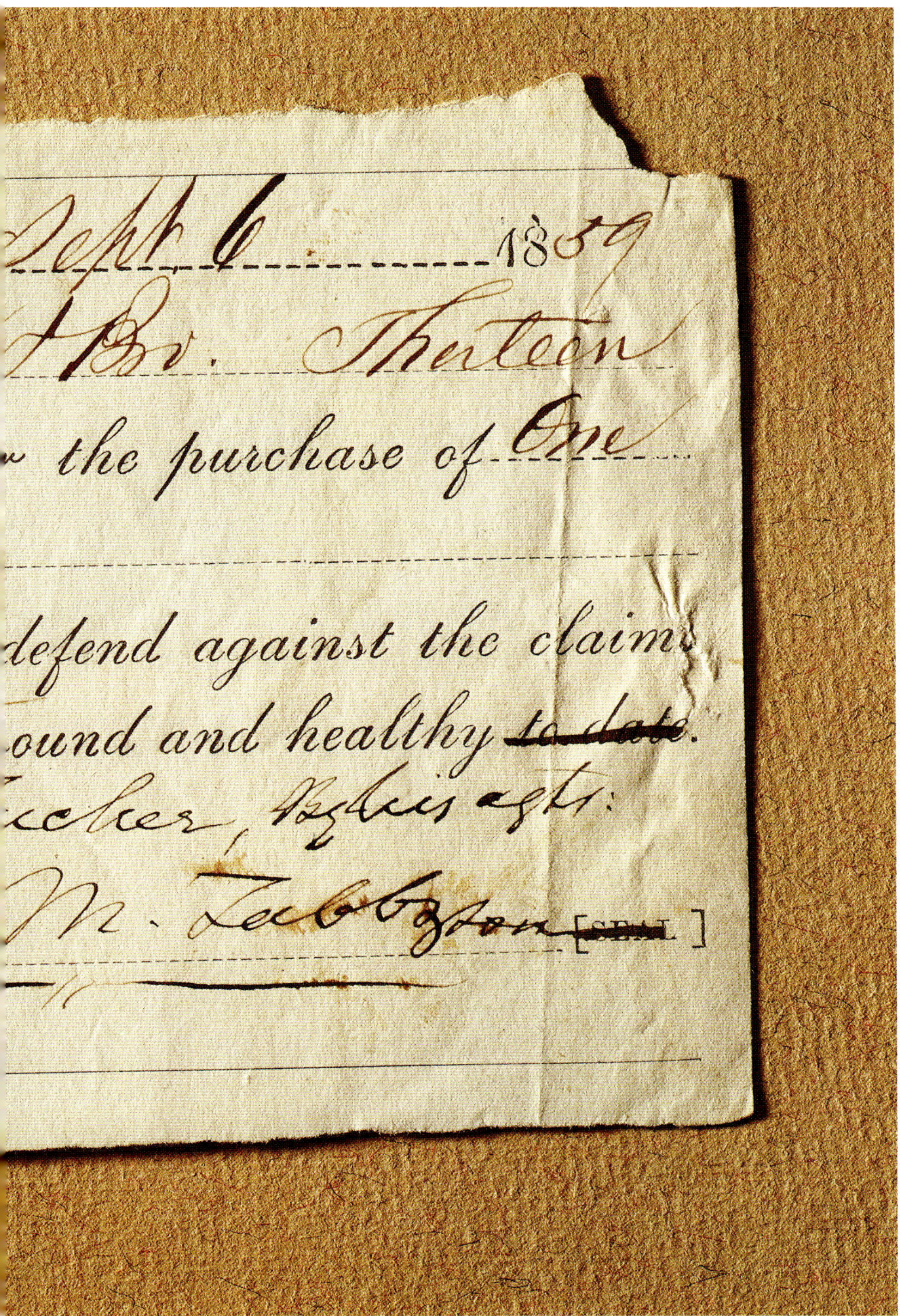

Sept 6 1839

Thirteen

the purchase of One

defend against the claim

ound and healthy ~~to date~~.

[SEAL]

Receipt for $1,310 for the purchase of "One Negro Slave named Susan"
1839
Manuscripts, Archives and Rare Books Division, Schomburg Center for Research in Black Culture

The institution of slavery was foundational to amassing and concentrating wealth in the United States, and this receipt serves as a clinical and visceral reminder of the American business of enslaving humans. The printed text on the paper suggests the frequency with which such forms were used, and the absence of any name but "Susan" shows the degree to which her fullness as a person was elided. The context in which this piece of American history is preserved matters greatly, insofar as the Schomburg Center's work to collect, preserve, and interpret black life and culture centers Susan's experience—rather than those who profited from her labor—creating the space to ask who she was, where she was from, and what her life was like.

Frederick Douglass (1818–1895)
"John Brown"
1881
Frederick Douglass Collection, Manuscripts, Archives and Rare Books Division, Schomburg Center for Research in Black Culture

The carnage of the Civil War and the failure of Reconstruction were still in living memory when the abolitionist, orator, author, and social reformer Frederick Douglass gave this lecture on John Brown's role in the raid on Harpers Ferry. Douglass's original text proposes to discuss John Brown as "among the world's greatest heroes and martyrs," but his emendations articulate a more modest ambition to "show him entitled to your respect, if not your entire approval." Despite this rhetorical scaling back, John Brown nevertheless emerges in Douglass's telling as a hero in the fight against slavery, before whom the prospect of freedom was "shadowy and uncertain." This typescript shows Douglass to be the consummate statesman and speaker, modulating his tone to persuade his audience about a controversial figure in a time of continued unrest, when the full extent of the gains won in the Civil War were still to be determined.

JOHN BROWN.

~~It is~~ not to fan the flame of sectional animosity, now, happily in the process of rapid, and, I hope, permanent extinction; not to revive and keep alive ~~active~~ a sense of shame and remorse for a great national crime, which brought its own punishment in loss of treasure tears and blood; not to recount the long list of wrongs inflicted upon the colored race by more than two centuries of cruel bondage; ~~not to seek in the labyrinths of far off centuries for deeds and qualities to stir men's blood and kindle enthusiasm;~~ but to pay a just debt long due, to a great historical character of our own times and country, one with whom I was well acquainted, and whose confidence and friendship it was my good fortune to share, is the object of my lecture this evening. I wish especially to give you such facts, recollections and impressions as I have of John Brown ~~of h in connection with his raid and its consequences~~. ~~the raid upon Harper's Ferry, the main fact in the life of John Brown, and the one which gave his name a place among the world's greatest heroes and martyrs.~~ as will show him entitled to your respect, if not your entire approval.

In its bearings upon the question of slavery, the importance of the raid upon Harper's Ferry by John Brown cannot well be over estimated, or over stated. Aside from the late tremendous war, of which it was in some sense, the beginning, ~~and a part~~, I know of no incident in all the thirty years of conflict with slavery, which will be remembered longer,

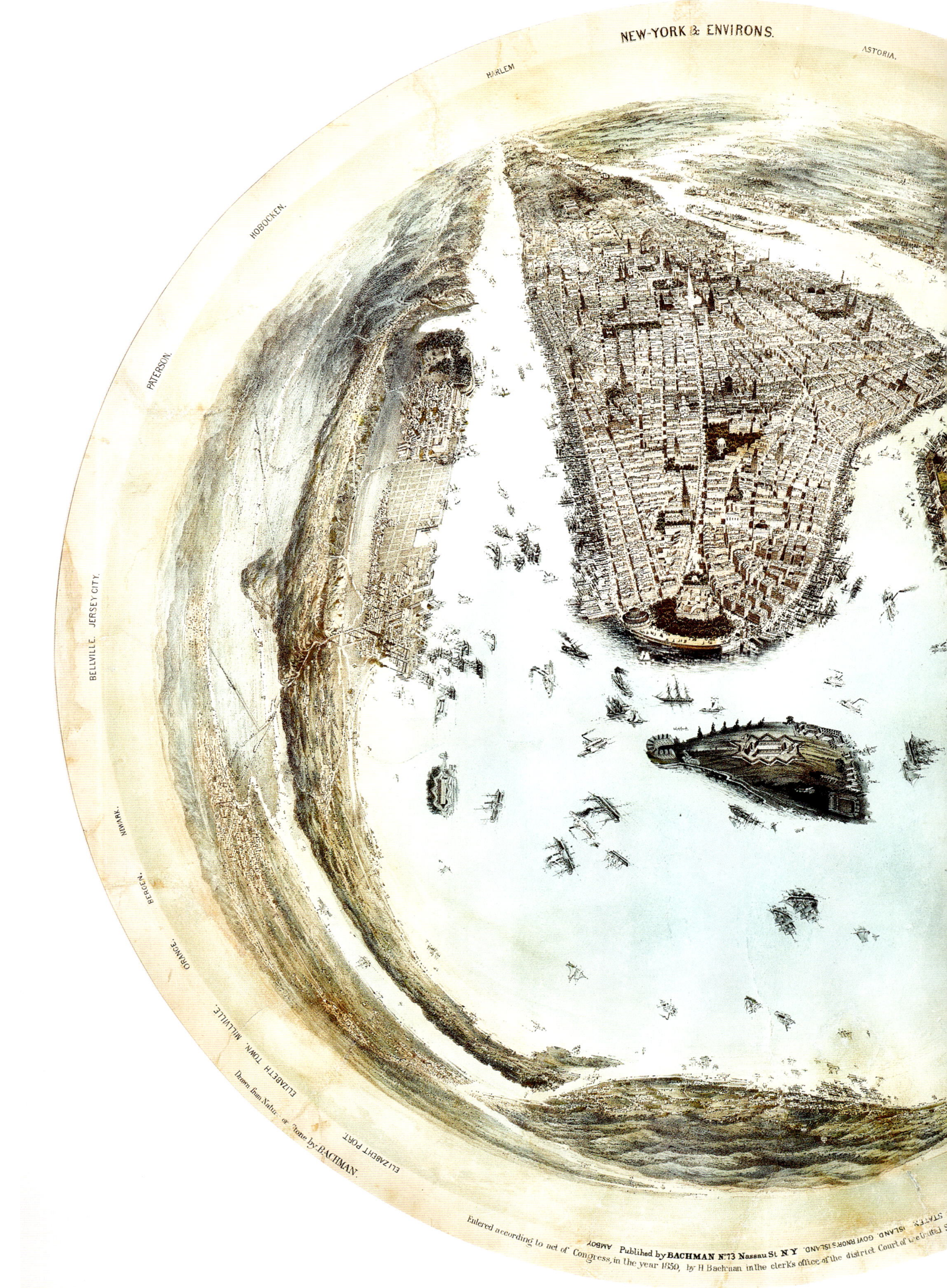

NEW-YORK & ENVIRONS.
HARLEM
ASTORIA.
HOBOCKEN.
PATERSON.
BELLVILLE. JERSEY CITY.
NEWARK.
BERGEN.
ORANGE.
ELIZABETH TOWN. MILLVILLE.
ELIZABETH PORT.
AMBOY
ISLAND. GOVERNOR'S ISLAND.
STATEN
Drawn from Nature on Stone by BACHMAN.
Published by BACHMAN No. 73 Nassau St N.Y.
Entered according to act of Congress, in the year 1859, by H Bachman in the clerk's office of the district Court of the United S

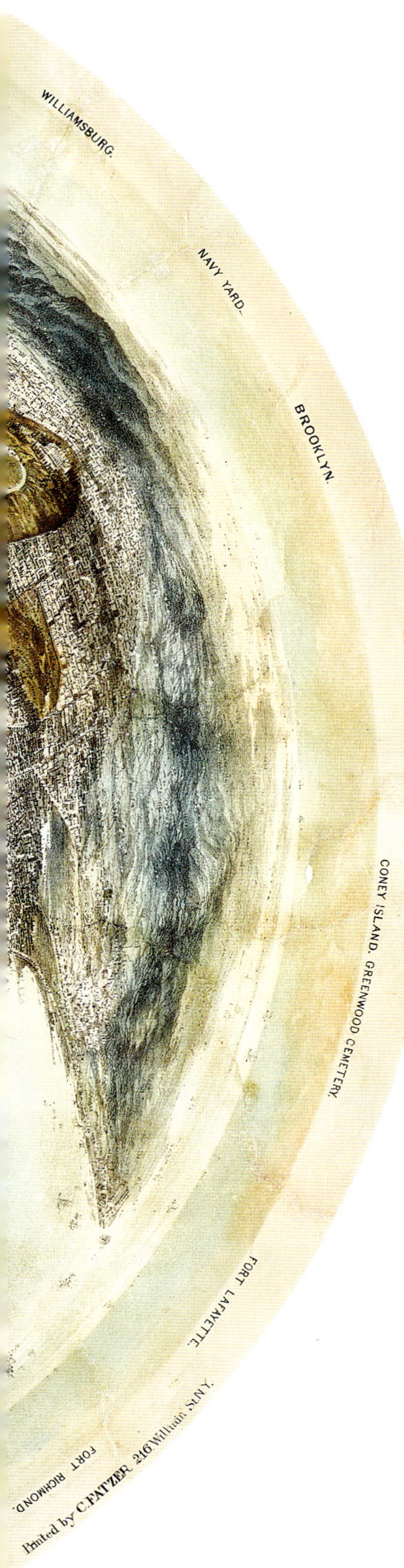

John Bachmann (1814–1896)
New-York & Environs.
Hand-colored lithograph, 1859
The Miriam and Ira D. Wallach Division of Art, Prints and Photographs, Print Collection

A specialist in lithographic city views, the Swiss printmaker John Bachmann immigrated to New York in 1848. Here, Bachmann departs from his more common bird's-eye views by visualizing New York City and its environs through an imaginary fish-eye lens, and at a height well beyond that of a bird's flight. Picturing New York City as the focal point of an imaginary globe, Bachmann creates an idea of the city as the world's literal and figurative center. Views like this were among the most popular commercially produced type of lithograph in the mid-19th century, serving to decorate private homes and municipal buildings as well as to buoy optimism in modern urban life. Part of the Library's Eno Collection of more than 700 views of New York City in all its phases, Bachmann's lithograph helps build an important picture of the metropolis in the mid-1800s.

Poster issued by the War Department: "$100,000 Reward! The Murderer of our late beloved President, Abraham Lincoln, is still at large. . . ."

New York: Geo. F. Nesbitt & Co., April 20, 1865

Rare Book Division

The assassination of President Abraham Lincoln on April 14, 1865, occasioned a nationwide search for perpetrator John Wilkes Booth and his co-conspirators. For twelve days following the murder, Booth and his accomplice, David Herold (misidentified here as Daniel C. Harrold), eluded capture until Union cavalry cornered them in a barn in northern Virginia. Refusing to surrender, Booth was ultimately shot by one of his pursuers and died a few hours later.

The manhunt for Booth, then the largest in the country's history, involved thousands of soldiers, police officers, and civilians. A wide distribution of "Wanted" posters greatly aided the effort by raising public vigilance in the pursuit of the fugitives. The present example, issued in New York City, serves today as a prized but tragic reminder of a pivotal moment in America's past.

War Department, Washington, April 20, 1865.

$100,000 REWARD!

THE MURDERER

Of our late beloved President, ABRAHAM LINCOLN,

IS STILL AT LARGE.

$50,000 REWARD!

will be paid by this Department for his apprehension, in addition to any reward offered by Municipal Authorities or State Executives.

$25,000 REWARD!

will be paid for the apprehension of JOHN H. SURRATT, one of Booth's accomplices.

$25,000 REWARD!

will be paid for the apprehension of DANIEL C. HARROLD, another of Booth's accomplices.

LIBERAL REWARDS will be paid for any information that shall conduce to the arrest of either of the above-named criminals, or their accomplices.

All persons harboring or secreting the said persons, or either of them, or aiding or assisting their concealment or escape, will be treated as accomplices in the murder of the President and the attempted assassination of the Secretary of State, and shall be subject to trial before a Military Commission and the punishment of DEATH.

Let the stain of innocent blood be removed from the land by the arrest and punishment of the murderers.

All good citizens are exhorted to aid public justice on this occasion. Every man should consider his own conscience charged with this solemn duty, and rest neither night nor day until it be accomplished.

EDWIN M. STANTON, *Secretary of War.*

DESCRIPTIONS.—BOOTH is 5 feet 7 or 8 inches high, slender build, high forehead, black hair, black eyes, and wears a heavy black moustache.

JOHN H. SURRATT is about 5 feet 9 inches. Hair rather thin and dark; eyes rather light; no beard. Would weigh 145 or 150 pounds. Complexion rather pale and clear, with color in his cheeks. Wore light clothes of fine quality. Shoulders square; cheek bones rather prominent; chin narrow; ears projecting at the top; forehead rather low and square, but broad. Parts his hair on the right side; neck rather long. His lips are firmly set. A slim man.

DANIEL C. HARROLD is 23 years of age, 5 feet 6 or 7 inches high, rather broad shouldered, otherwise light built; dark hair, little (if any) moustache; dark eyes; weighs about 140 pounds.

GEO. F. NESBITT & CO., Printers and Stationers, cor. Pearl and Pine Streets, N. Y.

QUEEN'S THEATRE,

PARAGON STREET.

On FRIDAY, June 23rd, 1848

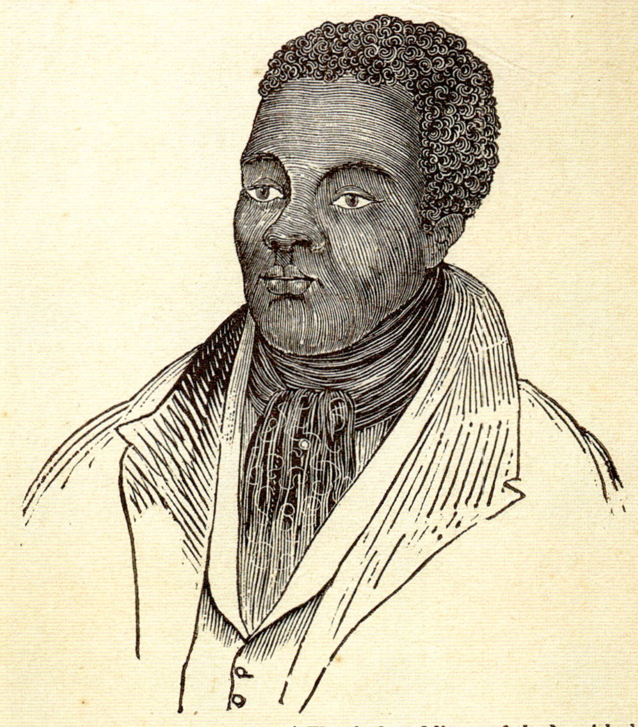

" Mislike me not for my complexion, | The shadowed livery of the burnished sun."

FOF THE BENEFIT OF

MR. IRA ALDRIDGE, THE

AFRICAN ROSCIUS

AND HIS

LAST APPEARANCE.

First and only Night of

THE SICILIAN MARINER!

Bertram......................The AFRICAN ROSCIUS.
Imogine..Mrs. CARLTON.

First and only Night of

THE VIRGINIAN MUMMY!

The Mummy............by the............AFRICAN ROSCIUS.

NEGRO MELODIES, by the AFRICAN ROSCIUS

First time these Twenty-five years of the Nautical Drama, entitled

ROBINSON CRUSOE.

Man Friday..............by the..............AFRICAN ROSCIUS.

For full Particulars see BILLS of the Day.

STAGE MANAGER..........Mr. MELVILLE HILL.

☞ Doors open at Seven o'Clock; Performances commence precisely at Half-past.
Private Boxes, 3s.; Dress Boxes, 2s. 6d.; Upper Boxes, 1s. 6d.; Pit, 1s.; Gallery, 6d.

John Howe, Printer, Old Corn Exchange, 50, Market Place, Hull.

Queen's Theatre (Hull, England) program featuring Ira Aldridge (1807–1867)
June 1848
Billy Rose Theatre Division, Library for the Performing Arts

By the time the actor Ira Aldridge headlined at the Queen's Theatre in Hull, England, he was firmly established as one of the greatest Shakespearean actors of his time. Born a free African American in New York City and inspired by performances at the free black African Grove Theatre, he joined its short-lived acting company in the early 1820s. In 1824, he moved to England to escape discrimination against black actors, reinventing himself as African royalty and finding a more welcoming theater community. Over the next four decades, Aldridge received critical praise and toured widely in Great Britain and Europe, most often playing African or Moorish characters in Shakespearean and other popular dramas of the day. Ephemeral broadsides for Aldridge's performances are extremely rare; this example displays the depth of his repertoire and offers insight into the ways in which artists of color navigated through institutional racism in the 19th century.

Tintype of Walt Whitman (1819–1892) and Bill Duckett
ca. 1886
Rare Book Division

In 1886, the American poet Walt Whitman sat for this portrait with his friend, traveling companion, and likely romantic interest, Bill Duckett. The picture itself represents just one of the nearly 130 known images of Whitman, who, over the course of his career, became the most photographed literary figure of the 19th century.

The New York Public Library is recognized today as a premier repository of works by and about Whitman, and therefore as a necessary destination for those conducting research on the author. This tintype image, drawn from the Rare Book Division's Oscar Lion Collection, is indicative of the many rarities—books, manuscripts, and photographs—to be found among these rich, deep holdings of Whitmaniana.

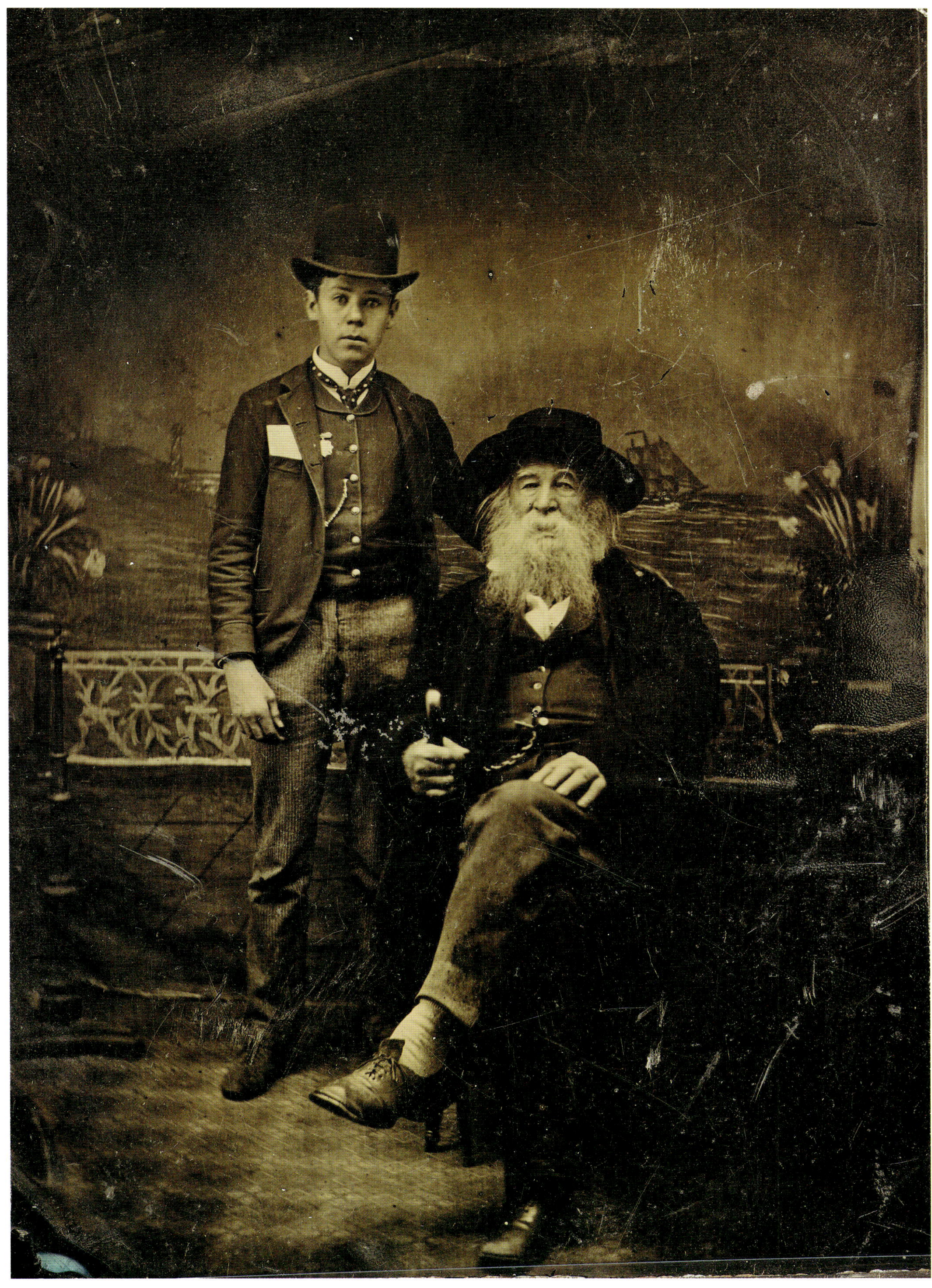

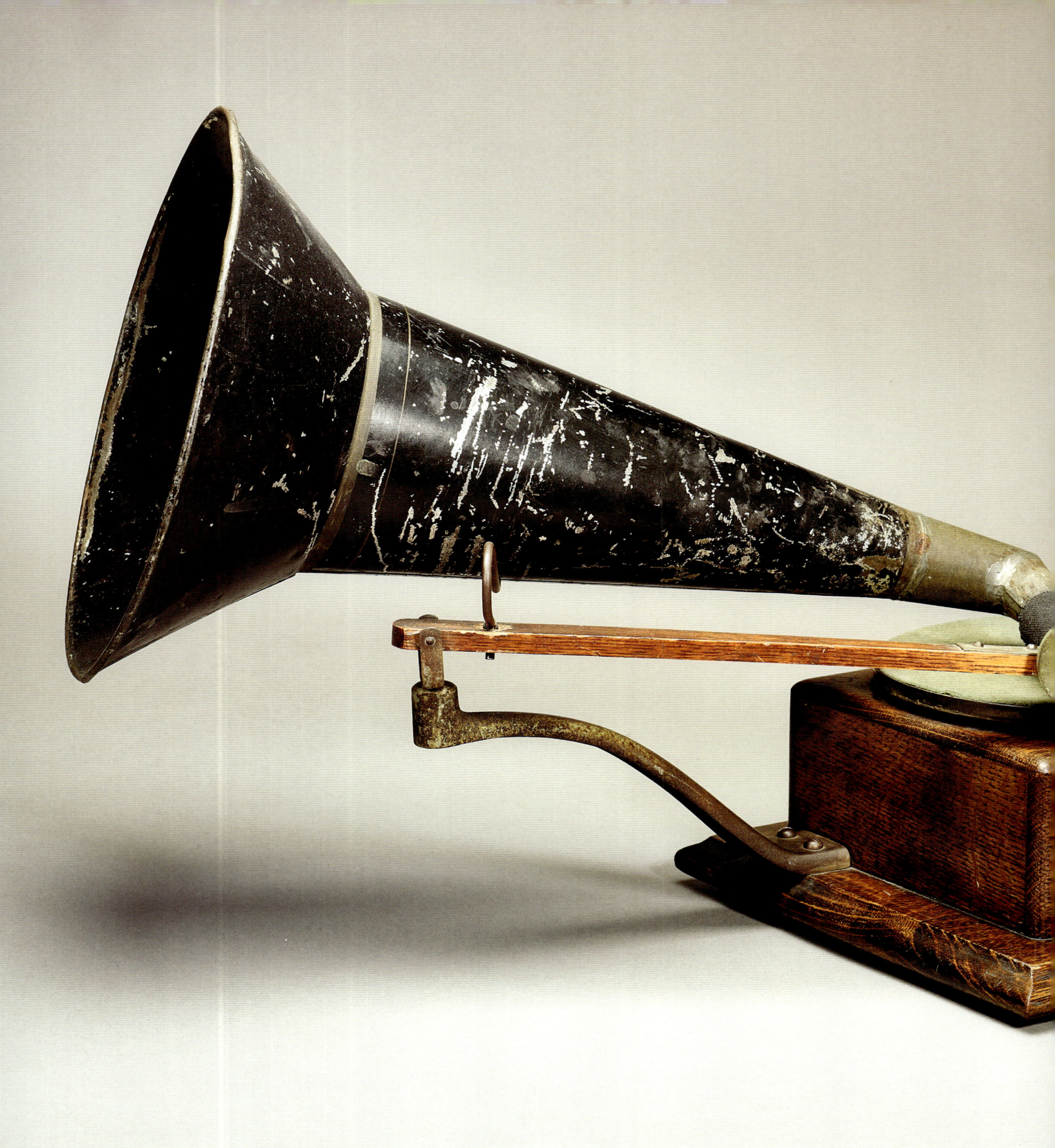

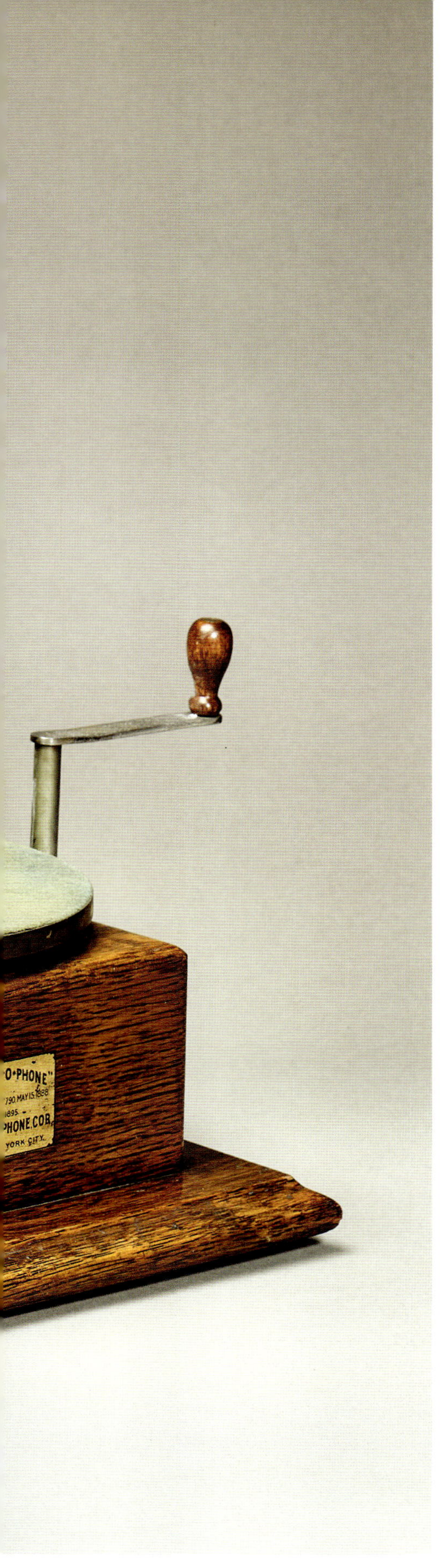

Emile Berliner (1851–1929), inventor
"Berliner Gram-O-Phone"
ca. 1895–1897
Rodgers and Hammerstein Archives of Recorded Sound, The New York Public Library for the Performing Arts, Dorothy and Lewis B. Cullman Center

Emile Berliner invented and patented his Gramophone record player in 1887, at a time when Thomas Edison had cornered the market in sound recording and playback with his cylinders and cylinder players. Fresh from the success of his invention of a transmitter, which the Bell Telephone Company bought and incorporated into its business, Berliner set up a sound lab in his Washington, D.C., apartment. There, he revolutionized sound recording by inventing a method of recording onto flat discs rather than cylinders. By 1895, he had secured enough financial backing to create the Berliner Gramophone Company. His gramophones needed several modifications before becoming a commercial success—a spring motor supplanted the hand-crank mechanism, and shellac proved better than rubber-based discs—but flat discs and players soon became the favored format. Among the many benefits that Berliner touted, the fact that flat discs took up considerably less space may have been the most appealing to consumers.

Recording from Amelia Earhart's (1897–ca. 1937/39) international broadcast

May 22, 1932

Rodgers and Hammerstein Archives of Recorded Sound, The New York Public Library for the Performing Arts, Dorothy and Lewis B. Cullman Center

In 1932, the aviator Amelia Earhart published *The Fun of It: Random Records of My Own Flying and of Women in Aviation*, the second of three books documenting her own experiences as well as those of other influential female pilots of her time. Her transatlantic flight, begun May 20, 1932, marked the first crossing of the Atlantic by a solo female pilot and commemorated the fifth anniversary of Charles Lindbergh's initial voyage. Although conditions required Earhart to land in Ireland rather than in France as originally planned, she officially ended her voyage on May 22 in London, where her address to the large and admiring crowd was broadcast internationally. Excerpts from that broadcast were recorded onto this five-inch souvenir disc and distributed with the first edition of *The Fun of It*.

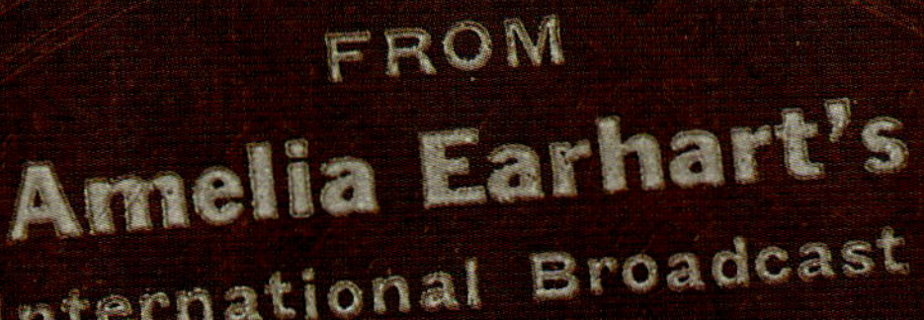
FROM
Amelia Earhart's
International Broadcast

DURIUM PRODUCTS INC.
NEW YORK
MADE IN U.S.A.
TM REG.
In London
May 22
1932
As picked up in New York
by
SILVERTONE

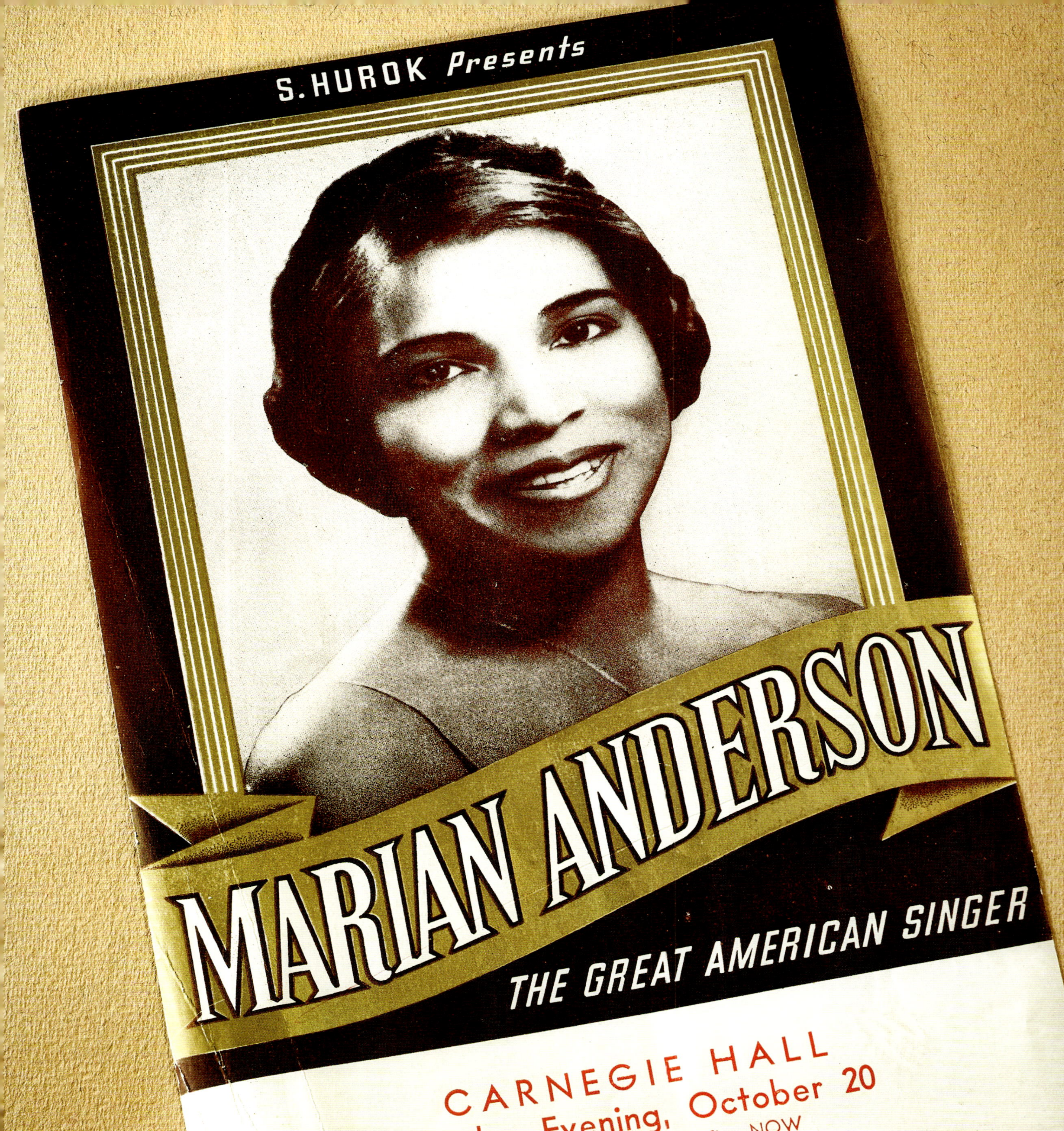
S. HUROK Presents
MARIAN ANDERSON
THE GREAT AMERICAN SINGER
CARNEGIE HALL
Sunday Evening, October 20
Seats on sale at box office NOW
(Steinway Piano)

Marian Anderson (1897–1993) at Carnegie Hall flyer
Music Division, The New York Public Library for the Performing Arts, Dorothy and Lewis B. Cullman Center

Among the most influential singers in American history, the contralto Marian Anderson is best known for her powerful 1939 recital on the steps of the Lincoln Memorial in Washington, D.C.—a concert arranged in part by First Lady Eleanor Roosevelt after the Daughters of the American Revolution denied Anderson access to Constitution Hall because she was black. By 1939, Anderson had established herself as a major touring artist, both in the United States and abroad. She began making recordings with Victor Records in 1923 and gave her first Carnegie Hall concert in 1928. In 1955, Anderson became the first African American on the roster of the Metropolitan Opera.

Aretha Franklin's (1942–2018) ASCAP membership form
ca. 1964
ASCAP Archives, Music Division, The New York Public Library for the Performing Arts, Dorothy and Lewis B. Cullman Center

The ASCAP Archives contain the business files of the American Society of Composers, Authors and Publishers (ASCAP), a New York City-based organization founded in 1914 that protects the intellectual property of its members. Part of the collection consists of membership forms from artists representing a range of popular and classical genres from around the world.

Aretha Franklin likely submitted her membership form around 1964 to document her authorship of the song "Without the One You Love," which she had recorded for Columbia Records in 1962. This was just the beginning of Franklin's long career as a songwriter. Also notable in her form is her response to the request to "kindly outline [a] brief sketch of your career with particular reference to activities in music, and citing factors that led you to music." Her response seems to emphasize her piano playing more than her singing: "Started out playing in Father's church, changed fields and now I record for Columbia Records play piano on most of my releases."

-63 pca

BIOGRAPHICAL DATA

1. NAME Aretha L. Franklin

2. ADDRESS 1721 Field st Detroit

3. PLACE AND DATE OF BIRTH Memphis Tenn. ~~[illegible]~~ March 25
(If you do not want year of birth publicized, please indicate. However, kindly include this information for our files.)

4. FATHER'S NAME Rev. C. L. Franklin

5. MOTHER'S MAIDEN NAME Barbara Siggers

6. MARRIED OR SINGLE ~~[illegible]~~

7. IF MARRIED, DATE OF MARRIAGE Single NAME OF SPOUSE

8. CHILDREN (if any): NAMES & ADDRESSES 3. Clarence + Edward Jordan, Franklin + Theodore Richard White II

9. EDUCATION (SCHOLASTIC AND MUSICAL) None

10. MEMBERSHIP IN MUSICAL ASSOCIATIONS, SCHOLARSHIPS, FELLOWSHIPS AND SIMILAR HONORS
Musicans local 802

11. KINDLY OUTLINE BRIEF SKETCH OF YOUR CAREER – WITH PARTICULAR REFERENCE TO ACTIVITIES IN MUSIC, AND CITING FACTORS THAT LED YOU TO MUSIC Started out playing in Fathers church, changed Fields And I now Record For Colombia Records play piano on most of My Releases. Elementary + high school classes.

12. LIST OF YOUR IMPORTANT WORKS Without the one you love.

13. PRINCIPAL HOBBIES Writing music, golf, bowling.

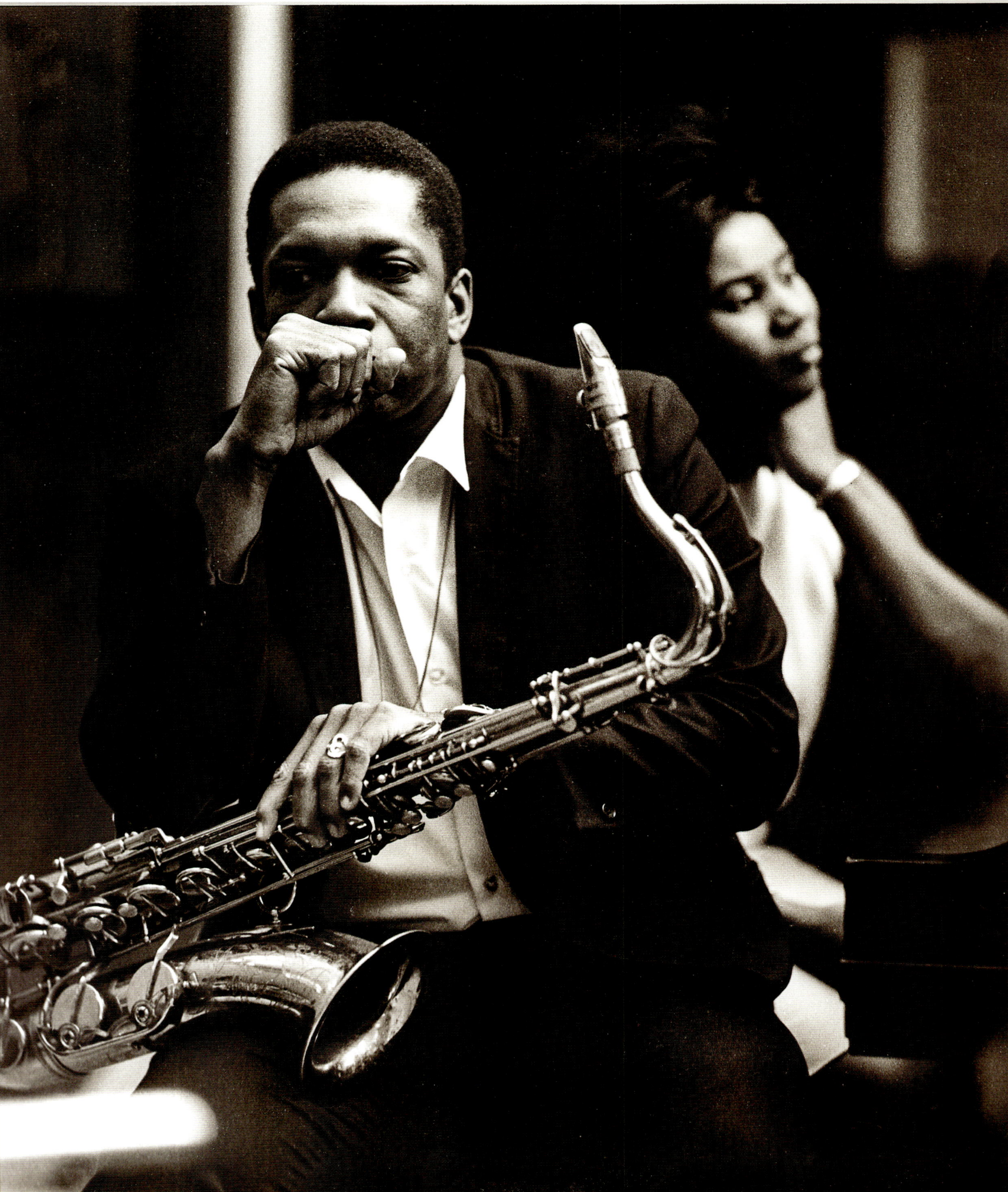

Chuck Stewart (1927–2017)

John (1926–1967) and Alice Coltrane (1937–2007)

Gelatin silver print, 1966

Photographs and Prints Division, Schomburg Center for Research in Black Culture

This image captures jazz great John Coltrane in Rudy Van Gelder's recording studio in Englewood Cliffs, New Jersey. Alice Coltrane, John's romantic and spiritual partner—an acclaimed jazz pianist and harpist in her own right—is visible in the background in her familiar supportive role to her husband. After Coltrane's untimely death at age forty, Alice carried on his musical mission and created her own legacy. Chuck (Charles) Stewart photographed not only the Coltranes but also nearly every jazz musician who worked in New York between the 1950s and 1970s. His personal relationships with some of these musicians enabled Stewart to capture them not only in performance, but also in rare intimate moments and moods. This photograph is one of a dozen by Stewart that the Schomburg Center acquired in 1982 as it sought out the works and perspectives of photographers of African descent.

Sonny Rollins's (b. 1930) notebook
1957
Sonny Rollins Papers, Manuscripts, Archives and Rare Books Division, Schomburg Center for Research in Black Culture

Musical genius is most often experienced through live or recorded performance. But the prolific American jazz tenor saxophonist Theodore Walter "Sonny" Rollins is that rare musician who has also extensively documented his music, creative process, and studied craft. Simple spiral notebooks like this one provide a glimpse into the work that informs and animates his music. This example includes practice notes and musings in what appear to be three different sessions, written in the midst of his watershed successes in the 1950s. Having established himself as a uniquely talented and innovative musician by the end of that decade, Rollins has gone on to become one of the most important and revered saxophonists in jazz history.

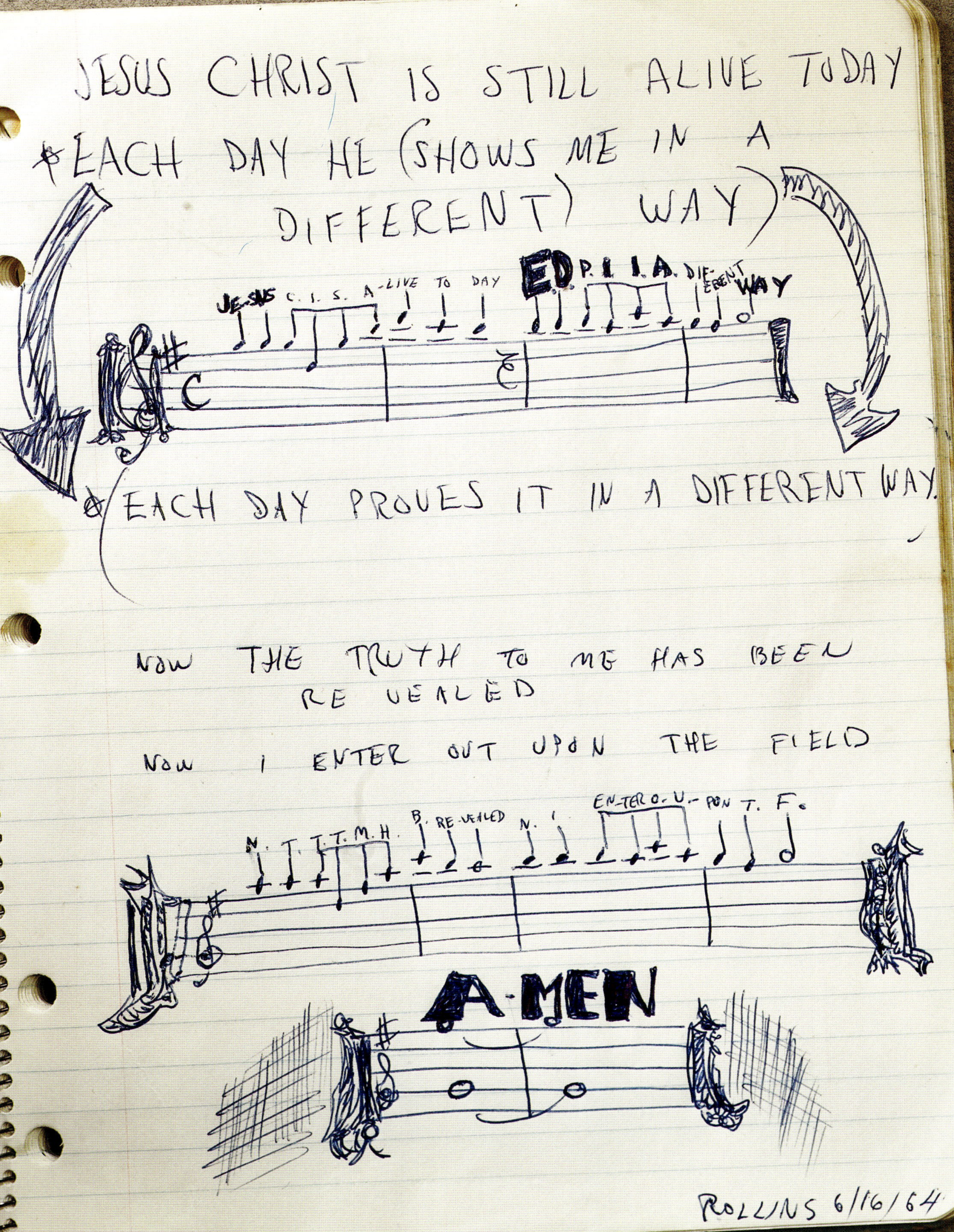
JESUS CHRIST IS STILL ALIVE TODAY
EACH DAY HE (SHOWS ME IN A DIFFERENT) WAY
JE-SUS C. I. S. A-LIVE TO DAY
ED. P. I. I. A. DIF-ERENT WAY
EACH DAY PROVES IT IN A DIFFERENT WAY.
NOW THE TRUTH TO ME HAS BEEN RE VEALED
NOW I ENTER OUT UPON THE FIELD
N. T. T. T. M. H. B. RE-VEALED N. I EN-TER O. U.-PON T. F.
A-MEN
ROLLINS 6/16/64

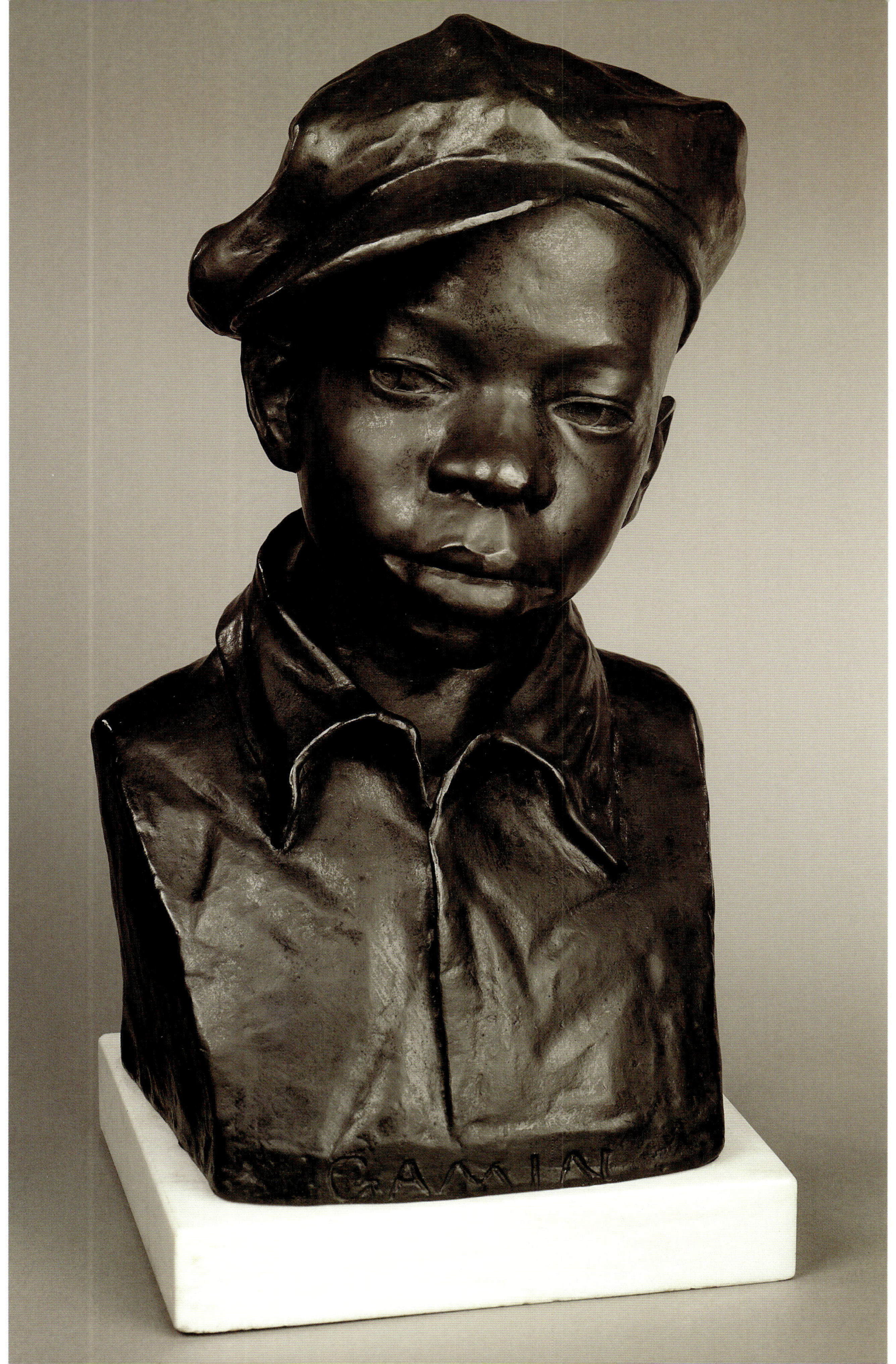
GAMIN

Augusta Savage (1892–1962)
Gamin
Bronze, ca. 1930
Art and Artifacts Division, Schomburg Center for Research in Black Culture

Augusta Savage, a key figure of the Harlem Renaissance, won international acclaim with her sculpture *Gamin*, modeled after her nephew. Growing up in northeast Florida, Savage fashioned clay ducks from the loamy soil before her artistic gifts were recognized at a county fair. She moved to New York in 1921 and attended the Cooper Union School of Art; a fellowship awarded for *Gamin* enabled her to study in Paris. On her return from Europe, she founded the Savage Studio of Arts and Crafts, which the painter Jacob Lawrence and the writer Ralph Ellison attended. She was appointed the first director of the Harlem Community Art Center in 1937.

Dizzy Gillespie (1917–1993), composer
Mel Dancy (1937–2016), lyricist
Signed, handwritten chord chart for "Brother K"
1973
ASCAP Archives, Music Division, The New York Public Library for the Performing Arts, Dorothy and Lewis B. Cullman Center

The jazz artist Dizzy Gillespie composed a piece called "Exotica" while on tour in 1968, but he changed the title to "Brother K" in response to the assassinations of Dr. Martin Luther King, Jr., and Robert F. Kennedy that year. Gillespie was a civil rights advocate who had participated in marches and protests; he even ran for president of the United States in 1964 as a write-in candidate. The singer Mel Dancy later wrote lyrics that overtly linked the song to King, and Gillespie's publishing company, Dizlo Music Corporation, copyrighted the melody and lyrics in 1973. The song's first commercial release came that same year in a live instrumental version appearing on the album *The Source.* Gillespie inscribed and gave the sheet music to the American Society of Composers, Authors and Publishers (ASCAP). The sheet music is significant both as a handwritten relic of a seminal figure in jazz composition and improvisation and as an artistic response to pivotal events in American history.

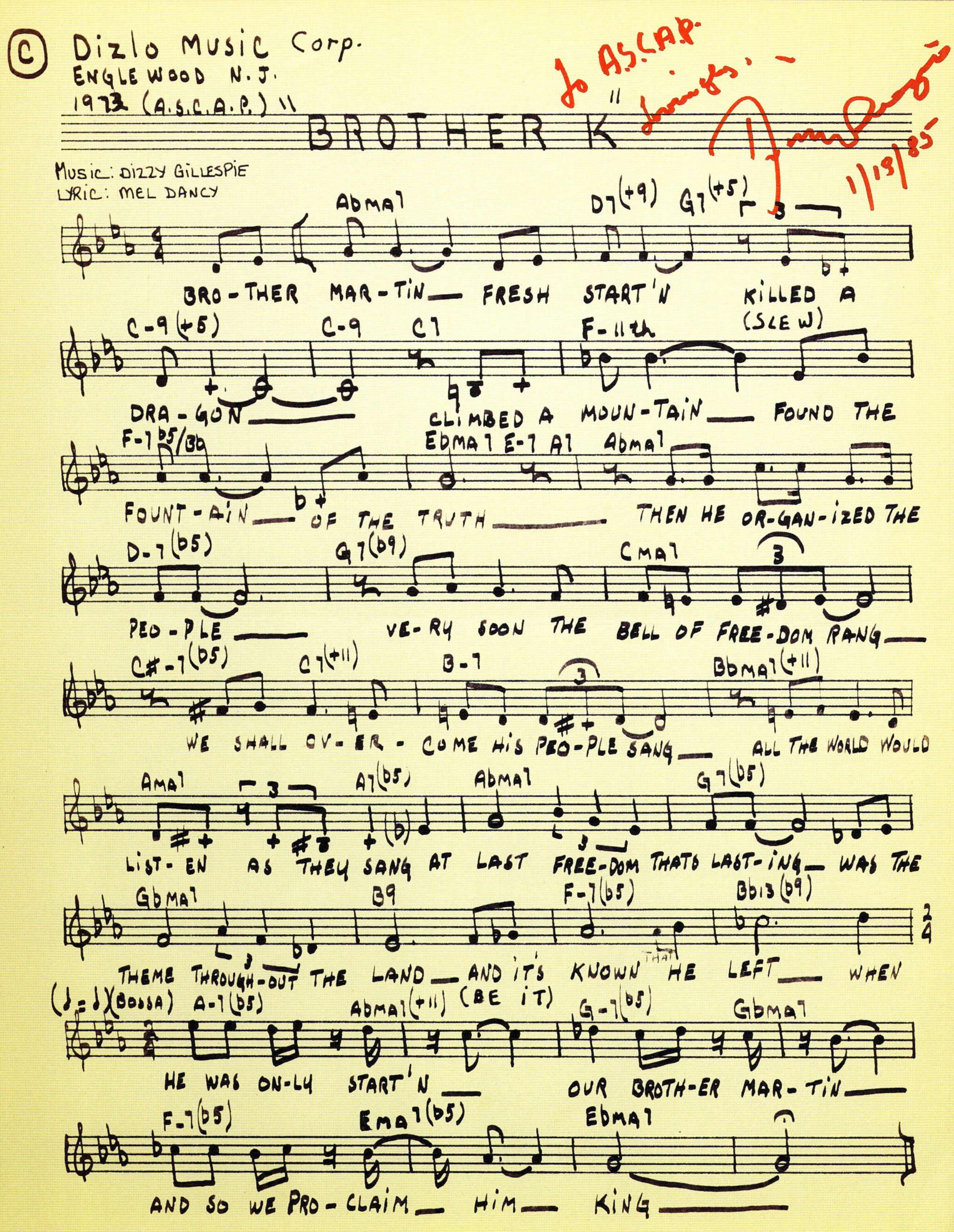

© Dizlo Music Corp.
ENGLEWOOD N.J.
1973 (A.S.C.A.P.)
"BROTHER K"
To ASCAP
1/18/85
Music: DIZZY GILLESPIE
LYRIC: MEL DANCY
BRO-THER MAR-TIN FRESH START'N KILLED A (SLEW)
DRA-GON CLIMBED A MOUN-TAIN FOUND THE
FOUNT-AIN OF THE TRUTH THEN HE OR-GAN-IZED THE
PEO-PLE VE-RY SOON THE BELL OF FREE-DOM RANG
WE SHALL OV-ER-COME HIS PEO-PLE SANG ALL THE WORLD WOULD
LIST-EN AS THEY SANG AT LAST FREE-DOM THATS LAST-ING WAS THE
THEME THROUGH-OUT THE LAND AND IT'S KNOWN THAT HE LEFT WHEN
(BOSSA) (BE IT)
HE WAS ON-LY START'N OUR BROTH-ER MAR-TIN
AND SO WE PRO-CLAIM HIM KING

THE

Charter

OF THE

CITY

OF

NEW-YORK;

Printed by Order of the Mayor, Recorder, Aldermen and Commonalty of the City aforesaid.

TO WHICH IS ANNEXED,

The Act of the General Assembly Confirming the same.

NEW-YORK,
Printed by *John Peter Zenger*. 1735.

The charter of the city of New-York; printed by order of the mayor, recorder, aldermen and commonalty of the city aforesaid

New York: John Peter Zenger, 1735

Rare Book Division

In 1734, John Peter Zenger, the second printer to set up shop in New York City, was arrested for publishing seditious libels directed at the colonial governor, William Cosby. Zenger was acquitted of all charges in a trial that became a landmark in American legal history: it laid the groundwork for the precedent that statements, however unflattering or defamatory, are not libelous if they can be proved true.

On his release from prison Zenger set about completing the long-delayed printing of the second charter of the City of New York, known as the Montgomerie Charter. Perhaps as a veiled provocation toward Cosby, Zenger wrote in his newspaper, *The New-York Weekly Journal*, "The Printer, now having got his liberty again, designs God willing to Finish and Publish the *Charter of the City of New-York* next week."

Harry Crosby (1898–1929)
The Sun
Paris: Black Sun Press, 1929
Rare Book Division

As specialized products of the book arts, miniatures—that is, books measuring less than three inches in height and width—have delighted bibliophiles for centuries. The Library's Rare Book Division holds several thousand such miniature publications, ranging from Bibles and dictionaries to short-story collections and works of verse. One notable example of this latter genre is Harry Crosby's poem "The Sun." Issued in 1929 by the author's own Black Sun Press, the book, in fact, qualifies as a micro-miniature, measuring as it does barely one inch by one inch.

While the quality of Crosby's verse is debatable, the importance of his publishing enterprise is without question: it was from his press that landmark works such as James Joyce's *Ulysses* and Hart Crane's *The Bridge* first appeared. Charmingly, the Library retains the envelope in which Crosby mailed his tiny volume, addressed simply to "The New York Public Library | U.S.A."

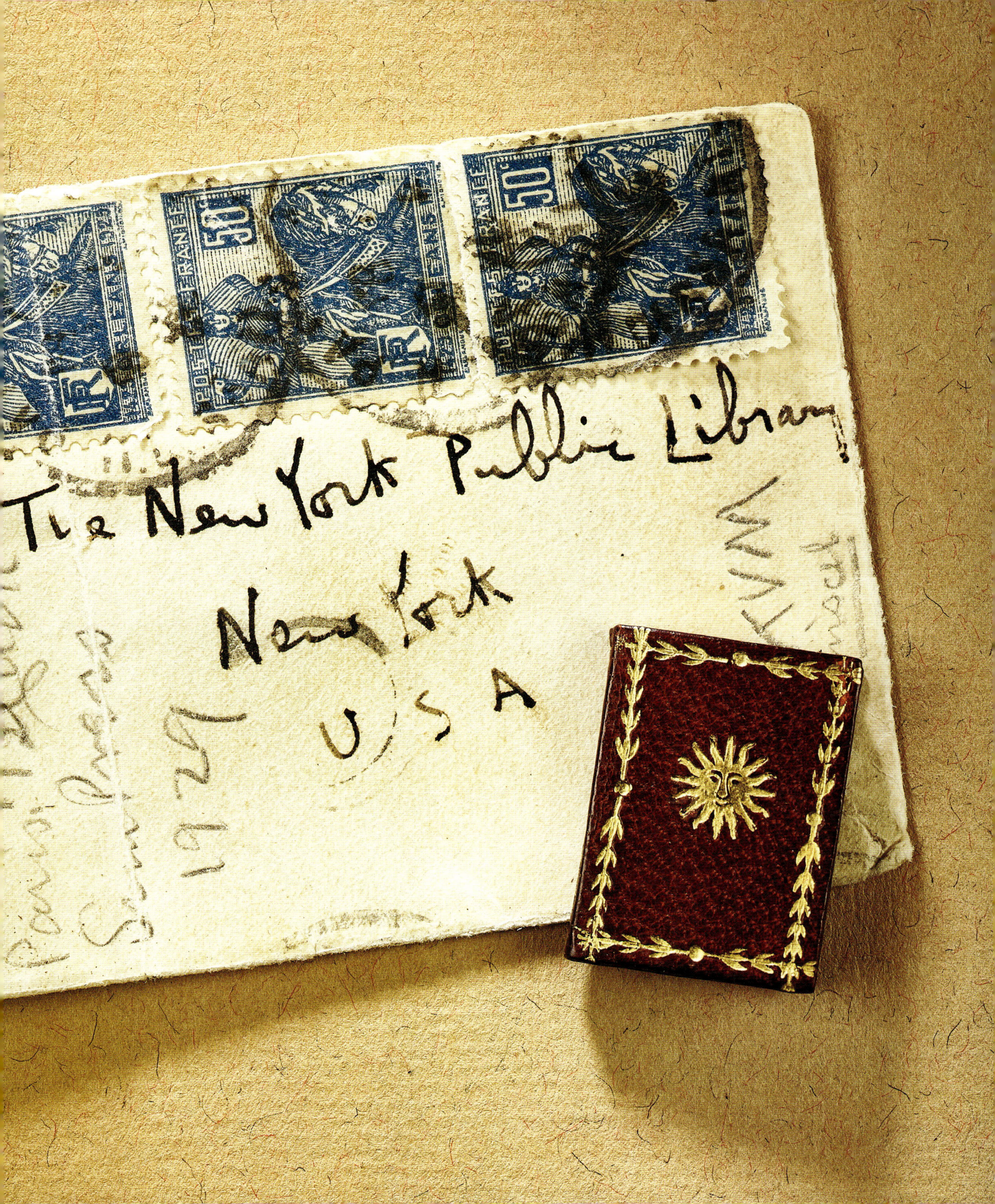

The New York Public Library
New York
USA
50

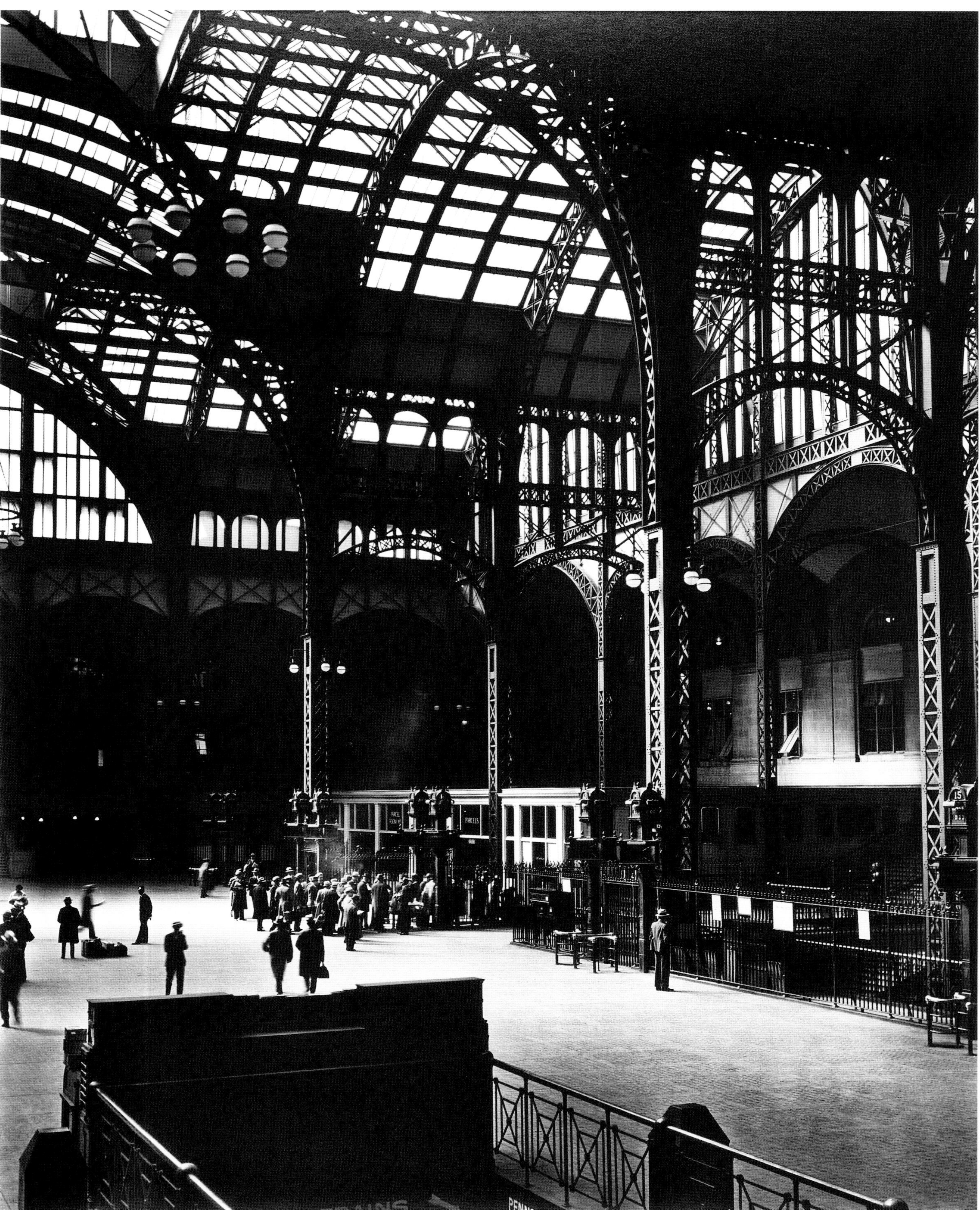
PARCELS
TRAINS

Berenice Abbott (1898–1991)

Penn Station

Gelatin silver print, 1934 (printed later)

The Miriam and Ira D. Wallach Division of Art, Prints and Photographs, Photography Collection

Berenice Abbott first learned photography while working as Man Ray's darkroom assistant in Paris, where she established herself as a portrait photographer and met the noted French photographer Eugène Atget. His views of Paris inspired her to capture the contrasts of old and new when she returned to New York in 1929. Her work earned the support of the Federal Art Project in 1935 and eventually led to the book *Changing New York*, which was released in conjunction with the New York World's Fair in 1939. Abbott included Penn Station in her documentation. Opened in 1910, the railroad hub was a masterpiece of Beaux-Arts style, and Abbott focused on conveying its structural magnificence rather than its function. She photographed the interior from several different viewpoints, which represent just a few of the thousands of photographs from the project that the Library owns.

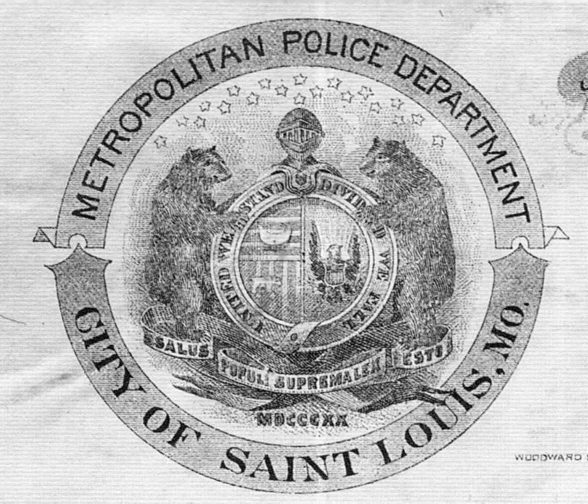

JOHN W. CAMPBELL, Chief.

OFFICE OF

Chief of Police.

WOODWARD & TIERNAN PRT'G CO. ST. LOUIS

St. Louis, Mo., Aug. 28, 1899.

We, the undersigned, do hereby certify that we stripped Harry Houdini stark naked, sealing up his mouth with plaster, and hand-cuffed and leg-shackled him chaining his hands to his feet; and he successfully extricated himself from everything locked upon him, using the Department's irons, this being done in the office of the Chief of Detectives where he was left alone, with absolutely no chance of confederacy.

[illegible] Asst and Acting Chief Police
W. Desmond Chief of Detectives
Thos J. Ward Secy of Board
E. E. Sumner Mgr West End Hotel
Peter Reynolds Capt. Police
Jas H. Smith Asst Chief of Detectives
C H Jones Secy to Chief of Police
Roscoe T. Abbott Asst " "
W. C. McCarty Reporter Post Dispatch
[illegible] Chronicle
[illegible] Reporter St. Louis Star

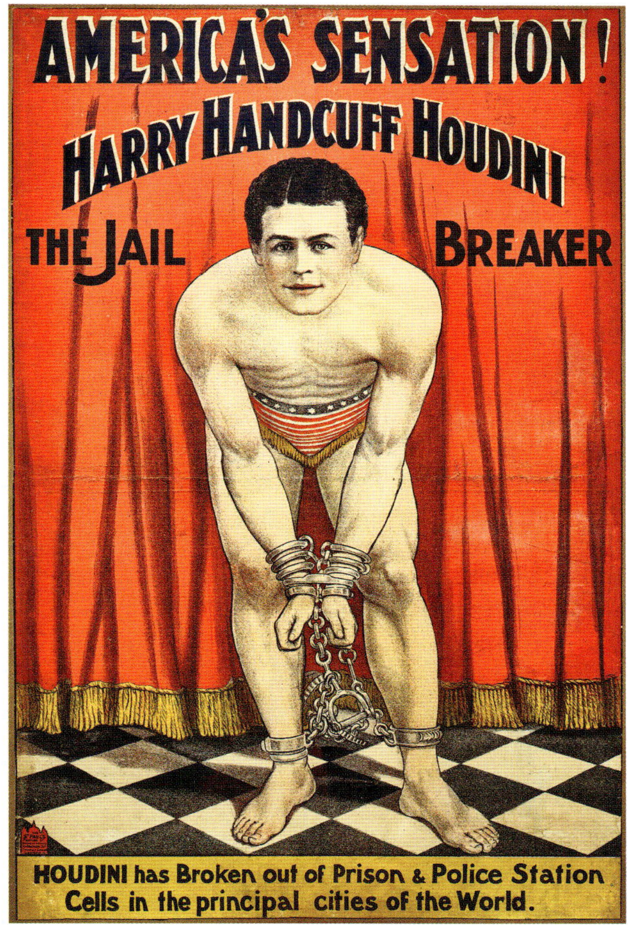

St. Louis, Missouri, police certification of the escape of Harry Houdini (1874–1926)
1899
Billy Rose Theatre Division, The New York Public Library for the Performing Arts, Dorothy and Lewis B. Cullman Center

"America's Sensation! Harry Handcuff Houdini" poster
London: St. Paul's Printing Co., ca. 1900
Billy Rose Theatre Division, The New York Public Library for the Performing Arts, Dorothy and Lewis B. Cullman Center

In the mid-1890s, Harry Houdini was a struggling magician finding little recognition in card tricks and sleight of hand. By 1898, he was seeking out police and civic leaders across the United States to witness his seemingly inexplicable escapes from regulation handcuffs, shackles, and other restraints. This document from Houdini's visit to St. Louis in August 1899—one of seventy-eight extremely rare "police certificates" the Theatre Division holds—bears the signatures of eleven witnesses, including the chief of police, the chief of detectives, and a reporter for the *St. Louis Post-Dispatch*, all swearing there was "absolutely no chance of confederacy" in his extrication. In 1900 vaudeville booking agent Martin Beck encouraged Houdini to take his escape act to England, where he received great acclaim. This poster is among the earliest issued on his British tour, depicting Houdini poised at the brink of stardom. The Library's rare collection of Houdiniana traces the intersection of magic, promotion, and celebrity at the dawn of the 20th century.

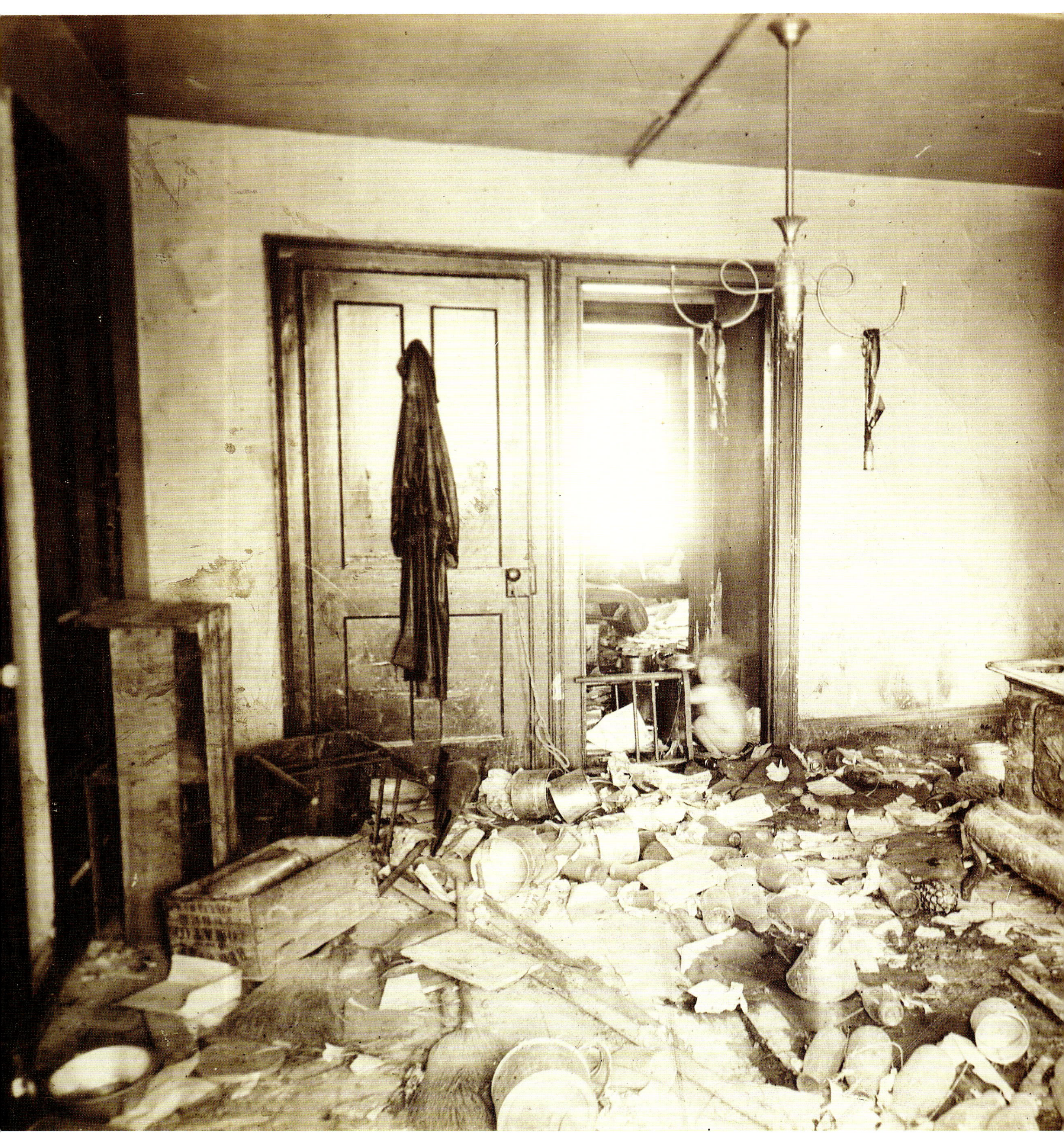

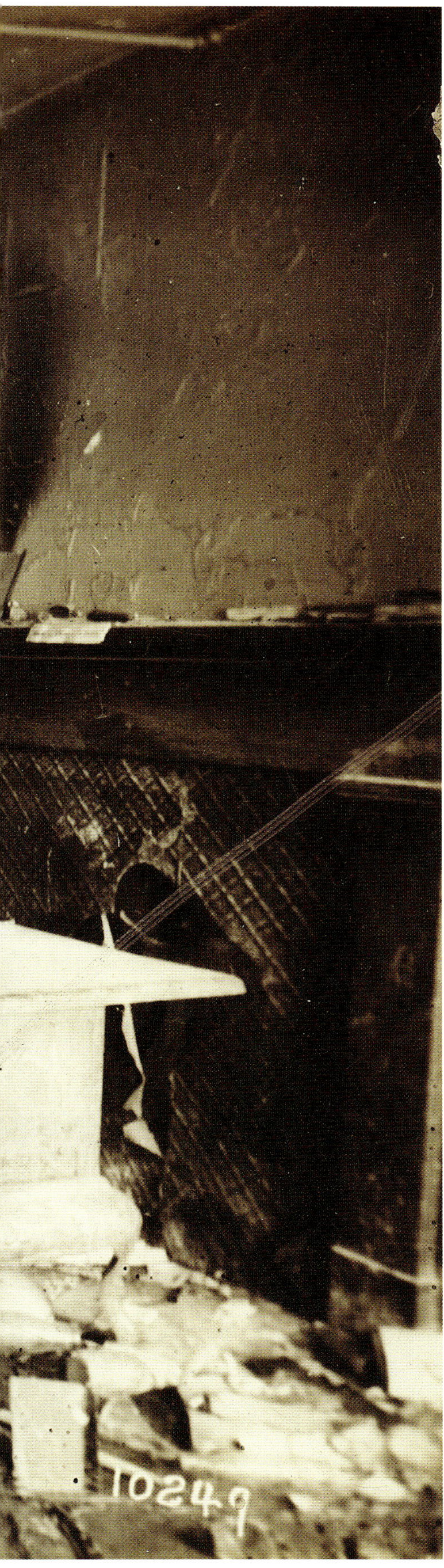

New York City Tenement House Department

Plate 10249: "One of the dirtiest and most unsanitary rooms ever found by the Tenement House Department. Cleaned by order of Department" from the series *New York City Tenement House Department Photographic Prints Illustrating Conditions and Problems of Tenement Housing 1902–1922*

ca. 1909

Irma and Paul Milstein Division of United States History, Local History and Genealogy

Jacob Riis's groundbreaking 1890 publication, *How the Other Half Lives*, presented photographic evidence that led to greater and more visible efforts to ameliorate the squalid living conditions that the urban poor experienced by reforming public policy.

In 1898, Lawrence Veiller, the organizer and first Deputy Commissioner of the New York City Tenement House Department and the director of a charitable group's Tenement House Committee, said that the Committee's chief aim was to "make a general study of the tenement house question." He launched a comprehensive method for documenting every tenement building in New York City (already in excess of 80,000 in 1902) in a card file. The Committee's photographs, in a style reminiscent of Riis's jarring visuals and combined with dramatically worded descriptions, were intended specifically for communication with the public. This image includes a glimpse of a child in the background, blurred by the camera's long shutter speed—a phantom alerting the viewer that this seemingly abandoned space is actually very much occupied.

Victor Prevost (1820–1881)
Central park in 1862
New York, ca. 1862
Rare Book Division

Victor Prevost studied photography in France under Paul Delaroche and Gustave Le Gray and was one of the earliest photographers to work in New York City. Prevost established a studio at Broadway and Bleecker Street upon his arrival in 1850, but he achieved only limited commercial success and ultimately gave up photography as a career in 1857. He continued, however, to take photographs of major construction projects in the city, the most important of which are his images of the then-new Central Park. Shot mostly during the summer of 1862, these photographs reveal a rapidly changing landscape as the once-rural Manhattan north of 59th Street gave way to urban development.

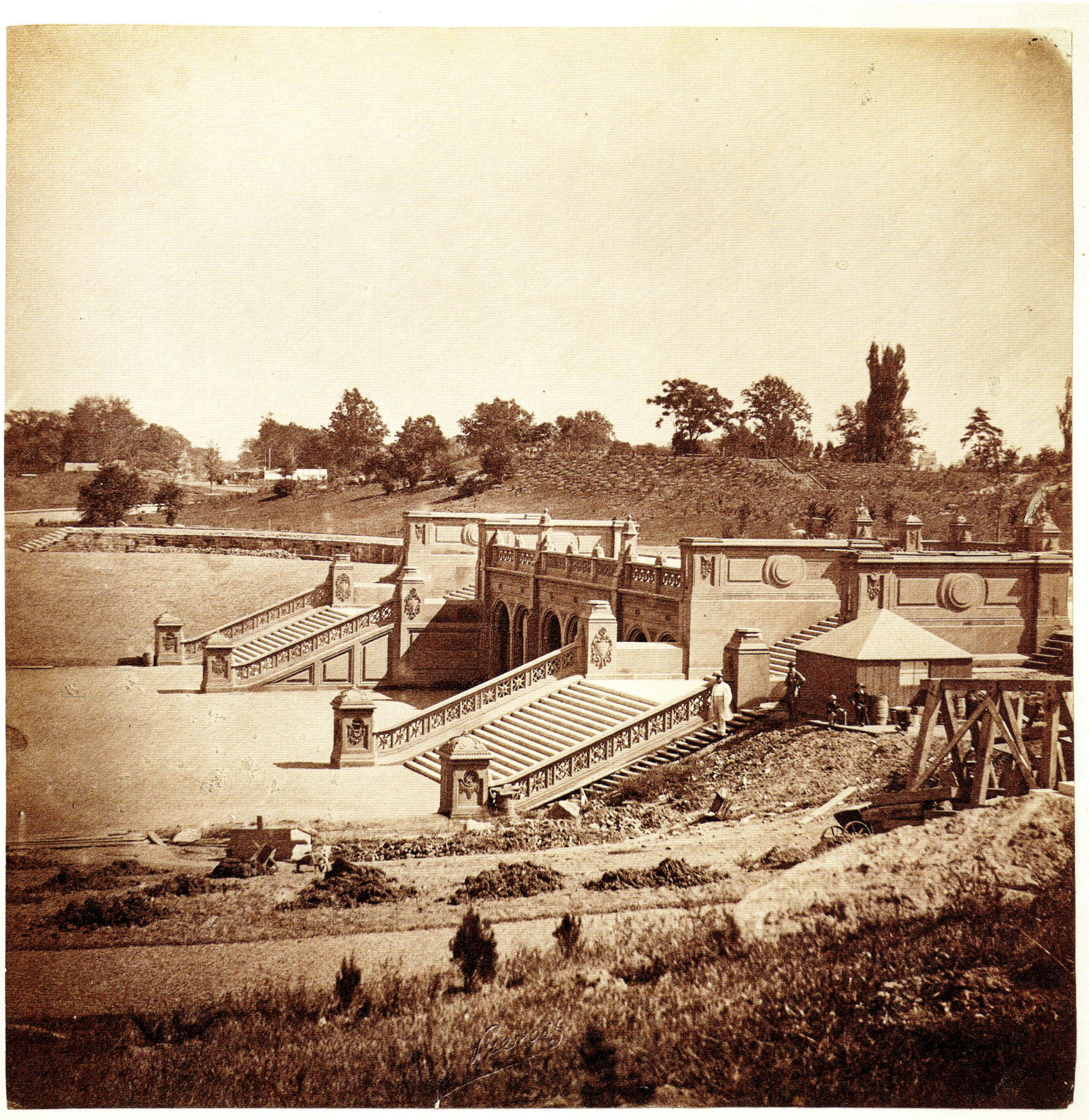

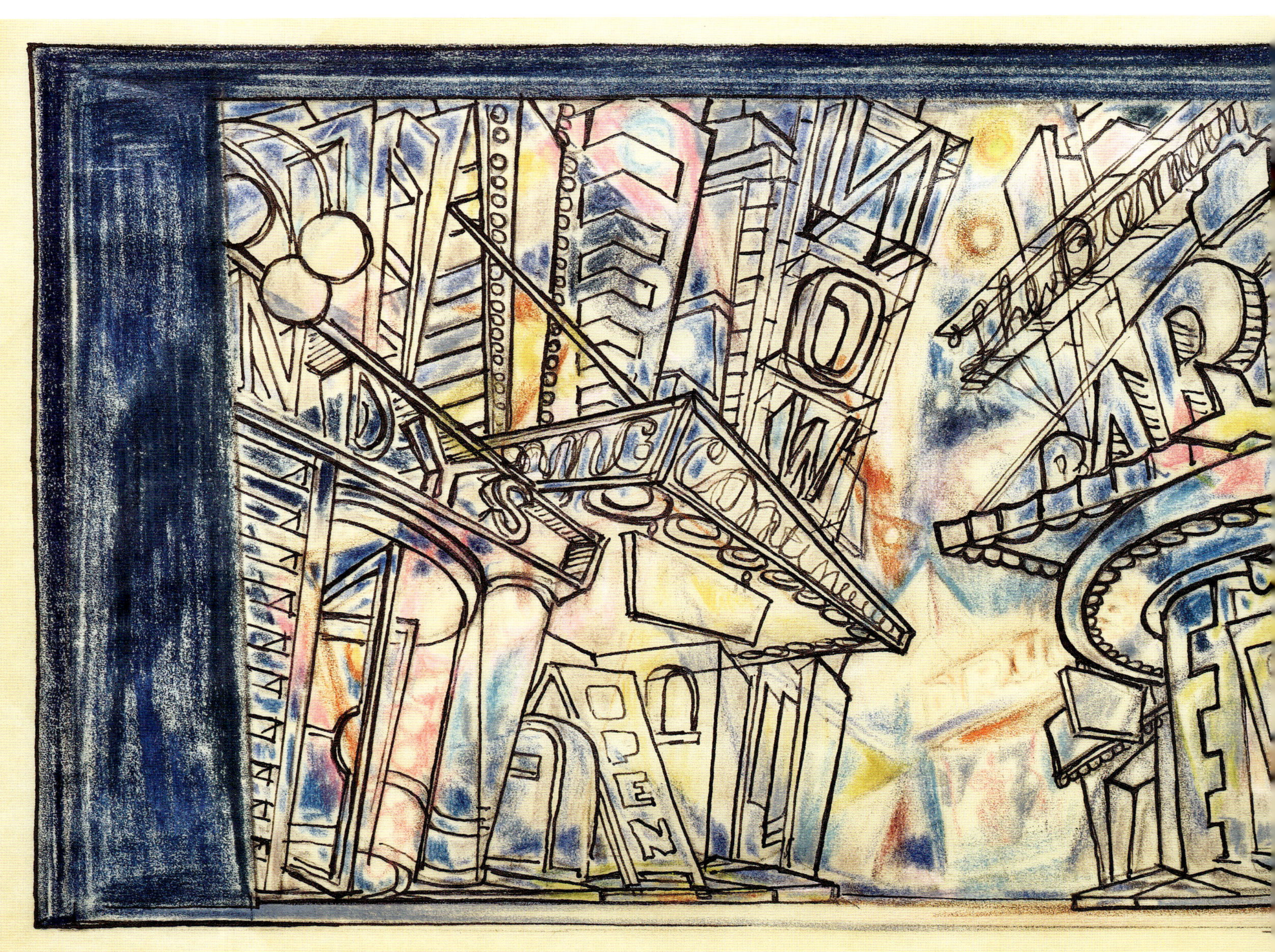

OPEN

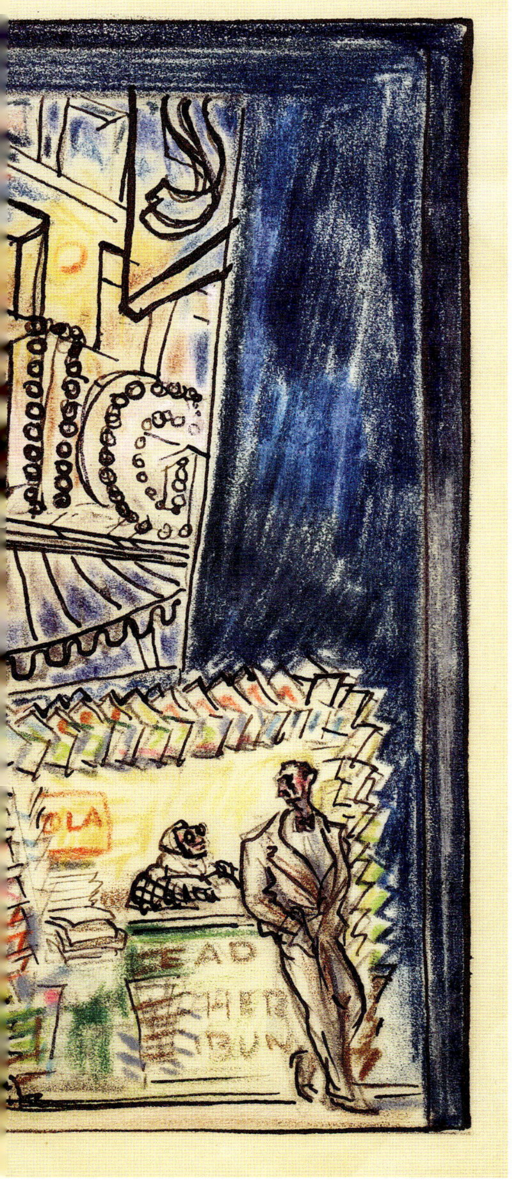

Jo Mielziner (1901–1976), designer and artist
***Guys and Dolls* "Street Scene A" design**
Colored pencil on tracing paper, 1950
Billy Rose Theatre Division, The New York Public Library for the Performing Arts, Dorothy and Lewis B. Cullman Center

Jo Mielziner was one of the most celebrated and prolific set, costume, and lighting designers of the 20th century. Mielziner's vision gave three-dimensional life to the original productions of the theatrical masterpieces *1776*, *Annie Get Your Gun*, *Carousel*, *Cat on a Hot Tin Roof*, *The Crucible*, *Death of a Salesman*, *Gypsy*, *The King and I*, *Pal Joey*, *South Pacific*, and *A Streetcar Named Desire*, among many others. For generations of designers and historians, Mielziner has been seen as an artist's artist, deftly conveying theatrical narrative and all its energy, pathos, fear, and joy through the seemingly simple act of placing color on a two-dimensional surface. In his designs for *Guys and Dolls*, the 1950 Broadway musical adaptation of Damon Runyon's short story "The Idyll of Miss Sarah Brown," Mielziner used tracing paper and vibrant colored pencil to convey the riotous activity of the musical's caricature of New York's Times Square (called "Runyonland" in Abe Burrows's script).

Hugh Ferriss (1889–1962)

"Chrysler Building" from *The Metropolis of Tomorrow*

New York: Ives Washburn, 1929

The Miriam and Ira D. Wallach Division of Art, Prints and Photographs, Art & Architecture Collection

While no building he designed was ever constructed, Hugh Ferriss was known as an eminent draftsman of other architects' work. Commissioned in 1916 to speculate about how new zoning laws might one day affect the urban landscape, Ferriss executed a series of influential drawings envisioning the way that setbacks might generate thousand-foot structures such as the Empire State Building. These chiaroscuro designs, guided by Ferriss's interest in psychology, also explored the ways in which various skyscraper models could represent differing mental states and foster radical social change. The Chrysler Building, here depicted under construction, temporarily attained the status of the tallest building in the world. The building's remarkable Art Deco design by William Van Alen featured a 125-foot-tall spire, a black granite and white marble base, and the first American use of a permanently bright stainless steel. Stylized gargoyles refer to the American Eagle and Chrysler automobiles' steel hood ornaments. Ferriss's futuristic work, eventually published in book form, influenced the design of components of the 1939 New York World's Fair and the United Nations' headquarters—not to mention the invention of Batman's Gotham.

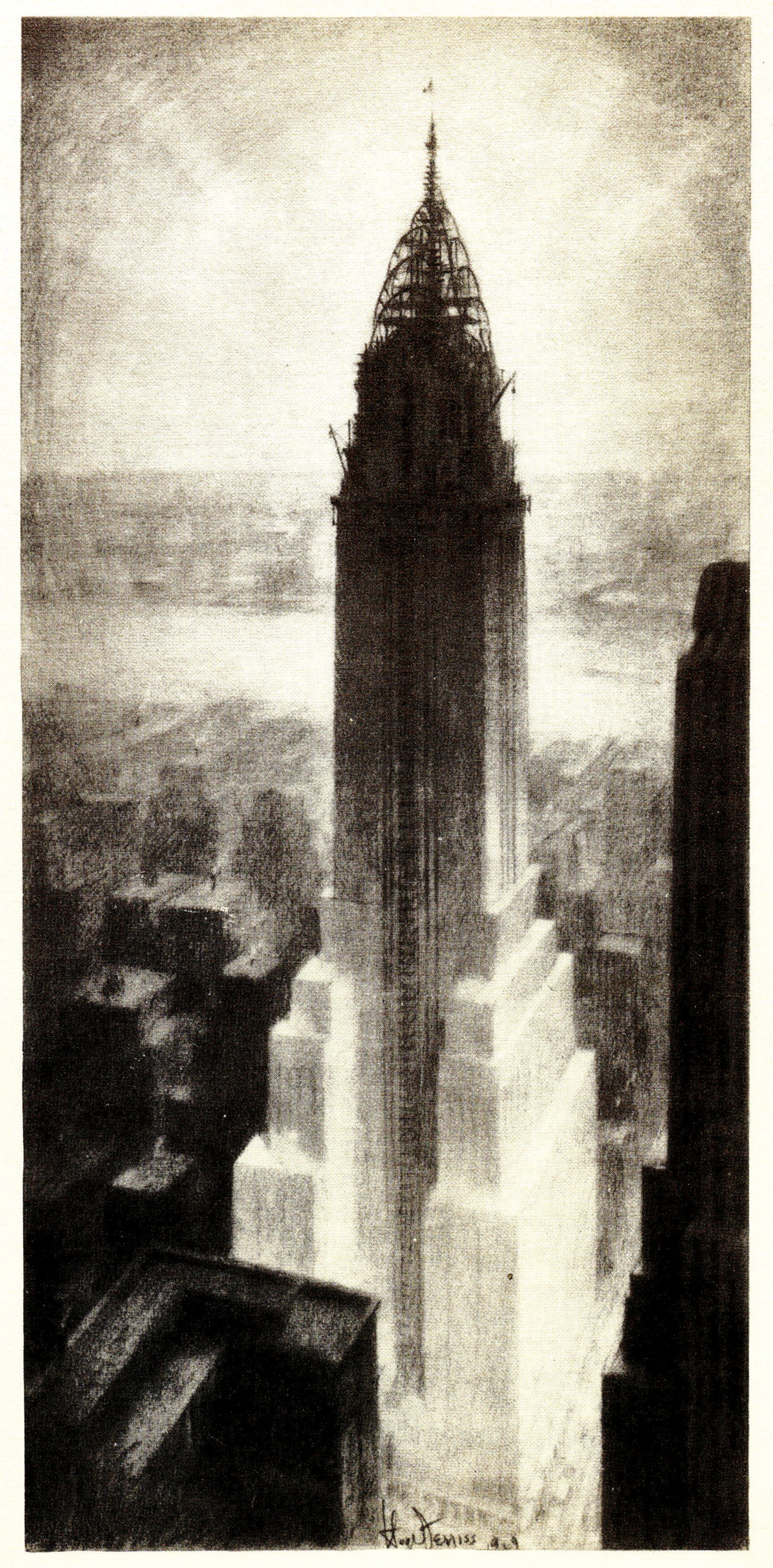

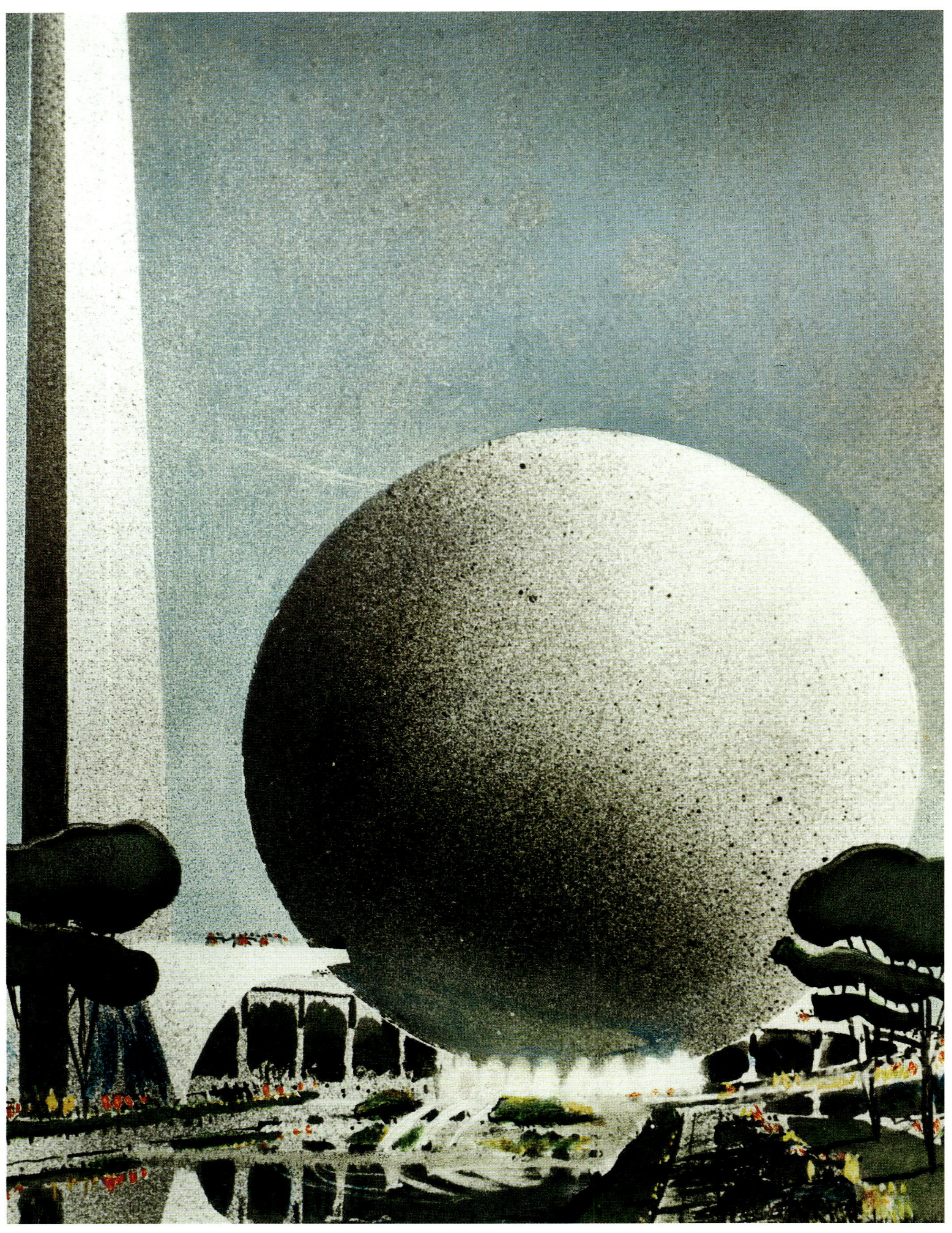

Wallace Harrison (1895–1981) and J. André Fouilhoux (1879–1945)
Trylon and Perisphere
Hand-colored photograph, 1939
Manuscripts and Archives Division

Wallace Harrison and J. André Fouilhoux, the architects of the two most iconic structures of the 1939 World's Fair shown here, coined the names Trylon and Perisphere for the obelisk and orb, respectively. New York City Parks Commissioner Robert Moses, considered the city's "master builder," had teamed up with the city's Department of Sanitation to transform an old ash dump in Queens into the sprawling grounds of the World's Fair in the new Flushing Meadows Park. The 600-foot-high Trylon and 180-foot-wide Perisphere are still recognized as symbols of the Fair. The Perisphere housed the "Democracity" exhibition, depicting "the city of the future." While "Building the World of Tomorrow" was the theme of the Fair when Albert Einstein spoke at its opening, the start of World War II prompted organizers to change it the following year to "For Peace and Freedom." The Trylon and Perisphere were both dismantled at the Fair's closing in 1940.

Carleton E. Watkins (1829–1916)

The Yosemite Valley from Inspiration Point

Albumen print, 1865–1866

The Miriam and Ira D. Wallach Division of Art, Prints and Photographs, Photography Collection

Carleton Watkins was not the first to make pictures in Yosemite, or from Inspiration Point—a granite shelf off the Mariposa Trail that offers sweeping views of the Yosemite Valley below—but he was inarguably the most daring and influential 19th-century artist to do so. When Watkins embarked on his first trip into Yosemite in 1861, he brought with him a new camera designed to record highly detailed images on glass plates measuring 18 by 22 inches, by far the largest of their day. This was no easy feat; the arduous journey required assistants and a pack of mules to transport 2,000 pounds of fragile equipment both into and out of the valley. By the time Watkins returned to Yosemite in 1865, and in part due to his dramatic, large-scale compositions, President Abraham Lincoln had signed a bill to preserve Yosemite in perpetuity—thus paving the way for the future National Park System and a conservation movement that is still ongoing.

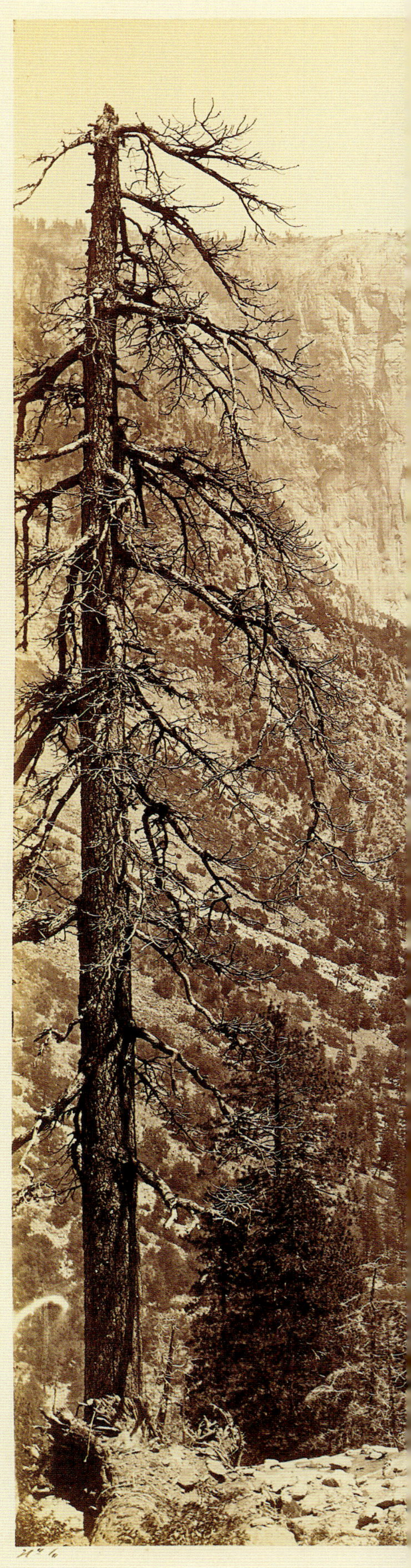

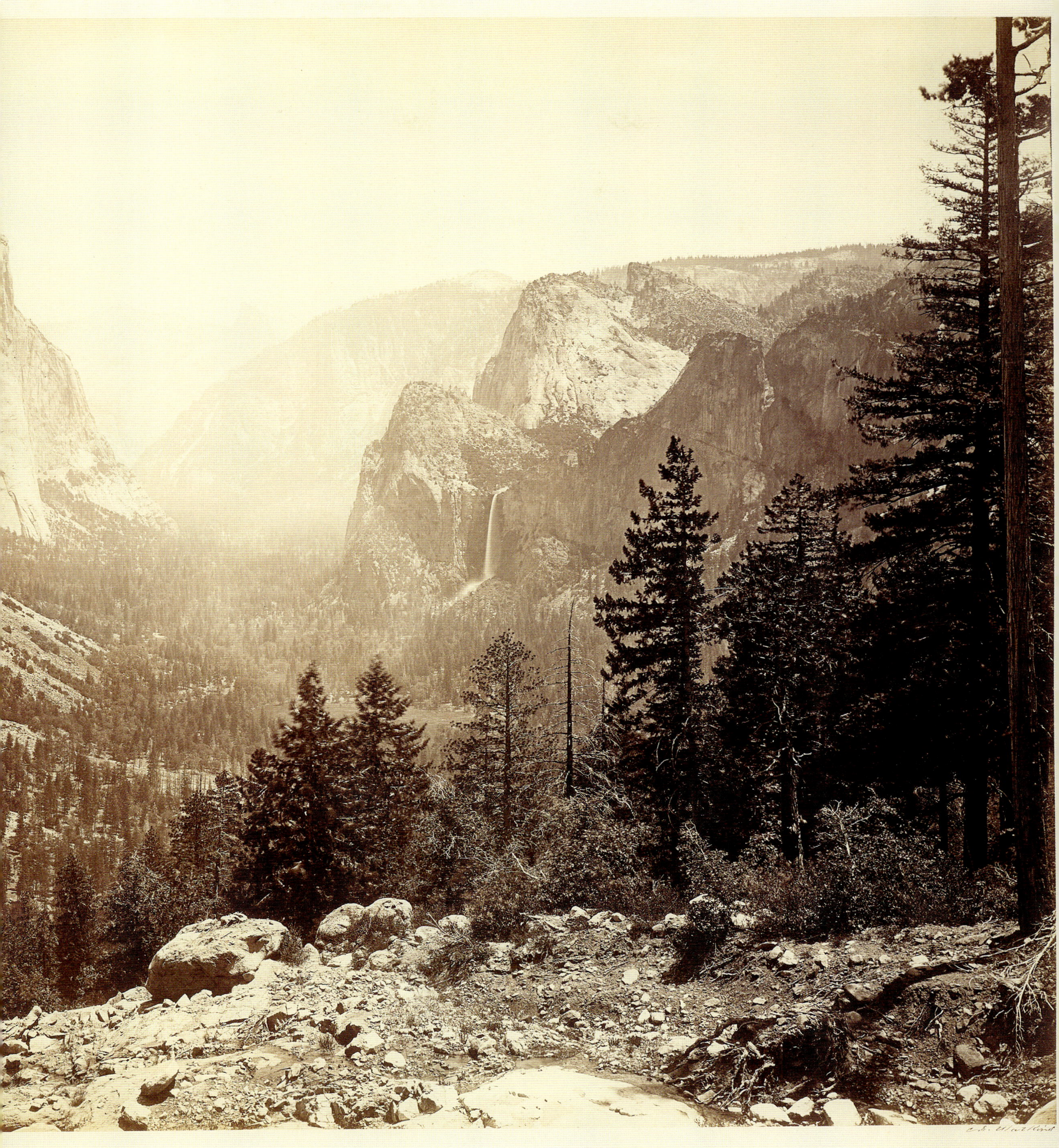

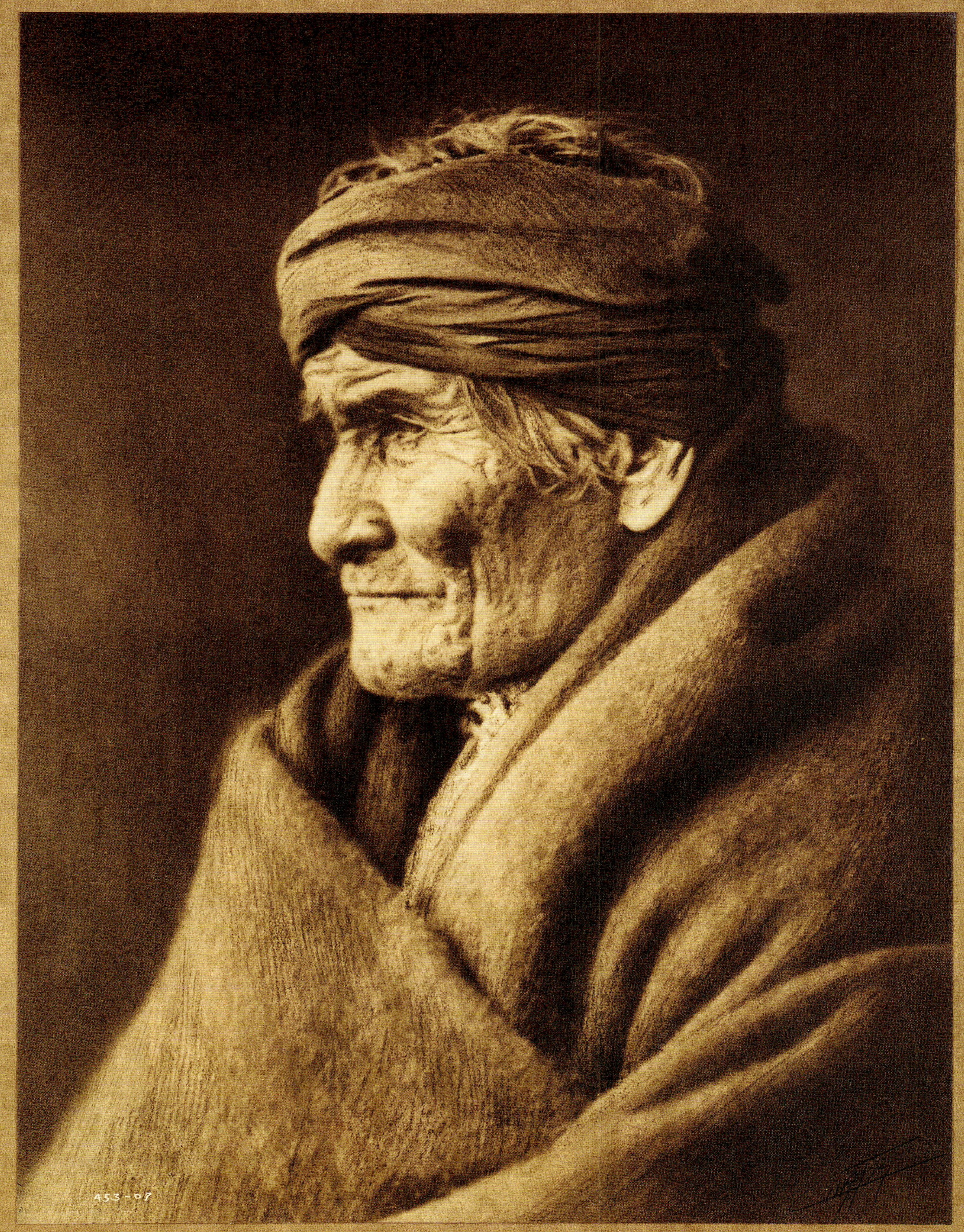
453-07

Edward Sheriff Curtis (1868–1952)

Geronimo-Apache* from the series *The North American Indian

Platinum print, ca. 1907

The Miriam and Ira D. Wallach Division of Art, Prints and Photographs, Photography Collection

Edward Curtis made this photograph of Geronimo in 1905 while he was in Washington, D.C., for the second inauguration of Theodore Roosevelt. Curtis was on his East Coast exhibition tour to gain financial backing for his monumental project, *The North American Indian*, which aimed to record in sound, film, text, and photographs the life, culture, and environment of all of the still extant American Indian tribes who continued to live on their lands and practice their traditional ways. Curtis approached J. Pierpont Morgan, who at first refused to help, but the beauty of Curtis's photography convinced Morgan of the project's merit. Around 1911, Morgan donated one hundred exhibition prints from the series to the Library, including this one.

Gertrude Parthenia McBrown (1898–1989), author
Loïs Mailou Jones (1905–1998), illustrator

The Picture-Poetry Book

Washington, D.C.: The Associated Publishers, Inc., 1935
Jean Blackwell Hutson Research and Reference Division, Schomburg Center for Research in Black Culture

Associated Publishers, a black-owned and -operated publishing house founded by Dr. Carter G. Woodson, issued *The Picture-Poetry Book* in 1935. It was the first book of poetry by the dramatic artist, historian, and author Gertrude P. McBrown and featured illustrations by the budding artist Loïs Mailou Jones. Jones was born in Boston and trained at the School of the Museum of Fine Arts, Boston (now part of Tufts University). She began her career as a textile designer, but due to racial and gender discrimination, she decided to study fine art. She achieved her first success in Paris in the 1930s. Inspired by the styles of African, Caribbean, and African-American masters whose work she most admired, Jones strove to humanize the figurative representation of blacks. Jones was also a noted educator who taught painting and related subjects at Howard University for forty-seven years, counting David Driskell, Elizabeth Catlett, and Robert Freeman among her illustrious students. She received recognition in her lifetime through exhibitions as well as representation in important museum collections. This volume is included in the bibliography *The Black Experience in Children's Books* that was compiled by Augusta Baker, who was the Library's first African-American administrator and renowned for her contributions to children's literature.

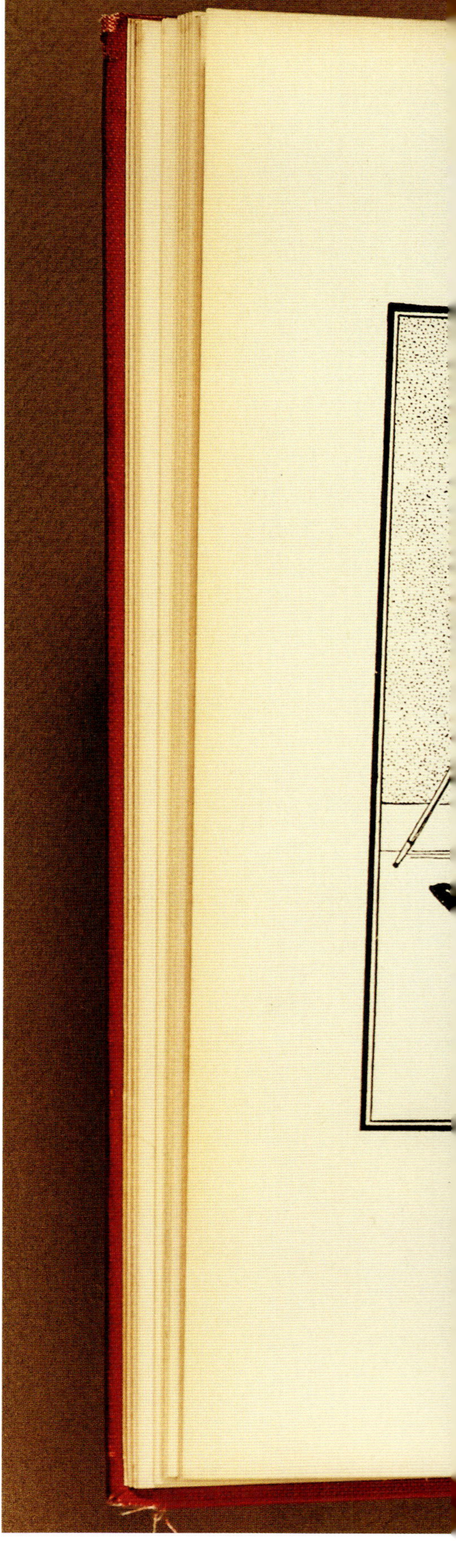

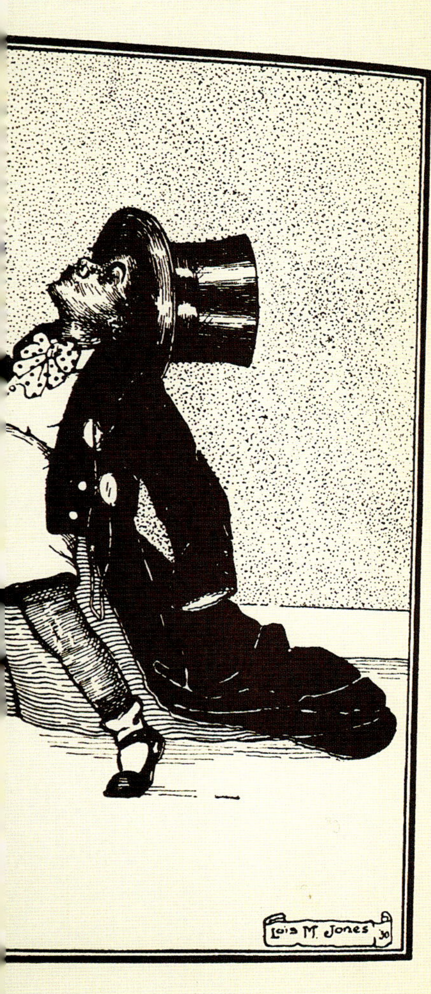

A Lawyer

I'm going to be a lawyer when I grow,
I'll sit up late by the big desk light
And write long papers every night;
I'm going to be a lawyer when I grow,
Daddy is a lawyer and he walks just so.

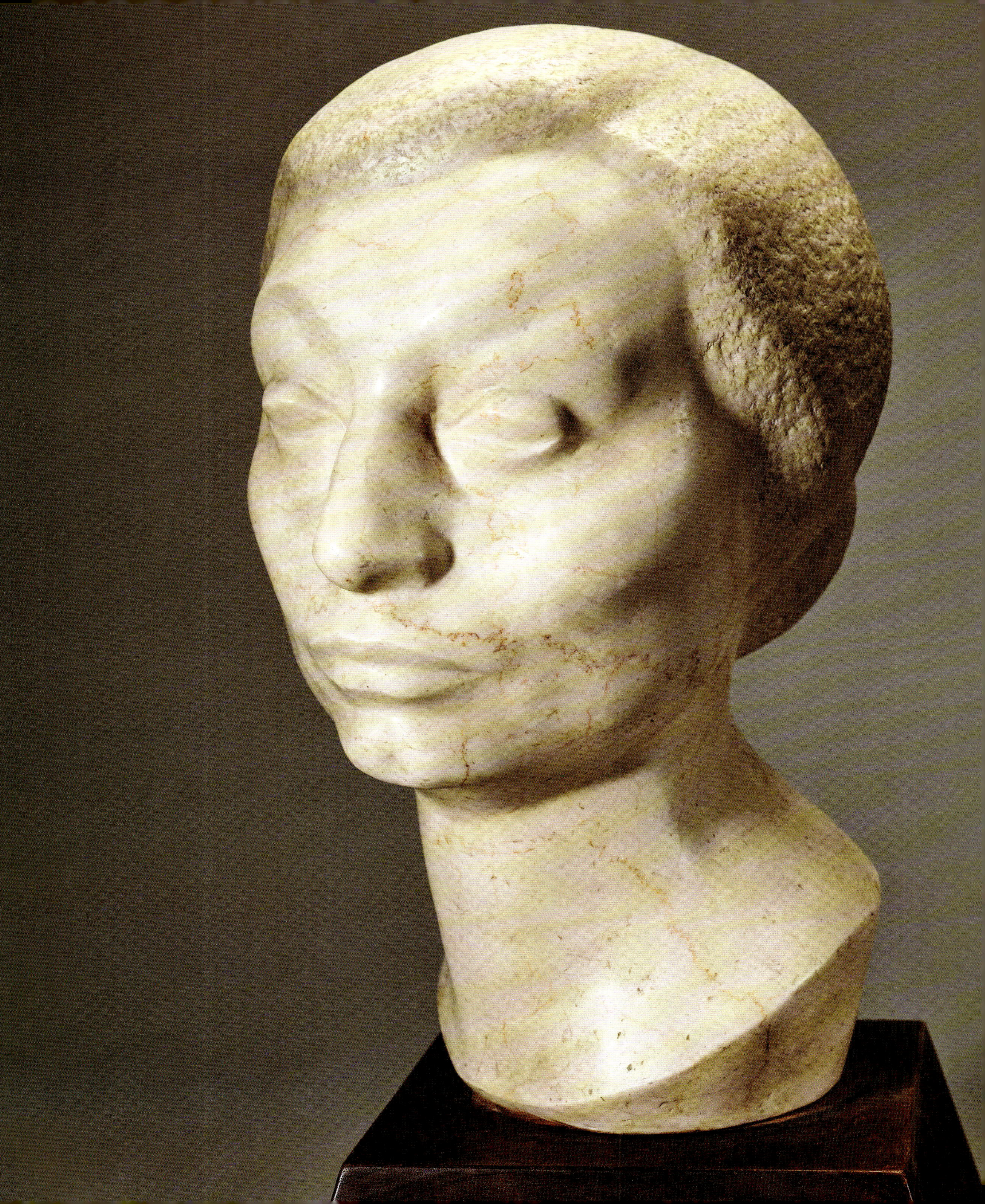

Isamu Noguchi (1904–1988)
Portrait bust of Aline MacMahon (1899–1991)
Botticino marble, 1937
Billy Rose Theatre Division, The New York Public Library for the Performing Arts, Dorothy and Lewis B. Cullman Center

Although best known for his abstract and conceptual sculpture, landscape designs, and furniture, the Japanese-American artist Isamu Noguchi began his career sculpting portrait busts. He returned to the form often during his decades-long career. Many of Noguchi's friends and subjects were members of the creative community in New York City, where he produced much of his work. The actress Aline MacMahon made her New York stage debut in 1921 with the experimental Neighborhood Playhouse company, and later found recognition as an actress on Broadway and in Hollywood. In 1930, MacMahon gave Noguchi money to travel to East Asia; in 1937, Noguchi repaid her with this bust. The sculptor found particular inspiration in MacMahon's elegant and serene countenance, playing the rounded forms in her hair against the planar lines of her contemplative face. MacMahon donated her personal archive and this bust to the Theatre Division shortly before her death.

Lorraine Hansberry (1930–1965), adapted by
Robert Nemiroff (1929–1991)
To Be Young, Gifted, and Black
ca. 1966
Lorraine Hansberry Papers, Manuscripts, Archives and Rare Books Division, Schomburg Center for Research in Black Culture

To Be Young, Gifted, and Black was an Off-Broadway play about the African-American playwright Lorraine Hansberry, adapted from her published and unpublished works after her premature death by her ex-husband and collaborator, Robert Nemiroff. This first page of a draft script features several elements of Hansberry's oeuvre, including fragments of her views on art and a scene from *A Raisin in the Sun*, the enormously successful play that in 1959 made history as the first work by an African-American woman to be produced on Broadway. The play catapulted Hansberry to fame at the age of twenty-nine. *To Be Young, Gifted, and Black* takes its title from a phrase of Hansberry's. It captures the celebration and possibilities of black experience and talent that Hansberry both embodied and dramatized in her life and work.

PART ONE

~~PART I PROLOGUE~~

Prologue

THEME MUSIC UP: a jaunty, swinging, Black ~~xxx~~ melody, which continues under the RECORDED VOICE of ~~LO... H...~~ — "

LORRAINE HANSBERRY ~~(ON TAPE)~~

My name is Lorraine Hansberry. I am a writer. I suppose I think that the highest gift that man has is art, and I am audacious enough to think of myself as an artist — That there is both joy and beauty and illumination and communion between people to be achieved through the dissection of personality. ~~--~~ That's what I want to do. I want to reach a little closer to the world, which is to say to people, and see if we can share some illuminations together about each other. . . .

RUTH and ~~LIGHTS UP on~~ WALTER LEE YOUNGER, ~~in pajamas or bathrobe and his wife RUTH in housecoat.~~ a young black couple in their early thirties, enter: SHE in housecoat; HE, somewhat behind her, in pants and undershirt.

WALTER

(Embracing her from behind)

You look young this morning, baby.

RUTH

(Indifferently)

Yeah?

LORRAINE HANSBERRY ~~(ON TAPE)~~

I happen to believe that most people, and this is where I differ from many of my contemporaries, or at least as they express themselves, I think that virtually every human being is dramatically interesting. Not only is he dramatically interesting, he is a creature of stature whoever he is.

WALTER

Just for a second -- stirring them eggs. ~~It's gone now -- just for a second it was --~~ You looked real young again.

(Then, drily, releasing her)

It's gone now -- you look like yourself again.

THEY freeze.

RUTH

Man, if you don't shut up and leave me alone.

WALTER

First thing a man ought to learn in life is not to make love to no colored woman first thing in the morning. You all some ~~evil~~ e-e-evil people at eight o'clock in the morning.

RUTH

Oh, Walter Lee ...

~~(SHE folds her head on her arms over the table)~~

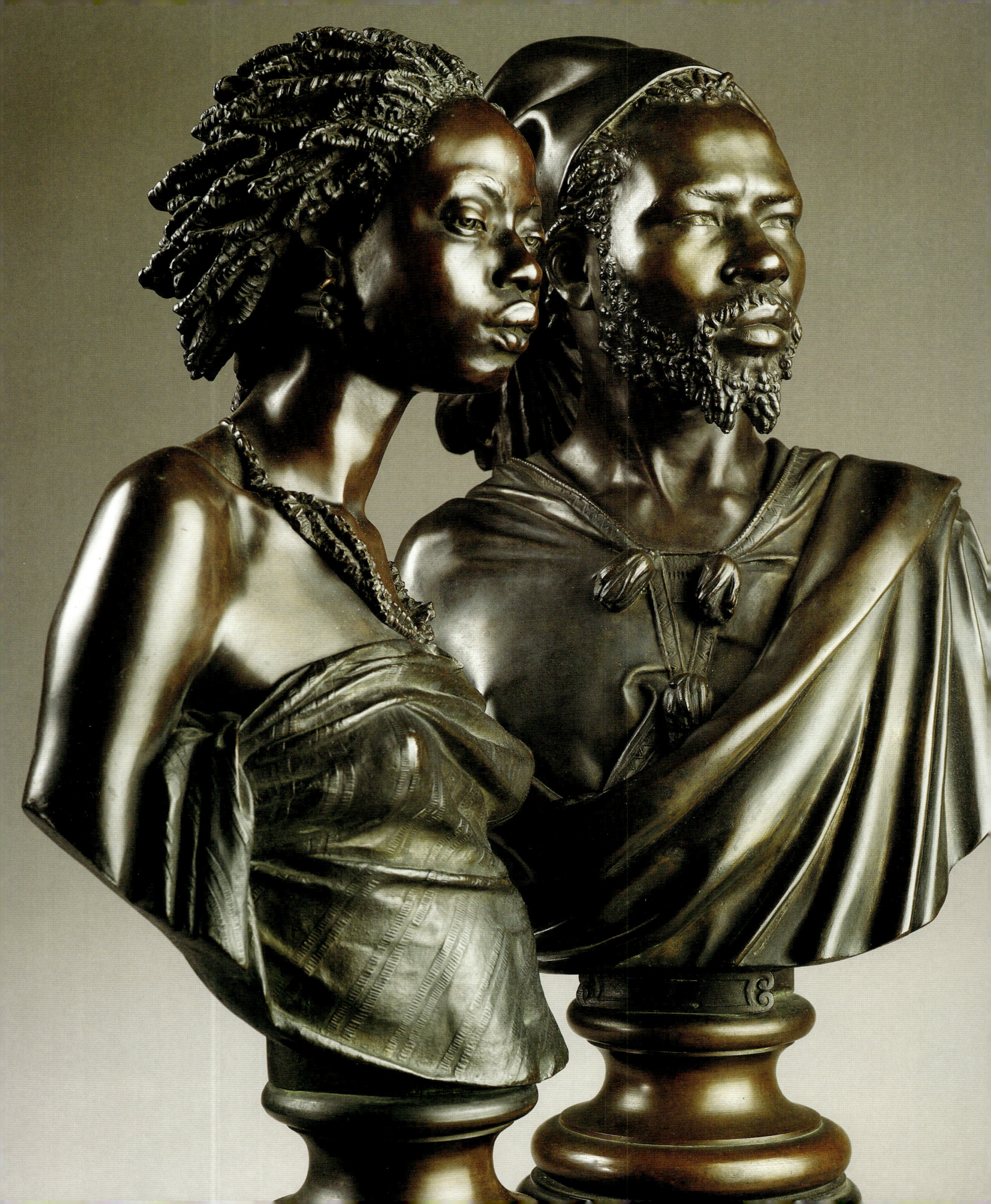

Charles Henri Joseph Cordier (1827–1905)
Vénus africaine
Bronze, 1852
Art and Artifacts Division, Schomburg Center for Research in Black Culture

Saïd Abdullah, de la Tribu de Mayac, Royaume de Darfour
Bronze, 1852
Art and Artifacts Division, Schomburg Center for Research in Black Culture

Charles Cordier's sculpture of Saïd Abdullah earned great renown not only for its splendor, but also for the dignity and pride it conveyed about its subject, an African man. Cordier submitted a plaster cast of the bust of Abdullah to the Paris Salon in 1848 and a bronze to the Salon of 1850, and he submitted both original bronze busts to London's Great Exhibition in 1851. Queen Victoria subsequently purchased them.

In 1926, grant money from the Carnegie Foundation enabled the Library to purchase Arthur Schomburg's collection of black cultural treasures for the 135th Street Branch of the Library. The money from the sale allowed Mr. Schomburg to embark on a collecting and research trip through France, where he purchased this pair of sculptures. They are believed to be the first acquisitions he donated to the Schomburg Collection. His papers show that on his return to America, Mr. Schomburg corresponded with a friend, requesting that he conduct research on the bronze busts he had purchased for the collection.

Maya Angelou (1928–2014)

Manuscript draft of *I Know Why the Caged Bird Sings*

ca. 1969

Maya Angelou Papers, Manuscripts, Archives and Rare Books Division, Schomburg Center for Research in Black Culture

Published in 1969, Maya Angelou's coming-of-age memoir, *I Know Why the Caged Bird Sings*, was an immediate national bestseller and a critical success. The first in a series of books that chronicled her life through the 1960s, this work helped to establish Angelou as a major figure in American letters. On this manuscript page from the book, Angelou captures the moment when she and her brother, Bailey, arrived in Arkansas to be raised by their paternal grandmother and presages the personalities that she and Bailey would later develop. With connections to activist, literary, and expat communities in the United States and Ghana, Angelou's work encapsulates the Schomburg Center's strongest holdings—stories of the struggles, triumphs, and everyday vicissitudes of black life.

"Caged Bird" Refile 1

My brother and I arrived in Stamps, Ark. with grey tags on our wrists and notes pinned on our clothes that stated Marguerite Johnson, Stamps Ark. and Bailey Johnson Stamps Ark. c/o Annie Henderson. I was three and Bailey was four, and we had travelled from Long Beach, California. The entire trip was for me like slides seen on a torn sheet. A porter in whose care we had been put, got off the train after he gave us to another porter. We ate sandwiches and cold fried chicken and sometimes Bailey made me stretch out, and ordered me to sleep, then went away. and the windows Some people said we were good children and that Bailey was "a little man". and then we were being met by our grandmother Henderson who was so big, and brown, and her hair stood on end like a teddy bear. I was told later that Bailey cried when he first saw our destination, and begged to be sent back to his mother Dear, but that I simply said that I was hungry. How unlike the the personalities we later developed. I was to become the dramatic character, and Bailey, the cold, precise, calculated one.

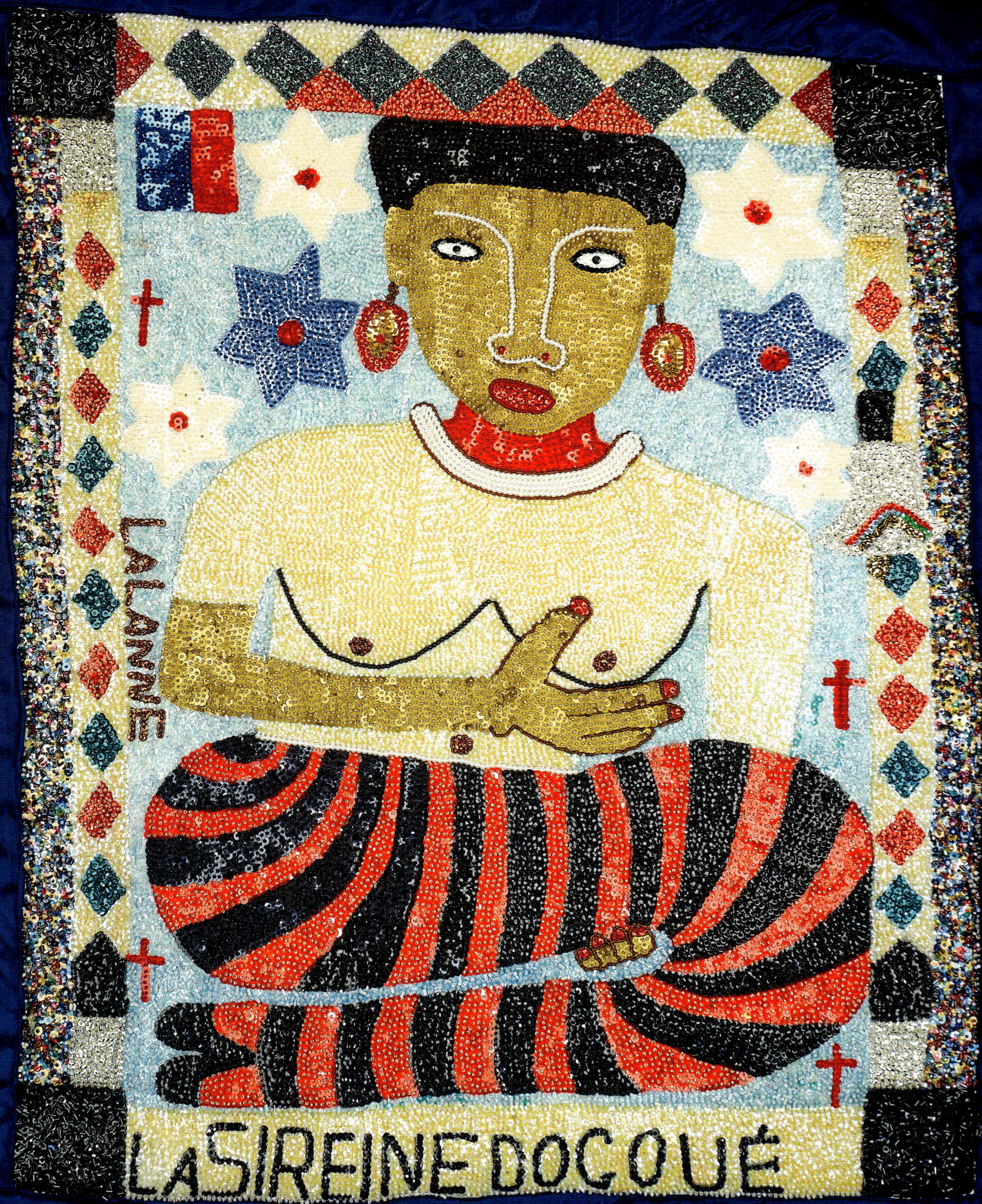
LALANNE
LA SIREINE DOGOUÉ

"La Sireine Dogoué" *vèvè* flag
ca. 1990
Art and Artifacts Division, Schomburg Center for Research in Black Culture

Elaborately decorated with sequins and beadwork, *vèvè* flags derive from the beliefs and practice of Haitian Vodou, or Voodoo. They are carried at the commencement of ceremonies in which followers call on spirits, known as *loa*, to receive offerings, grant requests, and settle grievances, among other functions. *Loa* are not deities themselves; rather, they are supernatural beings who act as intermediaries between humans and the supreme deity, called Bondye. This *vèvè* flag signifies the spirit La Sireine Dogoué, a mermaid-like figure who, along with her male counterpart Agoue, exercises control over all things aquatic.

Cartier, designer and manufacturer
***Adios, Argentina* cigarette case owned by Cole Porter (1891–1964)**
14-karat gold, ca. 1934
Billy Rose Theatre Division, The New York Public Library for the Performing Arts, Dorothy and Lewis B. Cullman Center

"Another openin', another show" . . . and another cigarette case. Cole Porter's wife, Linda Lee Thomas, famously presented her songwriter husband with a cigarette case on the opening night of his musicals. His hit musical comedies include *Anything Goes* (1934) and *Kiss Me, Kate* (1948), and a number of his songs—"I Get a Kick Out of You," "I've Got You Under My Skin," "Begin the Beguine," and many others—are renowned as jazz standards. Although there was never to be an opening for the ill-fated, unproduced movie musical *Adios, Argentina*, for which Porter wrote the classic song "Don't Fence Me In," the project was memorialized with this cigarette case given as a Christmas present in 1934. The case, designed and manufactured by Cartier, bears the inscription, "Adios, Argentina XMAS 1934" and an engraved caricature of Porter at his piano. This is just one of the many artifacts in the Billy Rose Theatre Division documenting the work of musical theater composers and lyricists.

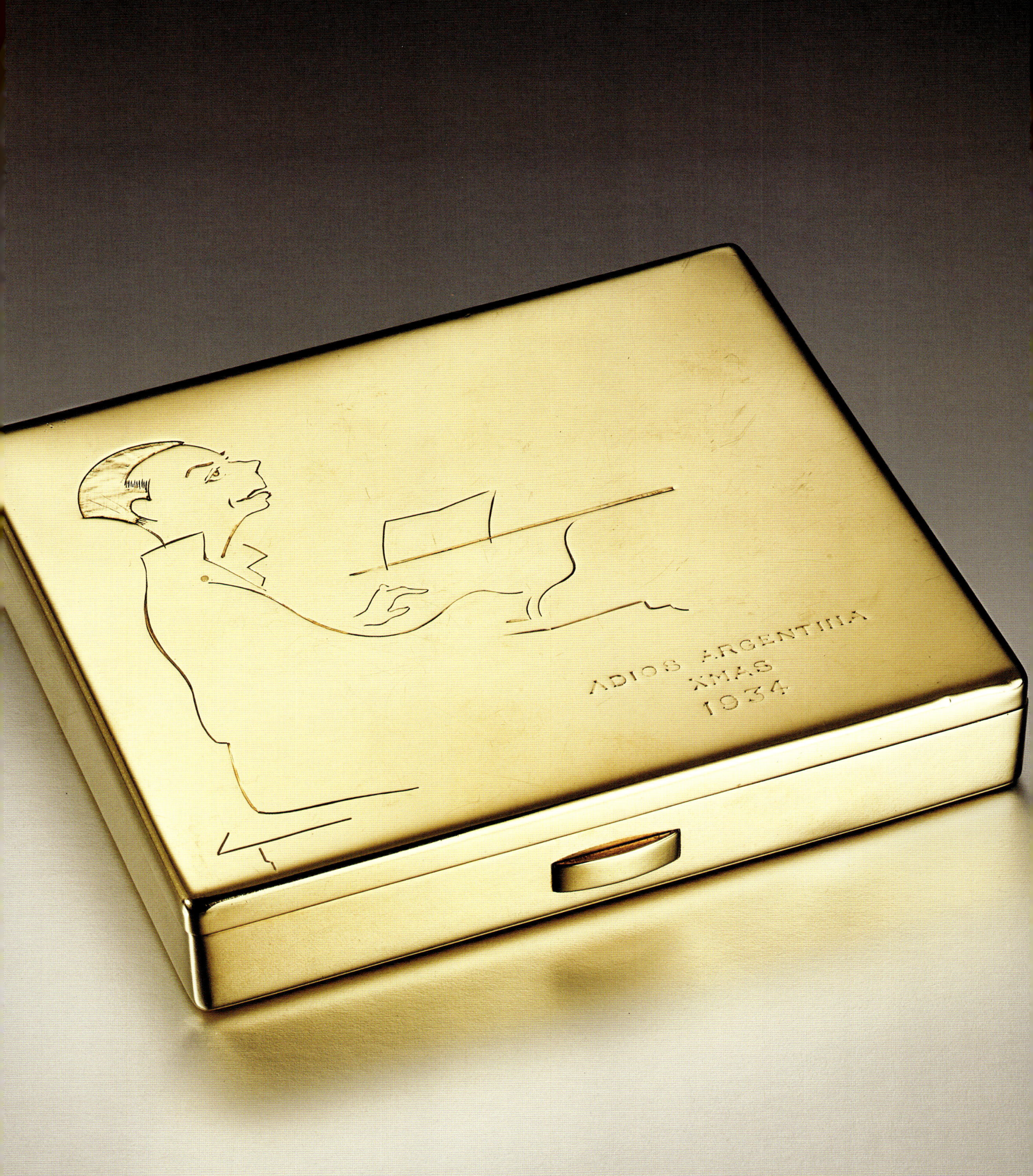
ADIOS ARGENTINA
XMAS
1934

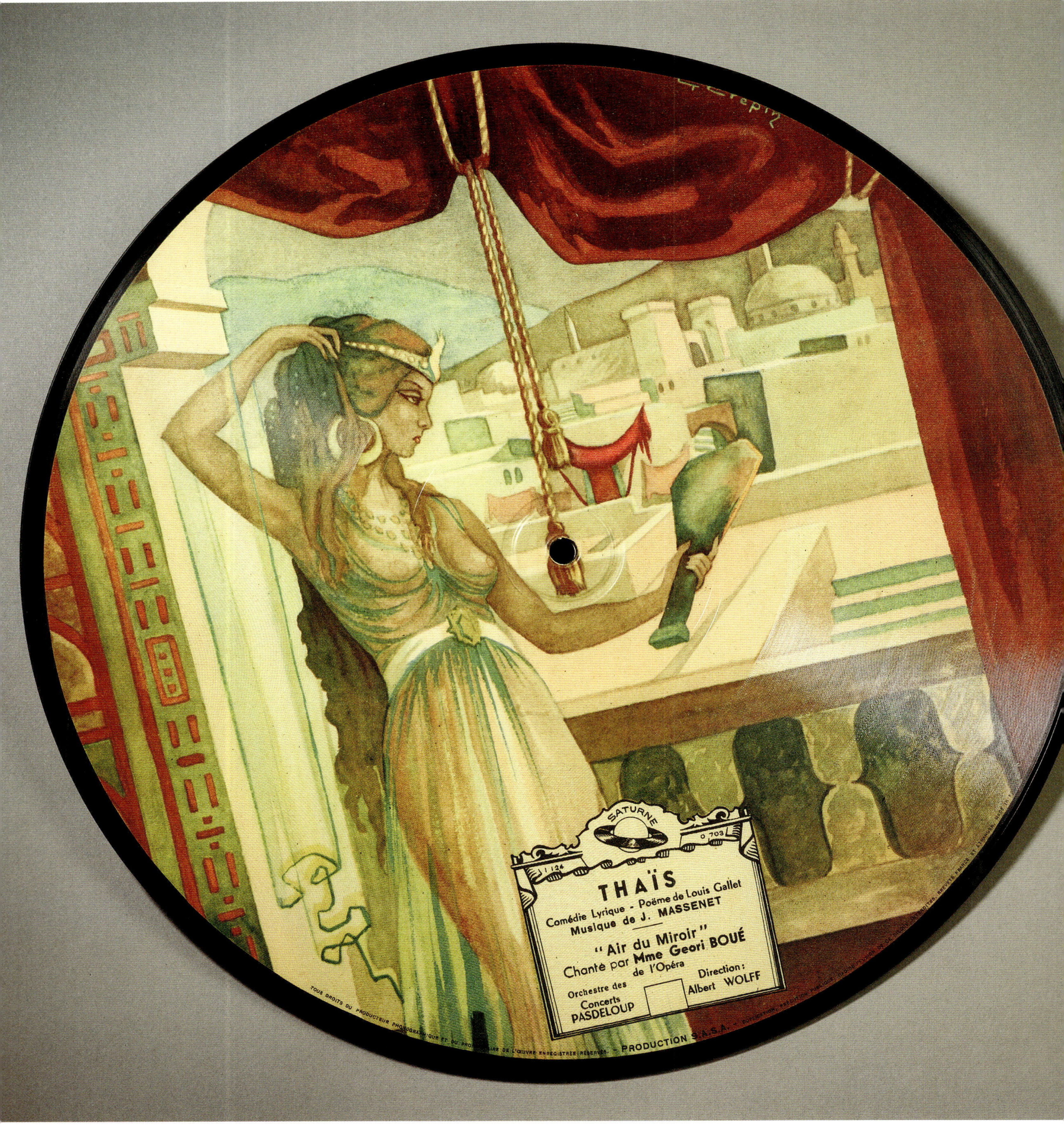
SATURNE
I 126
O 703
THAÏS
Comédie Lyrique - Poëme de Louis Gallet
Musique de J. MASSENET
"Air du Miroir"
Chanté par Mme Georí BOUÉ
de l'Opéra
Orchestre des
Concerts
PASDELOUP
Direction:
Albert WOLFF
PRODUCTION S.A.S.A.

Géori Boué (1918–2017), with the Orchestre des Concerts Pasdeloup, conducted by Albert Wolff (1884–1970)

"Air du Miroir" from *Thaïs*, composed by Jules Massenet (1842–1912)

Saturne Records O-703, 78 rpm, ca. 1950

Rodgers and Hammerstein Archives of Recorded Sound,
The New York Public Library for the Performing Arts, Dorothy and Lewis B. Cullman Center

Though the medium of recorded sound is meant to be heard rather than seen, several record labels throughout the 20th and 21st centuries have incorporated artwork not just into album covers or deluxe packaging but also, in the case of picture discs, onto the actual records.

Sometime around 1950, the Paris-based Saturne record label began a relatively short-lived series of picture discs, containing repertoire that included opera, dance music, spoken word, and jazz. The example here features an aria from Jules Massenet's opera *Thaïs*, as sung by the soprano Géori Boué. She also sang on the first recording of the full opera, released in 1952 on Urania Records. The disc's illustration shows the title character, Thaïs, an Egyptian courtesan. The New York Public Library is one of two known libraries to own a copy of this disc.

Lock of Ludwig van Beethoven's (ca. 1770–1827) hair
ca. 1827
Music Division, The New York Public Library for the Performing Arts, Dorothy and Lewis B. Cullman Center

Ludwig van Beethoven changed the trajectory of Western music through a combination of ingenuity and sensitivity applied to traditional genres, such as the string quartet. At the time of his death in 1827, mourners commonly snipped lockets of hair from their loved ones and from celebrities as mementos. The composer's hair had particular iconic value as a visible manifestation of the "untamed" creativity that distinguished his compositions and piano playing. We know of at least five parties who cut locks of the composer's hair. According to one source, visitors began to do so two days before Beethoven died.

The lock of hair now in the Library's collection most likely belonged to the Beethoven Association, a New York City society that held Beethoven-themed concerts from 1918 to 1940 and collected important editions of the composer's works. When the association dissolved, its collection came to The New York Public Library's Music Division.

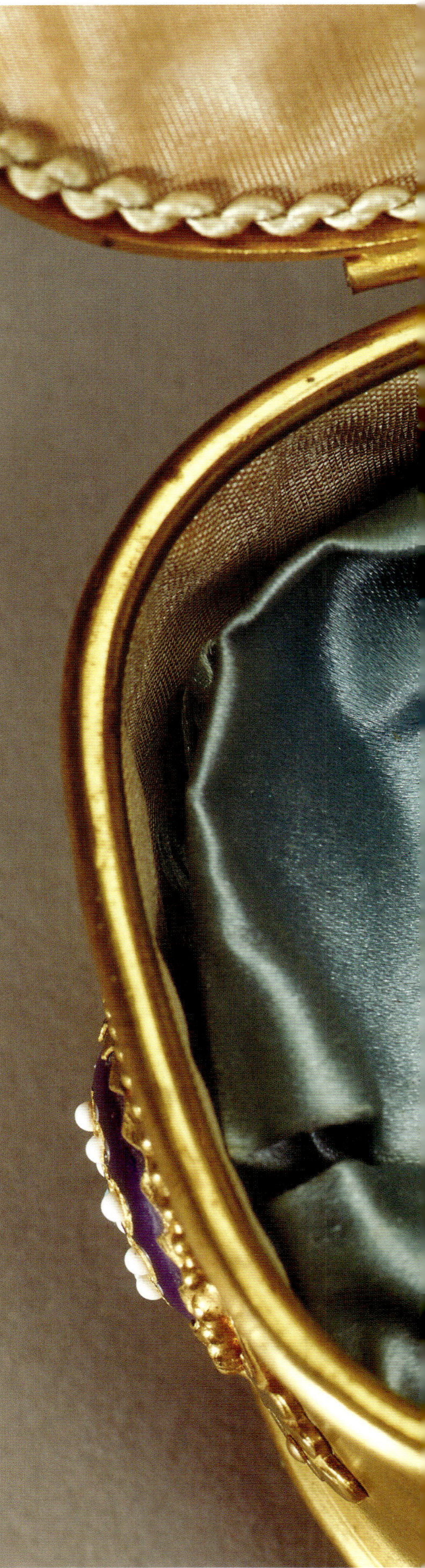

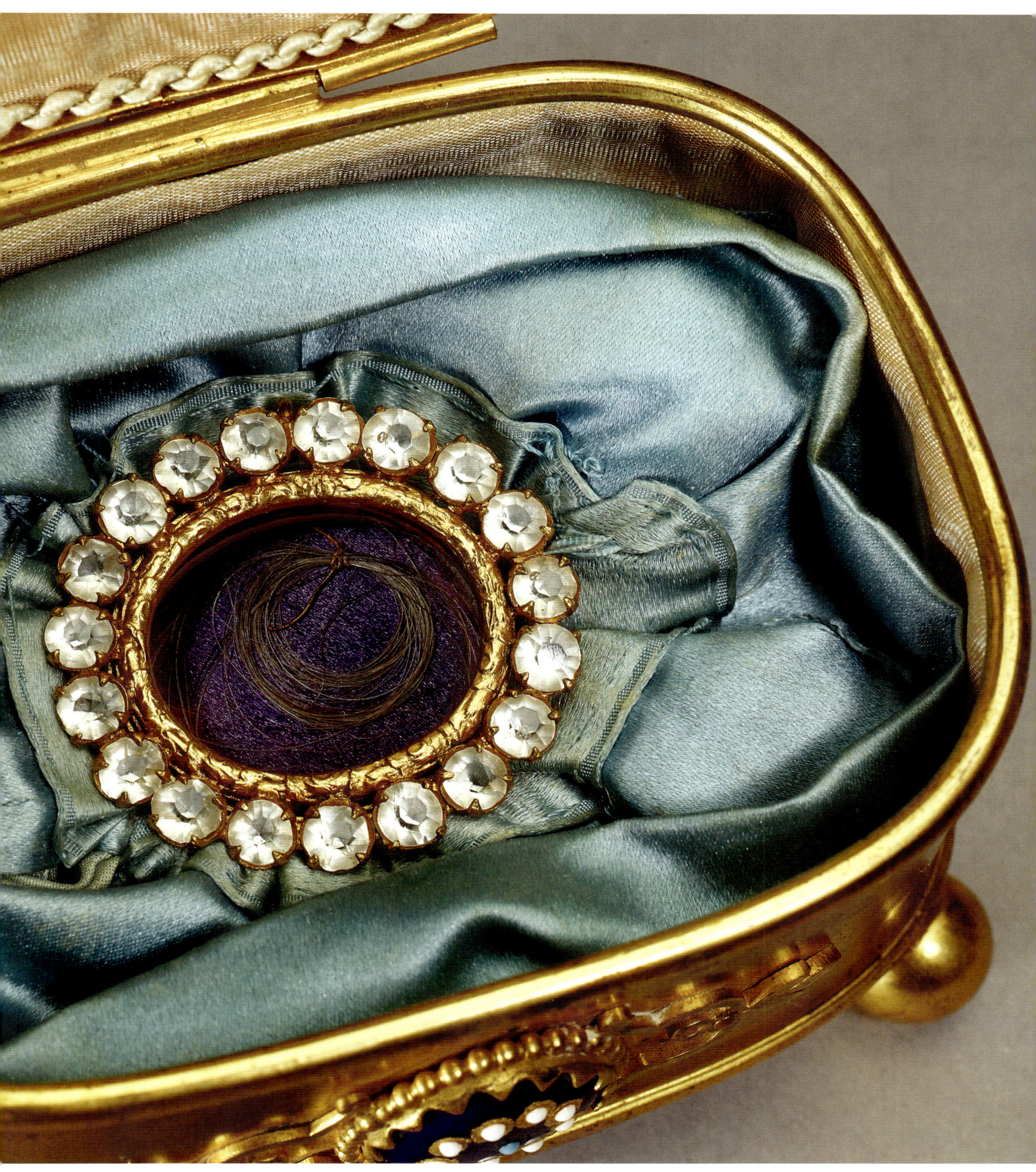

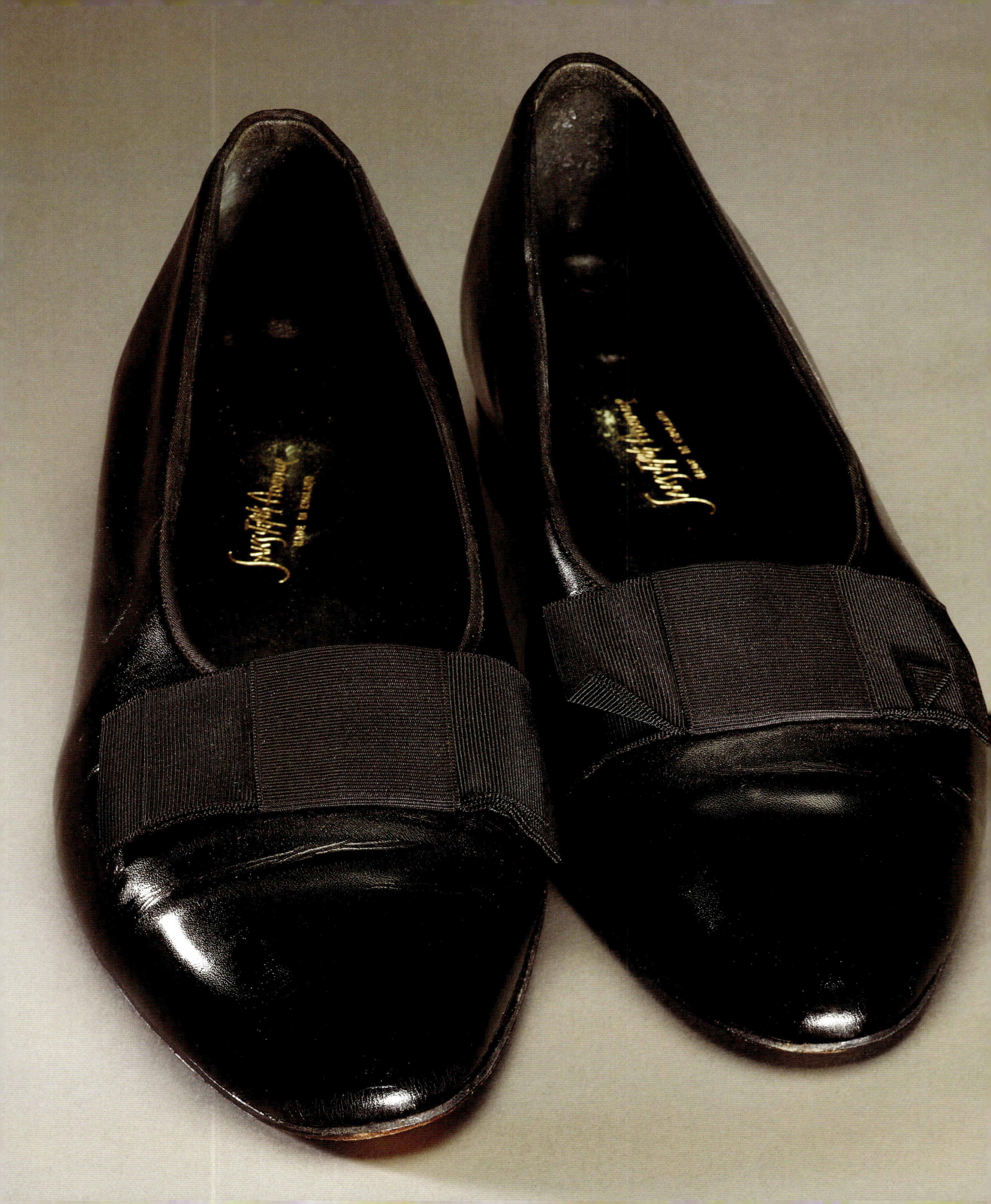

Dress shoes worn by Arturo Toscanini (1867–1957)
ca. 1950
Music Division, The New York Public Library for the Performing Arts,
Dorothy and Lewis B. Cullman Center

Arturo Toscanini, the legendary Italian conductor of the La Scala, New York Philharmonic, and NBC Symphony orchestras, used his entire body to produce the precision, acoustic balance, and emotional pacing he sought from his ensembles. Toscanini's celebrated recordings belie the intense physicality that produced them: his methods resulted in dozens of broken batons and chronic pain in his right shoulder and arm.

This pair of Toscanini's shoes testifies to the physical dimension of his artistic practice. The British shoemaking company Alan McAfee Ltd. (also commissioned to make several pairs for Fred Astaire) handmade them for Saks Fifth Avenue, and Toscanini personalized them by scoring the soles to increase their traction. He was evidently determined to avoid the fate of Sir Thomas Beecham, the English conductor who, in 1932, had fallen off the podium while filling in for Toscanini at a rehearsal of the New York Philharmonic.

The New York Public Library proudly holds a number of Toscanini's personal effects, along with the maestro's personal correspondence, recordings, annotated scores, and books.

Lionel Mapleson (1865–1937)

Early opera recordings on wax cylinders

1900–1904

Rodgers and Hammerstein Archives of Recorded Sound, The New York Public Library for the Performing Arts, Dorothy and Lewis B. Cullman Center

The Mapleson cylinders are among the rarest objects belonging to The New York Public Library. Named for Lionel Mapleson, their creator and the librarian of the Metropolitan Opera, they are a collection of more than one hundred cylinder recordings of live Metropolitan Opera performances made primarily between 1900 and 1904. At a time when sound recording was in its infancy, these cylinders allowed for a live recording with full orchestra and performers—a feat that was not otherwise accomplished until the advent of electrical recording in the late 1920s. Mapleson captured on his cylinders a number of legendary performers who never made commercial recordings, among them Marcella Sembrich, Jean de Reszke, Nellie Melba, Louise Homer, Emma Calvé, and David Bispham, thereby providing documentation of notable artists as well as invaluable examples of performance practice at the start of the 20th century. Attesting to their significance, the National Recording Registry at the Library of Congress chose the Mapleson cylinders as one of its twenty-five selections in 2002, the registry's inaugural year.

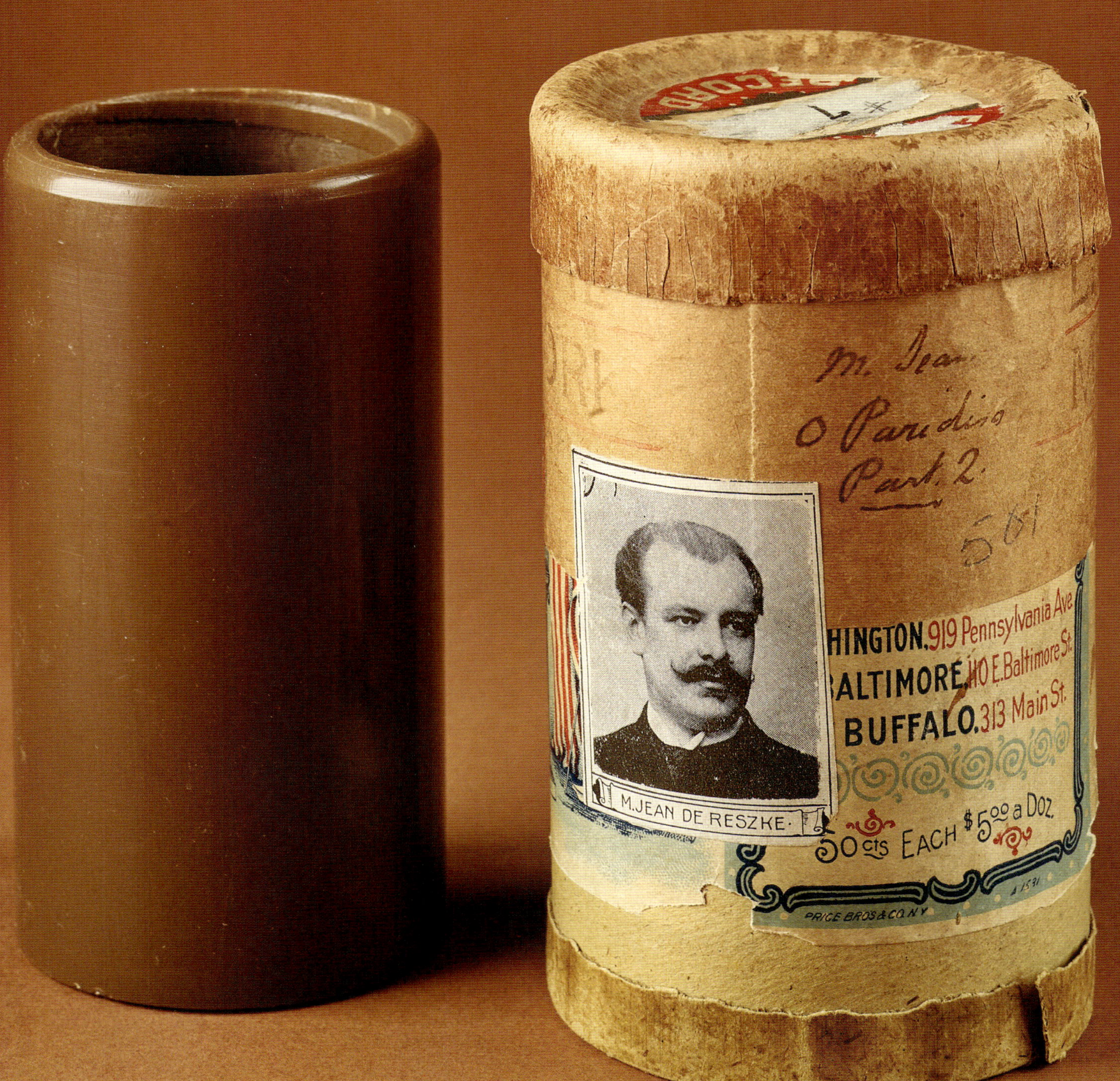
M. Jean
O Paradiso
Part 2
501
HINGTON. 919 Pennsylvania Ave.
BALTIMORE. 110 E. Baltimore St.
BUFFALO. 313 Main St.
M. JEAN DE RESZKE
50 cts EACH $5.00 a Doz.
PRICE BROS & CO. N.Y.

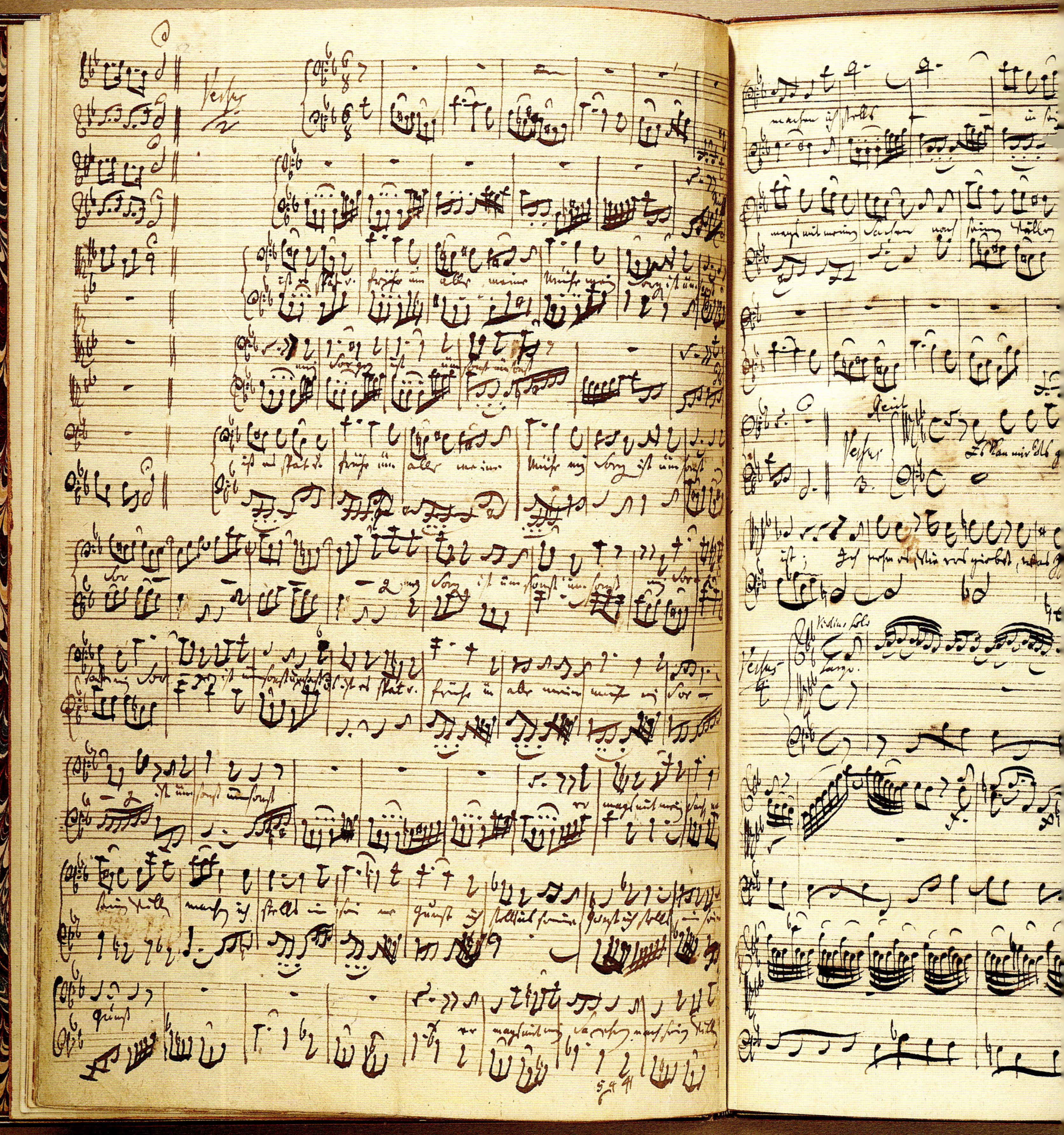
Versus 2
Versus 3
Recit
Versus 4
Violino Solo
Largo.

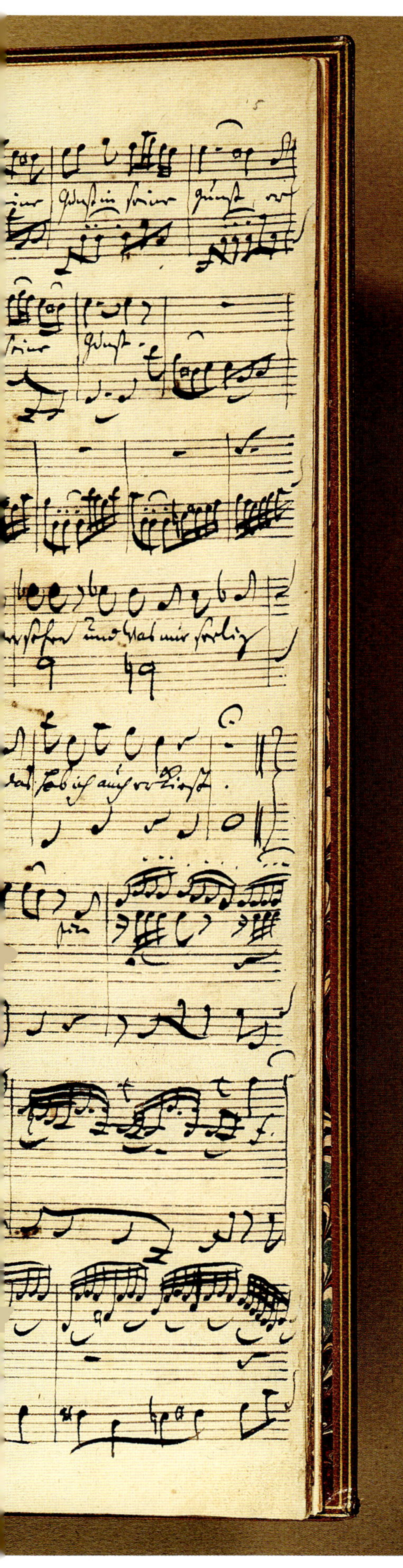

Johann Sebastian Bach (1685–1750)
"In allen meinen Taten"
ca. 1732–1735
Music Division, The New York Public Library for the Performing Arts, Dorothy and Lewis B. Cullman Center

Johann Sebastian Bach was a prolific and virtuosic composer of the Baroque period, now regarded as one of the greatest composers of all time. Bach wrote this cantata no. 97 sometime between 1732 and 1735. While he composed most of his cantatas for specific days in the Church calendar or for celebratory occasions, we know very little about the origins or use of "In allen meinen Taten" ("In all my actions"). At the conclusion of the sixth section, an unidentified hand wrote "Nach der Trauung" ("after the wedding procession"). This inscription once led to the conclusion that Bach wrote the cantata for a wedding, but the more recent consensus opposes this assumption; the piece lacks characteristics present in cantatas that Bach wrote expressly for weddings.

The whereabouts of this manuscript remained unknown from Bach's death in 1750 until Frederick Locker-Lampson purchased it from an unidentified collector in 1872. By the early 20th century, it was in the collection of Christian Archibald Herter. His companion, Lillie Bliss, donated the manuscript in honor of Herter to The New York Public Library in 1932.

Merce Cunningham (1919–2009)

Choreographic notes for 1984 *Event*

Jerome Robbins Dance Division, The New York Public Library for the Performing Arts, Dorothy and Lewis B. Cullman Center

This choreographic notation was made to prepare for a 1984 *Event*. *Events* were composed of various dances in the Cunningham repertory, edited together to make a unique collage and designed to be danced in nontraditional performance spaces such as museums, gardens—and even The New York Public Library. (Cunningham made an *Event* for the Jerome Robbins Dance Division in 2007.) Cunningham began adapting dance to unconventional spaces in 1964 and contributed considerably to the popularity of performance in museum spaces today. His methodology of chance operations has led many to assume that his work was predominantly improvisation, but this document shows that he used his astute understanding of space to synchronize a complex tapestry of group and solo entrances and exits. The notation is directional, temporal, and spatial—a perfect example of Cunningham's choreographic genius.

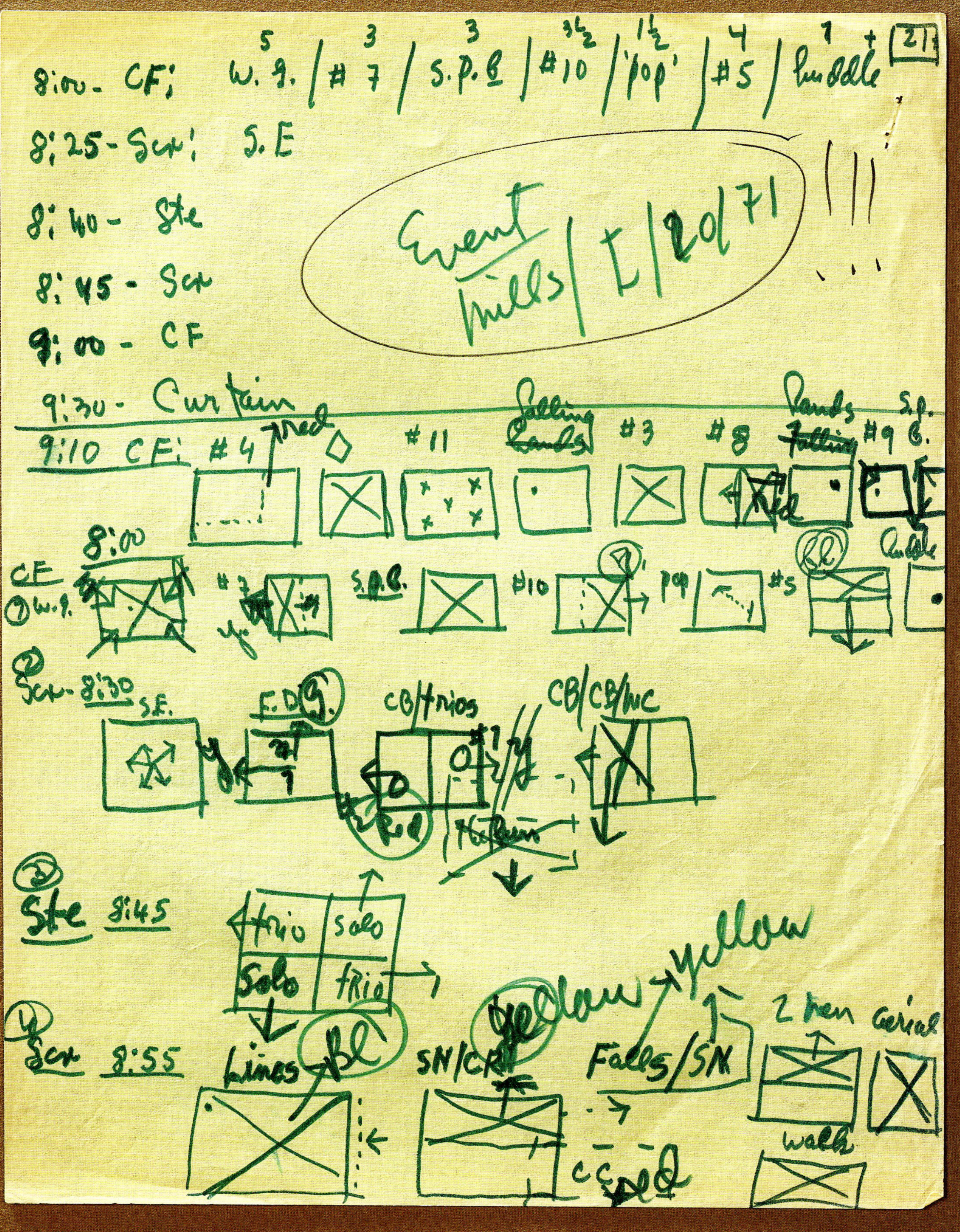

8:00 - CF: W. G. / #7 / S.P.B / #10 / 'pop' / #5 / huddle
8:25 - Scr: S.E
8:40 - Ste
8:45 - Scr
9:00 - CF
9:30 - Curtain
Event
9:10 CF: #4
#11
#3
#8
#9
8:00
CF
S.P.B.
#10
pop
#5
huddle
S.E.
CB/trios
CB/CB/WC
Ste 8:45
trio
solo
solo
trio
Scr 8:55
Lines
SN/CR
Falls/SN
yellow
yellow
2 men
aerial
walk

To reveal

0'00" FOR YOKO ONO AND TOSH

IN A SITUATION HAVING MAXIMUM AMPLIFICATION OR NONE

ACT ETC.

朝

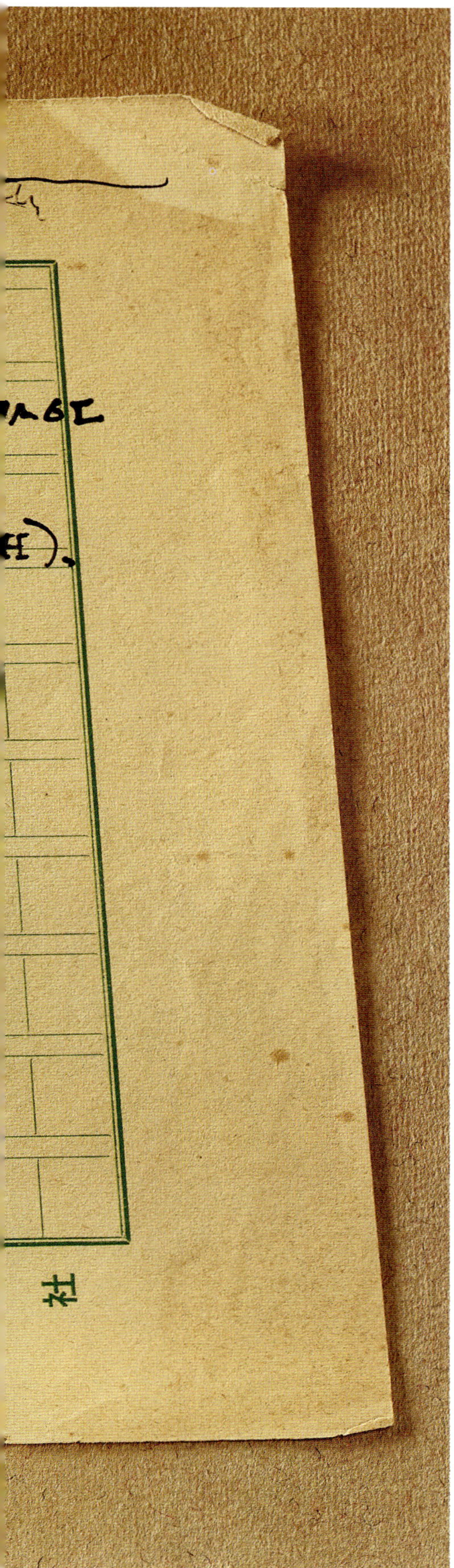

John Cage (1912–1992)

Manuscript sketch for *0′00″: solo to be performed by anyone in any way*

1962

Music Division, The New York Public Library for the Performing Arts, Dorothy and Lewis B. Cullman Center

Composer John Cage created experimental works that profoundly shaped music in the mid-20th century and made him a leader of the American musical avant-garde. Cage composed *0′00″* on paper he acquired during a 1962 visit to Tokyo, where he spent time with his friend Yoko Ono and her first husband, the composer Toshi Ichiyanagi. The final version instructs the performer: "In a situation provided with maximum amplification (no feedback), perform a disciplined action." As Cage notes elsewhere in the sketches, "The first performance was the writing of this manuscript." Cage typically eschewed politics in his music, but *0′00″* has proved to be among his most political works: participants frequently take the opportunity to perform an act of protest or resistance as their "disciplined action."

0′00″ also exemplifies the numerous interrelationships between the more than 300 compositions that make up the John Cage Music Manuscript Collection, which is under the stewardship of the Library's Music Division. Cage notes that *0′00″* "may be considered *4′33″* no. 2, for though there is activity, it is a 'silent piece.' It is also the third & last work in a series corresp[onding] to the 3 lines of Haiku poetry; Atlas E[clipticalis] is the first." Cage composed *4′33″* (the duration of the piece) for any instrument or instruments, instructing performers to not play during the three movements that make up the work. The pianist David Tudor premiered *4′33″* in 1952, and the work remains Cage's best-known composition.

Telegram from Igor Stravinsky (1882–1971) to George Balanchine (1904–1983)
1957
Jerome Robbins Dance Division, The New York Public Library for the Performing Arts, Dorothy and Lewis B. Cullman Center

On December 1, 1957, Balanchine and Stravinsky's artistic partnership reached its apex with the first staged performance of the ballet *Agon*, at New York's City Center of Music and Drama. The title is an ancient Greek word meaning "contest." *Agon* is not related to Balanchine and Stravinsky's other Greek collaborations, *Apollon Musagète* and *Orpheus*. Rather, the ballet is a study in abstraction, derived from two distinct inspirations: the 12-tone musical composition developed by composers Arnold Schoenberg and Anton Webern in the early 20th century, and the French court dances described in François de Lauze's 1623 French dance manual, *Apologie de la danse et la parfaicte méthode de l'enseigner tant aux cavaliers qu'aux dames*. Balanchine mimicked Stravinsky's 12-tone experimentations in his ballet of 12 movements for 12 dancers, and he named each section after dances in Lauze's book. This telegram was sent less than a week before the ballet premiered and shows the great affection between the two men.

CLASS OF SERVICE

This is a fast message unless its deferred character is indicated by the proper symbol.

WESTERN UNION

TELEGRAM

W. P. MARSHALL, PRESIDENT

1201

SYMBOLS

DL=Day Letter

NL=Night Letter

LT=International Letter Telegram

The filing time shown in the date line on domestic telegrams is STANDARD TIME at point of origin. Time of receipt is STANDARD TIME at point of destination

OA032

1957 NOV 27 AM 4 40

O LSJ014 NL PD=LOS ANGELES CALIF 26=

GEO BALANCHIN=

CITY CENTER BALLET 55 ST NYK=

TO YOU TO WHOM I DEDICATE AGON AM SENDING TODAY MY HEARTIEST WISHES FOR A GREAT SUCCESS YOUR BEAUTIFUL COMPOSITION HIGHLY DESERVES I AM IN THOUGHT WITH YOU=

STRAVINSKY=.

THE COMPANY WILL APPRECIATE SUGGESTIONS FROM ITS PATRONS CONCERNING ITS SERVICE

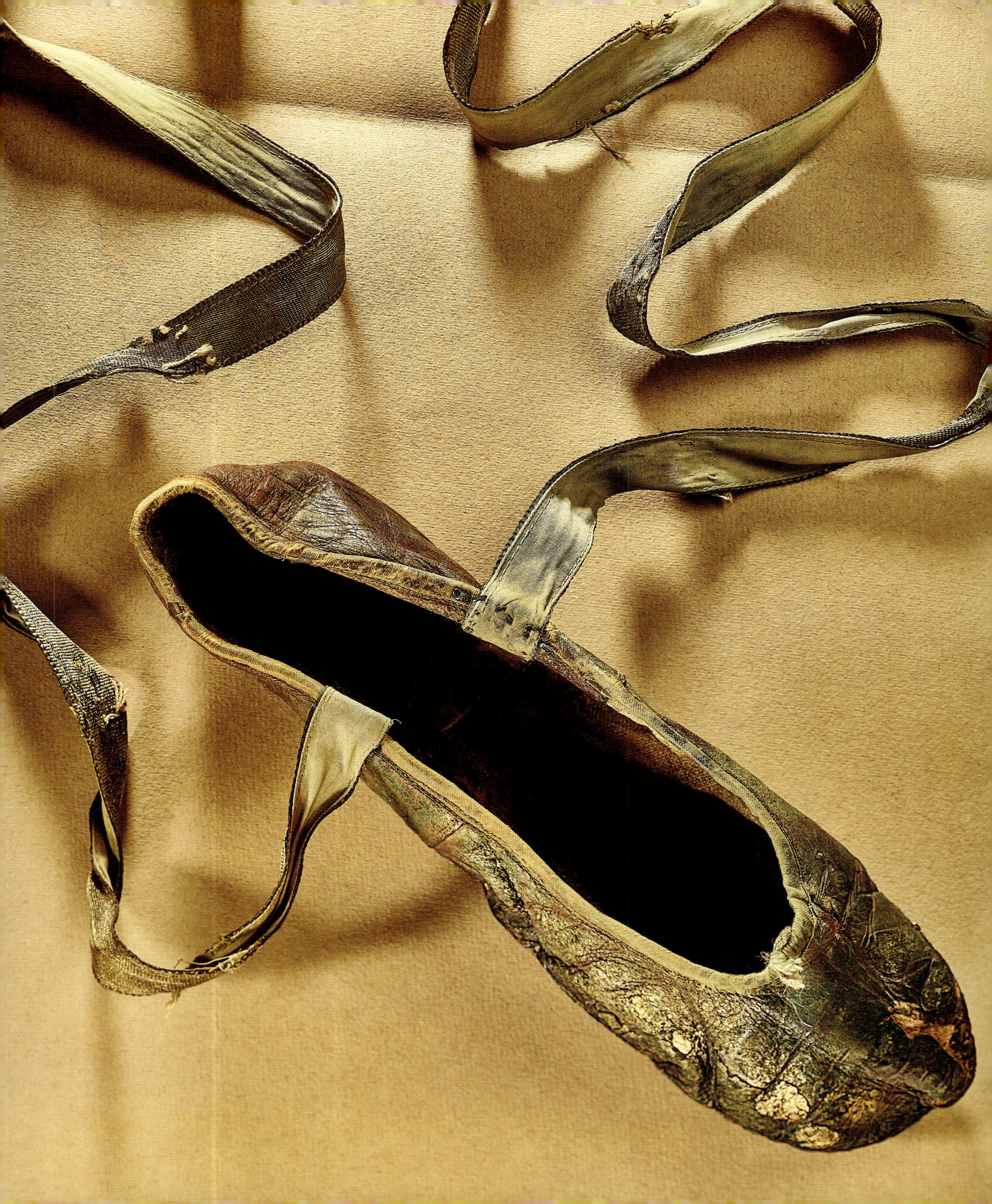

Coco Chanel (1883–1917)

Ballet shoe worn by Serge Lifar (1905–1986)

ca. 1927–1929

Jerome Robbins Dance Division, The New York Public Library for the Performing Arts, Dorothy and Lewis B. Cullman Center

This leather ballet slipper was once hand-painted gold, and its long ribbons could be tied in a crisscross pattern, evoking an ancient Grecian sandal. It was worn by Serge Lifar, the original interpreter of the role of Apollo in George Balanchine's first masterpiece, *Apollon Musagète* (now simply called *Apollo*), choreographed for Sergei Diaghilev's *Ballets Russes*. Balanchine was only twenty-four years old when his version of the ballet premiered in 1928, promulgating the neoclassicism that shaped 20th-century ballet. *Apollo* is often called a *ballet blanc,* literally a "white ballet"—typically referring to ballets danced in white in the Romantic period of the 1800s. In this case, however, the term alludes not only to the color of the costumes but also to a classical minimalism in choreographic style that became one of Balanchine's defining traits. French naïve painter André Bauchant designed the original costumes for *Apollon Musagète*, but Diaghilev premiered new versions by Chanel in 1929.

Jerome Robbins (1918–1998)

Diary, Volume 5

1973

Jerome Robbins Dance Division, The New York Public Library for the Performing Arts, Dorothy and Lewis B. Cullman Center

The dance division of The New York Public Library is named for choreographer Jerome Robbins, and his collection is one of the most complete archival examples of an artist at work in the world. Robbins' genius expanded beyond dance to painting, writing, and photography, outlets that helped him to process the world around him. Periods of intense creativity often overlapped with personal turmoil; in the 1970s, Robbins entered a period of great introspection and began an unparalleled, thirteen-year art project he referred to as "the diaries." From 1971 to 1984, Robbins produced twenty-four inimitable volumes, many of them double-sided, on Japanese accordion foldout notebooks. The diaries are partly personal journals, but they also contain travelogues, collages, watercolors, sketches, photographs, poems, dreams, pressed flowers, and creative ideas. This section, which comes from Volume 5, gives a glimpse into Robbins' visual style, sense of humor, preoccupations, and activities at the time of its creation.

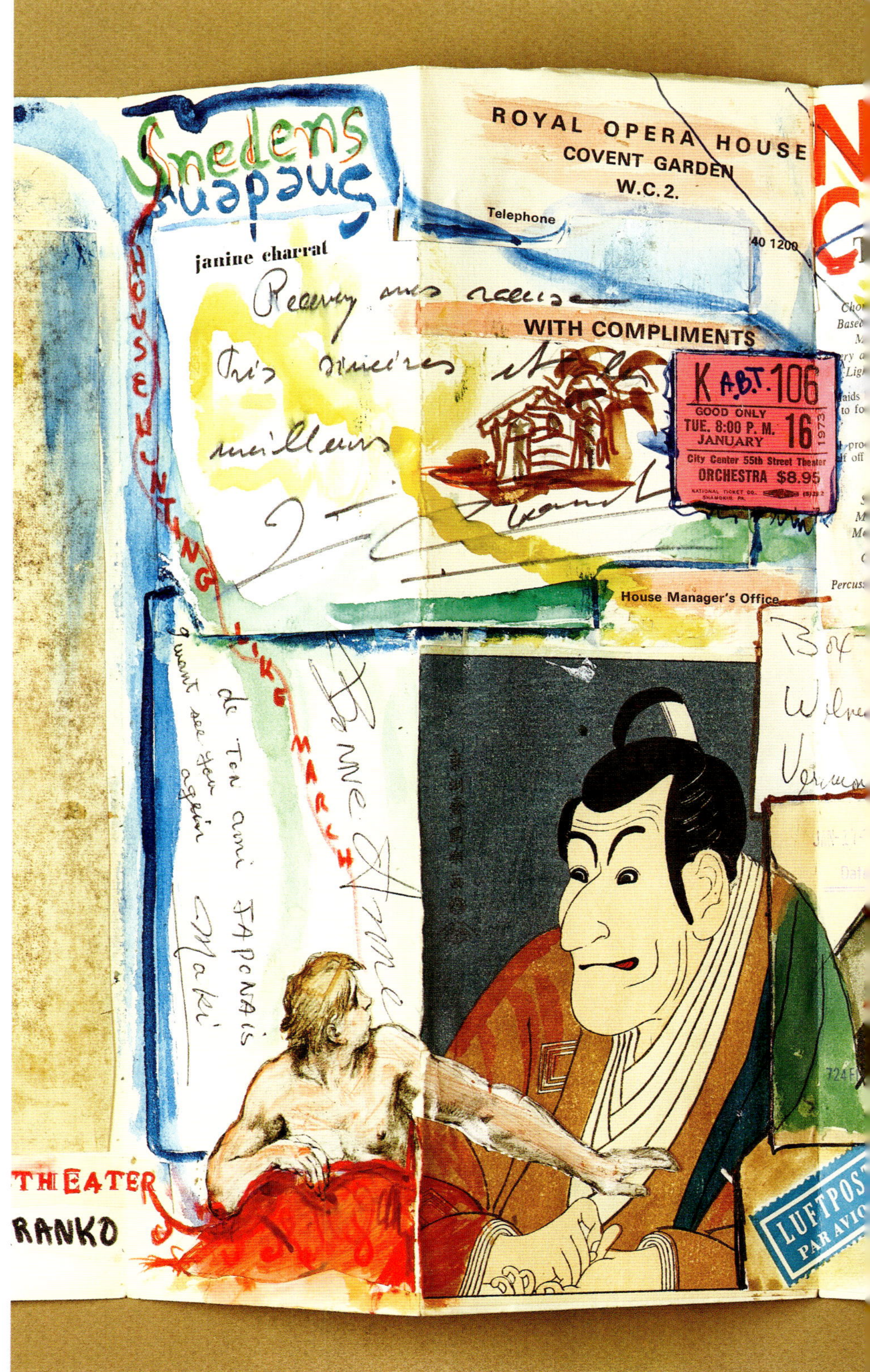

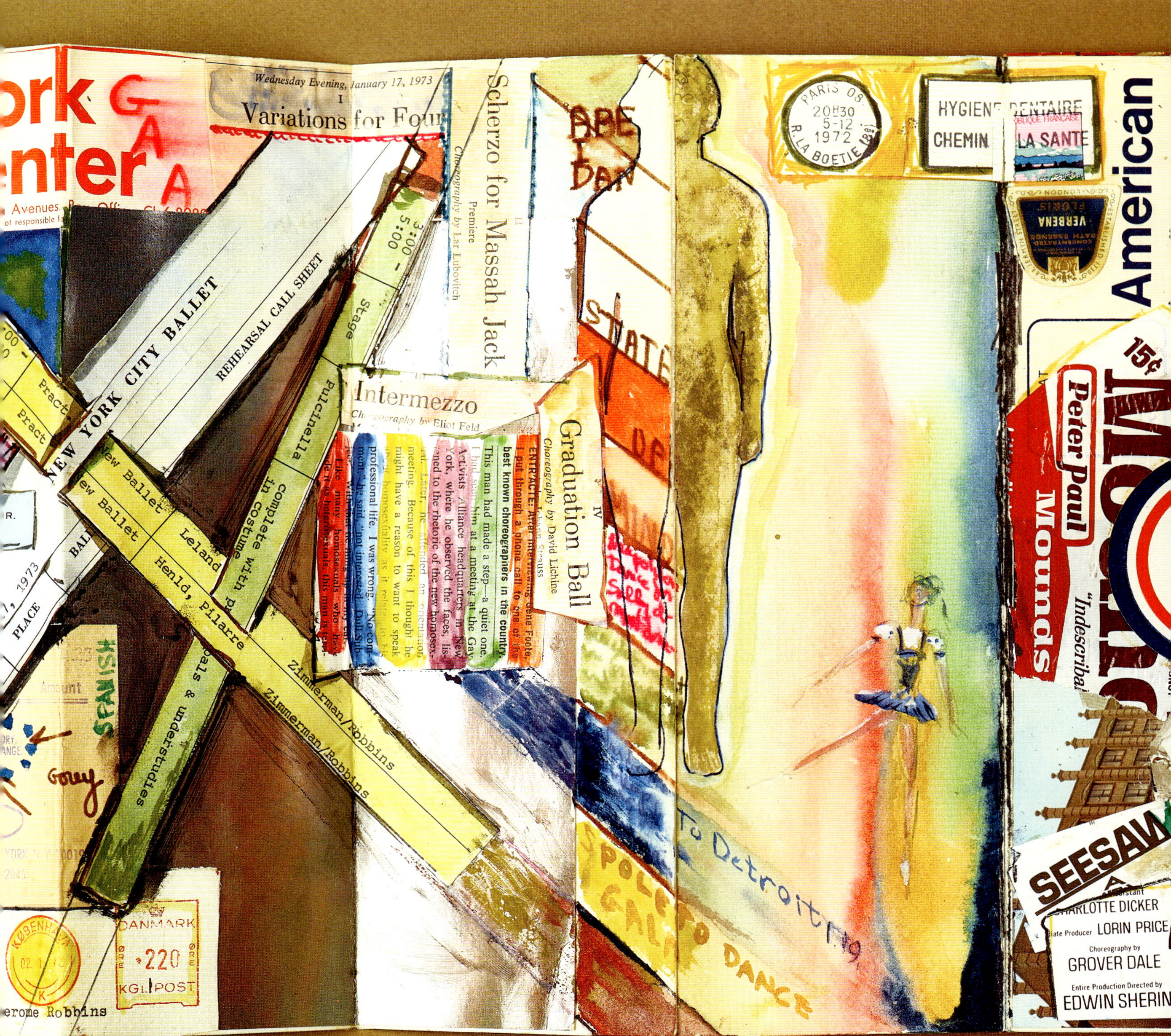

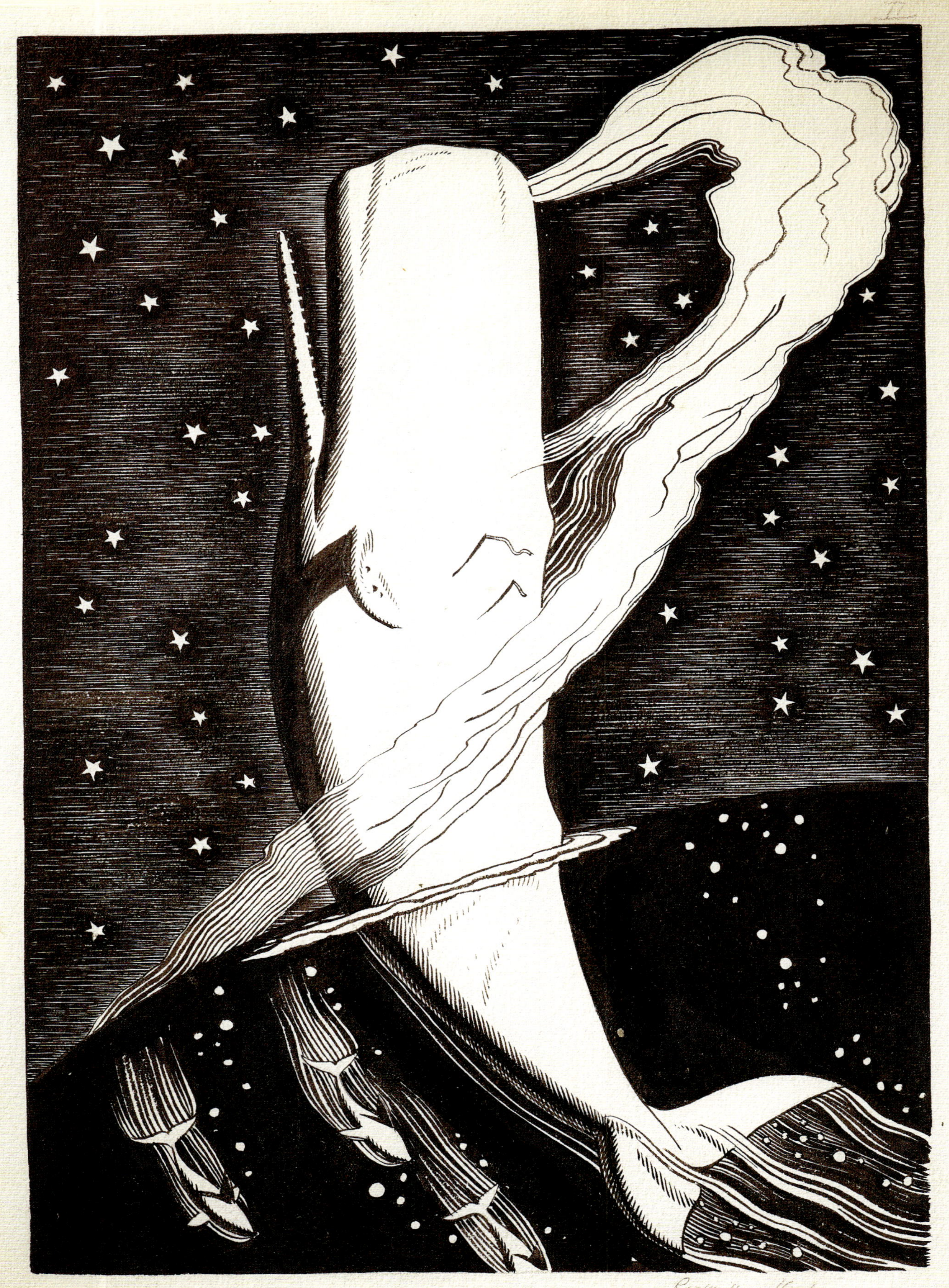

Rockwell Kent (1882–1971)

Illustration for Herman Melville's *Moby-Dick; or, The Whale*

Chicago: The Lakeside Press, 1930

The Miriam and Ira D. Wallach Division of Art, Prints and Photographs, Spencer Collection

No work of literature is more intimately associated with whales and whaling than Herman Melville's *Moby-Dick*, first published in 1851. This is one of Rockwell Kent's original drawings for a limited edition of Melville's masterpiece, published by Lakeside Press in 1930. With his interest in American Transcendentalism and knowledge of seafaring, Kent was particularly well-suited to illustrate Captain Ahab's monomaniacal quest for the White Whale. This illustration depicts the whale as Melville describes it in chapter 41, emerging from the ocean:

> *The rest of his body was so streaked, and spotted, and marbled with the same shrouded hue, that, in the end, he had gained his distinctive appellation of the White Whale; a name, indeed, literally justified by his vivid aspect, when seen gliding at high noon through a dark blue sea, leaving a milky-way wake of creamy foam, all spangled with golden gleamings.*

William Faulkner (1897–1962)

Erotic drawing of the author with Meta Carpenter Wilde (1907–1994)

1930s–1940s

Henry W. and Albert A. Berg Collection of English and American Literature

Meta Carpenter Wilde was the daughter of a successful cotton planter in Tennessee who trained as a concert pianist before going to Hollywood. There she worked as a model and music librarian before becoming secretary to the film director Howard Hawks, who made her his script supervisor in 1935. This set the stage for the beginning of her eighteen-year affair with William Faulkner, who was in Hollywood to work on the screenplay of *The Road to Glory*, which Hawks directed. During the early years of their relationship, Faulkner drew a series of erotic pencil sketches—eight pages of line drawings depicting their various sexual positions—that Wilde gave to the Library in 1972. She later donated the emended typescript of her memoir, *A Loving Gentleman: The Love Story of William Faulkner and Meta Carpenter*, which became a bestseller in 1976. This sketch, with its whimsical caption, is the final page in the series. Access to the drawings was restricted until 2008, and they have never been publicly displayed.

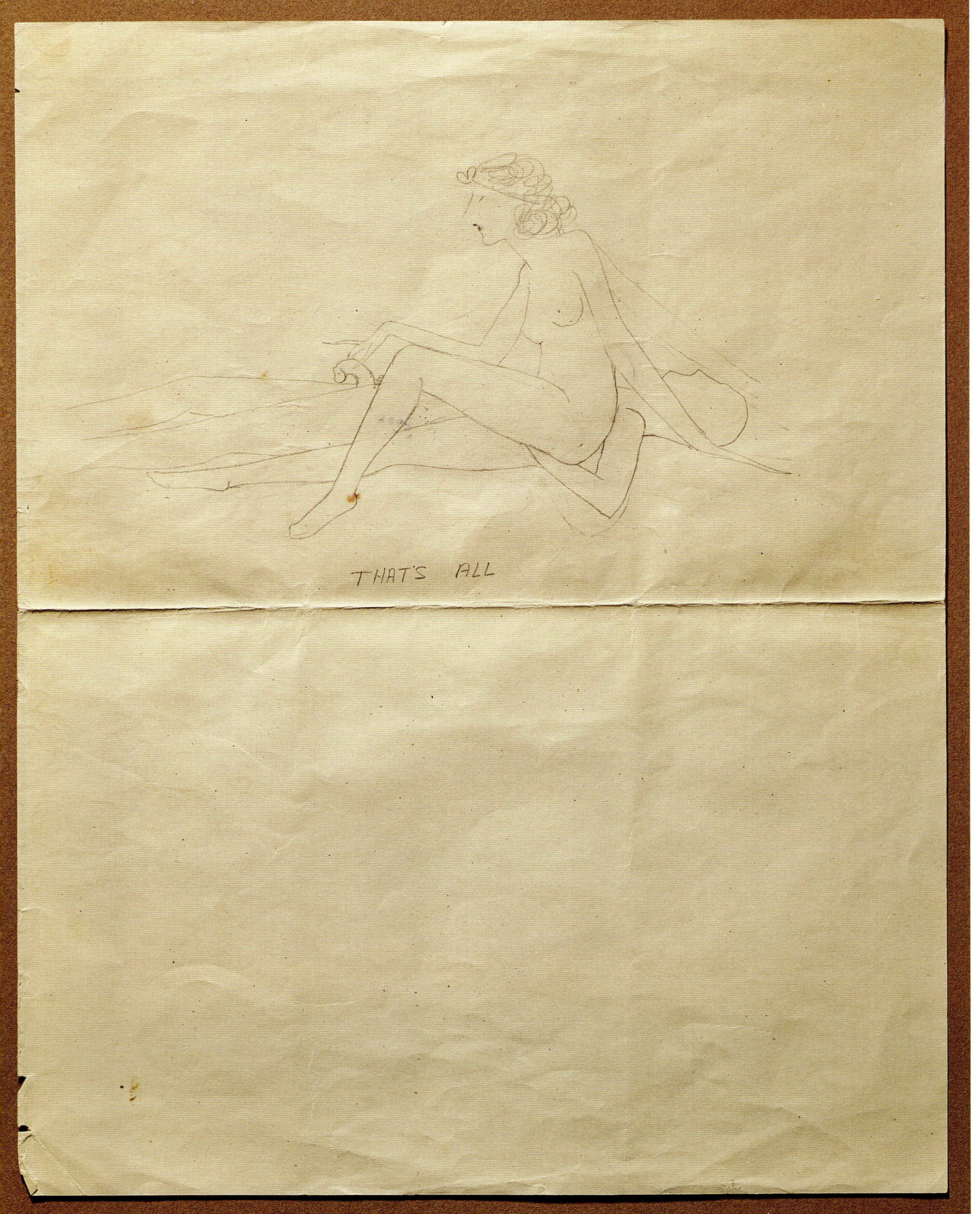
THAT'S ALL

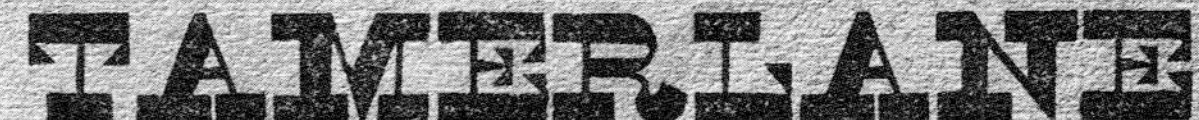

AND

OTHER POEMS.

BY A BOSTONIAN.

Young heads are giddy, and young hearts are warm,
And make mistakes for manhood to reform.—COWPER.

BOSTON:
CALVIN F. S. THOMAS.....PRINTER.

1827.

Edgar Allan Poe (1809–1849)

First edition of *Tamerlane and Other Poems*

Boston: Calvin Thomas, 1827

Henry W. and Albert A. Berg Collection of English and American Literature

This slender volume of poetry was Poe's first book. Published anonymously and at Poe's own expense, the book received no critical attention. Following the author's death at the age of forty, one scholar surmised that *Tamerlane* might never have been printed. No copies of the book were identified until 1859, and only twelve are now known to be extant. The New York Public Library holds two—this copy, which bears the signature of an early owner, Susan Saunders, on the cover; and a second copy, which was discovered in Maine in 1938. Although he never enjoyed financial security, Poe became one of America's most popular writers with the publication of his poem "The Raven" in 1845. Today he is remembered as the father of the modern detective story.

E.E. Cummings (1894–1962)

Valentine

Oil and crayon on cardstock, 1947

Henry W. and Albert A. Berg Collection of English and American Literature

Already twice married and well established in avant-garde literary circles, E.E. Cummings—famous for his eschewal of capital letters and poems like the 1952 "i carry your heart with me(i carry it in / my heart)"—met the love of his life in 1932: Marion Morehouse, an accomplished photographer and America's first supermodel. Throughout their long relationship, which lasted until Cummings's death, the poet drew and painted several valentines for Marion, often incorporating an elephant motif. Cummings's valentines are a private example of his considerable output as a visual artist. His abstract paintings appeared in the influential literary magazine *The Dial*, and in 1931 he published a selection of 99 examples of his visual art in a book titled *CIOPW*. (*CIOPW* is an acronym for charcoal, ink, oil, pencil, and watercolor.)

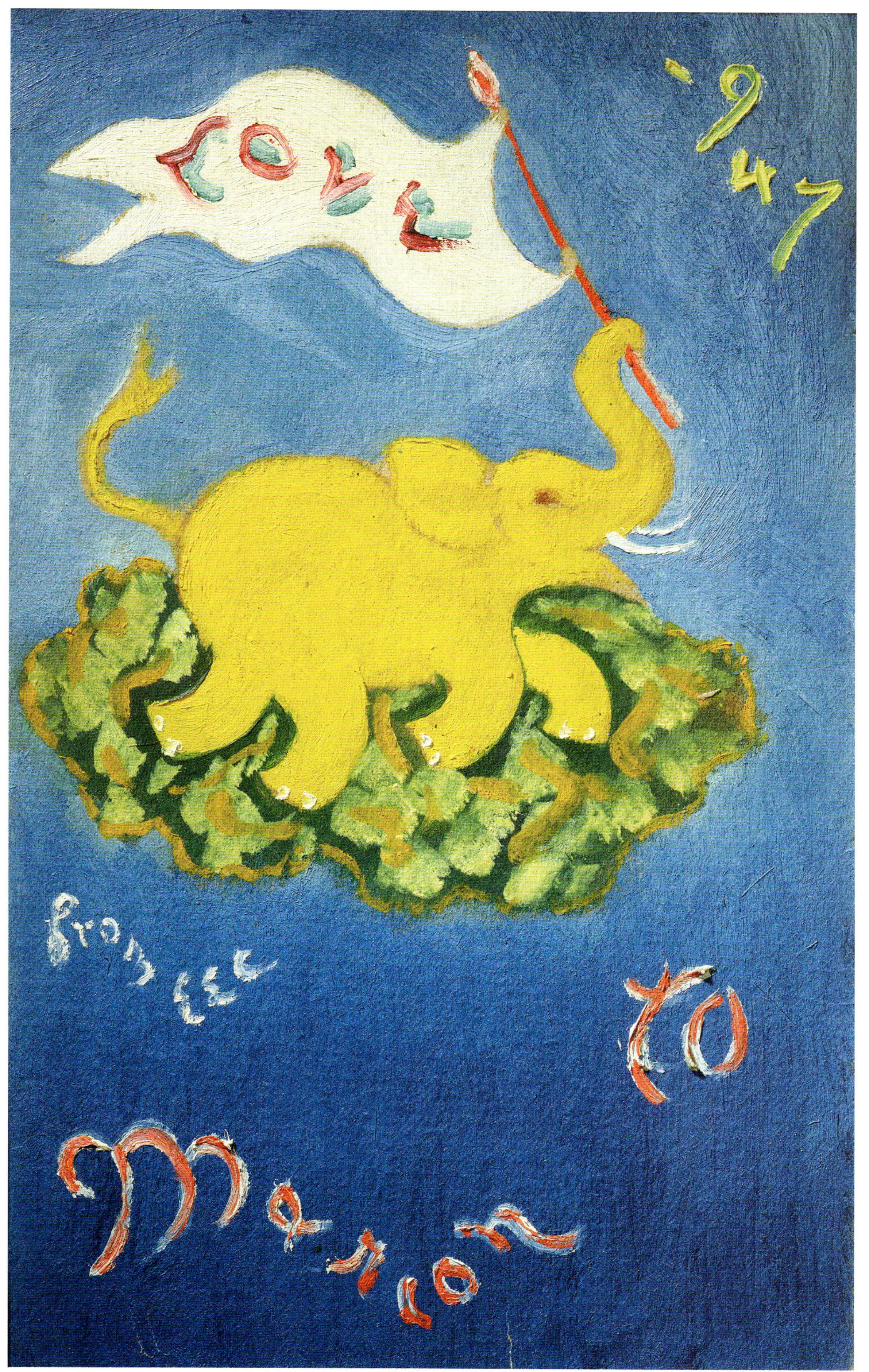
Love
1947
from eec
to
Marion

Jack Kerouac (1922–1969)
Diary from summer at Desolation Peak
June 18–September 26, 1956
Jack Kerouac Papers, Henry W. and Albert A. Berg Collection of English and American Literature

About a year before he published *On the Road*, Jack Kerouac spent part of the summer of 1956 working for the U.S. Forest Service as a fire lookout on Desolation Peak in Washington State. He lived in a one-room shack perched at the top of the 6,102-foot mountain. Almost entirely isolated, Kerouac recorded his innermost thoughts and meditations on Buddhism in this pocket-sized notebook. "I'd rather have drugs and liquor and divine visions than this empty barren fatalism at the top of a mountaintop," he recorded during his stay. Kerouac took the name of the mountain to heart: the word "desolation" appears in later poems and in his novel *Desolation Angels* (1965), which drew heavily on his experiences from that summer.

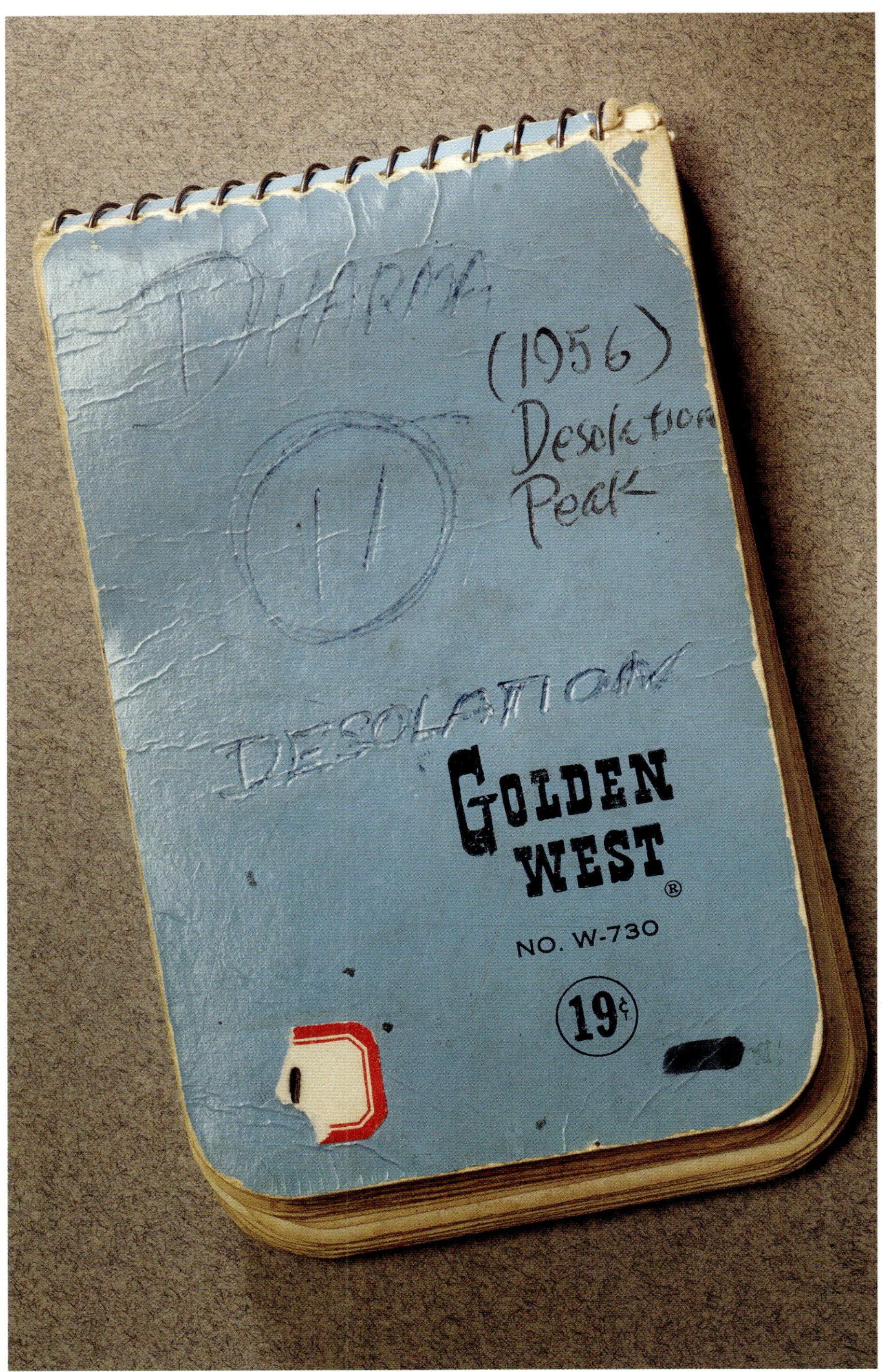

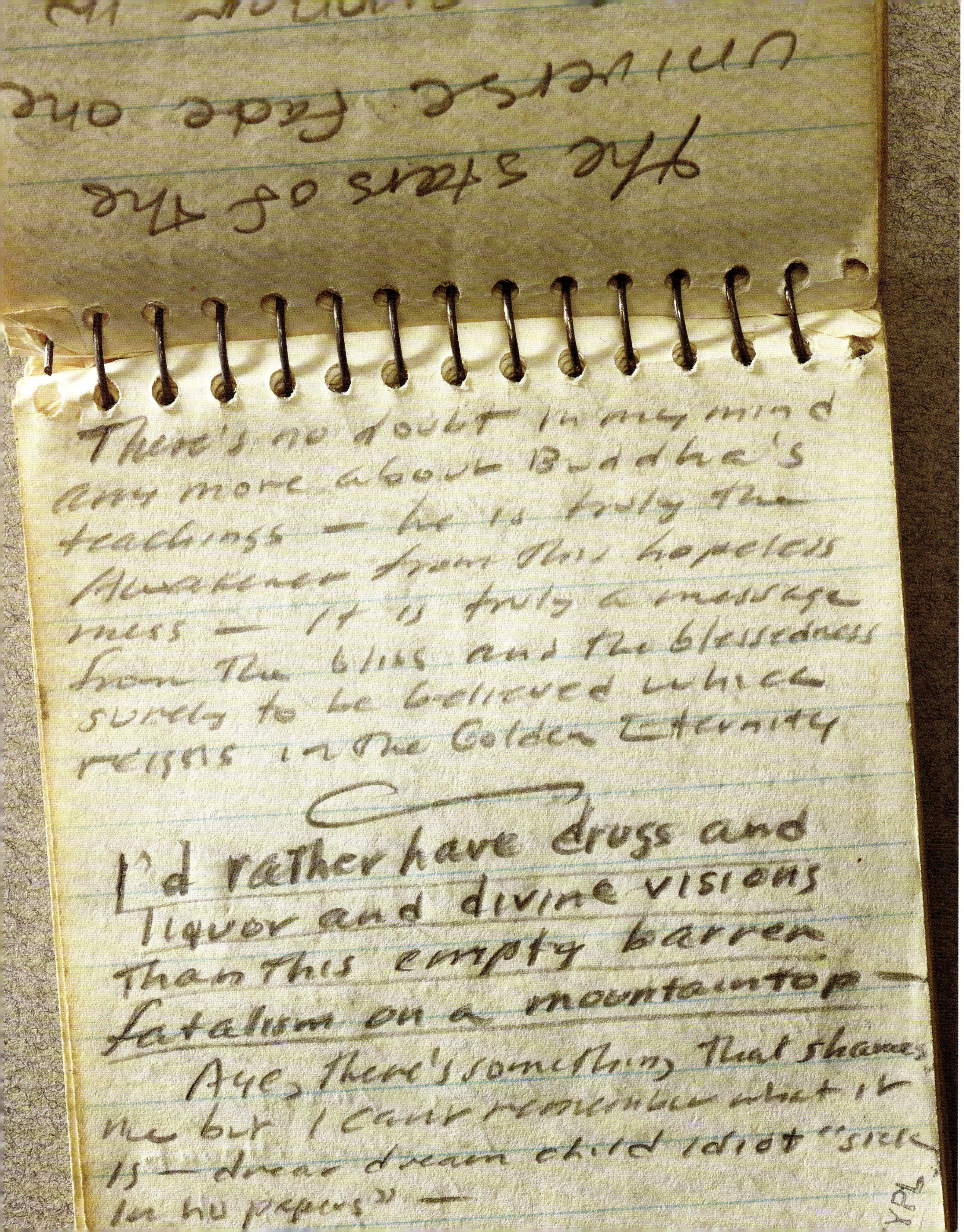

the stars of the
universe fade one

There's no doubt in my mind any more about Buddha's teachings — he is truly the Awakener from this hopeless mess — It is truly a message from the bliss and the blessedness surely to be believed which reigns in the Golden Eternity

I'd rather have drugs and
liquor and divine visions
than this empty barren
fatalism on a mountaintop —

Aye, there's something that shames me but I can't remember what it is — dear dream child idiot "sick in his papers" —

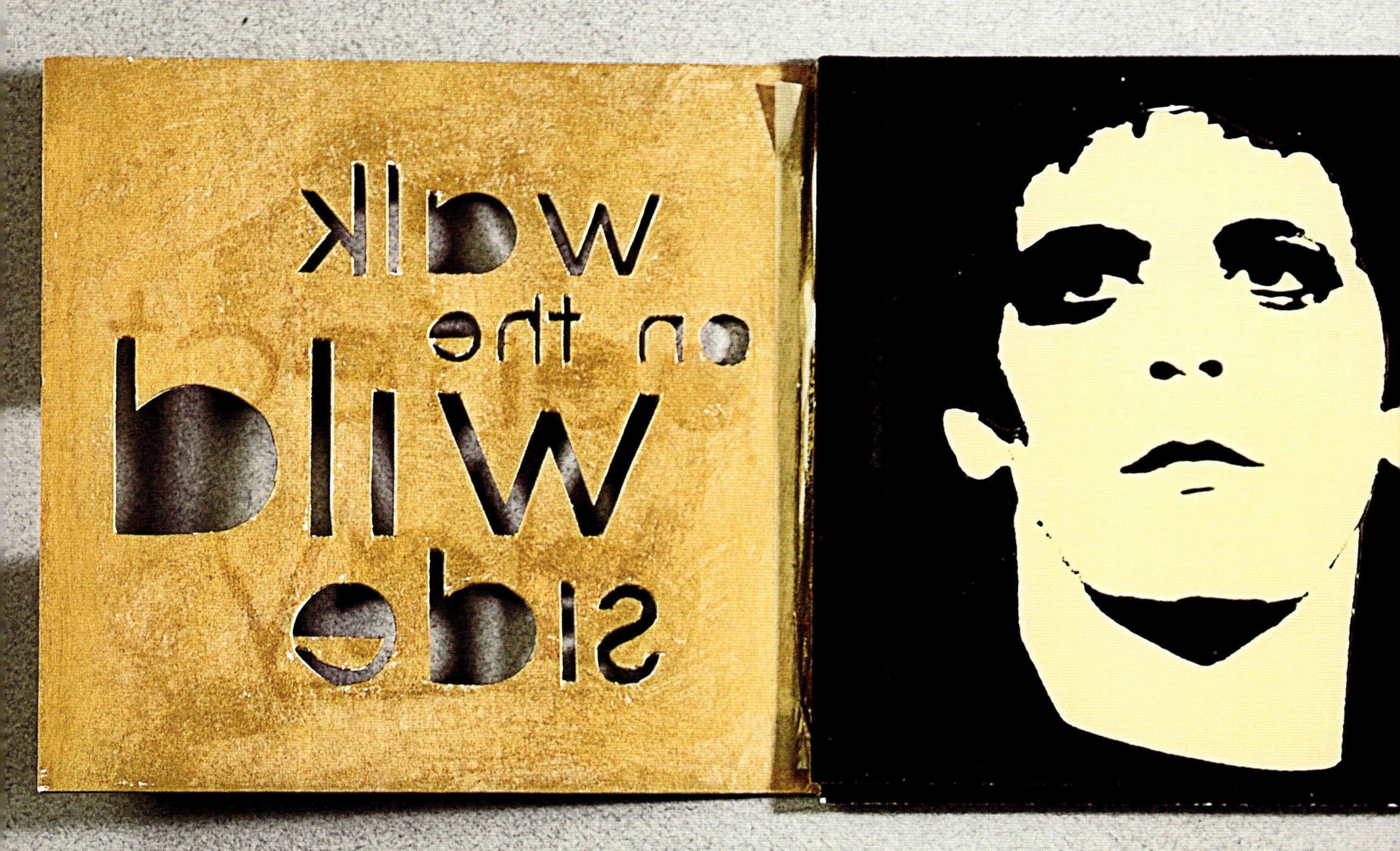
walk
on the
wild
side

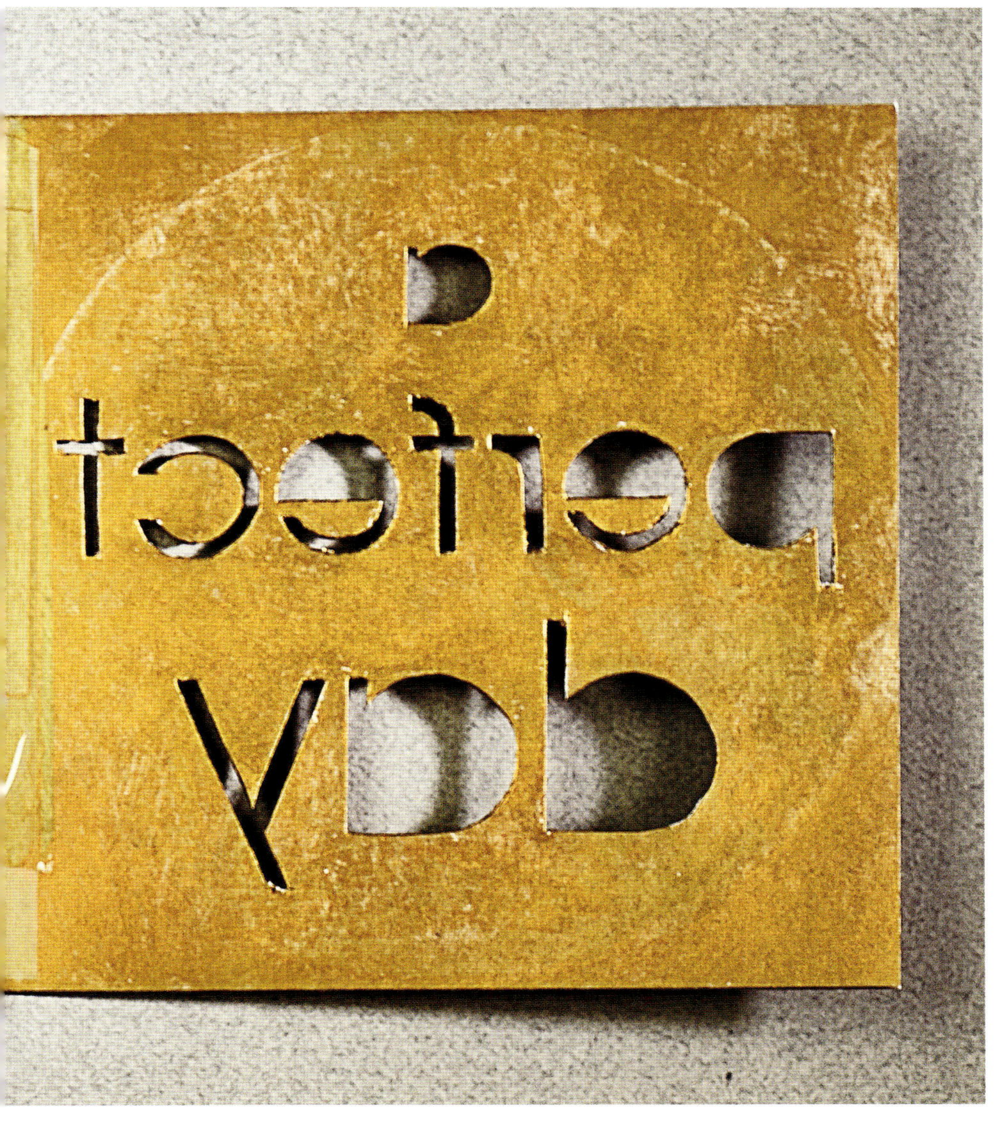

Mick Rock (b. 1948)

Mock-up for Lou Reed's (1942–2013) *Transformer*

ca. 1972

Music Division, The New York Public Library for the Performing Arts, Dorothy and Lewis B. Cullman Center

The iconic rock photographer Mick Rock designed this record jacket using his most famous shot of singer and songwriter Lou Reed. The photo, which went out of focus during development in the darkroom, struck both Rock and Reed as an ideal cover image for Reed's landmark solo album, *Transformer* (1972). The design exemplifies the synthesis of careful planning and happy accident that so often define the most enduring artistic expressions, although the special seven-inch record for which it was prepared was never released. This extraordinary artifact came to the Library as part of the Lou Reed Archive, which the Library acquired in 2017.

Timothy Leary (1920–1996)

The Psychedelic Experience . . .

Typescript, 1964

Timothy Leary Papers, Manuscripts and Archives Division

The Psychedelic Experience: A Manual Based on The Tibetan Book of the Dead (commonly referred to as *The Psychedelic Experience*) is a book on the study and use of psychedelic drugs coauthored by Timothy Leary, Ralph Metzner, and Richard Alpert, who worked together at Harvard University until they were removed from the faculty in 1963. Leary began writing the book in 1962 as part of the Zihuatanejo Project at the Hotel Catalina in Zihuatanejo, Mexico. He believed the psychedelic experience represented an "ego death" or "depersonalization" similar to that described in a translation of the *Tibetan Book of the Dead* by W.Y. Evans-Wentz. Leary became a counterculture icon during the 1960s, and many people regarded his book as he intended: as a guide on how to properly handle the psychedelic experience. John Lennon of The Beatles sings a quotation from the text in the song "Tomorrow Never Knows."

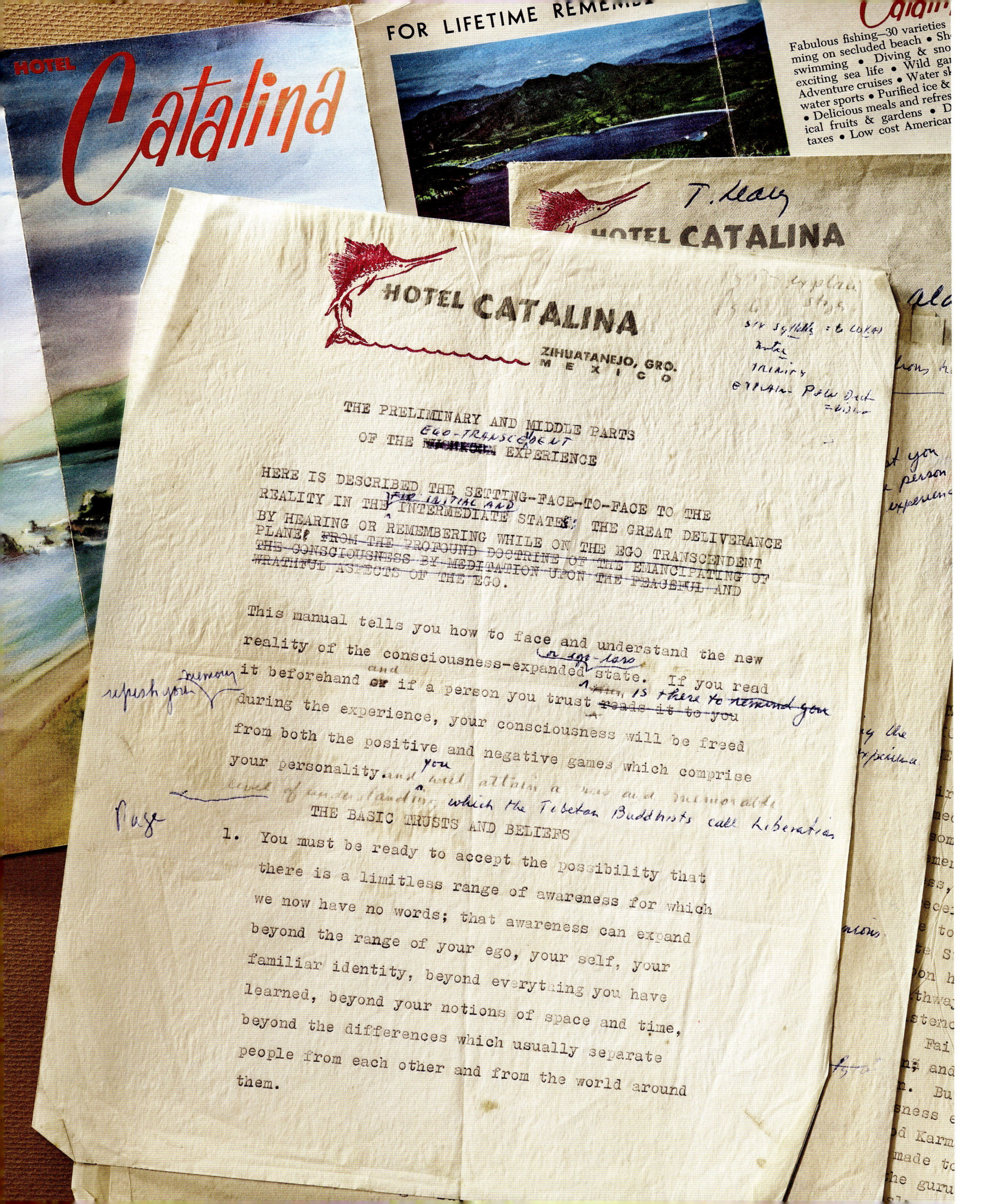

HOTEL CATALINA
ZIHUATANEJO, GRO.
M E X I C O

THE PRELIMINARY AND MIDDLE PARTS
OF THE EGO-TRANSCEDENT EXPERIENCE

HERE IS DESCRIBED THE SETTING-FACE-TO-FACE TO THE REALITY IN THE FOR INITIAL AND INTERMEDIATE STATES; THE GREAT DELIVERANCE BY HEARING OR REMEMBERING WHILE ON THE EGO TRANSCENDENT PLANE.

This manual tells you how to face and understand the new reality of the consciousness-expanded or ego-loss state. If you read it beforehand and if a person you trust is there to remind you during the experience, your consciousness will be freed from both the positive and negative games which comprise your personality and you will attain a new and memorable level of understanding which the Tibetan Buddhists call Liberation.

THE BASIC TRUSTS AND BELIEFS

1. You must be ready to accept the possibility that there is a limitless range of awareness for which we now have no words; that awareness can expand beyond the range of your ego, your self, your familiar identity, beyond everything you have learned, beyond your notions of space and time, beyond the differences which usually separate people from each other and from the world around them.

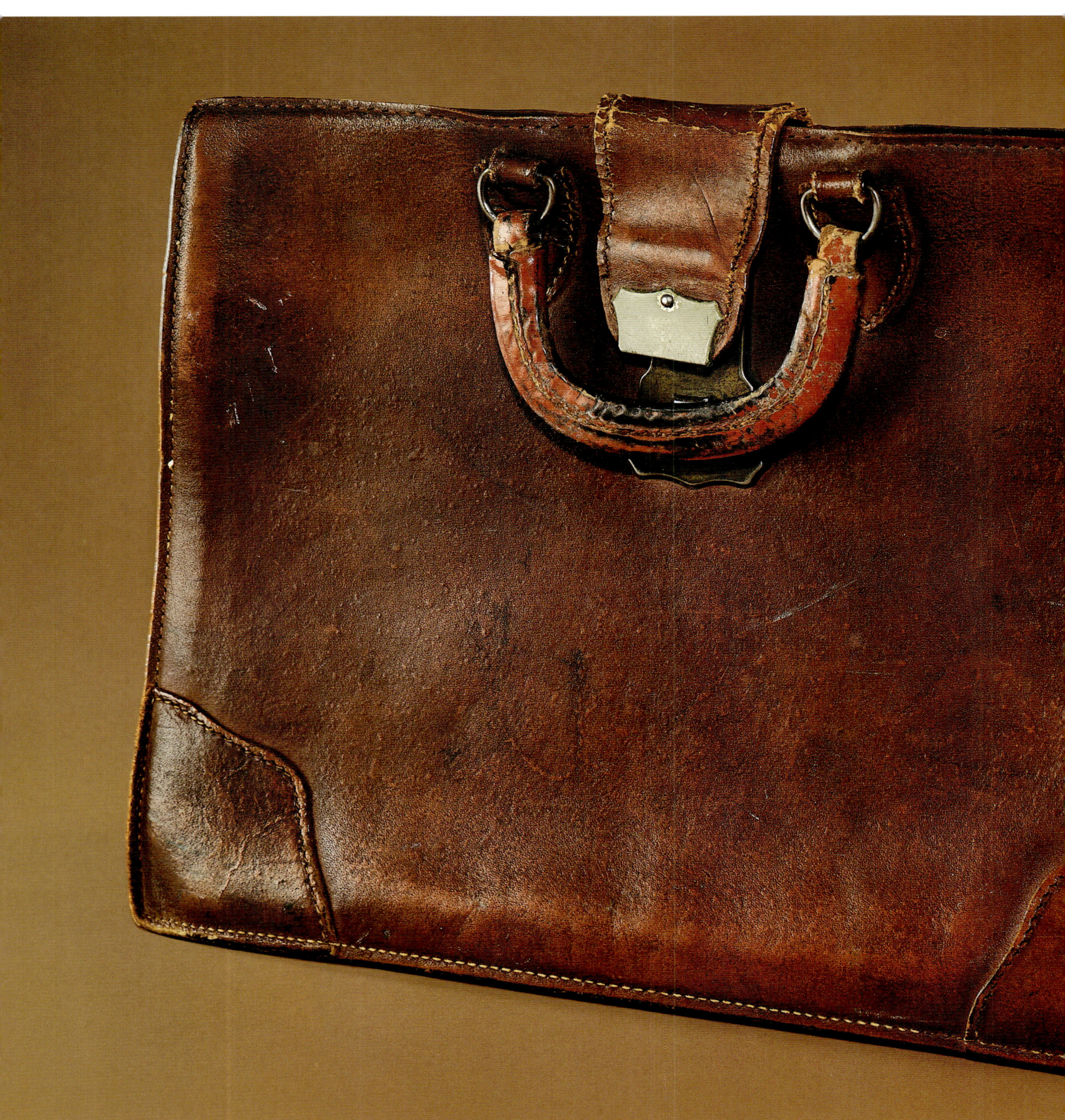

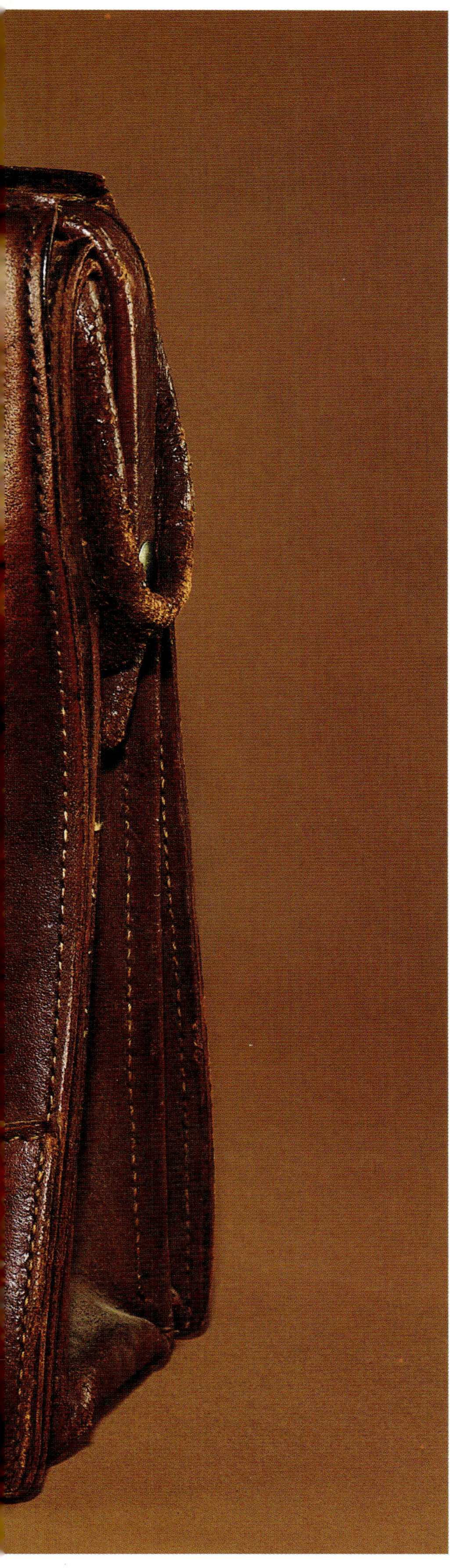

Malcolm X's (1925–1965) briefcase
Leather and brass, ca. 1965 or earlier
Malcolm X Collection, Manuscripts, Archives and Rare Books Division, Schomburg Center for Research in Black Culture

Malcolm X maintained a famously busy schedule, meeting with activists, religious and community leaders, students, scholars, and everyday people around the world and on the sidewalks and in the shops of Harlem. Much of the Malcolm X Collection documents the substance of those many meetings, conferences, and public presentations, and provides a glimpse of the charisma that drew so many people to him. Yet the collection includes only a handful of Malcolm X's personal effects. With very few commonplace items that were a part of his remarkable life accessible to the public, this briefcase is one such rare artifact and a testament to Malcolm X's tireless work.

Miniature locket album of Charles Sherwood Stratton, a.k.a. "General Tom Thumb" (1838–1883), and Lavinia Warren (1841–1919)
1863
The Miriam and Ira D. Wallach Division of Art, Prints and Photographs

This miniature locket, just one inch high, contains an album of photographs from the wedding of Charles Sherwood Stratton, better known as General Tom Thumb, and Lavinia Warren. He and his wife were famous for performing in P.T. Barnum's circus, part of the cast of "human curiosities" who sang and danced for the huge crowds that frequented Barnum's American Museum in lower Manhattan. Barnum hired Stratton when he was five years old and twenty-five inches tall; he would eventually grow to a height of only forty inches. Barnum publicized him as Tom Thumb, after the English fairytale about a man no bigger than his father's thumb. The wedding ceremony was held at Grace Episcopal Church in New York in 1863. Thousands of onlookers blocked the streets outside the church, and Barnum charged seventy-five dollars (the equivalent of 1,400 dollars in today's money) for admission to the reception at the Metropolitan Hotel. The Vanderbilts and Astors were among those who attended. Photographs of the wedding were mass produced as commemorative souvenirs. This locket contains a pullout concertina of twelve tiny albumen prints.

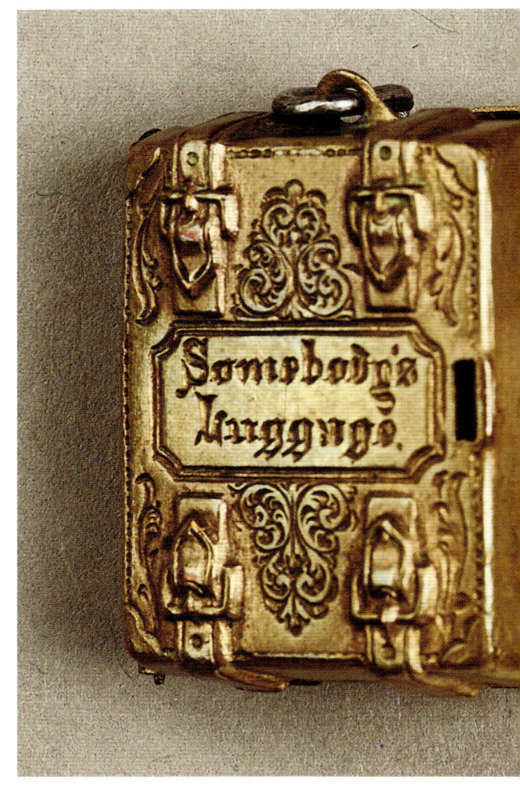

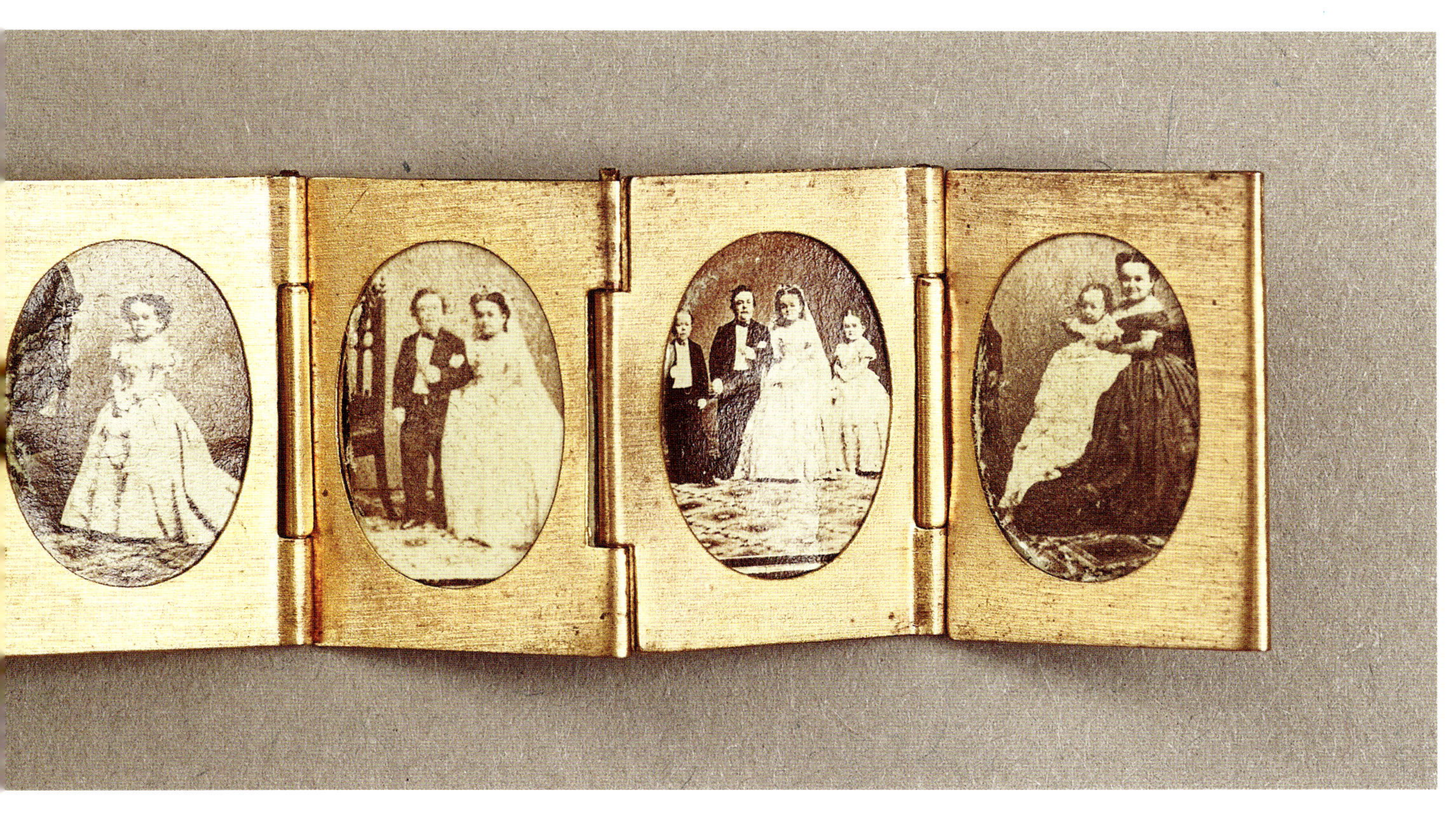

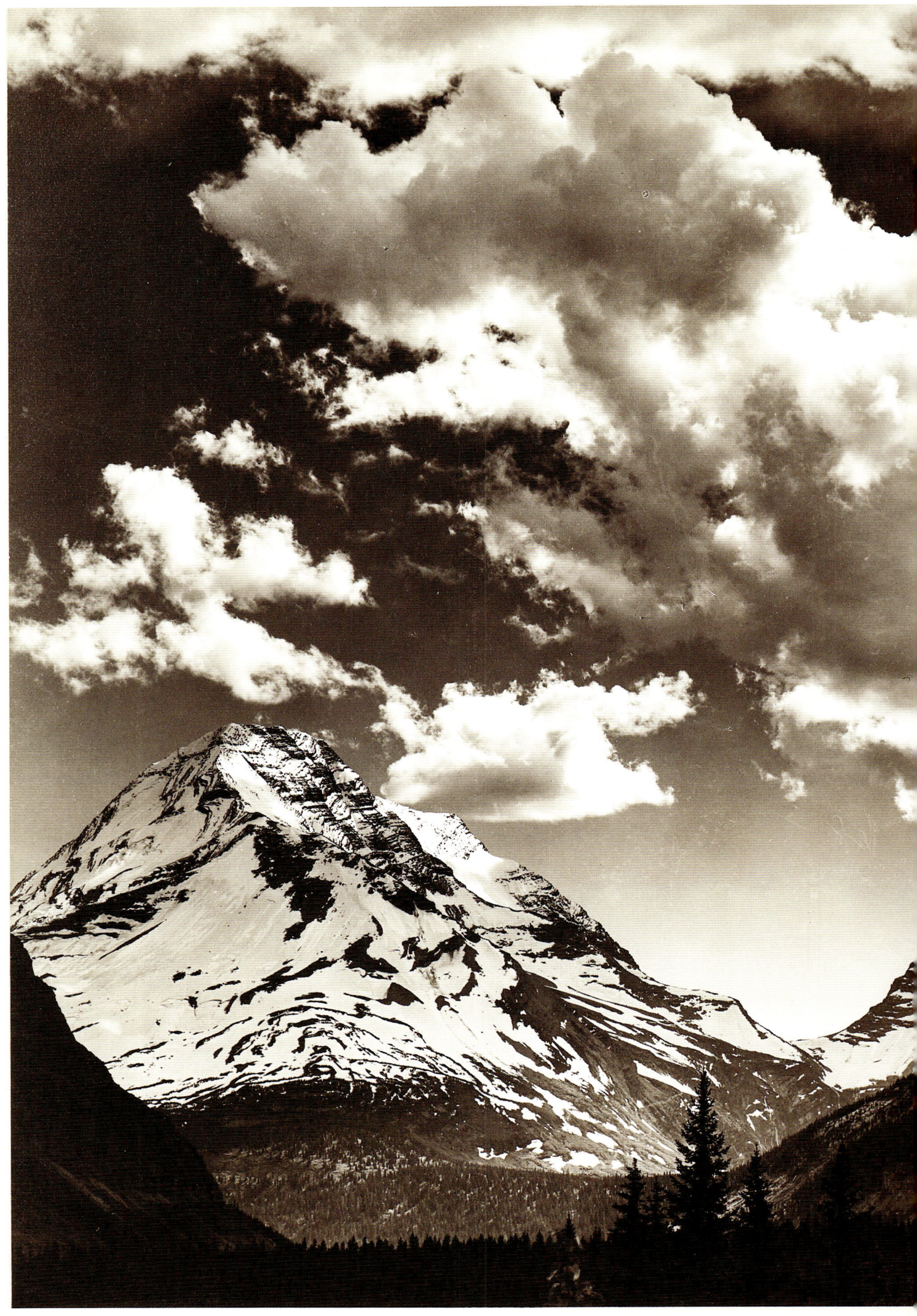

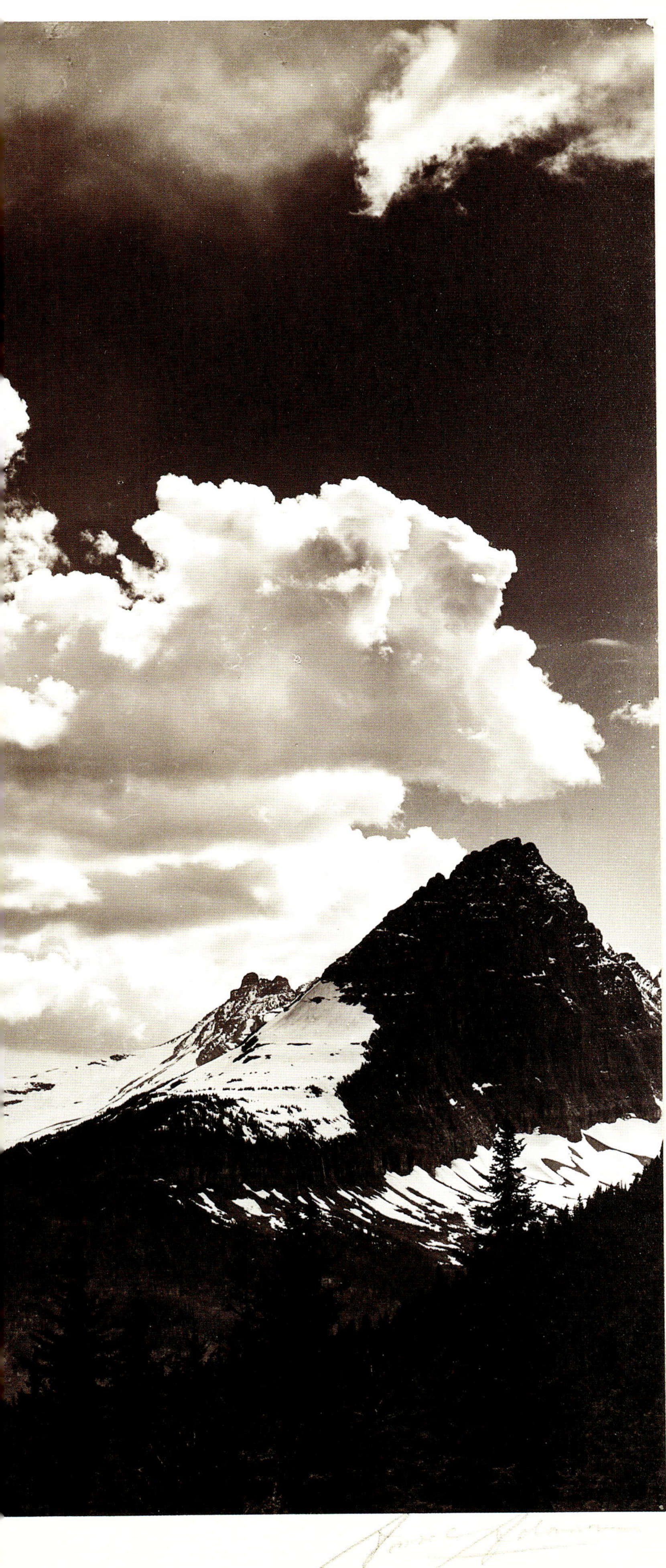

Ansel Adams (1902–1984)
Noon Clouds, Glacier National Park, Montana
Gelatin silver print, 1942, from *Portfolio II*, 1950
Rare Book Division

An iconic figure in 20th-century photography and environmental conservation, Ansel Adams channeled his passion for the American West—as well as his renowned mastery of darkroom craft—into an incomparable body of work that is synonymous with the unspoiled majesty of the landscapes found in the U.S. National Park System. Adams also played a vital role in establishing a collectibles market for fine-art photographs, creating his first limited-edition portfolio in 1927. Between 1948 and 1976, he produced another seven portfolios, which he personally edited and printed, to represent his epic body of work. This dramatic scene, with operatic clouds soaring above snow-capped peaks and trees silhouetted in the foreground, is exemplary of Adams's high style.

Moneta Sleet, Jr. (1926–1996)

Dr. King (1929–1968) in his study at home, Montgomery, Alabama

Gelatin silver print, 1956

Photographs and Prints Division, Schomburg Center for Research in Black Culture

Racial equality continues to prove an elusive goal in the United States, where ideals of justice, peace, and harmony feed the dreams of many. Dr. Martin Luther King, Jr., here contemplates one of his own sources of inspiration, Mahatma Gandhi, who led India to freedom from colonial oppressors during the first half of the 20th century. Though Gandhi's attitude toward blacks has raised concerns, his nonviolent methods of demonstration and protest set a critical precedent for King and the civil rights movement. The photojournalist Moneta Sleet, Jr., worked on the staff of *Ebony* magazine for more than forty years and was the first African-American photographer to win the Pulitzer Prize, awarded for his depiction of King's widow comforting her daughter at the assassinated leader's funeral. In 1989, John H. Johnson, the founder and publisher of Johnson Publishing Company (which published *Ebony*), donated a collection of Sleet's work to the Schomburg Center.

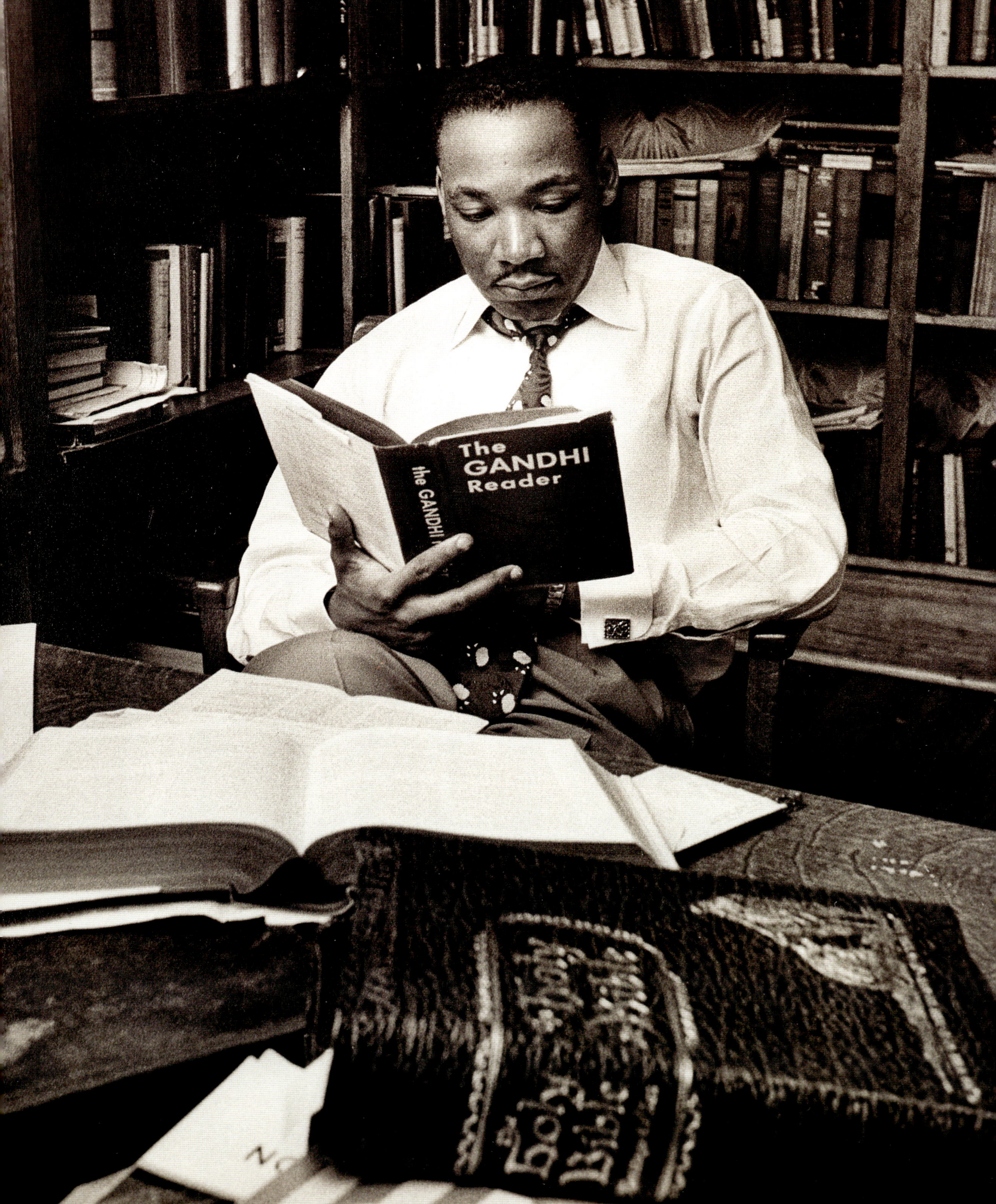
The
GANDHI
Reader
the GANDHI
Holy Bible

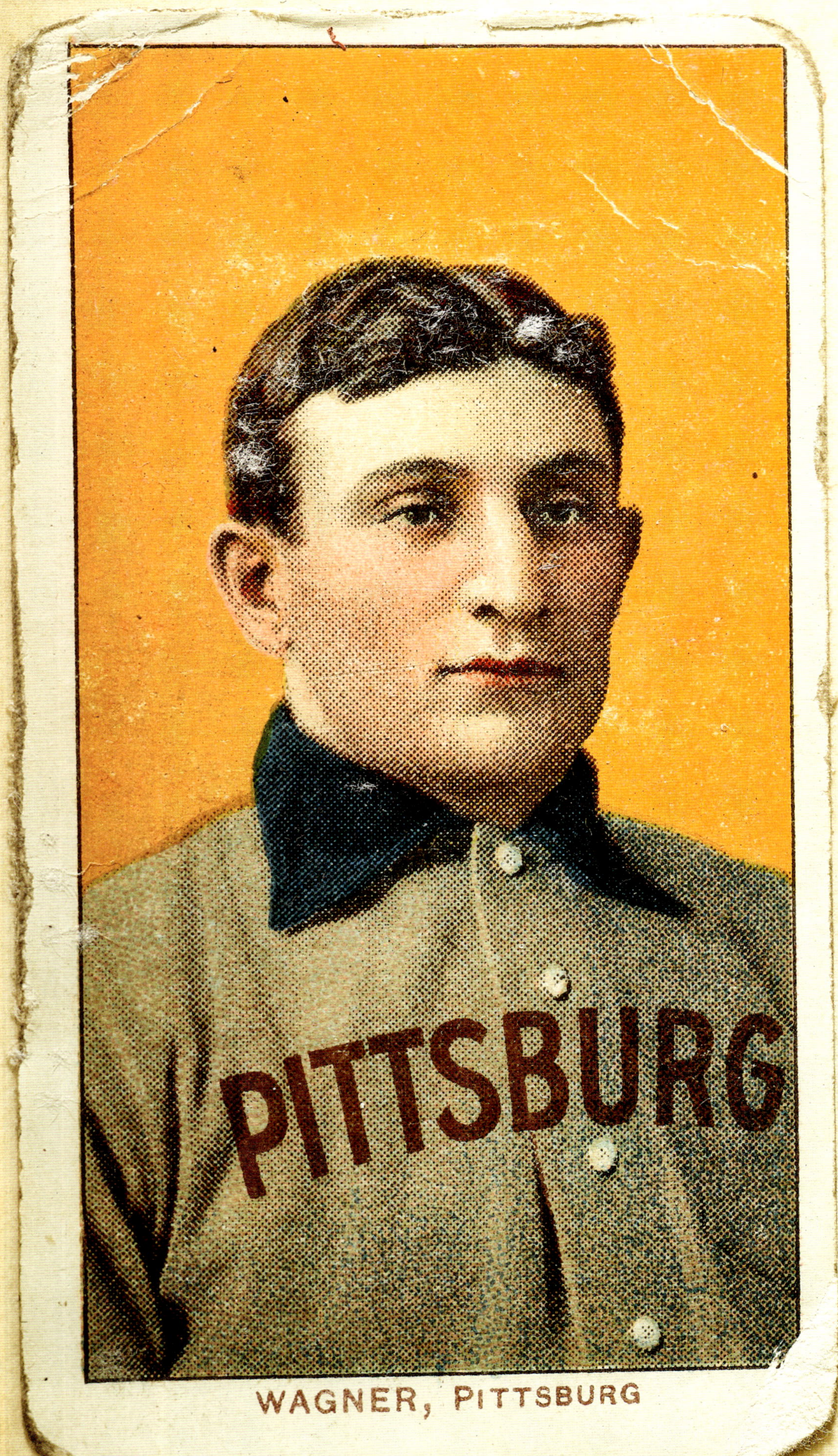
PITTSBURG
WAGNER, PITTSBURG

Baseball card depicting Honus Wagner (1874–1955)
ca. 1909
George Arents Collection

The Honus Wagner card is one of the rarest baseball cards. Wagner, who played shortstop for the Pittsburgh Pirates, asked that the American Tobacco Company stop production of his card, halting its manufacture almost before it had begun. Various explanations have been posited for Wagner's action. While it is popularly believed that he did not want children to have to buy packages of cigarettes in order to acquire his card, his decision to discontinue its printing may have been financially driven: he may have wanted greater monetary compensation from the company in exchange for using his likeness. Whatever his motivation may have been, it is quite likely that only a few hundred cards were ever produced; of these, only around sixty are known to survive. It is this scarcity that contributes to its fame and appeal, and today, baseball card collectors regard acquiring one as something of a holy grail.

Francis Scott Key (1779–1843)

First edition of "The Star Spangled Banner"

Baltimore: Carr's Music Store, 1814

Music Division, The New York Public Library for the Performing Arts, Dorothy and Lewis B. Cullman Center

Francis Scott Key, a lawyer and writer, conceived the poem that would become the lyrics of "The Star Spangled Banner" during the defense of Baltimore's Fort McHenry in the War of 1812 (1812–1815). The vivid description of the battle and America's victory spoke to the resilience of a young country. Today, the words and the soaring melody remind us of the lofty ideals of American democracy. The melody comes from an English drinking tune titled "The Anacreontic Song," or "To Anacreon in Heaven." "The Star Spangled Banner" became America's official national anthem in 1931. The Library's copy of the first edition is among only eleven known extant copies and is discernible from subsequent editions by the misspelling of "patriotic" as "pariotic" in the subtitle.

THE STAR SPANGLED BANNER

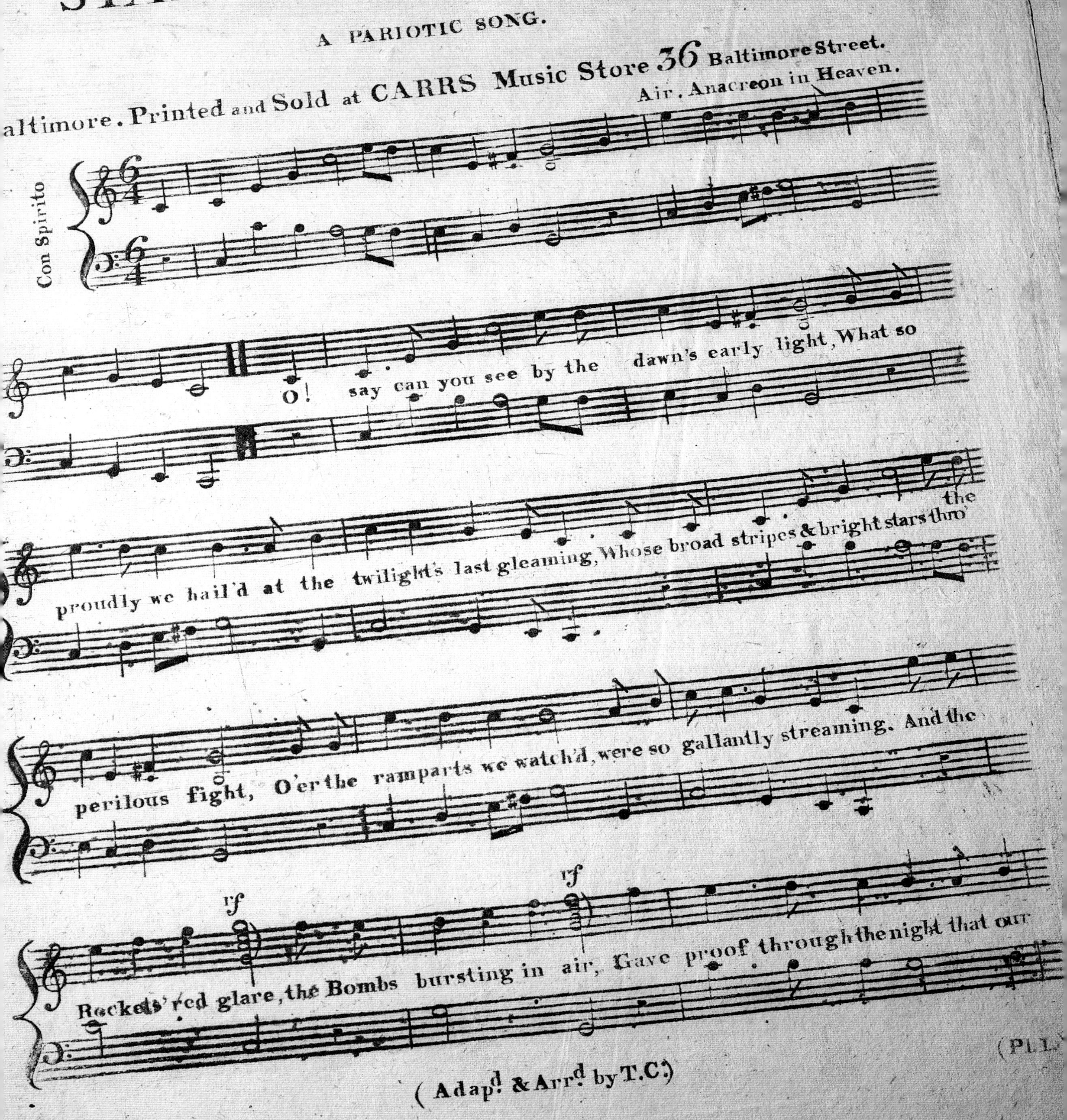

Acknowledgments

Thank you to the many without whom this book would not have been possible. We are indebted to the enthusiastic contributions of the following New York Public Library staff and consultants:

Project Staff
Project Oversight: Carrie Welch
Principal Photography: Robert Kato
Curatorial Associate: Sara Spink
Editor: Mim Harrison

Anne-Marie Belinfante, Cheryl Beredo, Guy Burak, Joshua Chuang, Stephen Corrsin, Elizabeth Cronin, Karen Davidson, Myriam de Arteni, Elizabeth Denlinger, Deirdre Donohue, Ian Fowler, Elizabeth Hays, Jonathan Hiam, Michael Inman, Benedict E. Kiely, Declan Kiely, Mary Catherine Kinniburgh, Matthew Kirby, Robert Kosovsky, Thomas Lannon, Tammi Lawson, Maira Liriano, Shola Lynch, Michael Mery, William Moeck, Angela Montefinise, Linda Murray, Carmen Nigro, Mary Oey, Susan Rabbiner, Douglas Reside, Annemarie van Roessel, Sara Spink, Carolyn Vega, Madeleine Viljoen, Klaus Wagensonner, Jessica Wood, Mary Yearwood, and Kevin Young

And to our partner colleagues at St. Martin's Press:

Editor: Michael Flamini

Elizabeth Curione, Alyssa Gemello, Laurie Henderson, Rebecca Lang, Karen Lumley, Mara Lurie, Hannah Phillips, Danielle Prielipp, Martin Quinn, James Sinclair, and Michael Storrings

Rights and Permissions

Pages 136–37.
Franz Kafka. *The Metamorphosis.*

Franz Kafka, Copy of *The Metamorphosis* owned and annotated by Vladimir Nabokov, 1946. Personal copy of THE METAMORPHOSIS. Copyright © Vladimir Nabokov, used by permission of The Wylie Agency LLC.

Pages 138–39.
Vladimir Nabokov. Scrapbook. February 20, 1946.

Vladimir Nabokov, Page from scrapbook containing hand-drawn diagrams and manuscript notes, ca. 1946. Excerpts from the Berg Collection by Vladimir Nabokov. Copyright © Vladimir Nabokov, used by permission of The Wylie Agency LLC.

Pages 172–73.
Virginia Woolf. *Mrs. Dalloway.*

Virginia Woolf, Manuscript draft of *Mrs. Dalloway*, 1922. © The Society of Authors as the Literary Representative of the Estate of Virginia Woolf.

Pages 184–85.
T.S. Eliot. *The Waste Land.*

T.S. Eliot, Manuscript draft of *The Waste Land*, 1914–1922. By Ezra Pound, from New Directions Pub. acting as agent, copyright ©2015 by Mary de Rachewiltz and the Estate of Omar S. Pound. Reprinted by permission of New Directions Publishing Corp.

Excerpts from THE WASTE LAND: A FACSIMILE AND TRANSCRIPT OF THE ORIGINAL DRAFTS INCLUDING THE ANNOTATIONS OF EZRA POUND. Copyright © 1971 by Ezra Pound. Reprinted by permission of Houghton Mifflin Harcourt Publishing Company. All rights reserved.

Pages 188–89.
Mark Twain. *A Connecticut Yankee in King Arthur's Court.*

Mark Twain, Manuscript of *A Connecticut Yankee in King Arthur's Court*, 1887. Courtesy of the University of California Press and Robert H. Hirst, General Editor, Mark Twain Project.

Pages 236–37.
Chuck Stewart. John and Alice Coltrane.

Chuck Stewart, John and Alice Coltrane, 1966. © Chuck Stewart Photography, LLC.

Pages 238–39.
Sonny Rollins. Notebook.

Sonny Rollins, Notebook, 1957. © 2019 Sonny Rollins.

Pages 268–69.
Isamu Noguchi. Portrait bust of Aline MacMahon.

Isamu Noguchi, Portrait bust of Aline MacMahon, 1937. © 2019 The Isamu Noguchi Foundation and Garden Museum, New York / Artists Rights Society (ARS), New York.

Pages 274–75.
Maya Angelou. *I Know Why the Caged Bird Sings.*

Maya Angelou, Manuscript draft of *I Know Why the Caged Bird Sings*, ca. 1969. Excerpt(s) from manuscript of I KNOW WHY THE CAGED BIRD SINGS by Maya Angelou, copyright © 1969 and renewed 1997 by Maya Angelou. Used by permission of Random House, an imprint and division of Penguin Random House LLC. All rights reserved.

Pages 292–93.
John Cage. Manuscript sketch for *0′00″: solo to be performed by anyone in any way.*

John Cage, Manuscript sketch for *0′00″: solo to be performed by anyone in any way*, 1962. © John Cage Trust.

Pages 294–95.
Telegram from Igor Stravinsky to George Balanchine.

Telegram from Igor Stravinsky to George Balanchine, 1957. © Fondation Igor Stravinsky, Geneva.

Page 298–99.
Jerome Robbins. Diary.

Jerome Robbins, Diary, Volume 5, 1973. ©The Robbins Rights Trust.

Pages 300–01.
Rockwell Kent. Illustration for *Moby-Dick.*

Rockwell Kent, Illustration for Herman Melville's *Moby-Dick; or, The Whale*, 1930. Rights Courtesy of Plattsburgh State Art Museum, State University of New York, USA, Rockwell Kent Collection, Bequest of Sally Kent Gorton. All Rights Reserved.

Page 302–03.
William Faulkner. Erotic drawing.

William Faulkner, Erotic drawing of the author with Meta Carpenter Wilde, 1930s–1940s. © Copyright 2020, Faulkner Literary Rights, LLC. All rights reserved. Used with permission, William Faulkner Literary Estate, Lee Caplin, Executor.

Pages 306–07.
E.E. Cummings. Valentine.

E.E. Cummings, Valentine, 1947.

From "LOVE TO MARION FROM EEC" [ELEPHANT] by E.E. Cummings. Copyright by the Trustees for the E.E. Cummings Trust.

Pages 310–11.
Mick Rock. Mock-up for Lou Reed's *Transformer.*

Mick Rock, Mock-up for Lou Reed's *Transformer*, 2013. Photo © Mick Rock 1972, 2019.

Pages 182–83.
Gisèle Freund. Photograph of James Joyce chatting with Sylvia Beach and Adrienne Monnier.

Gisèle Freund, Photograph of James Joyce chatting with Sylvia Beach, the owner of Shakespeare and Company, and Adrienne Monnier, 1938. Photo Gisèle Freund/IMEC/Fonds MCC.

Index